Reform and Revolution

Readings in Latin American Politics

Reform and Revolution

Readings in Latin American Politics

———◆•◆———

edited by

Arpad von Lazar

Associate Professor
International Development Studies
The Fletcher School of Law and Diplomacy

Robert R. Kaufman

Research Associate
Center for International Affairs
Harvard University

Allyn and Bacon, Inc., Boston

Library of Congress Catalog Card Number: 68–8268

Printed in the United States of America

A nuestro amigos latinoamericanos . . .

PREFACE

The effort to construct an introductory reader for the study of Latin American politics requires a choice between several useful alternatives of organization and approach. One alternative is to collect short political histories or sketches of individual countries, so that the student might have a chronological and empirical framework on which to base comparative analysis. A second is to focus on groups which influence politics in most Latin American countries—the students, the military, the Church, etc. Still a third alternative is to group articles around a core question, hypothesis or thesis about the nature or direction of Latin American politics.

The selections included in this reader reflect a somewhat different set of objectives and a considerably more eclectic general approach. One purpose of the volume is to introduce the new student to some of the central questions that have concerned scholars of the area. A second is to preserve for the student at least some sense of the richness and complexity of the various Latin American polities. Accordingly, priority has been given to articles which refer empirically to single countries, but which also imply or treat directly issues relating to violence and stability, change and conflict, and reform and revolution. These three headings under which the articles are grouped are intended to serve as a broad and hopefully suggestive framework of organization, but no attempt has been made by the editors to fit the highly individual approaches and techniques of the contributors into a neat or precise thematic scheme. Many of the articles included raise issues which are relevant to all three general categories, and all speak for themselves.

Undoubtedly there are disadvantages to this eclecticism. There is much to say for a "straightforward" approach, which spells out or develops a set of propositions that are supported or refuted in the volume. Inevitably, moreover, the answers to analytical questions will ultimately depend on comparative efforts, which transcend the limits of single-country studies. In spite of these problems, it is hoped that this reader will fill a gap in the introductory literature by registering some, if not all, of the increasing variety of viewpoints, techniques, and concerns that have been brought to the study of the area. The "open-endedness" of the reader mirrors the open-endedness of the current state of Latin American studies themselves.

The number of persons who contributed sympathetic assistance to the authors in the preparation of this volume is unfortunately so large as to preclude naming them individually. However, gratitude must be paid to Ronald A. McCrea, research assistant at the Fletcher School of Law and Diplomacy, for his valuable research and editorial assistance, and to the editors of Allyn and Bacon, Inc., for their patience and understanding throughout this enterprise.

CONTENTS

INTRODUCTION

"I have so much to do, I am going to sleep." So says a Savoyard proverb, an exquisitely tempting one for students of Latin American affairs. When we face the plethora of problems in Latin America our frustrations abound and hope may wane. The doom-sayers set the following terms of the problems: violent social and political revolutions in the Castro style versus social stagnation and unwarranted economic backwardness.

Still, we may usefully challenge the sufficiency of these terms. In the first place, Latin America is not easily subject to generalization. There is considerable diversity among the different countries. Some, such as Ecuador, Bolivia, and Paraguay, are truly *under*-developed. Others, such as Argentina, are not so much basically underdeveloped as lagging behind their potentials. Still others, placed between the first two cases on an imaginary scale of development, appear to subsist from crisis to crisis.

In the second place, the countries of the Southern Hemisphere do not share the heritage of recent colonialism so common to African and some Asian countries. They are not the creations of the twentieth century post-colonial Cold War competition, they have a distinct political history. The issue of anti-colonial struggle and formal national independence has been resolved for more than 150 years.

The contemporary *latino* world is a world of traditions. A Chilean or an Argentinian can summon a veritable treasure of historical memories and identifications—battles won or lost and great heroes, revolutionaries, and statesmen.

While the shared experience of national existence over a century and a half reinforces the *latinos'* sense of national identity, it also heavily influences their contemporary outlook and posture

1

toward the problems and issues of modernization. *Latinos* thus takes offense if problems in their countries are compared with those in Africa or Asia.

But we might ask whether, at base, the general issues are not really the same. Isn't the conflict the same here as in other places— between the old and the new, between traditional values, behavior, and institutions on the one hand and the urgent demand for change on the other? Aren't the prospects for resolving the stagnation-change conflict set on two avenues, one leading to repressive stagnation and one leading to revolution?

The modern evidence suggests that these desperate dichotomies have lost much of their appropriateness. The choices of paralysis or violent revolution no longer describe the case adequately. In many countries the debate appears to be not *whether*, but rather *what kinds of*, reforms shall occur, and *what methods* should be used to bring them about. On the other hand, it is possible to ask whether reformist rhetoric masks a fundamental inertia, in which the issue of broad, "structural" reform is not relevant to the aspirations of any social group.

Whether genuine or superficial, the euphoria of the modernizing consensus fades only when the demand is made for specifics. Precisely how will changes be brought about? Who will feel these changes, and how? How fast should they occur? The answers to such questions provide the basis for reform or for revolution. Changes *do* occur. But not all change is instrumental in fulfilling the developmental needs of the countries of Latin America. If the conflicts that exist do not have to lead necessarily to revolution, neither is it guaranteed that change will be meaningful. It follows logically that the student of Latin American affairs must focus his attention on the principal actors if he is to assess and predict how the case for change short of revolution will fare.

THE UPPER CLASS

Latin American upper classes, landed or urban, are the most logical groups to be immediately and directly affected by the nature and outcome of the debate over the nature and means of change. Their image has been that of a traditional sector defending its privileges and vested interests in the face of all changes. Some have said that the power of the upper classes could be broken only by depriving them of their economic power base, be that land, industry, or control of banks. Others have said that only the ferocity of a violent revolution could settle once and for all the issue of upper class domination over all aspects of social life.

But are the upper classes as static and unbending as one has been led to suspect? To the contrary, in some cases the history of the past few years suggests that they have learned to compromise with skill and to accept losses where necessary in order to maintain their chances for survival. They have learned how to slow down the very process that aimed at their elimination. Part of this disposition to make concessions may be traced to the fact that in modern Latin American societies the dividing lines between social classes have become blurred and intertwined by a certain degree of upward and downward mobility. This has fused both the composition and the nature of economic interest in these groups.

In Chile, the upper class took part in disassembling parts of its own power base. Members realized that it was an inevitable step demanded by broad segments of society and knew that they could salvage some of their past power and influence by compromise and participation. Thus, members of this sector employed political skills, influence, wheeler-dealing, and an ability to communicate through intricate channels to influence decisions and their implementation. In other countries of course, flexibility has not been manifest, and pure political power has slipped from the hands of the upper class. What makes the difference?

THE MIDDLE CLASS

Considering the European experience of an earlier age, it has generally been expected that the development and growth of the Latin American middle class would serve to implement those cultural and political changes that are demanded by industrialization and modernization. Rarely did any consideration of developmental phenomena exclude extensive reference to this allegedly reform-oriented "middle sector."

The actual performance of the middle sectors in those countries where they have assumed control of the legitimate decision-making apparatus has not fulfilled these expectations. Instead, they seem generally to have solidified traditional social structures and to have adopted policies effecting economic stagnation.

The exponents of the "middle-sector catalyst" theories generally began their studies by emphasizing the section's extremely hetero-geneous make-up. They also emphasized traits or values which were allegedly common to all members in that group. Often ascribed to the middle sectors were an obsession for modern indus-trialization, particularly the development of heavy industry, and the endorsement of the right, or even the responsibility, of state intervention to effect it. The members of the middle class were seen as highly nationalistic and as placing high priorities on broadly based educational opportunity. It is, generally speaking, an urban class and represents a broad cross-section of vocational groups—professional, academic, bureaucratic, certain levels of the military, and certain levels of the clergy.

Performance and the good use of hindsight have pointed out the inadequacies of theories which extol the middle class as innovators of radical changes. In the first place, it would be asking quite a bit in the Latin American context to accept the idea that a group so admittedly heterogeneous would endorse a common value system or, agreeing upon common goals and methods of achieving them, would be able to manipulate political power effectively to gain desired results. As for the traits that are allegedly held in common by the members of the middle class, a number of questions might be raised. Why was there an "obsession" for modern industrializa-tion? What was behind the highly self-conscious nationalism? and how much of this nationalism was, after all, economic nationalism? When consideration was given to this, why was little attention de-voted to the degree to which its members accepted the traditional values and symbols of status and prestige such as land and property ownership?

It was not, after all, concerted effort on the part of Latin Ameri-cans which brought industry to Latin America but rather the dictates of world politics. Industrialization came to Latin America by "accident." Some *latinos* early hailed industrialization as the instrument which would produce painless social, political, economic, and cultural changes in Latin America. The European precedent was the basis for this assumption. However, they failed to recognize that the industrial processes had not brought ready solutions to social and political questions, but rather had intensified the prob-lems and made the finding of solutions more imperative.

Basic in this failure of the middle sectors to effect the anticipated social and political modernization is their unwillingness or inability to create a system of rewards within the context of the middle class itself. Instead, the rewards of industrialization and other twentieth-century economic innovations have been utilized by the members of the middle sectors to create an opportunity to assume the aristocratic trappings of traditional society—such as leisure time and a landed estate.

The degree of egalitarianism which accompanied the nineteenth-century industrialization of Europe is not always found in the present Latin American experience. But as more persons from the middle sectors acquire wealth or career opportunities based on desirable skills, more persons have a vested interest in maintaining to some extent the status quo—with increased social and economic mobility, of course. The possibility of attaining most of the materialistic status symbols valued by the traditional social system makes many members of the middle sectors less than eager to destroy traditional culture and institutions. Meaningful change cannot be effected so long as traditional values are capable of satisfactorily awarding status and prestige and so long as the avenues of social mobility remain relatively open to members of the middle sectors with necessary training and skills.

Chile and Uruguay are two interesting examples of the defensive reform orientation, the limited obstructionism of the *latino* middle class and its preoccupation with a true Veblenian habit of "conspicuous consumption." Chile is a well-developed welfare state, but it is a welfare state *only* for those who have created it and for whose benefit it was created: the middle class.

In countries with a significant middle-class population, the welfare state is bursting at the seams for the simple reason that needed institutional reforms—i.e., changes in the structuring and functioning of the system—are beyond the scope of acceptability for the politically vociferous and predominating middle class. In Uruguay and, to a certain degree, in Costa Rica and Argentina, highly complex democratic institutions appear to process massive social demands with delirious energy. Debate occurs, laws are sometimes passed; but output remains near zero. It amounts to what one student of these trends has called "dynamic stagnation."

We see, then, that the middle class can be reform-oriented and desirous of change only up to the point at which it begins to affect its status quo—the limits of which are often more narrowly

defined by the middle class than by the old oligarchy. The upper
class in some cases has learned both the art of compromise and
the ability to be versatile about safeguarding resources. Not so the
middle class.

THE MILITARY

Modern technological and scientific changes have basically altered
the nature and outlook of Latin American armies, which are woe-
fully inadequate to exert an international role. At the same time,
the demands of internal security—meaning counterinsurgency—
have moved the preparational emphasis toward police action and
the civic action functions of the armed forces. Appropriately, a
new type of officer, the *tecnico-officer*, is coming of age: a scien-
tifically trained man, usually U. S. educated, less image- and
hierarchy-conscious, and representing a wider scale of popular distribution in terms of family background.

Traditionally Latin American armed forces have been considered
the "guardians of the constitution"—the nonpolitical forces that
have both the capability and the vested "authority" to oversee the
general development of society and political life. Meddling in
politics has been persistent, however, justified by the argument that
the army is enforcing "order" in face of the inability of other
elements to avoid political chaos. Given the present day demands
for development and the general clamor for modernization, most
Latin American armed forces have revamped their public image.
Much is said about civic military programs, the military's commitment to modernization and economic development, and the general civic educational functions the armed forces perform.

How far is this image relevant to the overall issue of change
within the reformist or revolutionary context? The facts are that
the armed forces of present day Latin America tend to be internally modernizing (they upgrade the structure and capabilities of
themselves) and externally conservative. The internal modernization is directly related to status considerations, while the relative
external conservativism reflects a concern for the maintenance of
traditional institutions and values. By and large the armed forces
of Latin America accept modernization—or at least the idea of it—
only as long as it does not involve the possibility of changes in
social "status quo" through "turmoil" and social conflict. This

prospect of social conflict and confrontation is abhorred, and high preference is accordingly assigned to suppressing it. The military accepts *some* aspects of representative democracy but not all and certainly not all of the consequences of the give-and-take implied by the functions of democratic institutions and processes. This is the essence of the famed concept of *autocracia timida*.

What is the long range perspective? Modernization and involvement of the military in civic action programs will in no measure diminish the probability of the armed forces meddling in the affairs of the state. There will be as many coups in the future as there have been in the past, while the format and the style of interference will change as the process of internal modernization reshapes values and aspirations in the officer corps. The point here is that what we are witnessing might be far more significant than the mere manipulation of political capabilities by a military regime. Modernizing authoritarian or semi-authoritarian systems in Latin America must rely, to an increased extent, upon the introduction of policies that in themselves induce support for the system. For example, the modernizing elements of the present regime in Argentina do not want to freeze the system and society in the status quo but to effect changes that generate popular support. This development is characterized by the desire of the power wielders, the military elite, to get the populace to identify itself with the basic values and authority pattern of their governing. The premise upon which the present military regimes base their hopes is this: they will be able to carry out a continuous process of controlled relaxation of pressures and thus turn a military-authoritarian rule into a military-civilian regime of consent and controlled modernization.

THE CAMPESINO

Finally, the major question must be asked: Whither the peasant, the *campesino*? It is to his fate that the claims for modernization are deeply answerable, and it is he, finally, with whom all sectors must reckon, for he is the mass man.

The centuries-long dream of agrarian reform—of owning the land one toils—is emerging as a realistic proposition throughout the hemisphere. And while some economists may still argue validly against the wisdom of meeting the food production problem with agrarian reform, a larger consideration is making such arguments inconsiderable. On this issue turns the possibility of mobilizing the *campesino* politically, and concerns about production and marketing structures pale next to this consideration. In a very real sense, the time has come when Latin American governments may contemplate the abandonment of agrarian reform only at their peril.

The fact is that the *campesino* wants the land. As long as his demand is not fulfilled, he remains a politically exploitable force of revolutionary dissent. Chile's example suggests that the *campesino*, when given the opportunity to express his political preferences freely, opts for the choice that offers the most reward for the least sacrifice. This disposition can permit a demagogic proposition or a reformist solution, and not necessarily a revolutionary path of action. The peasant, generally, is a conservative and cautious element with only peripheral commitment to ideology or abstract causes. The *latino campesino* is certainly no exception. Peasants become advocates of the revolutionary path only so long as it is construed for them as the only possible solution or when they are confronted with it as an accomplished fact, as happened in Cuba during 1958 and 1959. Their basic attitude is one of caution and distrust combined with a fast-developing concern for economic interest. This attitude makes perfectly consistent the emergence of a relatively independent and indigenous *campesino* union movement throughout Latin America. The distinctiveness of this movement is in its independence, which pervades the efforts both to create institutions and to develop a sense of style for political participation and involvements.

We wonder if anyone could suggest an answer if asked, "Whither the *campesino*?" If answers do not abound, so much the better. Perhaps the *campesinos* will provide the free-wheeling political force of undetermined ideological predisposition that could shake up the traditional *danse macabre* performed by the interplay of sectors commonly viewed as significant on the political scene. A most embarrassing thought for left and right alike!

THE LABOR UNIONS

Labor unions, youth and student organizations, and the Church represent added elements of concern within this societal framework of stresses and strains. Organized labor has a conspicuous role in the modern political life of such countries as Argentina, Chile, Bolivia, Venezuela and Peru, while offering a shifting pattern of influence in the rest of the continent. Labor unions generally command sizable sets of voting blocs, even if these blocs have remained fairly constant—at times stagnant—in terms of their organizational growth and manipulative capabilities. As we have already mentioned, the issue of *campesino* unionization represents a new trend with drastically new variables introduced into the political spectrum.

YOUTH AND STUDENT ORGANIZATIONS

To state that student and youth groups are in the forefront of political action is an elaboration upon the obvious. Student politics is totally integrated into the national political cycle. University students are members of political parties which often operate within the confines of the university; indeed to be a political leader at the university level often means the first step toward national political prominence. Universities tend to become the center of political extremism or opposition, where the government cannot reach without risking the serious consequences of popular disturbances or even a collapse of the government. High degree of emotional involvement, radical-idealism, political extremism and nationalism are viewed by us as the norms of university youth behavior for some time to come, thus lending a supporting climate to a politics of conflict in Latin America.

THE CHURCH

Latin America is in the almost exclusive religious domain of the Catholic Church. The political and social impact of the Church's stand on any given issue of national political, social, or economic relevance is uniformly felt throughout the continent. The traditional conservative identification of the Church has recently changed considerably under the pressure of two significant developments. First, the Church itself has moved considerably toward a progressive position in the fields of economic and social justice. It has taken a positive stand on such reform measures as agrarian reform, the broadening of political bases, *campesino* unionization, and problems of poverty, illiteracy and hunger. Second, the emergence of Christian Democratic parties in Latin America, with political views of reformist and social revolutionary nature, helped to change the assumption that a pro-clerical and Catholic stand can be only conservative and pro-status quo. In confronting a changing and conflict-ridden world, the Church quite naturally becomes a small universe reflecting in its internal life the very same confrontations the continent is beset with: the revolutionary defiance and desperation of a Camillo Torres, the reformist zeal and enthusiasm of an Archbishop Larrain and the traditionalist-conservative hesitation of an Argentine or Colombian hierarchy.

ENGINEERING CHANGE

The question remains as to how far Castroite and revolutionary theorems and schemes, however enthusiastically espoused, are valid within the highly divergent, specific environments of other Latin American countries. Is the Chilean *campesino*, beneficiary of the land reform, also a vehicle for social reform? Could the highlands Indian of the Bolivian *altiplano* become a mainstay of revolutionary action under all circumstances? At this stage, the road for the proponents of violent revolutions is a hard and arduous one. The fact is that the "masses" of Latin America are *not* on the move, and revolutionary politics remains in the realm of hit-and-miss propositions of strategic expediency.

Fidel Castro is continually contrasted with the reformist image of an Eduardo Frei from Chile, Belaunde from Peru, or Betancourt from Venezuela. These men are identified with the concept of a "peaceful and democratic" path to social change and development. Their efforts to bring about much needed changes rest on the assumption that the democratic-parliamentary representative system they work with is, or will be, capable of accommodating policies that will bring about changes of such dimensions as to negate the validity of the violent revolutionary assertions. Unfortunately, the road for the proponents of reformism is equally beset by pitfalls and problems. They have to be revolutionaries in their objectives and moderates in their choice of methods! They have to change the rules of the game while observing them!

All of these reformists confront the same phenomenon: the persistence of unreformed institutions and structures which prede-

termine the outcome of the political process and also discourage
efforts for change within the system. Because of this, how higher
institutions are developed and how much they resemble Western
political structures are very likely meaningless in terms of the
demands for political modernization. Indeed, the creation of political institutions might provide for controlled change with the
emphasis more upon control than upon the necessity for change.
An institutional division of power into legislative, executive and
judicial functions; a well-established bureaucratic apparatus; and
the fact that people and functionaries know what they are supposed
to be doing and actually perform according to these set demands do
not at all guarantee that the problems of development and modernization actually get solved or even receive a "fair hearing."
Development means more than just the mere existence of institutions and the availability of skills. It also means the constant consideration of newly created demands that emerge within the very
process of mobilizing for development. Such consideration requires
attitudes of flexibility and sacrifice.

Maybe we should carry this point one step further: is it possible
that the example of Frei et al. suggests that we should de-emphasize
the notion of development and begin to worry about change? The
economic criterion that is so deeply identified with the notion of
development is clearly not fulfilling the task of mobilizing resources
for performance in the optimal fashion at the level of politics. The
nature and scope of economic development are predetermined by
political considerations. And this is the point where, without institutional changes within the individual political systems, the Latin
American countries are merely postponing necessary decisions and
at the same time refusing to accept the consequences of the post-
ponement.

Thus, the problems that confront Latin America are threefold:
the problems of stability, legitimacy and efficiency. It can be well
assumed that the setting of modernization will not provide for a
general state of political serenity. The challenges to political stability arise from the very conflicts that are inherent to the dynamics
of modernization. The problem of legitimacy emerges as new
groups and segments of society, such as the *campesino*, gain access
to the political arena and are mobilized for political action. How
long these new groups will accept the legitimacy of institutions
they have not participated in building and political practices they
were not asked to help develop is a question for any responsible

politician on the Latin American scene. The limits of efficient performance in the economic field are very clearly drawn and these limits will not be broadened unless political decisions are sensitive to the climate in which they are made.

But then, everyone wants progress and development. A few espouse the idea of change on the institutional level. Unfortunately, changes does not mean only the redistribution of income but also a new system of manipulating political skills and influence according to a new scale of preferences. This is unacceptable to many— certainly to vested interests and largely even to the middle class. What is the answer then—reform or revolution? As one ponders the available options, the answer likely to remain is that it depends upon one's perspective and purposes. Maybe it is this realization that makes us see Latin America through a glass darkly!

Part One

Political Stability and Instability

Few would disagree with the proposition that political conflict is somehow related to the process of social and economic development. The difficulty lies in defining the nature of this relationship. Frequently the political fabrics of many Latin American countries appear torn by an endless struggle between political elites, each of which seeks a security that is always beyond its reach. The selections by Thomas E. Skidmore and Abraham F. Lowenthal both point to the strong centrifugal pressures that exist in the dissimilar settings of Brazil and the Dominican Republic, posing permanent dilemmas for any developmentally oriented politicians or political regimes. Viewed from this perspective, development might well depend on the establishment of *any* political authority sufficiently strong to limit the threat of opposition groups and to elaborate and carry through an economic program of one sort or another.

Viewed from another perspective, however, it can be argued that the politics of many Latin American countries are depressingly stable. In countries like Chile and Uruguay, durable constitutional procedures may themselves perpetuate traditional social status systems. *The Chonchol Plan,* written from the perspective of the left wing Christian Democrats, indicates that economic development in Chile may have to await an unsettling process of challenge and change to the country's democratic institutions. But how is this challenge to be organized? The difficulty is great in Chile, and the study of tensions within the Paraguayan opposition to the Stroessner regime holds out little hope that the Febrerista party can be an effective governing agent when and if it succeeds in coming to power. (See article by Paul H. Lewis.) Our two studies of Peru and Colombia, by James L. Payne and Robert C. Williamson, respectively, indicate that even violent challenges to existing regimes

13

may not lead to structural changes within the political system. In the first case, violence has become a mechanism of adjustment for the system itself. In Colombia it has become a diffuse backdrop, against which normal political activities continue.

The Search for a New Political Order

Thomas E. Skidmore

The overthrow of João Goulart was proof that normal constitutional processes had failed in Brazil. It was not the first time the Army had intervened to suspend combat among the politicians. The obvious precedent was 1954; but 1964 was profoundly different for several reasons.

The Army was for the first time united in an ideological stance against populism. This position was first clearly spelled out in February 1954 when "the colonels' memorandum" made an implicit case for Goulart's dismissal as labor minister. Their anti-populism was, however, muted in the subsequent generals' ultimatum, which brought about Vargas' suicide in August 1954. Now, even the pro-legality moderates had been forced to the conclusion that populist politicians could not be trusted to preserve the delicate social equilibrium on which Brazilian democracy rested.

It was the apparent breakdown of this equilibrium which had converted the moderate military to an offensive conspiracy. They believed that the Goulart regime had decided to incorporate a new guard into the political elite while threatening to exclude the old guard altogether. The "old guard" comprised the leadership of the hybrid political system created by Vargas. It included old-style politicians (typified by the PSD), middle-class spokesmen (most prominent in the UDN), and the journeymen functionaries of the PTB—a labor party created by Vargas and not the outgrowth of an independent working-class movement. The "new guard" were the leaders of the radical left, such as the left-wing labor leadership

(CGT, PUA), radical nationalist student cadres (UNE, AP), and the professional politicians of the radical left (Leonel Brizola, Max da Costa Santos, and other members of the *Frente Parlamentar Nacionalista*). The violent language of the new guard indicated that they sought a monopoly of political power which would for-ever end the politics of compromise. Whether true or not, this is what the old guard and the moderate military had come to believe in March 1964. The Army, therefore, prepared to fight a civil war against whatever cadres the radical left could mobilize.

THE VICTORS AND THE VANQUISHED

The Goulart government collapsed so quickly that even the "re-volutionaries" were surprised. Instead of taking a stand in Rio de Janeiro, or in Brasília, or in Rio Grande do Sul, Goulart fled Brazil, leaving his bewildered supporters isolated in the face of the rapidly mobilizing "revolutionaries." But the political forces that brought down the Goulart government were far from united. That soon became evident as the revolutionaries contemplated the sudden vacuum of power created by their boldness.

Who were the victors of March 31? Most important among their number were the aggressive young military. Adamant in their anti-political attitude, they had no desire to finish their intervention by simply delivering power to a different group of civilian politicians, as had happened in 1954, 1955, and 1961. The "hard-line" military had been the earliest conspirators and had waged a long campaign to convert their moderate elders. The latter thought in terms of the Army's traditional role as the guardian of the political equilib-rium, and could not contemplate the vision of a Brazil governed indefinitely by men in uniform. It was the aggressive younger officers who pushed their senior colleagues to a more militant position.

Although it was the military who had intervened to rescue Brazil from "corruption" and "communism," there were some civilians who believed they were the victors. These were the anti-getulista civilians of neo-liberal views. They were led by conservative politicians, such as Bilac Pinto, who had been long-time conspira-tors, and public figures such as Júlio Mesquita Filho, owner of *O Estado de São Paulo*. The civilian conspirators believed they had at last triumphed over the legacy of Getúlio Vargas. Their claim of victory was another expression of the syndrome of 1937—compounded with frustration over the incomplete victory of 1954, the setback of 1955 and the bitter frustration of 1961. When Getúlio Vargas committed suicide, the lines of conflict were drawn: on one side the populist politicians mobilizing the new mass vote; on the other side, the military, the middle class, and the old elite who feared that the populists might push Brazil toward a realm of conflict in which the traditional techniques of political compromise would be scrapped in favor of more radical methods of government.

The apparent influence of the populists was magnified by the failure of the democratic left to find any significant institutional expression in the two decades after 1945. This failure was briefly disguised by Kubitschek's *tour de force* of improvisation, but the lack of responsible leadership in the early 1960's brought the crisis to the surface. When the "positive left" attempted its brief experiment in early 1963, San Tiago Dantas found that there was no organized political base to sustain his program. The PTB remained in the hands of unresponsive manipulators, and the "progressive" wings of the PSD and UDN were but ineffectual minority movements within their own parties. There was neither time nor leadership to organize a new party of the left. Furthermore, the center, representing middle-class opinion which wanted both honesty and reform, was also debilitated by disorganization. Seen in these terms, the failure of Quadros in 1961, combined with the lack of a "respectable" democratic left, led directly to the clash of March 1964.

When the clash came, however, even the radical left collapsed. Its leaders had overestimated the militancy and organization of the masses and underestimated the panic they had provoked in the center. Put to the test, radical nationalism proved to lack both inner coherence and a firm social basis.

COUP OR REVOLUTION?

Was the political trauma of 1964 an authentic revolution? If defined in terms of a radical shift in the distribution of power among social classes or sectors, only time could answer that question. Could one at least conclude that the victory of the "Movement of March

31" portended a radical transformation of political institutions? That question received a partial answer less than two weeks after the coup.

Goulart had been deposed by a military revolt. His flight was not the result of action by the civilian political elite. On the contrary, the Goulart opponents in the Congress had not even attempted impeachment proceedings because they knew they lacked the necessary votes to win such a test, just as the anti-getulista opponents had lacked the votes in 1954. Although a majority of congressmen had grown deeply suspicious of Goulart's intentions, they were still not ready to try him on the grounds outlined in the Constitution. Their reluctance was hardly surprising. As professional politicians they were fearful of what an impeachment might bring in its wake. As a result, there was no centrist congressional leader prepared to champion a campaign to impeach the President. And the UDN militants who favored such a move, such as Bilac Pinto, were suspect figures to the majority leadership, made up of PSD stalwarts, who feared that an ouster of Goulart might turn into a general purge of the "ins."

In the days immediately following Goulart's flight from Brasília, there was a period of apprehensive maneuver among the old-style political elite. Many politicians, especially among the PSD and moderate wing of the UDN, attempted to act as if 1964 would be little different from the earlier crises of 1954, 1955, and 1961. The first sign of a real difference came, however, when the Congress conspicuously declined to formalize Goulart's ouster by failing to vote (no resolution was even introduced) that he had been *impedido* (the constitutional term meaning "obstructed" or "prevented") from continuing to exercise presidential powers. Marshal Lott had been able to extract such a vote against both Carlos Luz and Café Filho in November 1955. It had not been necessary in 1954 or 1961, when Vargas and Quadros had removed themselves from office. Why did the Congress in 1964 not attempt to repeat the vote of 1955? In part it was because the majority—still PSD-PTB as it had been in 1954—was highly apprehensive about its own future, and far more interested in thinking about the next President than in ratifying the inglorious exit of the last President. (In 1955 the President had already been elected and represented the PSD-PTB alliance.) The fact was that in 1964 the initiative lay with the soldiers, and the politicians knew it.

The Constitution provided for an election within thirty days if both the presidency and vice presidency should fall vacant. Political crises had come with such rapidity in the early 1960's that Brazil now lacked a Vice President who could succeed to the presidency. Unlike the crisis of 1954 when the Army endorsed Vice President Café Filho's inauguration, or 1961 when the advocates of legality got Vice President Goulart into the presidential palace, some new figure would have to be found. The politicians began to make soundings. Would it be an experienced PSD leader of center-left, such as Tancredo Neves, or an old-style politician, such as Gustavo Capanema? Perhaps a centrist general such as Amaury Kruel? Or a military-civilian patriarch such as Dutra?

What the speculation ignored was the most significant stuggle in progress behind the scenes. The extremist military, soon known as the "hard-line" (*linha dura*), were now anxious to seize control of Brazilian politics. In their view the recurrent interventions of the military since 1945 had solved nothing. They were determined not to repeat the mistake of delivering power to another subgroup of the political elite who might lead Brazil back to the cul-de-sac of "corruption" and "subversion." There would be no presidential election before the military "revolutionaries" could make certain that the political rule had been changed to their satisfaction.

From the moment he took office in the early morning hours of April 2, Acting President Mazzilli and the old-line congressional leadership were under intense pressure to expel from their legislative ranks those whom the military branded as unacceptable, and get from Congress emergency anti-subversive legislation. On April 7 the demand of the three military ministers, appointed by Mazzilli (except Costa e Silva, the War Minister, who had literally appointed himself on April 2[1] and was merely "retained" in his post by Mazzilli), became public knowledge. The legislation demanded by the military would give the Executive sweeping powers to purge the civil service, and revoke the mandates of members of the federal and state legislatures.

The leaders of Congress were not, however, ready to surrender

---

[1] Sometime on the night between April 1 and 2, General Costa e Silva simply announced to a group of assembled officers that he was assuming "the functions of Commander in Chief of the National Army." This was reported in *Correio da Mañha*, in its issue for April 2, 1964. Later, Costa e Silva claimed that he had already assumed command of the conspiracy on March 16, 1964. His claim was immediately disputed by General Mourao Filho, who considered himself the father of the revolt. *O Estado de São Paulo*, April 4, 1964.

their powers. The conservative leaders of the UDN and PSD drafted their own version of an emergency act which made it clear that they did not share the hard-liners' diagnosis of Brazil's political problems. In short, the civilian politicians were unwilling to carry out the "surgery" to the extent and in the manner that the military demanded.[2]

The uniformed revolutionaries therefore took matters into their own hands. On April 9, 1964, the three military ministers, simply ignoring the politicians' draft of an emergency act, issued, on the authority which they arbitrarily assumed as the Supreme Revolutionary Command, an Institutional Act. The Act, which had been drawn up by Francisco Campos (author of the Constitution of 1937), gave the Brazilian Executive extraordinary powers to break the political deadlock. It began by stating that the Constitution of 1946 and the state constitutions were to remain in force subject to the modifications included in the articles of the Institutional Act. The new powers granted to the Executive included the following: (1) The power to submit constitutional amendments to the Congress, which would have only thirty days in which to consider the proposals, and need only approve them by a majority vote rather than the two-thirds vote required in the 1946 Constitution. The President was also given exclusive power to propose expenditure bills to Congress, and the Congress was denied the right to increase expenditures on any bills proposed by the President. The President was also given the power to declare a state of siege or to prolong such a state of siege for a maximum period of thirty days without congressional approval. (2) The Executive was given sweeping powers to suppress the political rights of political undesirables for ten years. This included the right to cancel the mandates of members of state, municipal, or federal legislatures. There was also an article suspending for six months the constitutional guarantees of job security in the civil service.

This act by the Supreme Revolutionary Command was a new response to the crisis of political authority that had been evident in Brazil since the mid-1950's. Quadros had complained that he lacked

---

[2] General Costa e Silva was later remarkably frank in describing this struggle with the congressional leadership, which he said had "consumed more of our energy than the actual military operation." Costa e Silva's comments were in a speech given early in May 1964 to the Chamber of Deputies, excerpts of which were reprinted in the *Boletim Informativo*, No. 86 (May 7, 1964), published by the Brazilian Embassy in Washington, D.C.

powers to deal with the Congress. Goulart repeated this complaint, had even proposed a state of siege in October of 1963 and had in early 1964 put forward a number of specific proposals for strengthening the hand of the Executive. The Institutional Act was therefore a new and decisive response to the apparent inability of the Brazilian Executive to command the necessary authority.

The action of the military in 1964 thus went beyond any other intervention since 1945 because the Army now came close to repudiating the political elite as a whole. The Institutional Act temporarily changed the rules of democratic politics. The implication was obvious: the politics of compromise had been discredited by Goulart's "overplaying" the democratic game. The Army intervention was a throwback to the anti-political message preached by Jânio Quadros: it was the "politicians" whose irresponsibility had brought Brazil to the edge of chaos.

THE AWKWARD ELECTORATE

The Institutional Act stipulated that an election of a new President and a Vice President should be held within two days of the Act's publication. It also specifically canceled the ineligibility clause in the Constitution, thereby making eligible for election military officers on active duty. This change was intended to make possible the prompt election of General Castello Branco, the coordinator of the military conspiracy, who was the overwhelming choice of the revolutionaries, both military and civilian. Castello Branco was duly elected as the new President on April 11. As if to assert its independence, the Congress elected as Vice President José Maria Alkmin, a PSD leader from Minas Gerais who had become a civilian ally of the military conspirators only as Goulart neared the end of his presidency.

Castello Branco soon proved to be a mediator between the hard-line military and the pre-constitutionalists among the revolutionaries. The two months from Castello Branco's election until the expiration on June 15 of Article X of the Institutional Act (giving the President time to revoke legislative mandates and suspend political rights), was the period of purge designated by the new government. Castello Branco was under pressure from the hard-line military to suspend the political rights of some 5,000 "enemies" of the new regime. By June 15, when the deadline ran out under the

Institutional Act, the political rights of 378 persons had been suspended.[3] They included three former Presidents—Kubitschek, Quadros, and Goulart—as well as six state governors, 55 members of the federal Congress, and assorted diplomats, labor leaders, military officers, intellectuals, and public officials. The accused were given no right of self-defense. Their punishment was frankly acknowledged by the government as an arbitrary act necessitated by the emergency conditions in Brazil. The fact that only a few hundred were involved represented a considerable victory for the moderates among the revolutionaries, who wished to keep the list of the purged to a minimum. Actually, there had been pressure to extend the time limit of Article X to November 9, which was the cutoff date for Article VII, the article that provided for purges within the Civil Service. Marshal Taurino de Rezende, the head of the general investigating commission, had publicly requested Castello Branco to extend the life of Article X, but the moderates won out and the article lapsed, as stipulated, on June 15.

The new government included a combination of political conservatives and technocrats. There were several ministers identified with the UDN, and the head of the Civil Household, Luis Vianna Filho, was an UDN stalwart. Economic policy was in the hands of Finance Minister Octávio Bulhões and Planning Minister Roberto Campos. Both were identified as outspoken advocates of vigorous anti-inflation measures.

The fundamental question was, of course, what political position the new government would take. During his initial months as President, Castello Branco attempted to dissociate his regime from the reactionary position of the extreme right-wing revolutionaries. He explained that the revolution had been made in order to ensure continued economic development and social justice for all. But the government's heavy emphasis on anti-Communism, coupled with the suspension of the rights of a national figure such as Kubitschek,

[3] Evidently no official summary has been published of the number of persons whose political rights were suspended by the Castello Branco government. Many different totals have appeared in press reports. The figure of 378, for the suspension of political rights in the period from April 1 to June 15, 1964, was given in a feature story in *Correio da Manhã*, April 1, 1965. The story also noted that approximately 10,000 government officials had been dismissed or forcibly retired, and that about 5,000 investigations (involving 40,000 persons) had been initiated. The suspension of political rights resumed after the government gave itself back its arbitrary powers by the second Institutional Act (October, 1965). It was under the latter that Adhemar de Barros was deposed as Governor of São Paulo in 1966.

suggested that the influence of the "hard-line" was great. It appeared that the extremists were poised to demand the resumption of emergency powers for use against any opposition that threatened the new government's monopoly of power.

From the outset, the Castello Branco government faced the problem of finding a political base. The regime soon realized that the program of economic stabilization, on which the President placed utmost priority, would take longer than the year and a half remaining of the Presidential mandate, then due to expire on January 20, 1966. The "gradualist" deflationary policy of Campos and Bulhões would not have achieved its objectives by the time of the presidential election scheduled for October of 1965. In July 1964, President Castello Branco reluctantly agreed to a congressional amendment which extended his term until March 15, 1967, at the same time setting the election for November 1966. This was explained as an extension of the temporary "cure" during which preparations could be made for a return to normal political life.

The first electoral test came in March of 1965, with the election for the mayor of São Paulo. The victor was Brigadier Faria, who had been publicly suported by Jânio Quadros. Although the prestige of the federal government was not directly at stake in the election, there were rumblings of discontent among the hard-line military, who argued that the government should not permit itself to undergo a direct electoral test in October, when the governorships of eleven states would fall vacant.

In July 1965 the political crisis deepened. Of the eleven states in which there were to be gubernatorial elections, two were of major importance—Guanabara and Minas Gerais. The incumbent governor (unable by law to succeed himself) was in each case a prominent UDN leader—Carlos Lacerda in Guanabara and Magalhães Pinto in Minas Gerais. Both had been prominent supporters of the anti-Goulart conspiracy, but both had grown outspokenly critical (Lacerda violently critical) of the economic stabilization program, which had become an enormous electoral liability because all sectors were being squeezed simultaneously. It was thus inevitable that in both states the election should be considered a test of the popularity of the federal government.

During July the Castello Branco government moved to increase its control over the electoral system by two measures. The first was an "ineligibility law" that barred from candidacy in the upcoming elections any former ministers who served in the Goulart presidency after the plebiscite of January 1963. This was a measure clearly designed to limit the effectiveness of the opposition and to make it less likely that the government would suffer important reverses in its first major electoral test. The second measure was a new Statute of Political Parties that was intended as the framework for a major reorganization of political activity in Brazil. This was a long-term measure that, it was hoped, would overcome the splinter party phenomenon and help give Brazil the quality which its new government said it had most notably lacked since the war—stability.

In August, as preparations for the elections became intense, the opposition in Guanabara and Minas Gerais attempted to nominate figures who soon proved anathema to the hard-line revolutionaries. In Guanabara the choice had first fallen to Hélio de Almeida, who was promptly ruled ineligible under the act passed by Congress in July. The second choice of the opposition was clearly intended to inflame the anger of the military hard-liners. It was the nomination of Marshal Lott, the "nationalist" general of 1955 and the ill-fated presidential candidate of 1960. Marshal Lott's nomination was narrowly victorious in a tumultuous PTB convention, but his candidacy was soon quashed by the electoral tribunal on the grounds that he lacked the necessary residence in the state of Guanabara. The tribunal, however, deliberated under intense pressure from the government, including a warning by President Castello Branco that declared enemies of the revolution would not be permitted to reach high office.

In Minas Gerais, the opposition attempted to nominate Sebastião Pais de Almeida, a leading PSD politician in Minas Gerais and Kubitschek's last Finance Minister. He was also a *bête noire* to the hard-line military because of his widespread reputation for buying votes. After Pais de Almeida was ruled ineligible, the PSD nominated another long-term Kubitschek protégé in Minas, Israel Pinhero. In Guanabara the PTB joined with the PSD and nominated Negrão de Lima, a PSD scion and a former official in the Kubitschek government. In both states the incumbent UDN governors endorsed their party's candidates—Roberto Resende in Minas Gerais and Flexa Ribeiro in Guanabara. The contest was, therefore, between Kubitschek-inspired PSD politicians and UDN politicians whom the electorate tended to identify with the Castello Branco government, despite the incumbent governors' attempts to establish an independent position for their nominees.

When the votes had been counted, Negrão de Lima and Israel Pinhero had won handily, although in the other nine states the prestige of the federal government was not compromised by the results. The reaction of the hard-line military was immediate and vehement to what they regarded as the electoral success of the opposition. They pressed President Castello Branco strongly during October to annul the results of the elections. There was even pressure to subject the winners to investigation by military tribunal. As a result, the President was forced to issue a new (Second) Institutional Act on October 27, restoring many of the special powers that had expired under the first Institutional Act. In return, the President was allowed to ensure the peaceful inauguration of the two newly elected PSD governors, but at the same time his wide-ranging second Institutional Act again revised the rules for politics in Brazil.

All political parties were to be dissolved. The Presidential election of 1966, as well as the gubernatorial elections, would be indirect (by the Congress for the President and by the state legislatures for governors), and the President retained the right, on his own discretion, to remove the political rights of Brazilians considered to be a threat to the security of the government. There were many other provisions to the new Institutional Act, including an increase in the membership of the Supreme Court from eleven to sixteen, the additional judges to be appointed by the President. This packing of the Court was a response to the Court's repeated rulings in favor of the liberation of political prisoners.

At the same time that the government had capitulated to the hard-line military, it attempted to institutionalize these changes and to establish clear limits. The new Institutional Act was to remain in force until March 15, 1967, the date on which President Castello Branco's successor would be inaugurated. The Act was therefore a compromise between the hard-line and the constitutionalists. It was also clear recognition by the government that in its search for a political base it would need to manipulate the political scene more fully than the "constitutionalist" revolutionaries had hoped would be necessary. For them the implication was deeply disturbing: for how long must the electorate be deprived of the right to choose directly their governors and President? And for whose benefit would the manipulation be used? Might this coup prove "revolutionary" by devouring its own children?

DEVELOPMENT AND STABILIZATION VS. DEMOCRACY: BRAZIL'S DILEMMA?

After Goulart's fall all of Brazil's essential problems remained to be tackled: the immediate problem of economic stabilization; social reform in agriculture and education; and most important of all, rationalization of the economy to promote further growth.

But what rationale would emerge to sustain an attack on these problems? How would a new social consensus be created and maintained? Since the late 1950's Brazil's ideology, insofar as it had one, was nationalism in the ambiguous form which enlisted support from both growth-minded neo-liberals and the moderate left. Kubitschek had proved able to govern in part because he took care *not* to give his government any clear ideological identification. Quadros had embraced a frenetic moralism, but combined it with a conspicuously independent foreign policy—including an outright refusal to follow American policy in Cuba. Goulart, as we have seen, played with the ideologies of both the moderate and radical left, finally appearing to opt for the latter. *No* elected President since 1950 had ignored the ideology of nationalism and the left which put it forward. Which way would Brazil go now?

In the twenty years since the end of the Second World War, Brazil had experienced an alternation between expansion and attempted stabilization. Since the exhaustion of foreign exchange reserves in 1947, the country had incurred growing foreign indebtedness. This foreign financing was a predictable and necessary result of the industrialization drive. Still, it deferred part of the cost of development and represented an increasing burden which amounted to a growing political liability for successive governments. From 1951 until 1964 one could characterize Brazil as caught in a deepening "credit crisis." The economic growth rate remained high, one of the highest in the world until 1962, but the extensive use of foreign financing meant that a growing percentage of scarce foreign exchange had to be used to service the debt. This credit crisis, which first became severe in 1959, recurred in 1961 when the Quadros government attempted orthodox stabilization measures. It was the single most important policy problem for the Goulart regime. The serious shortage of foreign exchange, a direct result of the declining price for Brazil's exports, as well as Brazil's failure to diversify her exports, became evident in the early 1950's. It was to be a principal restraint on continued development after the early 1960's. In short, Brazil was unable to find a new method of financing her development once she had incurred a level of indebtedness that reached the maximum of tolerance for her foreign creditors.

Along with the incurring of heavy foreign indebtedness, went a growing sentiment of political nationalism. This attitude, which had historic roots in Brazil and was now being nurtured by the organized left, blamed foreign incomprehension and ill will for Brazil's difficulties in maintaining economic development. In practice, the nationalist explanation was often little more than the search for a convenient scapegoat. What it concealed was the inherent difficulty of mobilizing domestic resources for economic growth, particularly for an ambitious rate of growth.

As with so many developing economies, a full-scale mobilization of resources is what Brazil conspicuously lacked during its "developmentalist" drive of the 1950's. In order to mobilize resources, three steps are necessary: (1) a sound technical assessment of the situation; (2) the selection of a strategy for action; (3) the construction of a reliable political base for the strategy adopted.

The first step requires a determination of the stage of development reached and of the potentials and bottlenecks for the next stage. There was considerable agreement in the early 1950's about the proper diagnosis of the Brazilian economic situation. The studies of ECLA, the BNDE, and the Joint Brazil-United States Economic Development Commission laid the groundwork for the industrialization drive that produced successful results in the Kubitschek presidency. The specific barriers were identified: the lack of sophisticated technology, the lack of equipment, and the lack of incentives for domestic and foreign producers. These barriers were overcome by an intelligent combination of government policies that encouraged the rapid development of a sophisticated industrial base in Brazil. One can say with confidence that the technical assessment of the economic situation in Brazil in the early 1950's—despite minor disagreements—was virtually unanimous among the technocratic elite. Inded, it is difficult to find another country in Latin America where the diagnosis was so widely shared or the government policy so fully supported.

The second step involves the selection of a strategy for development. In the Brazil of the early 1950's, governments alternated between a nationalist and a moderately "cosmopolitan" policy, an alternation most dramatic during the presidency of Vargas between 1951 and 1954. The Kubitschek government proved willing to embrace a mixed strategy based on maximum use of public and private resources both domestic and foreign. The nationalist emphasis was less pronounced than in the Vargas period, although the credit crisis of 1958–59 found Kubitschek taking a nationalist way out. It was his political gamble for the preservation of his own image and the fulfillment of his "target program." The 1950's then, may be seen as a period in which Brazil pursued a mixed strategy, relying on private and public investment, both foreign and domestic, to develop the industrial base and the social capital necessary for an industrializing economy.

The third step requires the devising of a political strategy to ensure the public support for the development strategy adopted. This necessitates in the first instance an assessment of the lines of party support and secondly an evaluation of the class and sectional basis underlying the party structure. It is at this point that the Brazilian case becomes interesting and complex. The political base chosen for the developmentalist drive of the 1950's was first articulated by Vargas in 1950. By forming an unlikely alliance of the PSD and the PSP, along with his own PTB, Vargas was able to achieve a near majority in the presidential election of 1950. But he failed thereafter to strengthen the political base for a continuation of the developmentalist drive he had begun by 1953. Kubitschek merely extended the Vargas strategy to its ultimate potential without developing any new line of political strategy. What this strategy lacked most conspicuously was any clear-cut party commitment, either to the diagnosis of the economic situation or to the policy chosen for development. Kubitschek's principal support was the PSD, a notably non-ideological party whose support he maintained by a generous use of political rewards for the "ins." In the short run, this pragmatic attitude toward basic questions in economic analysis and developmental strategy was advantageous. It helped to submerge latent disagreements and to avoid policy conflicts over relative class roles in the developmentalist drive. In the long run, however, the avoidance of basic questions in politics was to prove disastrous when the character of political leadership deteriorated under Quadros and Goulart.

An illuminating way to look at the "revolutionary" regime, and to compare it with past governments, is to examine the way the Castello Branco regime has been tackling these three steps in the basic task of mobilizing resources for development. As for the first step, it has merely endorsed a technical assessment of the economic situation which had been in the air since the early 1960's. This diagnosis laid priority on the need to achieve a slowdown in the rate of price increase as an essential prerequisite for further economic development. It had been inherent in the Quadros stabilization policy in 1961 and had been the basis of Furtado's Three-Year Plan, outlined in December 1962. But no government had spelled out the assessment in such detail as did Roberto Campos and Octávio Bulhões in mid-1964. They went farther than the previous diagnoses in fixing the federal government's responsibility for controlling inflation and in emphasizing the need to diversify Brazil's export trade as the key to breaking the foreign exchange bottleneck. There was also a clearer emphasis upon bottlenecks in Brazilian institutional structure: the obsolete capital market, the privileged groups within the organized labor movement, the ill-organized monetary system, and the faulty distribution structure for agricultural products. All these weaknesses had been stressed previously, especially in the Furtado Three-Year Report, but there was a new single-mindedness on the part of the government to carry out the changes to which the diagnosis pointed.

In the strategy for development, the Castello Branco government diverged sharply from the policies of previous regimes. There was first of all a strong emphasis on the need to satisfy the international financial authorities and principal foreign creditors as a prerequisite for further development in Brazil. This meant the commitment to a rigorous anti-inflation program. At the same time, the new government sought to rehabilitate the role of the private sector, which it thought had been denigrated by the Goulart regime. The Goulart regime had emphasized the public role in a mixed strategy. The Castello Branco regime sought to emphasize the private role.

There was at the same time a new commitment to strengthening and improving the machinery of public administration. Tax collection—long notorious for its laxness—was tightened by introducing techniques of automated record-keeping. Delinquents were subjected to more prompt prosecution; they found themselves not only subject to fines but also forced to pay a percentage premium (computed according to a government-established rate under a policy called "monetarization") to compensate for the decline in the real value of the tax bill caused by inflation in the interval since the bill had been originally incurred.

A potentially powerful new government instrument for inducing change in the agrarian sector was the Agrarian Reform Bill passed

by the Brazilian Congress in November 1964. The law placed
primary reliance on a progressive land tax as a stimulus to more
efficient utilization of land. Although the law gave many safeguards to rural landowners (strict limits on the government's power
to expropriate, guarantees against currency depreciation for holders
of government bonds paid in compensation), the amount of real
reform would obviously depend on the attitude and determination
of the administering authorities. As a first step, the Agrarian Reform
Institute (IBRA) in 1965 began an ambitious computer-aided
cadastral survey of all rural land holdings. When completed, this
would be the first such nation-wide survey ever conducted in
Brazil. It was a further example of the "technocratic" approach that
characterized the Castello Branco government's approach to social
problems.[4]

It was in the third area—of political support for the new strategy
—that the Castello Branco government found most difficulty. In
essence, it encountered the same problem which every postwar
Brazilian government had faced: the overwhelming political un-
popularity of any effort at anti-inflation policies. This became
obvious to Vargas in 1953, the Café Filho government in 1955, the
Kubitschek government in 1958–59, the Quadros government in
1961, and Goulart, especially after early 1963. The Castello Branco
government chose as its way out a policy which the Goulart
government appeared to have been considering in 1964: a frankly
anti-democratic solution. Since the economic diagnosis suggested
that there was no alternative to a rigorous anti-inflation program
and a constant attention to the need to renegotiate and settle foreign
accounts, the Castello Branco government relegated the return to
constitutional government to a secondary level. It carried through
what seemed to be the logic inherent in the desperate measures of
both Quadros and Goulart: a suspension of the normal democratic
process during a period of economic emergency. The suspension
of the political system existing between 1945 and 1964 therefore
had a direct connection with the rhythm of economic development and economic crisis which has been evident since the Second
World War. Faced with the problem of electoral reversals while

---

[4] The new law is analyzed in Robert E. Price, *The Brazilian Land Reform
Statute* [Research Paper: Land Tenure Center, University of Wisconsin]
(Madison, Wisc., April 1965, mimeo). See also James W. Rowe, "The 'Week
of the Land' in the Brazilian Sertao," *American Universities Field Staff
Reports Service*, East Coast South America Series, XII, No. 1 (Brazil).

pursuing an anti-inflation program, the Castello Branco government chose to change the rules of the electoral game so that it could not suffer defeat.

The recurrent historical question that arises out of an examination of the period from 1945 to 1964 is: when did an authoritarian solution to Brazil's political cul-de-sac seem the only possibility? At what point did the suspension of the democratic system become unavoidable? Even if one acknowledges that Brazil was extraordinarily ill-served by its two Presidents after 1960, the fact remains that the need for unpopular and painful choices in economic policy-making imposed grave limits on the potential for either charismatic or populist political leadership. What all political leaders discovered in this political system was the inadequacy of the party structure, the inability to control the political elite in the midst of a highly controversial policy-making crisis. In short, the lines of political authority were not sufficient to sustain the tasks of political leadership demanded by the crisis of the early 1960's.

Instead, there was a steady poisoning of the political atmosphere as the possibility of negotiation and compromise faded. The arguments of the extreme left and the extreme right bore a great similarity. Both accused their enemies of delivering Brazil to a foreign power. The left charged *entreguismo*, meaning a "sellout" to capitalist powers, particularly the United States. The right charged subversion and communism—a sellout to the Communist bloc. In between, there were varying charges of bad faith and anti-democratic sentiments that ranged from the suspicion of Peronism on the left to suspicion of reactionary militarism on the right. Essentially, there was a collapse of the belief that differing interests could be harmonized. The "creative tension" of the Kubitschek period dissolved into an increasingly acrimonious conflict between differing visions of Brazil's problems and potential.

Most important, during the last year of the Goulart presidency there was a growing suspicion that the equilibrium upon which Brazilian politics rested was about to be destroyed. Could it have become possible that Brazilian politics was a zero-sum game in which there were only winners and losers in the absolute sense but no negotiated solutions? The trauma of Goulart's overthrow in 1964 led to a suppression of open political bargaining and an attempt to impose short-term emergency solutions that included not only economic stabilization but also institutional reform.

What of the deeper causes of the breakdown in the political

system so carefully constructed in 1945–46? At that time Brazil reaffirmed her democratic ideals by rejecting the authoritarian system under which so much economic change and institutional innovation had taken place. In the following two decades the implicit goal was wider political participation—bringing a larger number of the public into the active political process. In 1964 the trend toward increasing public participation was cut short. In its place was substituted a semi-authoritarian system. The revolutionaries increasingly feared that they could not justify to a majority of the electorate their programs or their basic ideas. Elections were thus made indirect—not only the election for governor of twelve states in September 1966, but also the election of a new President in October 1966. When the Castello Branco government encountered serious resistance in attempting to impose its own candidates (under the label of the new government party, called ARENA) in the 1966 gubernatorial elections, it did not hesitate to purge the state legislature, as in Rio Grande do Sul in July 1966, or even to remove the governor, as in São Paulo, where the deposing of Adhemar de Barros in August removed the last of the leading civilian revolutionaries who still held high office.

By the fall of 1966 it was clear that the Castello Branco government had chosen (or felt itself forced) to close the political system farther and farther. The immediate justification was the need to continue an anti-inflation and economic development program that was acknowledged to be unpopular but nonetheless essential. It was the one issue on which Castello Branco demanded a commitment from General Costa e Silva, the consensus candidate of the military and therefore the certain successor. Only after Costa e Silva had effectively promised to continue the stabilization program did he receive Castello Branco's unqualified support in the presidential campaign. The election of Costa e Silva by the Congress in October 1966 was a foregone conclusion since the government party held a majority of Congressional seats. The opposition party, MDB, registered its protest by refusing to appear in the Congress for the *pro-forma* vote.

The government's turn away from the electorate, whatever its short-term justification, seemed to develop its own momentum. A regime that so pointedly refused to practice the arts of electoral politics found itself developing a rationale for longer-term authoritarianism. Above all, the closing of the political system—the purges of elected politicians, the constant changing of the rules to prevent significant victories for the opposition—made clear that any eventual return to open political competition would find the political elite and the public ill-prepared. The organization of new political groups appeared virtually impossible in the manipulated atmosphere created by the revolutionaries.

One question remains. What of the opposition? How could the forces of the left and center have fallen silent so quickly? The two important centers of consistent political opposition after 1964 were the radical university students and the progressive Roman Catholic clergy. It is significant that these were the only groups which remained secure in their respective ideological positions. The fact is that the left was deeply divided in the early 1960's, never more so than in the last year of Goulart's presidency. Among politicians and intellectuals identified with the left there lurked deep uncertainties about the soundness of their ideas and the reliability of their political strategy. Their apparent confidence had become recklessness in early 1964. The center? It was outflanked, outshouted, and disorganized. The voice of the center which represented the majority of the politically aware public (especially in the urban sector), failed to carry any significant weight either in the final crisis of 1963–64 or in the aftermath of the coup of March 31.

Three factors contributed to the increasing authoritarianism of the revolutionary government. Most important was the attitude of the military, which had been the direct cause of Goulart's fall and immediately emerged as the active censor of Brazilian political life. Despite frequent conflicts between the moderates and the "hard-liners" within the officer corps, the majority of the military agreed on the absolute need to prevent a return to populist politics. They constantly pressed Castello Branco to restrict the opposition whenever it threatened the monopoly of power that the revolutionaries claimed for themselves. A second factor was the disorganization and opportunism of the political elite that logically should have comprised the opposition. A third was the profoundly skeptical attitude of the general public. Arbitrary suspension of the political rules, for example, brought a minimal response. The public, disillusioned by the blunders and opportunism of the "politicians," appeared to be resigned, for the time being at least, to rule by technocrats under military tutelage.

The Dominican Republic:
The Politics of Chaos[*]

Abraham F. Lowenthal

For fifty years, Latin America was discussed in book after book in terms of a supposed triad of "oligarchy," church and military.[1] A strong, cohesive oligarchy was said to control politics and the economy, its members struggling among themselves for the top positions but never opening the competition to new participants. The oligarchy was said to maintain its hold through close relations with its natural allies, the leaders of the Church and of the Armed Forces. The bi-class nature of Latin-American society, it was said again and again, made it impossible for the countries of the area to sustain in practice the political institutions proclaimed by their constitutional documents.

This conventional approach to Latin America has proved inadequate as social scientists examine the area's history and current situation. During the past few years, the "middle sectors" have been discovered, eulogized, set up as the bulwark of the Alliance for Progress, and, more recently, re-examined in the light of the persistence of traditional values, attitudes, and consumption patterns.

[*] This essay stems primarily from my personal dissatisfaction with available literature on recent Dominican politics. Having worked in the Dominican Republic as a Ford Foundation Training Associate from 1964 to 1966, I experienced at first-hand many of the events others have discussed in print. Reading various published accounts after my return to the United States, I found it difficult to match my own perceptions and those of Dominican friends with the views others have recorded. Encouraged by Samuel Huntington, Robert Kaufman and others, I set out to analyze these discrepancies; this essay resulted. I wish to express my deep appreciation to the many persons who have contributed to my understanding of Dominican politics.
[1] Compare, for example, James Bryce, *South America: Observations and Impressions* (New York, 1912) with Frank Tannenbaum, *Ten Keys to Latin America* (New York, 1962). The analyses are remarkably similar.

Divisions within the monied class into agricultural, industrial, and commercial sectors, each with very different attitudes toward enterprise and toward politics, have been emphasized. The distinct roles of military institutions at various stages of national development have been noted and the phenomenon of "the middle-class military coup" has been analyzed. Splits within the hierarchy of the Catholic Church in given countries, and major differences in approach from country to country, have been discussed. The political attitudes of urban squatters and slum-dwellers, of university students, of various sectors of organized labor, and of different types of peasant organizations have been surveyed and dissected. Increased understanding of Latin America has heightened awareness of the region's dilemmas, particularly as evidence reveals the fundamentally conservative bias of many of the groups which only recently had been considered by the left as the likely promoters of revolution and had been wooed by the United States as potential allies for progress. In many countries of Latin America, it has become increasingly evident that neither revolution nor evolution will quickly emerge, and that familiar views are off the mark.

I

The "conventional wisdom" about Latin America is being discarded, bit by bit and sector by sector.[2] The available literature about any given Latin American country, however, often tends to reflect the old approach. The considerable body of recent writing on the Dominican Republic is typical in this respect. Concepts and phrases, born in other countries and contexts, continue to be applied in uncritical fashion to the Dominican case. Countless books and

[2] Many of the points to be raised in this essay suggest the general inadequacy of much of the standard literature on Latin America, but the argument from this point on is specifically limited to the Dominican case. For similar but more general discussions based on research elsewhere in Latin America, see James Payne, *Labor and Politics in Peru* (New Haven, 1965), and Charles Anderson, *Politics and Economic Change in Latin America* (New York, 1967), as well as Paynes's as-yet-unpublished Ph.D. Thesis, "Patterns of Conflict in Colombia" (University of California, Berkeley, 1966). Two volumes edited by Claudio Véliz, *Obstacles to Change in Latin America* (New York, 1965) and *The Politics of Conformity in Latin America* (New York, 1967), should also be consulted.

articles explain events in the Dominican Republic over the past five years in terms drawn straight from the "conventional wisdom." Political instability in the Dominican Republic before Rafael Trujillo's regime began in 1930 is said to have indicated merely the switching back and forth in office among members of the country's oligarchy of elite families, which is said to have "ruled the Republic —furnished its Presidents and generals, dominated its business and finance—for more than a hundred years."[3] After Trujillo's assassination in 1961, the conventional argument runs, political participation expanded, so that instability over the past few years has been of a wholly different type, reflecting a struggle between the oligarchy and the reformers, drawn primarily from the middle sectors.

The standard approach to contemporary Dominican politics summarizes recent history along the following lines: President Bosch, elected by the masses in 1962 against the candidate of the oligarchy, was toppled after seven months because he had alienated the oligarchy, the Church, and the military, the traditional wielders of power. Widespread desire among the Dominican people for a return to constitutional and reformist government under Bosch produced a popular uprising against oligarchic rule in 1965. The nascent Dominican Revolution, however, was put down by oligarchic-military forces, supported by the U. S. military intervention.

Proponents of this general approach to an understanding of Dominican politics differ in their knowledge of the relevant facts, in their ideological commitments and partisan zeal, and in the depth of their analyses. All of them, however, present variations of the themes here outlined. The best-documented, most dispassionate and least journalistic study yet available—a 1966 Ph.D. thesis by Howard J. Wiarda—offers substantially the same interpretation, albeit in more sophisticated terms. Explaining the aftermath of the Trujillo dictatorship, Dr. Wiarda concludes:

> In the Dominican Republic . . . the more traditional groups . . . the armed forces, the Church, and the business-professional-landholding elite—were considerably stronger and better organized than the more "modern" groups—the political parties, the labor sector, and the peasantry. When the traditional groups worked together, they were able to completely dominate the country.

[3] John B. Martin, *Overtaken by Events* (New York, 1967), p. 133.

This imbalance ultimately caused the failure of the first attempt to build a pluralist democracy, represented by the overthrow of the democratically-elected, constitutional, and reform-minded government of Juan Bosch and the break-up of the system . . . [resulting] in a chaotic and bloody civil war.[4]

Although accepted in almost every piece of writing on the Dominican Republic, the conventional phrases are very misleading. Mention of the Dominican oligarchy, for instance, suggests to those familiar with much of the literature on Latin American politics that there is a coherent, hereditary elite of large land-holders, tightly controlling economic and political power, reactionary in outlook and firmly opposed to social change. When one analyzes those whom Dominicans identify as comprising the oligarchy, however, one finds that there is no coherent group but rather several sets of families and groups with different origins and characteristics, many set against each other in politics and in other spheres of activity. One of these groups, the economically-powerful Santo Domingo commercial sector, in recent years has generally played the type of political role associated with the phrase oligarchy in Latin America. This group, however, is not characterized by hereditary privilege or secure position but by recent arrival to wealth and prominence. Its members are largely recent Spanish or Syrian-Lebanese immigrants whose fortunes have been made within the past forty years, or Dominicans whose rise to prominence was achieved by close ties to the Trujillo regime. Of the various monied groups in the Dominican Republic, the one which Dominicans identify as the most oligarchic is the set of families *de primera* (first families) who have maintained social prominence for several generations. These families, however, do not possess vast tracts of land. Nor are they, for the most part, staggeringly wealthy, even in the context of a poor country; others in the Dominican Republic, outside their social group, are wealthier. Members of this oligarchy

---

[4] Howard J. Wiarda, "The Aftermath of the Trujillo Dictatorship: The Emergence of a Pluralist System in the Dominican Republic." Ph.D. thesis presented in 1966 at the University of Florida. Quotation is from authorized abstract of thesis, published in *Dissertations Abstracts*, November, 1967, p. 18761. Although the present essay rejects several of Wiarda's interpretations, the author wishes to acknowledge the important contributions Dr. Wiarda has made to the literature on the Dominican Republic and to his own knowledge of Dominican affairs.

are not necessarily reactionary; many of them did not actively oppose President Bosch and some even protested his overthrow publicly when few Dominicans did. Former U.S. Ambassador John Martin expected, on the basis of American liberal prejudices, to dislike these oligarchs and to have to overcome their resistance to change, but he concluded after two years in Santo Domingo that this oligarchy was "one of the really hopeful groups in the Republic."[5]

More important, perhaps, members of this most oligarchic group do not seem to control either politics or the economy. The principal sources of wealth belong to the State, which fell heir to Trujillo's private empire, and much of the private sector is in the hands of foreigners or of the aforementioned recent immigrants, who are not considered *de primera*, although their current economic and political power is greater. Rather than dominate politics, this oligarchy seems to remain aloof; many of its members stay in provincial Santiago and other cities of the interior precisely to avoid the political atmosphere of the capital city. What distinguishes the most continuous and best-known oligarchy in the Dominican Republic, then, is not economic or political power but social prestige, particularly what Dominicans call *abolengo*, the distinction of lineage in a society conscious of family and color.

The Dominican families of *abolengo* do not lack influence. On the contrary, in a society which accepts and values social distinctions, the capacity of this group to define itself, to admit or exclude others, is a major source of power. What Juan Bosch has called the "caste" of those *de primera* does exist in the Dominican Republic and has been able, for a variety of reasons, to preserve a greater degree of continuous influence than any other group in Dominican society.[6] First, being of a distinguished family creates the presumption that an individual is *un hombre serio*, whose opinion is worth consulting. Second, the very fact that these families have generally abstained from politics and developed sources of wealth independent of the violent oscillations of the country's politics has enabled them to preserve a comfortable economic position. Third, these families have usually been able—perhaps because of their color and self-image as well as because of their education and foreign language competence—to exert predominant influence on

[5] Martin, *op. cit.*, 134. See, generally, 133–136, 443, 715–16 and *passim*.
[6] See Juan Bosch, *Trujillo: Causas de Una Tiranía Sin Ejemplo* (Caracas, 1959), perhaps the single most useful study of Dominican society.

foreign individuals, institutions, and governments, which have always played a major role in Dominican affairs. What is being stressed here, however, is that this group, which expands to incorporate some of the upwardly-mobile through marriage, does not possess the political and economic attributes the term "oligarchy" connotes.[7]

The appearance of certain respected family names in the roster of Dominican presidents, which Martin cites to support the oligarchy concept, also turns out on further examination to be misleading. Some of the oligarchic presidents came to office from outside active politics. Often they were turned to—usually at the insistence of the Catholic Church or foreign interventionist forces— precisely because of their prestige and their standing above, or at least aside from, the political fray; characteristically they have lacked domestic sources of power. Furthermore, several Dominican presidents whom Martin would identify as oligarchs probably because of the current status of their descendants, seem actually to have been ambitious rural leaders of modest means who attained political power and then married into families of *abolengo*. Politics in the Dominican Republic has not been the province of the racially light, socially prestigious oligarchy but rather of racially mulatto, socially mobile men on the make.

Conventional references to the political role of the Dominican Armed Forces are usually framed in terms of "military intervention in politics." The 1963 overthrow of President Bosch, for instance, is often said to have resulted from a "series of conflicts . . . between Bosch and the armed forces . . . which grew steadily more severe," and the events of 1965–66 are commonly discussed in similar terms.[8]

The phrase "military intervention" and much of the relevant literature suggest a particular relationship between "the military" as a corporate entity on the one hand, and the civil political process on the other. The military, the phrase implies, remains apart from politics until and unless certain conditions exist, at which point the officers feel impelled to intervene. While this description may accurately explain the role of the armed forces in some countries,

[7] For a systematic effort to expose widespread misuse of the term "oligarchy," see James Payne, "The Oligarchy Muddle," *World Politics*, April, 1968, p. 439–453.

[8] See Howard J. Wiarda, "The Politics of Civil-Military Relations in the Dominican Republic," *Journal of Inter-American Studies*, October, 1965, p. 480.

and at some stages of political development, it cannot be usefully applied in the Dominican case. Far from being a professional institution dedicated to certain principles which impel its occasional entry into politics, the Dominican Armed Forces have never had any significant function beyond politics, except for plunder. The rival military groupings, which struggled with each other before American occupation authorities created the National Constabulary, existed primarily to advance the prospects of political rivals and to help them secure the spoils. Established during the U.S. occupation of 1916–1924, the Dominican Army was the vehicle for Trujillo's rise to power, and the Armed Forces then became Trujillo's main instrument of control.

Following Trujillo's death in 1961, the Dominican Armed Forces were quickly deprived of leadership. First, the entire Trujillo family and many leading *Trujillista* officers were ousted, and then potential strong-man General Pedro Rodríguez Echavarría—whose actions at the Santiago Air Base had been instrumental in removing the Trujillos—was also exiled. Since that time, all of the generals and admirals of the Trujillo era, together with almost everyone who has attained those ranks since 1961, have been retired or sent abroad. As a result of this leadership vacuum, the Dominican Republic has experienced a return to the competition characteristic of the period before the national military establishment was created. Now, however, the struggle goes on within the Armed Forces rather than among private bands. As competition for high military office has intensified, factions have arisen within the armed forces to struggle for power and a chance at the spoils, and they have naturally linked with civilian groups competing for office. Since Trujillo's death, the Dominican Armed Forces have been an integral part of the country's political process, indeed the locus of power and the major arena of conflict.

The history of the past few years in the Dominican Republic may best be viewed as a constant struggle among changing alliances of civilian and military cliques, not in terms of confrontation between civilian authority and the military establishment. In fact, since the exile of the Trujillos and Rodríguez Echavarría in 1961–62, there has never really been anyone able to speak authoritatively for the Dominican Armed Forces as a unit. The two Ministers of the Armed Forces who have remained in office for any length of time—General Viñas Román and the current chief, General Pérez y Pérez—gained and retained office precisely because of their lack of a substantial personal following, which made them acceptable to contending factions. Constant strife within the Dominican Armed Forces in recent years has caused frequent shifts of key personnel, the cashiering or reinstatement of officers and enlisted men, exile or assignment abroad for many officers and premature retirement for scores of others. On two occasions the struggle has even led one sector of the Armed Forces to strafe another, and less violent demonstrations of strength—including troop and tank movements and airplane maneuvers—have been almost commonplace.

Given this setting, it becomes evident that the 1963 coup was not a simple crisis of civil-military relations but was largely the result of a successful effort by Bosch's civilian opponents to enlist the support of military factions. The 1965 overthrow of Donald Reid Cabral which precipitated the "revolution," in turn, resulted precisely from the successful attempts by Bosch, his partisans, and others (mainly carried out after Bosch's overthrow) to cultivate support among other factions in the Dominican Armed Forces.

Some writers, including Bosch himself, who recognize the existence of factions within the Dominican Armed Forces, portray the strife in 1965 as pitting the "young and honest" colonels committed to constitutional government against the old order of established generals. This view, reflected in a number of books and articles about the 1965 Dominican crisis, does not hold up under examination. The crisis certainly divided Dominican society, bringing together a coalition of the aggrieved in support of the "constitutionalist" (pro-Bosch) cause and organizing on the anti-constitutionalist side some of the country's most retrograde elements. Longstanding economic and social deprivation and the immediate discomforts caused by severe drought made thousands of people in Santo Domingo willing to take to the streets and even to battle against General Wessin's tanks. There does not seem to have been any appreciable difference, however, between the top military leadership of the two sides—the established military chiefs and most of their constitutionalist rivals—with respect to previous ideology or degree of honesty. The main organizer of the pro-Bosch movement, Col. Fernández Domínguez, had cooperated closely with the anti-Bosch chief, General Wessin, in the 1962 ouster of General Rodríguez Echavarría. The eventual leader of the constitutionalist forces, Col. Caamaño Denó, had been against Bosch in 1963 and had headed the "public safety" police, one of the key objects of constitutionalist attack in 1965.[9] Some of the constitutionalist chiefs even took advantage of the short-lived movement to make the kind of personal profits characteristic of high military office in the Dominican Republic.

The major distinction between the military leaders on either side of the 1965 civil war was that of age and rank; the established leaders were of higher rank precisely because they had prevailed in previous struggles to reach the top. Dispassionate analysis of the 1965 revolution, in fact, would reveal the participation on the constitutionalist side, at least in the first days of the crisis, of some of the Dominican Republic's most discredited ex-generals, including Belisario Peguero, Atila Luna, and Santiago Rodríguez Echavarría. Some of the principal constitutionalist officers were fighting primarily to win reinstatement in the Armed Forces, from which they had been fired. All these leaders, as well as a varied collection of civilian and military personalities and groups, were brought together mainly by the fact of being "out" or, as Dominicans would say, "*abajo.*"

II

Enough has been said already to show that much of the available literature on the Dominican Republic provides superficial explanations which turn out, upon more careful examination, to be inadequate. Perhaps the single most important weakness of this literature is its failure to convey the violent instability of Dominican politics. Phrases and concepts which apply to analyzing events within a framework of order and established institutions lose much of their meaning when applied to the politics of chaos.

By any measure, Dominican politics has always been particularly unstable. It is true that four men (Báez, Santana, Heureaux, and Trujillo) ruled for more than half of the years that the Dominican Republic has exercised sovereignty, but when one looks beyond this statement at the whole of Dominican history, a different pattern emerges. Even without counting the numerous self-proclaimed regimes which never won national control or international recognition (there have been six of these since 1962 alone), the Dominican

[9] Fernández and Caamaño were both, it might be added, sons of leading Generals of the Trujillo era.

Republic has had more than fifty regimes (more than one a year) in the years that it was not governed by any of the four executives mentioned above. The many presidencies of Báez and Santana, moreover, were generally brief; the two knocked each other out of office several times in the nineteenth century and never managed to stabilize the country. Only three Dominican presidents—Heureaux, Caceres, and Trujillo—managed to establish firm control, to put a temporary end to rival configurations of power, and to last in office as long as six years at a stretch. Each of these three presidents, significantly, finally lost power only through assassination.

With respect to civil violence, the pattern is equally clear, notwithstanding Harry Eckstein's measure of unequivocal and equivocal acts of violence between 1946 and 1959, which showed the Dominican Republic to have the least violent record in Latin America.[10] There was little overt violence during the Trujillo period, except during three abortive invasions of the Dominican Republic by exiled opponents, but the regime killed hundreds of Dominicans—not to mention thousands of Haitians—in the course of thirty-one years of suppression. Before Trujillo, constant armed strife brought death to thousands; there were even periods in which one could legally be shot on sight for returning to the country from political exile without official permission.[11] Since 1961, of course, civic violence has been especially marked. From 1961 to 1965 there were scores of deaths from police clashes with demonstrators, from a short-lived guerrilla movement, and from riots during labor conflict. Some three thousand Dominicans are believed to have died in the 1965 struggle, and well over one hundred have been killed since then in various ways: in a renewed confrontation between the contending military groups, in civil-military clashes, in student and labor demonstrations and riots, and especially from terrorism and political assassination.[12]

[10] See Harry Eckstein, "Internal War: The Problems of Anticipation" in *Social Science Research and National Security* by Ithiel de Sola Pool and others (Washington, 1963), pp. 102–147. Eckstein's figures were based on *The New York Times*, which presumably did not record the many politically-motivated deaths the government-controlled Dominican press did not report.

[11] See Julio Campillo Pérez, *El Grillo y El Ruiseñor: Elecciones Presidenciales Dominicanas* (Santo Domingo, 1966), p. 126.

[12] There have been numerous nonfatal acts of political violence as well. Within the past two years, for instance, such prominent Dominican political figures as General Antonio Imbert, PRD Senator Rafael Casimiro Castro, and 1J4 leader (and alleged US agent) Luis Genao Espaillat have been badly wounded.

Instability has also been evident in other ways, less easy to measure in simple terms for comparative purposes, but more important
in terms of the political system's capacity to function. Of particular
interest and significance is the striking lack of institutional strength
or continuity. The instability of political parties might not show
up on a simple listing of Dominican parties from 1960 to 1968, for
instance, because the four major parties of 1961–62—the PRD,
UCN, Fourteenth of June (1J4) and PRSC—would all still be listed
in 1968.[13] A more informed analysis, however, would reveal some
remarkable discontinuities. The three leaders who returned from
exile in 1961 to organize Juan Bosch's PRD campaign—Angel
Miolán, Ramón Castillo, and Nicolás Silfa—are all out of Bosch's
party now and each has served in Balaguer's government, along with
the former Secretary-General and the former Finance Chairman of
the PRD, as well as the persons elected President and Vice-President
of the Senate and President of the Chamber of Deputies in 1962 on
the PRD ticket, Bosch's Ambassador to the United States, and
others from the PRD.[14] Almost all of the 1961 leadership of the
1J4 has deserted that party by now, some to join the PRD, the
PRSC, or the PR, and many to join the Dominican Communist
Party (PCD) or one of its several rivals for the claim of Marxist-
Leninist orthodoxy. The UCN, unquestionably the strongest Dominican political organization in 1961, has since disintegrated into
several unimportant factions, one of which polled a handful of
votes in 1966 in support of Balaguer's candidacy, another of which
was stirring opposition to the Balaguer government in 1968. In
1962, the PRSC was generally considered a moderate leftist party
with a promising future; by 1966, it had split into three factions.
One 1962 leader, Mario Read Vittini, formed a right-wing party
(PDC) which supported Belaguer in the 1966 election, but Read
declared himself in opposition to Balaguer early in 1968. A second
group, which had captured official control of the party in a struggle
which featured a physical battle for possession of the party headquarters, supported Bosch in 1965 and in the 1966 election but has
since parted company with Bosch, while many of the leaders of the

---

[13] Even such a simple listing, however, would reveal the fact that the party
currently in power, the P.R. of Joaquín Balaguer, did not exist six years ago,
when all four of the mentioned parties favored exiling Balaguer.

[14] The last six individuals mentioned are, respectively: Antonio Martínez
Francisco, José Brea Pena, Juan Casasnovas Garrido, Thelma Frías de
Rodríguez, José Rafael Molina Ureña, and Enriquillo del Rosario.

third faction, including former PRSC President Guido D'Alessandro and Víctor Hidalgo Justo, are now serving in the Balaguer government.

This turbulent pattern is not adequately reported in the literature on Dominican politics, perhaps because foreign journalists and scholars are rarely in Santo Domingo long enough to realize that the configuration they see at any given moment is ephemeral and that preconceived labels cannot be usefully applied. While the literature on Dominican politics generally tags key personalities as "conservative" or "liberal" or in other ways suggests that they have fixed ideological affinities, many Dominican politicians have pursued courses which can best be understood simply in terms of self-advancement. Miguel Angel Ramírez Alcántara, who had co-operated closely with Bosch in exile, was one of Bosch's most vociferous opponents in 1963. Very strongly opposed to Balaguer in 1961–62, Ramírez had by 1968 joined the Balaguer government and had even disbanded his party, declaring its objectives to have been fulfilled. Virgilio Mainardi Reyna—like Ramírez Alcántara, a regional leader with national ambitions—has attempted to gain prominence within and outside the PRD, alternatively backing and opposing Bosch as the situation seemed to demand. Horacio Julio Ornes, chief of the PRD party, was tagged in some reports and articles early in 1963 as a moderate leftist because he had instructed his followers to vote for Juan Bosch, but Ornes very soon turned out to be one of Bosch's main critics and was one of those who signed the agreement creating a government to replace Bosch in September, 1963.

Similar switches have occurred in the reverse direction as well. Pedro Manuel Casals, an outspoken critic of Bosch who was chosen to be Minister of Finance in the first post-coup government of 1963, played a leading role in the 1965 effort to restore Bosch to the presidency. In fact, the six-man Negotiating Commission of the pro-Bosch Constitutional Government of 1965 included only one man who had supported Bosch in 1962.[15] One of the six, Héctor Aristy, had been involved in such a spectacular variety of movements that even Dominicans tend to call him an opportunist; it is a clue to the volatile nature of Dominican politics that the others are not so regarded. When politics is as chaotic as in the Dominican

---

[15] The loyal Bosch supporter was Antonio Guzmán, a close friend of Bosch since their boyhood, who was later chosen by Bosch as his running-mate in the 1966 election.

Republic, switching loyalties or positions in the political spectrum bears little cost.

Close analysis of labor union politics, of student and university politics, of the composition of high and middle levels of the bureaucracy, and particularly of the politics of military factions would probably show similarly unstable patterns. Labor unions and confederations have organized, split, reorganized, and split again.[16] Student groups in changing alliances have fought each other for control of the University of Santo Domingo and many secondary schools; they have employed violence not only against government authorities but against each other, and have kept the University closed on many occasions. From Trujillo's death to early 1968, none of the elected rectors of the University of Santo Domingo managed to retain office through a full two-year term.

No government ministry has escaped the prevalent pattern of instability. In the seven years that Dean Rusk has served as U.S. Secretary of State, the Dominican Republic has had fourteen Foreign Ministers recognized by the U.S. Government, besides several representing regimes with which the U.S. did not officially deal. There has been similar turnover in every other Cabinet post and in the leadership of quasi-governmental institutions like the Corporación de Fomento Industrial (CFI) established as autonomous entities to protect them from political pressures.[17] Nearly complete turnover of government personnel down to intermediate levels of the bureaucracy have occurred in most departments with almost every new executive. Indeed, when incoming President Balaguer left many PRD sympathizers in government positions, a new organization—the *Comisión pro Mejoramiento Reformista*—arose to protest the President's having allowed *Reformista* supporters to go unrewarded while permitting members of the opposition to retain government jobs.

To sort out the politics of military factions over the past few years would require a separate essay, or at least the space to provide detailed biographical information. Suffice it to say that men like the brothers Rodríguez Echavarría and the brothers Fernández,

---

[16] See Howard Wiarda, "The Development of the Labor Movement in the Dominican Republic," *Inter-American Economic Affairs*, Vol. 20 No. 1, pp. 41–63.

[17] Although formally autonomous, the CFI has had ten presidents in six years; each new appointment has followed either a change of government or the resolution of a political crisis.

the cousins Montás Guerrero and Belisario Peguero, Francisco Caamaño Deñó, Francisco Rivera Caminero, Braulio Alvarez Sánchez, Neit Nivar Seijas, Pedro Benoit, Elías Wessin y Wessin and others appear, again and again and in different combinations, in the events of these years; such figures are usually either in high military office or scheming to get there. The pattern of military politics has by now become quite predictable. Officers reach the top, generally accumulate a small fortune, and then are sent abroad, often at the ultimate expense of the United States Government. Once abroad, they often undertake efforts to regain power and influence, much in the style of the Dominican *caudillos* exiled in the last century. Alliances among cliques are formed for tactical purposes, and splits develop quickly; the task of those in power is always to keep one step ahead of the groupings of plotters.

Dominican politics over the past few years, in short, has resembled a kaleidoscope of constantly shifting groupings of "outs" against equally temporary alignments of "ins," of alliances of those *abajo* against those wanting to *quedarse arriba*. There has been almost no institutional continuity, very little consistency with respect to program or ideology, and not even much loyalty to personal leaders.

Perhaps the key characteristic of recent Dominican politics has been the predominance of very direct, virtually naked, confrontations among groups in conflict. The tactics employed by each group since 1961 have tended toward increasingly undisguised and unrefined displays of power, directed more often at replacing the government than at forcing it to take specific actions. Students and university politicians have issued *manifiestos*, circulated leaflets, fomented repeated strikes, demonstrated, marched on the Palace, rioted, clashed with police and army units, and physically occupied the university campus and administrative offices in order to oust an entire slate of university officials on political grounds. They have also supplied recruits for a brief guerrilla uprising and for the *comandos* of the constitutionalist movement. Labor unions have employed public appeals, mass meetings, and limited strikes, and have organized *turbas* (gangs of ruffians) to physically remove management officials they wished to replace on political grounds. Labor unions have also either initiated or lent themselves to various general strikes, including an almost totally effective national general strike in 1966, called to pressure the Provisional Government to send abroad the Minister of the Armed Forces. They also formed *comandos* for the constitutionalist movement. Businessmen gave an impressive demonstration of their power in the November-December, 1961, strike against the remnants of the Trujillo regime. Similar tactics were employed by a smaller group of merchants as part of the campaign to topple Bosch in 1963, and also by a group which organized a counterstrike against the general strike of 1966. Business and commercial groups have even organized and supported terrorist paramilitary groups which have probably outdone the extreme left in committing acts of violence since 1965.

Even the Church, although it has been very conscious of its standing together with the social elite as one of the few elements of continuity in Dominican life, has sometimes exerted its power directly. The Dominican bishops have issued various pastoral letters and other public appeals and actively participated in negotiations to establish a provisional government in 1965. Individual priests have even drafted documents for competing politicians.[18]

Various other groups have not only employed speeches, propaganda, meetings and the like but, more importantly, have engaged in subversion and conspiracy, encouraging military factions to coup and countercoup. The military groups, in turn, have acted to overthrow governments and to establish others, to prevent governments from executing specific policies, and often to suppress opposition. As each group in conflict exerted its power directly, the military groups were always able to prevail until the 1965 crisis. The escalation of violence in 1965, including the arming of irregular forces by the pro-Bosch group, produced the decision by the Air Force and the Armed Forces Training Center, wielders of the ultimately most powerful force, to strafe their Army opponents and the civilian population. It was the effects of this decision, the ultimate step in the politics of chaos, which deepened the 1965 crisis and set the stage for the U.S. intervention.

The particularly chaotic nature of very recent Dominican politics, it will be argued below, stems largely from the effects of the Trujillo period, particularly from the rapid increase in the number of active participants in the political process without the concomitant development of effective institutions. All through Dominican history, however, the country has lacked institutional means by which groups might present their demands and obtain satisfaction.

---

[18] During 1963, mass Christian Reaffirmation meetings were used to mobilize opposition to Bosch, but the initiative for these efforts seems to have been from outside the Church hierarchy.

Groups and individuals have conflicted directly for control of
executive power at the local or national level. Force has always
been the arbiter; "he who bears the bayonet of armed insurrection
or of the organized army has decided the outcome of elections,
before or after the electoral act."[19] Only Heureaux, Cáceres and
Trujillo, the strongmen of Dominican history, have been able to
gather sufficient power (and have had sufficient lack of moral
scruples) to suppress the otherwise incessant struggle. The rhythm
in Dominican history between harsh dictatorships and unsuccessful
attempts at other forms of government reminds one of Hobbes:
"During the time men live without a common power to keep them
all in awe, they are in that condition which is called war, and such
a war is of every man against every man."[20]

III

The major purpose of this essay has been to show that available
literature on the Dominican Republic does not convey the chaos
which has characterized recent Dominican politics. It should be
noted as well that the available literature also fails to explain con-
vincingly the prevalent instability of politics in the pre-Trujillo
Dominican Republic. The two most important books in English
on the Dominican Republic, *Naboth's Vineyard*, by Sumner
Welles, and *Overtaken by Events*, by John Bartlow Martin, both
isolate the problem of political instability as the key to the Dominican Republic's woes and to continuous U.S. involvement. The explanations they offer for this constant instability are far from
satisfying, however. Welles divides Dominican history into two
types of regimes, the "strong" and the "well-intentioned." He
argues that the Dominican tragedy is that the Dominican people's
noble aspirations have time and again been thwarted by "bad"
leaders.[21] Except for some references to the ill effects of the Haitian
occupation and of the return to Spanish rule (1861–1865), however, Welles makes little effort to explain what brings bad leaders
to power in the Dominican Republic, what keeps good leaders out,
and why neither type can maintain himself in office. Welles'

[19] Campillo Pérez, *op. cit.*, p. 11.
[20] Thomas Hobbes, *Leviathan*.
[21] See Sumner Welles, *Naboth's Vineyard: The Dominican Republic, 1844–
1924* (New York, 1928), especially p. 900 ff.

analysis is much more an acceptance of partisan Dominican views about political history than an explanation of that history.

John Martin writes that, as U.S. Ambassador in the Dominican Republic in 1962–63, he always repeated publicly what Welles had said but that he often wondered "whether political scientists are not nearer the truth when they say that people get the kind of government they deserve."[22] At a later point in his book, Martin spells out what he means: "Vanity, pride, posturing, rigidity, hopelessly grandiose dreams, volatility and instability, an almost child-like refusal to assume responsibility: these were flaws in Bosch's character as they are flaws in the Dominican character."[23] What makes Dominicans allegedly less able than others to control these faults and what prevents them from establishing political institutions which withstand human frailties is not discussed, however. Martin writes feelingly about the effects of political instability in Dominican society, but his proposed solution—a binding referendum at the end of the first and third years of an elected president's term to reduce the incentive to coup—betrays his misunderstanding of the nature and depth of the problem.

To find more adequate explanations for the volatile pattern of the last few years, one would have to study in depth many aspects of Dominican history, for the roots of current problems undoubtedly lie in the country's extraordinarily unfortunate past. A thorough analysis of Dominican history cannot be presented here, but it is appropriate to conclude this essay by suggesting, at least in tentative form, some possible causes of the Dominican Republic's violent political instability. At the risk of excessive oversimplification, this brief discussion of possible reasons for contemporary Dominican political chaos will be divided into a cursory examination of three types of causes: those rooted in Dominican history before Trujillo, those due to the effects of the Trujillo era, and those attributable to developments since Trujillo's death.[24]

The era of *caudillo* politics, from the beginning of the Dominican Republic's independent history to the U.S. occupation in 1916, was very much like the early history of other Latin American

[22] Martin, *op. cit.*, p. 22.
[23] *Ibid.*, p. 716.
[24] For his knowledge of the pre-Trujillo period, the author is particularly indebted to the various works of Dr. Harry Hoetink, especially those published in recent issues of *Caribbean Studies*, and to the ideas Dr. Hoetink has expressed in personal correspondence.

countries, but with a lag of some thirty or forty years equivalent to the delay the Dominican people experienced in achieving national independence.[25] Rival leaders and their armed bands fought back and forth across the Dominican countryside all during the nineteenth and early twentieth centuries, taking over provincial forts or disappearing into the hills as their fortune changed, sieging the capital when they were confident of control of most of the countryside. A rhythmic process marked the period: *pronunciamiento*, declarations of support, battles, siege of the capital, takeover, provisional government, and then some form of legitimizing election, followed by dissension—often involving a split between the president and one of his erstwhile allies in the Cabinet—and finally by a counter-*pronunciamiento* and the renewal of the cycle.[26] Defeated leaders often went from the presidency into foreign exile, then returned to lead rebellious bands in a new assault on the capital. Semi-institutionalized means developed to keep the struggle within certain bounds. The right of asylum, exile, and safe-conduct were respected, and foreign intervention—by diplomatic efforts or even by show of military force—was often used to arrange the transfer of power from the vanquished to the victor.[27]

The struggles of the nineteenth century divided the country's politically active population into followers of Buenaventura Báez and Pedro Santana, indistinguishable in terms of ideology or program, and consequently referred to as *rojos* and *azules*.[28] By the early twentieth century, the main political leaders were not Báez and Santana, but Juan Isidro Jiménes and Horacio Vásquez. Like the earlier *rojos* and *azules*, the *jimenistas* and *horacistas* were

[25] For a valuable comparative reference, see R. L. Gilmore, *Caudillism and Militarism in Venezuela, 1810–1910* (Athens, Ohio, 1964). Except for the time lag, Gilmore's analysis of Venezuela applies in many respects to the pre-Trujillo Dominican Republic.

[26] Perhaps the best concise description of late nineteenth and early twentieth century Dominican political history is Luis F. Mejía, *De Lilís a Trujillo* (Caracas, 1944).

[27] In one case a U.S. warship's commander intervened during hostilities in a coastal city to establish a neutral zone and even to define a line, the crossing of which by either side would signify victory and bring an end to the battle. See Mejía, *op. cit.*, p. 45.

[28] For further comments on the lack of ideological or programmatic distinctions between Báez and Santana (and their followers) see Pedro Troncoso Sánchez, "Posiciones de Principio en la Historia Política Dominicana" *Journal of Inter-American Studies*, Vol. IX, p. 187. Troncoso argues that the absence of political dialogue over issues retarded the development of mature politics in the Dominican Republic.

constantly changing groupings, as supporters crossed from one party to another and back.

The issues from year to year were primarily economic. Each group came to office pledged to end corruption in the administration of public funds. In reality, however, *caudillo* politics tended to be mainly a struggle for revenue, for jobs and favors, and for the opportunity to control the customs-houses and other sources of wealth.

Three aspects of this long period of *caudillo* politics distinguish the Dominican Republic's history from that of many other countries in Latin America; those differences help account for the ease with which Rafael Trujillo came to dominate Dominican society in 1930 and perhaps also for the disorder which has followed Trujillo's death. First, throughout its independent history the Dominican Republic has lacked a powerful oligarchy. A series of emigrations by elite families, particularly after the Spanish withdrawal in 1795 and during the Haitian occupation of 1822 to 1844, eliminated from Dominican society many who might otherwise have dominated the country's economy and politics. The few white, socially-prestigious families remaining in the Dominican Republic in the late nineteenth century were not wealthy or powerful but insecure. The elite's fragile position, their ability to monopolize social prestige alone, together with the fear of renewed Haitian domination, account for the persistent search for a "protector nation" to exert sovereignty in the Dominican Republic. Failing to exercise political control, the traditional elites lacked confidence in the results of national independence.

Second, the Dominican Republic has also lacked a strong, well-entrenched Church. The Spanish withdrawal of 1795 had already drastically weakened the Church and after 1822 the Haitian occupation authorities set out deliberately to destroy what was left of the Church as an institution, to expropriate its property, and to deport foreign priests. By the time the Dominican Republic's independence was proclaimed in 1844, the Church was practically crushed. Since then, the Church has never regained wealth or political power, and has characteristically been a cautious, dependent institution, forced to accommodate itself to political upheavals and to accept the conditions imposed by the few strong governments in Dominican history.

Third, the Dominican Republic before Trujillo never developed a national military institution. The Dominican Republic's unusual experience of having European colonization followed immediately by Haitian occupation deprived the country of the experience of a national "war of independence" shared by most countries in the hemisphere. By 1844, it did not require much military effort to persuade the Haitian authorities to withdraw. No sooner had the Haitians left than the Dominican military chiefs split; they exiled Juan Pablo Duarte, the national hero, within weeks of achieving independence. From that time until the U.S. occupation of 1916– 1924, the Dominican Republic never had a national military force but rather small bands of armed men loyal to competing *caudillos*.

From the time of independence until the U.S. occupation of 1916 ended the period of *caudillo* politics, then, the Dominican Republic was not characterized by a powerful triad of oligarchy, church and military, but rather by exactly the reverse: an insecure grouping of elite families, a weak and dependent church, and no national military institution. As a result of these conditions, a power vacuum existed which was filled by the continuous, virtually unchecked struggle of *caudillos* and their adherents. The intensity of the persistent struggle and its supposed effects on U.S. security and financial interests, eventually produced the U.S. military intervention of 1916 and the establishment by U.S. authorities of an occupation government. U.S. officials analyzed the pattern of Dominican politics, attributed the constant turmoil largely to the absence of a national military institution, and set out to establish the *Guardia Nacional*, the national constabulary. By organizing a relatively effective institution in a society almost totally lacking in institutions, U.S. authorities helped make it possible for the head of the newly-established force, General Rafael Trujillo, to seize power and to retain control for over thirty years. Given the weakness of the traditional elites and of the Church, as well as the desire of the U.S. Government to disengage itself from involvement in Dominican affairs, it was not difficult for General Trujillo to consolidate power through his domination of the new Armed Forces.

The Trujillo era in the Dominican Republic has been comparatively well-researched, but no available work has adequately analyzed the effects of the Trujillo period on the Dominican polity.[29]

---

[29] The best available work on Trujillo, Robert Crassweller's *Trujillo: Life and Times of a Caribbean Dictator* (New York, 1966) does not deal at all with the lasting consequences of the Trujillo period. Other works on the Trujillo era worth consulting include Howard Wiarda, *The Trujillo Dictatorship: Caudilloism or Totalitarianism* (U. of Florida, forthcoming);

To understand Trujillo's legacy, one should study at least four different results of the era, some of them purposeful but most of them unintended. By eliminating the last of the regional *caudillos* (fighters like Desiderio Arias) and by his bloody resolution of the problem of Haitian encroachment in the border areas, Trujillo performed the function of "unifying dictator." The Dominican Republic was a collection of separate towns and villages in 1930, but the Trujillo era saw the integration and definition of the Dominican political community. Political conflict, much of which had been strictly local up to 1930, was bound to concentrate on control of the national state after the Trujillo period.

Second, and closely related, was Trujillo's role as an "economic nationalist." By purchasing from foreign owners—on behalf of the state or in some cases for himself or for members of his family—such enterprises as the electric company, the six branches of the National City Bank, sixty percent of the national sugar production, and a host of other enterprises large and small, Trujillo transformed the pattern of the Dominican economy, bringing control of much of the national wealth into Dominican hands. When all of the holdings of the state and of the Trujillo family—including many other enterprises which Trujillo and his colleagues had begun or expanded—became public patrimony after Trujillo's assassination, it became clear that the dictator had created a state economic apparatus far more valuable as a prize than the one he had taken over in 1930.[30] Politics has always been an important means of access to revenue in the Dominican Republic; as a result of the Trujillo period, the economic stakes of political conflict are higher than ever.

Third, in his never ending desire to accumulate power and profit, Trujillo brought capitalism and the beginning of industrial development to the Dominican Republic, albeit in distorted and inefficient form and for his own ends. Trujillo, his family, and their colleagues

---

Jesús de Galíndez Suárez, *La Era de Trujillo: Un Estudio Casuístico de Dictadura Hispanoamericana* (Santiago, Chile, 1956); Juan Bosch, *Trujillo: Causas de Una Tiranía sin Ejemplo* (Caracas, 1959); Arturo Espaillat, *Trujillo, The Last Caesar* (Chicago, 1964); and German Ornes, *Trujillo: Little Caesar of the Caribbean* (New York, 1958). There are also a number of hagiographic works published under the auspices of the Trujillo regime.

[30] As a result of the assumption by the state of ownership of all the properties of the Trujillo family, the Dominican Republic in 1968 has a higher percentage of its Gross National Product in the public sector than any country in the hemisphere except socialist Cuba.

began or greatly expanded a considerable number of industries, mostly of the primitive import-substitution type: flour, peanut oil, cement, glass, paper, paint, etc. The industrial work force expanded almost fourfold between 1936 and 1956, and electricity production multiplied fifteenfold in the same period.[31] Trujillo's policies destroyed the fragmentation of the previous import-export trade patterns, in which each region of the country operated independently out of its own port; Santo Domingo (called Ciudad Trujillo) was built up as the commercial, financial, and administrative center of the country as well as the nation's political capital. Rapid urbanization, the swift expansion of government activities, and the beginning of industrialization brought two new social groups into being in Santo Domingo: an urban proletariat and the "middle-sector" of industrialists, bureaucrats, managers, and professionals.

The effects of these socioeconomic changes on Dominican society and politics after Trujillo's death were profoundly destabilizing. What occurred was not simply a return to *caudillo* politics, for Dominican society had changed considerably since 1930. A proletariat had been born, but no meaningful labor organizations had been allowed to form. The new middle sector had grown, but without any cohesion other than dependence on Trujillo, who had made its rise possible. Interest and professional associations had been permitted no function beyond praise of Trujillo; they were discredited and virtually in atrophy.

Hundreds of thousands of Dominicans had been made to feel part of the nation during the Trujillo era, especially through the establishment of a powerful national radio network, but no means had been established to organize these new participants. Political parties, except for Trujillo's own, had been banned. Associations had not been formed except to serve the dictator. The Dominican Republic faced the classic problem of "praetorian politics": the expansion of political participation outpaced the creation of political institutions.[32]

[31] Figures taken from Dominican government publication *21 Años de Estadísticas Dominicanos* (Cuidad Trujillo, 1957) show the industrial work force in 1936 to have been 20,301; in 1956, it was about 75,000. Electricity production was 13.4 million KW in 1936; 204.5 million KW in 1956. The Dominican Republic's total population during this period barely doubled.

[32] See Samuel P. Huntington, "Political Development and Political Decay," *World Politics*, 17, (April, 1965), pp. 386–430. Many of the ideas in this paragraph and in other passages of this essay have been influenced by Professor Huntington's articles and lectures, and by his forthcoming book, *Political Order in Changing Societies* (New Haven, 1968).

Finally, Trujillo's style and method—his consistent regard for legal niceties in the execution of monstrous crimes, his brutal practice of raising men from obscurity to power and then ousting them in *desgracia*, his shrewd stimulation of personal rivalries and jealousies, his love of bombast and show—all had lasting effects on the conduct of Dominican politics. By his own blatant cynicism, Trujillo encouraged a skepticism about public activities which has impeded the development since his death of institutions based on loyalty and trust. Perhaps the most corrupting effect of the Trujillo period on the Dominican polity has been the set of attitudes and expectations these years aroused.

Various aspects of the post-Trujillo period have heightened the problem of instability in Dominican politics. Political participation has expanded dramatically, as is evidenced by the fact that well over a million citizens have voted in each of the two national elections since Trujillo's death. Political awareness and activity have been facilitated by the sevenfold multiplication of radio receivers during the five years from 1960 to 1965 and by the almost equally pronounced proliferation of competing radio stations and publications.[33] Only in the most recent period have *campesino* federations, cooperative movements, community development organizations, labor unions, and the like been emerging to channel the activities of these new participants.

Another cause for disorder in the post-Trujillo Dominican Republic has been the sudden rise in the Dominican people's level of expectations after Trujillo's death. According to evidence gathered by Lloyd Free in 1962, it appears that, once liberated from the dictator's reign, Dominicans expected immediate and dramatic improvements in their own personal situations. Free reported that Dominicans rated their past and present personal positions lower than did nationals of some fifteen other nations studied, but that Dominicans expected remarkable improvements within five years.[34] Applying an analysis of the gap between expectations and fulfillment similar to the "J-curve" hypothesis formulated by James

[33] The Dominican Republic had about 100,000 radio receivers in 1960 and over 700,000 in 1965, according to figures obtained from the Dominican Government's *Dirección General de Estadísticas*. See, also, T. D. Roberts et al., *Area Handbook for the Dominican Republic* (Washington, 1966), pp. 226–238.

[34] See Lloyd Free, *Attitudes, Hopes, and Fears of the Dominican People* (Report issued in June, 1962, and republished in 1965 by The Institute for International Social Research, Princeton, New Jersey).

Davies, Free concluded that "an extremely dangerous situation of popular discontent and frustration, fraught with dangerous upheaval, exists in the Dominican Republic."[35] The events of 1965 seem to have borne out Free's perception.

The sudden exposure of the Dominican Republic to external political influences has been partly responsible for the quick rise in expectations and also for some of the intensity of political strife. Whereas Dominicans had been discouraged from travel during the Trujillo period, many thousands have been abroad in the past seven years, and they have brought back new ideas, wants, and information. Foreign books and periodicals have entered the country freely and Dominicans have been an especially receptive audience for foreign radio broadcasts, particularly those of The Voice of America and of Radio Havana.[36] Because the Dominican Republic's political life opened up—with Trujillo's death—just weeks after the Bay of Pigs, the country has been a particularly central object of Cold War politics. External agents, including not only leftists trained in Cuba but also anti-Castro Cuban exiles and American personnel, have helped to unsettle Dominican affairs. Most important, recent Dominican politics has been very affected by imported ideologies and rhetoric, much of it introduced by Dominican leaders formerly in exile and some of it fostered by United States policy. Phrases and ideas which did not arise from Dominican experience have nevertheless helped to stimulate political unrest.

A fourth factor contributing to the instability of recent Dominican politics has been the effects of American policy. While aiming always to promote stability, the United States Government has probably increased destabilizing pressures. Within the five years from 1960 to 1965, the United States first imposed sanctions on the Dominican economy, then granted the Dominican Republic massive amounts of aid, next cut off the aid program entirely, and finally resumed its aid program on a limited scale. These various measures, which had the effect of facilitating the rapid expansion of Dominican imports in 1962–63 and then helping to force the Dominican government to impose unpopular austerity policies in

[35] *Ibid.* Compare James C. Davies, "Toward a Theory of Revolution," *American Sociological Review* 27 (February, 1962), pp. 5–19.

[36] According to a study prepared for the U. S. Government, "in 1964 the Dominican radio audience was the largest in Latin America in terms of percentage of the total audience listening to foreign broadcasts." See T. D. Roberts *et al., op. cit.,* 238.

1964–65, heightened the discontent which fueled the 1965 explosion.[37]

The observation that United States policy has contributed, albeit unintentionally, to the instability of recent Dominican politics suggests a fundamental question which must be considered in a subsequent essay: The historic effects of the United States on the Dominican polity. The literature on United States-Dominican relations tends to focus almost exclusively on the U.S. military interventions in Santo Domingo. These interventions, however, are only the most dramatic and controversial episodes in a long history of deep American entanglement. Politically, the United States has often participated intimately in Dominican affairs, as is demonstrated in remarkable detail in the accounts of Sumner Welles and John Bartlow Martin, each written after its author had finished two years as the responsible U.S. official in the Dominican Republic. Economically, the U.S. role in the Dominican Republic has always been significant. From 1916 until 1947, in fact, U.S. currency was actually the legal tender of Dominican commerce. No country in the world had a larger percentage of its trade with the United States in 1967 than the Dominican Republic, and U.S. investments have historically been of considerable importance in the export sector of the Dominican economy: sugar, fruit, and more recently, bauxite. Culturally, the United States—particularly the institutions and practices introduced by the occupation authorities from 1916 to 1924—has been the dominant foreign influence in this century. Increasingly, too, the Dominican Republic is tied to the United States by migration patterns. More Dominicans have entered the United States on immigrant and visitor visas during recent years than residents of any other country in the hemisphere but Mexico.

The United States, in short, has been and still is a major, continuing influence on Dominican society and politics. Although nominally sovereign and independent, the Dominican Republic has never been able to escape the shadow of the United States; it has suffered the positive disadvantages of dependence without gaining the possible advantages of annexation. By failing to consider the total influence of the United States on the Dominican Republic, this essay—like other available interpretations of Dominican politics —leaves a major gap.

---

[37] A related but separate destabilizing influence has been the extreme fluctuation in the world price of sugar, which intensified the import boom early in the Trujillo period and worsened the foreign exchange crisis of 1964–65.

The Chonchol Plan[*]

[EDITORS' NOTE: The excerpts below offer an interesting insight into the ideological and practical trials that beset a reformist and non-Marxian social revolutionary political force in the process of solving developmental problems.

After the April 1967 municipal elections the National Council of the ruling Chilean Christian Democratic Party (PDC—*Partido Democratacristiano*) designated a technical-political commission to clarify the nature of tasks to be solved and the available and preferable paths to be chosen during the years 1967–1970. This study group was headed by Jacques Chonchol, influential ideologue of the PDC in charge of implementing the government's crucial agrarian reform policy.

The significance of this document lies in its ambiguity in trying to develop a scheme for a so-called "noncapitalistic" way of development while by and large adhering to the traditional tenets of Chilean parliamentary democracy. It proposes a gradual transferal of economic power from the traditional vested interests to the public sector, thus also effecting a transfer of political power and influence. Some of the ideas presented are clearly Marxian with a generous sprinkling of populist idealism and notions of communitarian collectivism. The measures promoted are not far from, if not identical with, those advocated by Chile's traditional leftist parties, socialist and communist. In addition, the document reflects the competitive tensions that exist between the more militant youthful-technocrat members of the PDC leadership and the moderate entourage of President Frei. The report stresses the importance of "correct" relations between the party apparatus and the gov-

* Translated by Carmen D. Deere from *P.E.C.* (Santiago de Chile), No. 239, July 28, 1967.

ernment, expressing it by suggesting that the latter should be subordinated to the former. Regardless of the narrowly local implications of this debate, some points might appear relevant to a broader
universe than just the PDC: the issue of pluralism and its feasibility
in a developmental setting and the problems of reconciling revolutionary goals with reformist methods.]

After the election of the councilmen at its meeting last April,
the National Council of the P.D.C., examined the results of those
elections and made an analysis of the political situation. It was
decided to appoint a political-technical commission to prepare a
report, in no more than sixty days, which would help the Party
to recondition its political strategy to the new circumstances, in
order to accomplish the programmed goals.

This report should direct its efforts towards a definition of the
immediate tasks in order to prepare Chile for a noncapitalist way
of development, in accordance with the course determined by the
Second National Congress of the Party. The commission in charge
of outlining the tasks was to direct its work according to seven
basic criteria, which were agreed upon by a unanimous vote of
the National Council and which are the following:

1. The total use and control by the state of the basic mechanisms
of the economic system, the effective implementation of the national plan, and the subordination of the budget and of credit to
these new programmed tasks.

2. The determination of strategic areas which should be incorporated into the public domain, and the procedures which should be
applied to the new activities.

3. The determination of the sectors in which the state will impose the constitution of *Sociedades Mixtas* [ED. NOTE: corporations
with the participation of public and private funds] in relation
either to national or foreign enterprises, guaranteeing in all cases
public control in the constitution of capital and in the administration of the enterprise.

4. The determination of statute for the private sector, to be
clearly written and established on the following principles:

    a. A tributary system of prices and credit established in such
       a manner as to grant just utility margins; and

    b. Sectoral requirements of reinvestment, production, pro-
       ductivity, standardization, quality, and export, etc.

5. To prepare systematic programs of development for the artisan
and small and medium-sized industry, cooperatives, and other ad-

vanced forms of industrial and agricultural production, guaranteeing them the necessary supply credit, the supply of primary materials, technical assistance and commercial facilities.

6. To restudy the national economic program of investment and to determine the percentages and quantity which, until 1970, will correspondingly contribute to public investment, popular savings, and the reinvestment of profits by the capitalist sector.

7. To lay out a plan for compensation and price policy in such a manner that the workers will have institutionalized opportunities to participate in its formulation, and the government will have effective technical and legal methods to control costs and rises in prices.

* * *

THE "REVOLUCION EN LIBERTAD"

The meaning of the presidential election of 1964:

The presidential election of 1964 was in our judgement much more than a simple electoral campaign. It directed an authentic public process to the situation with which our country struggled, and permitted clarifications and convergences that went beyond the two dynamic candidates who aspired to the government, to give origin to a truly national ideology that for the first time in our history permitted a positive definition in favor of profound changes in the Chilean economy and society.

We should remember several positive traits that characterized those months:

a. The presidential election of September, 1964, was the first held, not only without the participation of a candidate of the right, but additionally, with programs clearly directed against the privileges of the dominant groups.

b. The debate that was then produced and that reached an unprecedented maturity and depth, permitted [the emergence of] a collective "dose of conscience" about the "integral crisis of Chile," as Jorge Ahumada called it. The populace understood that the existence of misery, of economic stagnation, of large, exploited and unorganized majorities, of the lack of effective political representation, of external dependency and other things were interrelated and were the result of the inefficiency and injustice of the capitalistic system, the official ideology or practice of the government leaders that have led us in the last fifty years.

The capitalistic system and the "integral crisis of Chile," parties of the right and stagnation became synonymous concepts for the populace. The elements of a noncapitalist ideology were being consolidated, creating a climate of weariness and even desperation in some [ED. NOTE: presumably the right wing]. Those who opened their eyes to this new reality found intolerable situations of economic or social inferiority that until recently they had considered normal. The central idea of our propaganda, affirming that "all had to change," interpreted exactly this state of dominant intention.

c. The most representative political parties changed their traditional structure in order to transform themselves into social movements that could attempt to actively express the most important social forces in our country. The Christian Democratic Party, particularly, received massive influence from these sectors; the industrial workers, peasants, urbanites and youth have come to be, along with groups largely of the middle class, the sociological base of the Party and its external image.

d. In the eyes of these sectors the "Revolucion en Libertad," more than a governmental program with goals and defined stages, was a varied entity of longing and public aspirations; a rapid and substantial change was expected of the Frei government, accompanied by an essential betterment in their standard of living.

An active popular myth accompanied this attitude and in many ways cast shadows on certain difficulties (presupposed limitations, politics, etc.), that inevitably we would face.

All these factors determined that the tasks that our government should fulfill in order to respond to the legitimate aspirations it advanced were of a breadth that does not allow comparison with those fulfilled before. More than creating a good government we were setting in motion a revolution.

*   *   *

DEFINITION AND APPLICATION OF A NONCAPITALIST WAY OF DEVELOPMENT

Diverse sectors alien to the Christian Democratic Party have insisted on presenting the central formulation of our Second National Congress as an aggressive design on the plans of the government, or as an eagerness to go beyond the content of the September program. Not just a few have tried to make it seem a proposition of theory completely alien to the Chilean reality. Many have made an error.

The Party knows perfectly well that the work in the next three years will encounter limitations of two kinds:

a. It should be encompassed within the criteria formulated in the presidential program of 1964.

b. It cannot go beyond limits allowed by the financial possibilities of the country as expressed in the annual national budget.

This plan of action does not propose the lessening of the aspirations of the construction of a new society, for in this context this will be possible.

A few complementary explanations will help clear up our objectives:

a. First of all, it is necessary to remember that our assumption of government coincided with a very important moment in the evolution of our economy, in that there was a necessity of initiating a second industrial expansion in order to create industry of capital gains and large industrial complexes (petrochemical, cellulose, expansion of iron and steel, etc.). All the scientists agree that at the beginning of this decade the process of industrialization based on import substitution ended; therefore, the creation of an industrial sector which we are supporting was a fallacious demand in terms of our development.

This is not only an economic problem, but also a decisive matter of political importance that could define the nature of our development. Who makes the investment effort in these undertakings? Who takes possession of the installations and obtains the profits? This is the vital question, for if these dynamic industries were to pass into the definitive control of the capitalist sector, national or foreign, the Chilean economy and society would inevitably be a capitalist one in the next decades.

It would be perfectly possible, as a result, that by following that route and the proposals of those who direct the country, Chile would pass from a rudimentary and inefficient capitalist structure to a modern and efficient structure. This is what constitutes the danger of capitalist reconstruction or the introduction of neocapitalism, against which all of the "militantes" [ED. NOTE: activists or cadre] of the Party have declared themselves.

This affirms the conviction that not just any form of economic development is acceptable to the Chilean public, and that this is not an ideologically neutral process. We, the Christian Democrats, desire an economic growth that will move us away from, instead of compromising with, capitalist criteria. We want progress, but we also desire that the major effort of the populace benefit the majority and not serve to consolidate the power of just a few economic groups. Because of this, we will never measure the success of our work with simple statistical criteria: more houses, more roads, more schools, more industry, more work. All this interests us, but we attach a requirement: that the dominant beneficiaries of the development process be the workers, the peasants and the middle class of the country.

The Christian Democratic Party consequently rejects as contrary to its postulates the alternative of converting itself into "the Party of Chilean development" without other specifications. It searches, conversely, for the perspective of orienting the obtainment of economic development towards the building of a "new society of workers": unified, democratic and popular.

b. The Chilean economy in the private sector is not exclusively a capitalist economy. This is without a question its dominant form, but next to it exist diverse forms of noncapitalist organization that act in the majority of cases in a deprived form, assuming a subsidiary, marginal and rear-guard role as passive collaborators of the capitalist producers.

Their significance, however, is greater than appears to be the case. "In Chile today there are fifty-six million artisan workshops and eight million small industrial enterprises that generate thirty-eight percent of the industrial product and employ 230 million people. More than a million people live off what small industry and artisan workshops directly produce." (Data from the "Presidential Message," May 21, 1967). Numerous equivalent organizations exist in the agricultural sector: agricultural cooperatives, communals, committees of small farmers, and today—constantly gaining in importance—settlements of the agrarian reform. In the case of dwellings, cooperatives of dwellings and the popular societies of self-construction are becoming more significant all the time.

This distinction, in any case, does not let us forget that the national economic mission as a whole is to supply the nation with a growing quantity of goods and services. It is important to remember that the two sectors should receive the stimuli suitable to their proper nature. This means that in the future the state will no longer stimulate capitalist enterprises solely in the desire that there be private enterprise in Chile; instead, it will be judged by the objective criterion of its function, that there be private enterprise where it produces results that justify its existence.

Meanwhile, in relation to the development of social producers, the state will promote within its plans the establishment of enterprises financed by the community effort and in which forms of ownership and distribution of profits will be introduced that will benefit the workers who are involved in this activity. Likewise the resources of public credit financing will be oriented in their favor, which will allow them to take charge of reproductive investments.

We have faith in the future economic possibilities of these popular producers who, joined in action and investment with the public sector, will constitute an authentic "social economy of the people." We believe it necessary to assign them important tasks in the development process.

c. This exercise in authority has shown us that progress in the construction of a social system presents three well-defined characteristics: it is dynamic, experimental and progressive.

It is dynamic, for an experience in progress creates its own instruments and mechanisms as it goes along.

It is experimental, for the new forms of production should be more efficient than the capitalist forms. This imperative of efficiency obligates us to look for systems that will assure higher levels of production and productivity.

It is progressive, for the action of the new producers extends itself to more extensive areas and activities. As L. J. Lebret [ED. NOTE: French Christian Democrat Sociologist, d. 1966] teaches us, "a social system is constructed by means of successive approximations."

*　　*　　*

In the judgment of the commission, in the capitalist scheme of development, it is impossible [to strive] for the harmonious realization of the five great goals indicated to be compatible with priorities. In the capitalist form of development a few goals are always sacrificed, or, as in most cases, they are left for later on, when the desired goals are only obtained in a very restricted way and after permanent and frequently bloody social and political fights. Because of this, the commission considers that only a noncapitalist way of development will permit the attainment of the simultaneous realization of these goals, all of which constitute the insubstitutable foundation of a progressive and democratic society where human solidarity would be the fundamental sustenance of the social and economic system.

This is how the Second National Congress of the Party understood it when it affirmed the inevitable necessity for Chile to move forward along a noncapitalist way of development which is characterized by the following fundamental traits:

a. The democratic planning of socioeconomic life that involves the mobilization of the material and human resources of the country, in search of goals whose priority is to be determined by balanced development that is at the same time decentralized.

b. The rapid increase of communal forms of production.

c. A fast, drastic and massive agrarian reform that will end the "latifundio" and establish forms of rural ownership that are not patronal, strengthening the experiences of the communal type that are more realistic.

d. The extension of the control or dominion of the community over the centers of economic power and basic activities.

e. The adaptation of the noncapitalist state structures to the development process, permitting the active participation of the people in the decision-making centers. In this process the state cannot be neutral, but rather will be the means of transformation.

f. The determination of a statute for private enterprise that will continue to operate outside of the public sector. In this sense, private enterprise may realize income-yielding investment economic activity, but will be subject to governmental planning and to the political power of the people. The same regulations apply to foreign capital.

The ideas put forth allow the conclusion that:

> *The noncapitalist way of development is related to designated tasks in order to assure the full realization of the goals of the program of the government of 1964, and to advance from that point of realization the construction of a communitarian social economic system that will succeed the capitalist regime.*

* * *

CENTRAL CRITERIA FOR THE APPLICATION OF A NONCAPITALIST WAY OF DEVELOPMENT IN THE PERIOD 1967-1970

This report limits itself to an examination of, and the proposal of, concrete means that within the next three and one-half years will permit the deepening of the "Revolucion en Libertad" in accordance with the central strategy we have defined, appraising with the most possible clarity the basic criteria under which we must work.

The basic principles that we enumerate should inspire our conduct. From each one of them a number of concrete propositions can be deduced, whose details and foundations may be found in different chapters of this report.

First: *That the state act as the fundamental, dynamic element of the economic development of Chile and that it effectively control and use the instruments and mechanisms of the economic system.*

Second: *The democratization of the Chilean economy, and particularly severing the alliance between the financial powers and industrial property.*

Third: *To delimit the fields of work and the "rules of the game" of the public sector and of the private capitalist sector in respect to the state. This supposedly will distinguish between areas that should absolutely belong to the public domain and those in which the state participates in "sociedades mixtas," either as the owner of the majority of social capital or as a minor partner with a right to vote in important matters.*

Fourth: *To establish a defined program of development and of expansion of the social economy of the people, in which an acceleration of a thorough agrarian reform stands out, confirming its top priority in the assignment of financial resources.*

Fifth: *To promote the organizational tasks of the people and to obtain their effective participation in the various levels of government as the only method of work compatible with a revolutionary process.*

*   *   *

POLITICAL CONDITIONS NECESSARY FOR THE EFFECTIVE APPLICATION OF THIS PROGRAM OF WORK

It is essential, finally, to understand clearly that it is not enough to have numerous propositions, concrete as they may be, to accomplish those results that we look for. It is necessary additionally, to define the internal and external political conditions that this program necessitates for its successful completion.

EXTERNAL CONDITIONS

Presently in Chile a form of political anarchy exists that affects almost without exception all of the political parties, as a consequence of our efforts to break the frame of a society in crisis.

The present program intends to be a conscious effort to loosen ourselves from whatever influences us in this matter in terms of past political structure and practices so that the political behavior that corresponds to the [ideals of] Christian Democracy, through popular rule, will emerge effectively.

Thus it will be possible to carry forth the "Revolucion en Libertad," obtaining the completion of the political goals conducive to its total execution.

a. We ought to prepare ourselves for an active confrontation with the right, especially with its ultra-reactionary groups. As a consequence of their total failure to gain electoral support, they intend from now on to destroy our plans with a major aggressive forcefulness, at any cost. For more than training our "militantes" to respond "a posteriori" to the concrete attacks they make on us, we must train them to discover and denounce among all sectors of the public the methods of falsification that the right uses in its work against all progressive governments; also, our "militantes" must make it known that the right spreads rumors and fabricates myths.

Our work ought to progress in the knowledge that the middle sectors understand that their substantial interests are opposed to those of the right. Concretely, our objective should be to reduce the right to the exclusive support of the oligarchical and "latifundista" sectors; in accordance with the objective criteria of the distribution of the land and the revenue in 1964, it could not then aspire to represent more than five percent of the national vote in the electoral process.

b. Our situation of political independence should not constitute a pretext in which to aggravate our political solitude. We should try to maintain a democratic and constructive dialogue with diverse national political forces, especially with those from whom we can gain support for the execution of this program.

c. The main task, however, is more in the area of social forces than that of political parties. *We ought to consolidate social and electoral support established upon the creation of an alliance of the people-progressive middle class*, which naturally will increase as social and economic measures like the ones this report proposes are implemented.

d. In this program designed to give the people power it would be difficult to explain that due to political reticence (not articulating Christian Democratic goals specifically) one would distort the goals of Christian Democracy and remove the base of social support for the tasks designated, aligning against them mutually competing forces with a purely distinctive intent.

It would be senseless if this attitude should damage the objectives that motivate Christian Democracy, or if it should alienate the social base supporting the [fulfillment of] the tasks outlined above; this [alienation] could result in the [emergence of a] movement uniting forces that would oppose the realization of the important task that is ahead of us.

INTERNAL CONDITIONS

The Party, as is its due, ought to resolve simultaneously two important problems:

a. The first refers to the relations between the Party and the government. In this aspect it is fundamental that both have the same strategy. It is not possible for the government to act with one determined strategy and the Party with another, whatever they be. If this occurs, we will live in permanent difficulties and misunderstandings which would weaken the action of the Party as well as the government.

This strategy should be elaborated in common accord and institutionalized in the most explicit mode possible; it ought to work with a concerted action. It cannot be defined by the Party without an awareness of the concrete problems confronting the government, nor solely by the government, should its future be that of the Party's.

If this strategy is defined together, later on the distribution of specific responsibilities would take place in a logical place: the government with executive and administrative tasks; the Party with the tasks of communicating the programs to the public and with the search for social support for the tasks of the government.

Outside of this area of agreement the Party has the right and the responsibility to continue in ideological and programmatic elaboration, looking for a definition of the goals for new stages, as President Frei expressed in his message.

b. It is indispensable to readjust the Christian Democratic Party internally to change it into an instrument capable of constituting the vanguard of the Chilean revolution.

We ought to outlaw in our new internal structure "assemblies" and electoral or "caudillista" tendencies in order to end the lack of political skill in our bases and the lack of leadership training.

It is necessary to transform the Christian Democratic Party into a Party with representative bases, organically incorporated into the direction of national developments; to convert it into a modern and efficient Party, capable of executing adequate political pedagogy among all "militantes," with an active ideological and political debate, and a preparation for its middle level and grass-roots leaders; in summary, a Party that is prepared to understand national campaigns in all sectors, in order to gain attachment to the strategy outlined.

Lastly, it is necessary to note not only our faults, but also the false images that our work has been projecting (impudence, sectoral division, lack of practical sense). We need urgently to determine precisely a new attitude that we shall demand from all our activists. Our future definitely depends on the testimony that each one of us projects in the conduct of each day. To the extent that the country sees us in the image of honesty, idealism and the spirit of work, our right will be recognized to direct and deepen the revolution and to advance in a noncapitalist way of development towards the construction of a new society.

Leadership and Conflict Within the Febrerista Party of Paraguay[*]

Paul H. Lewis

Roberto Michels, writing in 1915, said about political parties:

> Every party organization represents an oligarchical power grounded upon a democratic basis. We find everywhere electors and elected. Also we find everywhere that the power of the elected leaders over the electing masses is almost unlimited.[1]

This, in a nutshell, expresses his now famous "iron law of oligarchy"—the assertion that every party organization must sooner or later become dominated by a small elite of leaders who will use their power to perpetuate themselves, and will succeed in doing so even in the face of widespread opposition from the rank and file.

Michels is supported in this view by a more contemporary student of political parties, Maurice Duverger, who says that: "The leadership of parties tends naturally to assume an oligarchic form. A veritable 'ruling class' comes into being that is more or less closed; it is an 'inner circle' into which it is difficult to penetrate."[2]

The oligarchic concept of party organization rests upon two main assumptions: (1) that there is a low turnover in party leader-

From Paul H. Lewis, "Leadership and Conflict within the Febrerista Party of Paraguay," *Journal of Inter-American Studies*, Vol. IX (April 1967). Reprinted by permission.

[*] This study is based on field research in Latin America, February-November, 1964, supported by a Fulbright research grant. During this time scores of Paraguayan exiles were interviewed and Paraguay was visited.

A shorter version of this paper was read at the Thirteenth Annual meeting of the Southeastern Conference on Latin American Studies at the University of Miami, March 18–19, 1966.

[1] Robert Michels, *Political Parties* (New York: Dover Publications, 1959), p. 401.

[2] Maurice Duverger, *Political Parties* (New York: John Wiley—Science Editions, 1963), p. 151.

ship at all levels, and that when vacancies do occur only younger
men who are considered "safe" by the old elite are coopted; and
(2) that the party elite exercises complete control over all levels
and all branches of the party organization.

An opposing point of view, based on a pluralistic model of parties
is offered by Samuel J. Eldersveld in his *Political Parties: A Behavioral Analysis.*[3] Eldersveld rejects the concept of oligarchy in
favor of *"stratarchy"*—a term developed by Harold Lasswell and
Abraham Kaplan.[4] The concept of stratarchy assumes that power is
dispersed within any given party, that there is little or no unity of
command at the top, and that the leadership's power tends to become diluted at the lower levels. This leads Eldersveld to assert
that: (1) control over the lower party echelons is "minimal and
formal," and (2) there is a high rate of turnover in leadership at all
levels of the hierarchy.

The oligarchy versus stratarchy debate is far from resolved.
Neither approach has, so far, been shown conclusively to be universally applicable. I would like to suggest that the reason for this
is that the type of party studied determines to a large extent the
conclusions that a scholar will reach. For example, Eldersveld's
book is a study of American political parties in Wayne County,
Michigan. Leaving aside the obvious fact that Wayne County is a
rather small corner of the world on which to base a theory of
political parties in general, we can hardly be surprised—since
American parties are notoriously decentralized—that he arrives at a
pluralistic model.

On the other hand, Michels formulated his "iron law of oligarchy" from his experience with the German Social Democratic
Party. Several studies of the S.P.D. have been made since the
appearance of Michels' classic work and, to my knowledge, none
of them disputes his conclusions that that party is a monolithic
organization. Again, however, the S.P.D. may not be typical.
Duverger's work is more broadly comparative than Michels', but
even there it is generally agreed that the weakest part of his book
is his description of the American and Uruguayan party systems. Moreover, it seems that the premises with which researchers
start may tend to influence the conclusions they reach. Elite theory
has been developed principally by Europeans (Michels, Pareto,

[3] Samuel J. Eldersveld, *Political Parties: A Behavioral Analysis* (New York: Rand McNally, 1964).
[4] Harold Lasswell and Abraham Kaplan, *Power and Society* (New Haven: Yale University Press, 1950).

Mosca) and has enjoyed much greater acceptance among European sociologists and political scientists than it has from their American counterparts.

This paper will discuss the Febrerista Party of Paraguay in terms of alleged oligarchization in its leadership. The idea here is not to attempt to prove either the oligarchic or the pluralist concepts. In fact, to be frank about the matter, it is my suspicion that *neither* concept is applicable to all political parties. Rather, the two concepts may represent poles at either end of a continuum, along which individual parties might be placed. My limited purpose, then, is simply to suggest some point in this continuum at which to place the Febrerista Party. A secondary purpose is to indicate some of the problems involved in any attempt to shed some light on the oligarchy-pluralism controversy.

I have indicated that the rate of turnover in leadership is one index used by political scientists to determine how oligarchic or democratic a given party's organization may be. With respect to the Febrerista Party, the turnover has been relatively low, indicating that a certain degree of oligarchization in the party's leadership revolves around a conflict between generations. At this point, however, I should like to abandon the word "generation," which I believe connotes a rather orderly spacing of time periods, and to substitute the word "promotion"—a word the *febreristas* themselves use. The two concepts overlap; there is usually an age difference among promotions, but "promotion" refers not to the age of a party member, but to the era in which he joined the party. The utility of "promotion" is that it gives us some idea of the date when a member was recruited, as well as what sorts of political events may be associated with his decision to enter the party.

Febrerismo had its genesis in the Revolution of February 17, 1936, just after the Chaco War. The term *febrerista*, then, refers to that revolution. The revolutionaries claimed to be reacting against thirty years of corrupt Liberal Party rule, during which time the Liberals had taken a weak position with regard to Bolivian encroachments in the Chaco, had ruled undemocratically, had failed to promote any real social or economic progress in an agrarian country where *latifundios* occupied more than half the land, and had sold the Paraguayans' birthright by opening up the country to unrestricted foreign economic penetration.

The revolution was basically military in character. Its backbone was the Chaco War Veterans' Association, headed by Colonel Rafael Franco, who became the president of the new government.

Today, Colonel Franco is president of the Febrerista Party. Another important group during this period was the *Liga Nacional Independiente*, a small but influential group of nationalistic intellectuals. The men who staffed the Revolutionary Government were drawn chiefly from these two organizations. Finally, the revolutionaries set up their own official party—a forerunner of the Febrerista Party—called the *Unión Nacional Revolucionaria*. The Union's leadership was made up chiefly of notables from the Veterans' Association, the *Liga* and some left-wing dissident Liberals. These men I have named the *first promotion febreristas*.

The revolution lasted about a year and a half before the government was overthrown by conservative military sectors. The first promotion *febreristas* were forced into exile, but the counter-revolution did not put an end to *febrerista* activity in Paraguay. *Febrerista* clubs were formed in the universities and high schools, headed by younger revolutionaries who had been passed over by the counter-revolutionary purges. These clubs were fully autonomous and not linked in any formal way either with one another or with *febrerista* exile groups. By 1941 they had begun to form alliances with certain labor unions—especially the railway workers'—and with *pro-febrerista* elements within the military. Eventually they felt strong enough to attempt a few strikes and even an abortive *coup d'etat*. The members of these revolutionary clubs may be called *second promotion febreristas*. Their organizations arose independently of the old leadership, without any direct or formal support from the men of the first promotion.

By 1944 contacts between the revolutionary clubs within Paraguay and the exile organizations had become closer. Eventually a Committee of Revolutionary Organization was set up to coordinate their activities. This was a more or less informal body within [which] each group had an equal voice in deciding policy. By the following year the C.O.R. had given way to the *Concentración Revolucionaria Febrerista*—a sort of protoparty with an even more cohesive structure. Even within the *Concentración*, however, there was considerable autonomy. The jealousy shown by each of the member groups in protecting its own independence reflected, it would seem, a feeling on the part of the men of the second promotion that, while they admired the elder revolutionaries, they, too, had—through their risky clandestine activities—established their claim to an equal voice in *febrerista* councils.

The definitive structure of the *febrerista* movement, according to the *Concentración's* charter, was to await the calling of a national convention by the movement's leaders some time in the near future. This job was postponed, however. In 1946 Higínio Morínigo, then dictator of Paraguay, invited the *febreristas* to return from exile to form a coalition government with the Colorado Party and the military. This coalition lasted only a few months. A bloody civil war followed the expulsion of the *febreristas* from the Cabinet in January, 1947. The *febreristas* lost and fled again into exile. Those who did not leave in 1947 were soon forced out of the country by the Colorado Terror, during which political opponents were hunted down, jailed and often murdered. Defeated and demoralized, the *febreristas* were unable to regroup sufficiently to hold their national convention until 1951. This convention, held in Buenos Aires, formally instituted the Febrerista Party. Those who have joined since then we may refer to as *third promotion febreristas*.

Now the problem of oligarchization stems from this fact: in every *febrerista* executive committee, from the *Concentración* to the present—with one exception—most of the key posts have been held by men of the first promotion, even though they are by no means numerically superior. Which are the key posts? First of all there is the president of the party, a position which has always been held by Colonel Rafael Franco. Next, there are the first and second vice presidents. Given the scattered nature of an exile organization these become important posts because the vice presidents must often command in the absence of the president. Fourth, there is the secretary-general, who supervises the work of the various departments of the national executive committee. Finally, we should include the secretary of organization, who supervises the regional and local committees, acting as a link between them and the national executive.

Since 1944 six national executive committees have been elected by the national convention. (The party [works] on an indirect system: members elect delegates to the convention and the convention, in turn, elects the executive.) Elections were held in 1945, 1951, 1954, 1958, 1962 and 1966. Only in 1954 was a coalition of radical dissidents, of the second promotion, able to wrest control from the old leaders. Unfortunately, this coalition was fractionalized internally and broke up almost immediately after the convention, leaving the national committee divided and ineffective. In *all* of the other national executive committees the key posts, with the exception of that of the secretary of organization, were held by men of the first promotion—men who had also been leaders in either the Chaco War Veterans' Association, the *Liga Nacional Independiente*, the *Unión Nacional Revolucionaria*, or the cabinet of the Revolutionary Government. In many cases they had been leaders in several of these groups. To get a clear picture of what we are dealing with, let us focus on the election of the national executive committee in 1962.

Two lists of candidates presented themselves for election to the convention. One list, representing the more conservative wing of the party, might be called the institutionalist list. It favored reaching an understanding with the present Paraguayan dictatorship in order to achieve legalization. Once back in Paraguay, the institutionalists argued, the party could work for the gradual institutionalization of democracy. The second slate of candidates called itself List 17 Febrero. This group stood squarely on a platform of unrelenting warfare against Stroessner, and promised the eventual bloody overthrow of the old oligarchy in Paraguay. Leaving aside these political differences and looking only at the occupational background of the leading candidates from both lists, we find no real difference. This was definitely not a class conflict within the party. The differences in ideology cannot be explained as a clash between the middle class and working class members. Lawyers predominate on both sides, followed by economists, merchants, businessmen and doctors—with a sprinkling of military men and journalists. In short, *febrerista* leadership, whatever its ideological position, is almost uniformly bourgeois in its background.[5]

However, if we break the two lists down by "promotions" we find that they differed significantly:

INSTITUTIONALISTS		LIST 17 FEBRERO
First promotion	17	6
Second promotion	14	28
Third promotion	4	3

The suggestion is, then, that this was largely a generational conflict. A second look at the institutionalist list offers other sug-

[5] The institutionalist list was taken from a list of executive committee members elected by the 1962 convention (institutionalist). The List 17 Febrero list was taken from two manifestos signed by leaders of various *febrerista* factions who agreed to unite behind a single opposition candidate.

gestions of oligarchization: (a) eleven of the candidates were incumbents from the 1958 national executive committee; (b) six of them had been on the 1951 national executive committee of the *Concentración*; (c) six of them had been on the 1951 national executive committee; (d) five of them had been on the executive committee of the *Unión Nacional Revolucionaria*; (e) three of them had been on the executive committee of the Chaco War Veterans' Association; and (f) two of them had been in the Revolutionary Government.

Further evidence of oligarchization appears if we examine Tables I–IV. These trace the background of the men holding key posts within the party, from the period of the *Concentración Revolucionaria Febrerista* to the party split in 1962. It will be seen from these tables that (1) the key posts are dominated by men of the first promotion in all of the national executive committees, (2) most of the men holding key posts were members of previous national executive committees, and (3) most of the men holding key posts also held key posts in previous national executive committees. It seems an inescapable conclusion, then, that turnover in the party's top leadership has been relatively low. One must, of course, qualify this judgment by taking into consideration the fact that the radical faction was in command of the party from 1954 to 1958. Thus, by voluntarily stepping aside in favor of their opponents the institutionalist leaders cast doubt on the charges that they have behaved like oligarchs. However, since the institutionalists reassumed control in 1958 several of the radical leaders were expelled from the party. As the factional struggles have become severe and ideological lines have hardened, the party leaders have tried to impose greater discipline on the rank and file.

At this point we might ask: how serious a problem is this for the party? The answer is that it has become extremely serious. The tendency, since the launching of the Committee of Revolutionary Organization, has been towards centralization in the party's leadership. As their groups have lost autonomy, this has caused rather widespread resentment among many second promotion febreristas. Having been coaxed into compromising their freedom of action, they claim, they are now excluded from the party's seats of power. Some of the more rebellious ones have been expelled from the party, others have formed splinter groups, and still others have become inactive and apathetic in protest against what they consider

TABLE I. THE CONVENTRACIÓN REVOLUCIONARIA FEBRERISTA

Post (CRF)	Promotion	Rev. govt. 1936–37	UNR CEN	ANEC CEN	CENs Serving	Key Posts Held
Pres. #1	1	Pres.		Pres.	2	2
Pres. #2	1	Minister	Pres.		2	2
Vice-pres. #1	1	Minister			1	1
Vice-pres. #2	1			Vice-pres.	1	1
Sec. gen.*	1	Mayor	X	Vice-pres.	3	2
Sec. gen.**	1				0	0
Sec. org.	2				0	0

* 1945–47. Mayor refers to Asunción, the capital.
** 1947–51.
X is the member of CEN but no key post.

TABLE II. THE 1951 CEN

Post (1951)	Promotion	CRF CEN	Rev. govt. 1936–37	UNR CEN	ANEC CEN	CENs Serving	Key Posts Held
Pres.	1	Pres. #1	Pres.		Pres.	3	3
Vice-pres. #1	1	Pres. #2	Minister	Pres.		3	3
Vice-pres. #2	1	Vice-pres. #2			Vice-pres.	2	2
Sec. gen.	1	Sec. gen.	Mayor	X	Vice-pres.	4	3
Sec. org.	2	Sec. org.				1	1
On CEN		5		4			
Held key post		5		4			

TABLE III. THE 1958 CEN

Post (1958)	Promotion	1951 CEN	CRF CEN	Rev. govt. 1936–37	UNR CEN	ANEC CEN	CENs Serving	Key Posts Held
Pres.	1	Pres.	Pres.	Pres.	X	Pres.	4	4
Vice-pres. #1	1	Sec. gen.	Sec. gen.	Mayor	Sec. gen.	Vice-pres.	5	4
Vice-pres. #2	1		X		X		2	1
Sec. gen.	1					Sec. gen.	2	1
Sec. org.	2						0	0
On CEN		2	3		4			
Held key post		2	2		4			

TABLE IV. THE 1962 INSTITUTIONALISTS CEN

Post (1962)	Promotion	1958 CEN	1951 CEN	CRF CEN	Rev. govt. 1936–37	UNR CEN	ANEC CEN	CENs Serving	Key Posts Held
Pres.	1	Pres.	Pres	Pres.	Pres.		Pres.	5	5
Vice-pres. #1	1	Sec. gen.				X	Sec. gen.	3	2
Vice-pres. #2	1	Vice-pres. #2		X				3	2
Sec. gen.	1	X				Sec. gen.		1	0
Sec. org.	1	Sec. org.						1	1
On CEN		5	1	2		3			
Held key post		4	1	1		3			

to be a conservative party oligarchy, firmly entrenched and unresponsive to the opinions of the members.[6]

On the other hand, the institutionalists point to the fact that they are *elected* to their positions. Is this not democracy? Therefore, how can they be oligarchs?

Perhaps their point is well-taken, but it would be safer not to lean too heavily upon electoral results as accurate reflections of rank and file opinion. *Febrerista* elections, like many Latin American elections, are often marred by fraud. To be fair to the institutionalists, they are not the only guilty ones in the party. Nevertheless, it would appear that *febreristas* of all opinions tend to fall considerably short of their publicly-stated ideals of democracy and fair play when it comes to electing their own leaders. For example, in the 1962 elections a total of seventy delegates were elected to the convention. Of these, twelve institutionalists and seventeen List 17 Febrero candidates had their credentials challenged before the party's Supreme Electoral Tribunal for alleged fraud. And in the party's local committee of Posadas, Argentina, both sides were so blatantly fraudulent in their electoral practices that the Tribunal nullified the elections entirely and Posadas sent no delegates at all to the convention.

To cite one more example of how difficult it is to determine the degree of representatives of the party's leadership we might look at some of the bizarre manipulations that went on at the convention. Thirty-eight List 17 Febrero members carried credentials to the convention, as opposed to thirty-one institutionalists. Did this demonstrate a popular majority favoring List 17 Febrero? Not necessarily. After all, seventeen of those thirty-eight credentials had been challenged by the institutionalists as having been gained through fraud. Now, even though the Supreme Electoral Tribunal may approve challenged credentials, the plaintiff may look to the national convention as a court of last resort in such cases. Therefore, having failed to get the Tribunal to invalidate the List 17 Febrero credentials, the institutionalists decided to carry the fight to the

[6] In all fairness to the present *febrerista* leadership it must be mentioned that the 1966 National Executive Committee shows a liberalizing trend at work in the party. Out of twenty-five seats, only eight went to first promotion men. Also, of the five key posts only three (president, first vice president and secretary-general) went to first promotion men. Finally, a partial reconciliation was achieved with former List 17 Febrero leaders, some of whom are represented on the new executive. However, no real large-scale renewal of leadership was achieved and many rebels appear to have been lost to the party forever.

convention. At this point it is important to remember that the incumbent national executive committee was controlled by the institutionalists.

The party constitution requires that before a delegate can enter the convention floor he must go through a Commission of Powers, which checks his credentials to make sure that they are valid. In this instance the incumbent national executive committee appointed five men to the Commission of Powers: three institutionalists and two List 17 Febrero members. At the first meeting of the Commission the institutionalist majority decided that the Commission should not only check the validity of all credentials (*i.e.* to make sure that they had been dully authorized by the Supreme Electoral Tribunal), but that the Commission would decide the validity of challenged credentials. Decisions would be taken by a majority vote, of course.

The results of this maneuver might easily have been predicted. The List 17 Febrero members withdrew from the Commission of Powers and, when it became apparent that neither side was willing to compromise, each slate held its own convention, elected its own executive committee and claimed henceforth to represent *febrerismo*. Also, each convention expelled the other from the party.

Generational conflict and low turnover in leadership have not been the only factors weakening cohesion within *febrerismo*. Ironically, as we have tried to show, a trend towards the centralization of decision-making—which might be expected to promote a more united movement—has served to aggravate generational and ideological cleavages. This facet of internal conflict within *febrerismo* affords us still another opportunity to test the oligarchic thesis: in this case, that party elites will tend to acquire complete control over all levels of the organization.

Parallel to the centralizing trend has been a tendency to establish an increasingly hierarchical structure. Not only was power diffused in the Committee of Revolutionary Organization, the participants acted as equals. With the establishment of the *Concentración*, however, not only were the member groups less autonomous but there began to appear a regular chain of command, starting with a national executive committee and extending down to subordinate regional and local committees. Moreover, decision-making was coming to be a jealously guarded prerogative of the national executive. The *Concentración's* charter stated explicitly:

The National Executive Committee will establish contact directly with all the party organizations within the country and in exile, through its authorized organs. Correspondence will be exchanged directly with the presidents of the committees, and will be signed by the corresponding authorities of the National Executive Committee. No other form of contact will have official validity, nor should be taken into consideration by any party organization. Moreover, the official correspondence of the committees in exile, and of the Resistance Committee, should be directed to the corresponding organs of the National Executive Committee. Administrative correspondence will be signed by the Secretary General and the head of the proper department respectively. Political correspondence will be signed exclusively by the President and counter-signed by the Secretary General.[7]

In short, the era of free-wheeling autonomy for the revolutionary clubs of the 1938–1944 period was definitely at an end.

The culmination—or rather, the crisis—of centralization was reached with the first party purge, which coincided with the party's constituent convention in 1951, when the Febrerista Party was officially instituted. It would require too much space to describe all the complicated struggles and maneuverings which preceded the 1951 convention. Let it suffice to say, instead, that three major factions emerged at that time. One was led by the "Old Guard," the men of the first promotion. A second group was called the *Bloque de Defensa de la Revolución* (hereafter referred to as the *Bloque*, or the *bloquistas*. The third faction was a group of young *febreristas* led by a fast-rising *caudillo* named Ricardo Franco (no relation to Colonel Franco).

Briefly, the *Bloque* was a radical, pro-communist group which was organized in exile after the *febreristas* were driven from Paraguay in 1947. Impatient with what it considered conservative, "do-nothing" leadership it aimed at wresting control from the "Old Guard." The *bloquistas* were joined for a short time by Ricardo Franco, who planned to lead the insurrection, but when he failed to get elected president of the *Bloque* he withdrew. The Febrerista Party was torn for the next three years by a three-cornered struggle, during which the Resistance Committee became the main bone of contention. This committee was *febrerismo's* underground organization in Paraguay—the remnants of the party left behind after the civil war to struggle against the Colorado Terror. Whichever faction led the Resistance Committee, then, would benefit from its immense prestige among the exiles.

[7] Concentración Revolucionaria Febrerista, *Construyendo el febrerismo* (Buenos Aires: CRF, 1951), p. 85.

The outcome of this factional struggle had two important results. First, the *bloquistas* were defeated. Not only did the Resistance Committee leaders close ranks against them, but Ricardo
Franco came to a convenient understanding with the "Old Guard."
Cut off from any major support, either in Paraguay or in exile, the
Bloque was defenseless at the convention in 1951, and its leaders
were expelled from the party. Not only did this strengthen the
hold of the old leaders over the party apparatus, but it also fixed
the ideological boundaries of *febrerismo*: the party was hencefor-
ward identified firmly with the West, and with anti-communism,
and it explicitly rejected the notion that it should be an exclusively
working-class party.

As the factional struggle wore on, however, the Resistance Committee also suffered. Caught among the three factions, each of which
was attempting to impose its policies and leadership upon it, the
Committee eventually quarreled with each of them in turn. As a
result they found themselves intervened in 1951 by Ricardo Franco,
once he had reached his understanding with the "Old Guard" and
the *bloquistas* had been isolated. Intervention took the form of
"electing" a different slate of delegates to the 1951 convention from
the ones chosen by the Committee. Most of the Resistance leaders
resigned in protest, and the Committee rapidly dwindled in effectiveness.

Several other examples could be offered to show that the centralization of decision-making in the national executive committee
has resulted in greater ideological conformity and discipline over
subordinate organs. We have already presented the story of the
aftermath of the 1962 convention, in which the List 17 Febrero
members were expelled from the party. Other examples might
include, briefly, the expulsion in 1958 of the *Vanguardia Febrerista*,
a party faction advocating increased guerrilla warfare, as well as the
eventual purge of Ricardo Franco himself. Concerning the latter
case, Franco was accused in 1959 of misappropriating party funds
while acting as president of the Buenos Aires regional committee.
After denouncing him violently for several months in the party
press, the national executive committee formally intervened in the
Buenos Aires regional by simply setting up a parallel committee.
Party members were then informed that those who continued to
serve in Ricardo Franco's committee would face sanctions. Meanwhile, formal charges were brought against him in the Tribunal
of Conduct, which quickly recommended his expulsion. Within a
year he was isolated.

Despite these examples, however, it is still not entirely clear that the "Old Guard," institutionalist leadership in the national executive enjoys thorough control over lower party committees. Indeed, it would be fairly easy to indicate some factors which make such control impossible—at least for the present. In the first place one must take into account the physical dispersion of the Febrerista Party. Since much of the party is located in exile, scattered among Argentina, Brazil and Uruguay, it becomes extremely difficult for party leaders to coordinate their activities effectively. Given the vigilance of the Paraguayan dictatorship, the process of communication between lower committees and the national executive, and between those inside Paraguay and the exiles, is usually slow and inefficient. As a result, regional and local committees must of necessity be allowed to take the initiative in the management of their day to day affairs in order to cope with the unpredictable behavior of the dictatorship.

A second factor working against the national executive's effective control over the entire party apparatus is the economic condition of both the leaders and the followers, especially those in exile. This is a crucial point, for it is organization—bureaucratic control—which Michels considered essential for the development of an oligarchy:

> It is organization which gives birth to the dominion of the elected over the electors, of the mandataries over the mandators, of the delegates over the delegators. Who says organization says oligarchy.[8]

In the *febreristas'* case, however, the party has never been able to afford a full-time staff of professionally-trained administrators. Instead, party militants tend to be strongly motivated amateur politicians. The party treasury simply cannot support a class of professional politicians. Moreover, since the *febreristas* are not only out of power but persecuted as well, there is not even the hope of being able to use the party to obtain jobs. Therefore, much of the organization is little more than a paper plan, without a sufficiently trained staff or proper funds to make it operative. The meetings of regional and local committees seldom accomplish more than the political education of the membership and thus keeping alive the faith.

[Apparently], then, oligarchic trends do exist within the

8 Michels, *Political Parties*, p. 401.

Febrerista Party but they are mitigated by the environment in which the party operates. One cannot ignore the low rate of turnover in the leadership, for instance, nor the trend towards centralized decision-making in the national executive. At the same time, though, exile, physical dispersion and economic privation tend to reduce the effectiveness of control from the top. Lastly, the party ideology may be a factor in ameliorating oligarchic tendencies within the national executive. After all, *febrerismo* claims to be a democratic socialist movement; and while it would be naive to assume that the ethos alone would prevent oligarchization, it seems equally true that a general acceptance of democratic values may at least make leaders more responsible, make their power less absolute by providing for the possibility of challenge by alternative leaders. Even Michels concurs with this:

> . . . the democratic principle carries with it, if not a cure, at least a palliative, for the disease of oligarchy. . . . The labor movement, in virtue of the theoretical postulates it proclaims, is apt to bring into existence (in opposition to the will of the leaders) a certain number of free spirits who, moved by principle, by instinct, or by both, desire to revise the base on which authority is established.[9]

Finally, there is some evidence that the first promotion's hold on the party's national executive is slowly weakening. The 1962 crisis left *febrerismo* so weakened internally that a rapprochement between promotions was necessary to save it. This was reflected at the Fourth National Convention, in 1966, which brought several new men into the National Executive Committee. Some of these had even been supporters of List 17 Febrero in 1962. At the same time, fewer first promotion men held seats on the committee. This gradual decline of the first promotion is shown in Table V.

TABLE V.   REPRESENTATION ON THE CEN, BY PROMOTION

	1958	1962	1966
First promotion	15	11	8
Second promotion	10	10	14
Third promotion	0	4	3

[9] *Ibid.*, p. 406.

Table VI. The 1966 CEN

Post (1966)	Promotion	1962 CEN	1958 CEN	1951 CEN	CRF CEN	Rev. govt. 1936-37	UNR CEN	ANEC CEN	CENs Serving	Key Posts Held
Pres.	1	Pres.	Pres.	Pres.	Pres.	Pres.		Pres.	6	6
Vice-pres. #1	1	Vice-pres. #1	Sec. gen.				X	Sec. gen.	4	3
Vice-pres. #2	2	X	X	X					3	0
Sec. gen.	2	Sec. org.	Sec. org.						2	2
Sec. org.	1	X	X						2	0
On CEN		5	5	2	1		2			
Held key post		3	3	1	1		2			

X is member of CEN but no key post.

There has even been a slight relaxation of the first promotion's hold on the party's key posts. While it still has a majority of these, the second promotion has increased its representation slightly. Also, some of the first promotion notables are being replaced by lesser known men from their era. This suggests that the first promotion's looser grip on the party may be due more to natural attrition—since they are approaching their sixties and seventies—than to a desire to voluntarily step aside. In any case, the party's top leadership is being rejuvenated, albeit slowly. Table VI shows the distribution of key posts in the 1966 CEN.

In conclusion, then, our study of *febrerismo* leads us to reject both the pluralist and the oligarchic theses in their pure forms. Of the two concepts, the oligarchic seems to fit somewhat better the overall trend within the Febrerista Party, while Eldersveld's assumptions about stratarchy seems excessively optimistic. However, it is also clear that party leaders have limits to their power. The purges that took place within *febrerismo* since 1958 have weakened its effectiveness considerably. The 1966 National Convention indicates that the old leaders may have come to a belated understanding of the dangers to *febrerismo's* future that lie in a policy of excluding younger members from positions of responsibility. For, after all, what use is an elite without followers, and where are the followers to come from if new recruits are discouraged from active participation in party life? In the last analysis we may conclude that while the rank and file may have little to say about setting party policy, the continued existence of the Febrerista Party—or any other party—depends ultimately on a unity of purpose among the members. Thus, the form of organization—monolithic or egalitarian —is hardly more important than the values and norms which underlie it.

Democracy by Violence

————— ◆•◆ ————

James L. Payne

This study has presented the system of political bargaining and has explored its implications for the Peruvian labor movement. The first chapter treated trade union methods as dependent variables and suggested the independent variables which led the workers to select political bargaining as their major strategy. At the same time an attempt was made to show why other methods, namely legal enactment and collective bargaining, were largely rejected.

It was suggested that legal enactment was relatively ineffectual because (1) the chaotic, nonrepresentative condition of the electoral system prevented workers from using their votes in a concerted, meaningful fashion, and (2) the administration was unable to implement, autonomously, many of the laws that were passed or might be passed. In the case of collective bargaining, the depressed state of the labor market was seen as the fundamental variable discouraging the use of this method.

We concluded that political bargaining had been selected because, relative to other methods, it was most effective. The basic variable which determined the efficacy of this strategy was the insecurity of the president of a free regime in the face of civilian violence. This insecurity was traced back to other variables—the nature of political conflict and the role of the military—and then some underlying structural factors which contributed to the basic relationships involved were discussed. The connections between the variables are shown in Figure 12.

Once political bargaining was established as the product of these environmental factors, the analysis in the following chapters shifted to the labor movement itself. The trade union method was treated

Reprinted by permission of Yale University Press from *Labor and Politics in Peru*, by James L. Payne, pp. 268–283. Copyright © 1965 by Yale University.

as the independent variable and the various features—political party relations, structure, finances, etc.—as dependent variables. As much as possible, these features were analyzed in their relationship to the bargaining pattern employed by the worker organizations.

FIGURE 12.

Schematic Representation of the Principal Variables in the Political Bargaining System

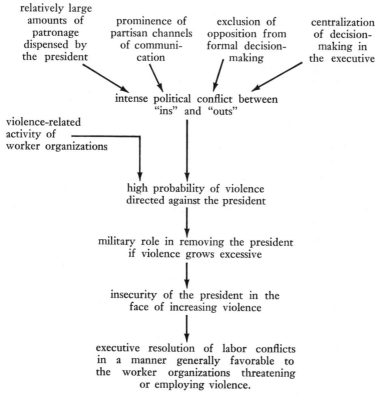

In addition to being a trade union method, however, political bargaining represents at the same time a system of political interaction. In the following pages this pattern will be discussed from the perspective of the political scientist, making explicit some of the implications of our findings. Nothing said, however, should be taken to mean that political bargaining is considered the only pattern of decision-making in Peru. Other arenas, such as the electoral process, Congress, the courts, and lower administration, should not be disregarded if one seeks a complete picture of the political system. Political bargaining is designated as an important, even dominant, pattern, but not one which operates to the exclusion of all others.

In its broad outlines political bargaining has much in common with constitutional democracy as it is practiced in the United States. In both patterns the decision maker is responsive to citizens because they may threaten his tenure of office if they are dissatisfied with his policies. But the mechanisms whereby this responsiveness is achieved are quite different in the two systems. In a constitutional democracy the officeholder is made insecure through elections. He is prompted to respond to citizen demands because otherwise, he fears, votes will be mobilized against him.[1] In political bargaining it is the possibility of military intervention that the executive fears. And it is civilian violence which tends to provoke a coup against the incumbent president. Consequently the president seeks to reduce the probabilities of extensive civilian violence by satisfying the demands citizens make upon him. These two analogous patterns are diagramed in Figure 13.

In Peru, then, there exists an interesting reversal of the proverbial exchange of bullets for ballots. But the product of this exchange is not the chaotic open warfare usually envisaged by democratic

FIGURE 13.
Political Bargaining and Constitutional Democracy: Basic Decision-making Mechanisms

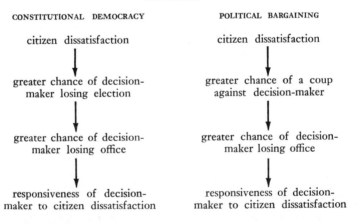

CONSTITUTIONAL DEMOCRACY

citizen dissatisfaction
↓
greater chance of decision-maker losing election
↓
greater chance of decision-maker losing office
↓
responsiveness of decision-maker to citizen dissatisfaction

POLITICAL BARGAINING

citizen dissatisfaction
↓
greater chance of a coup against decision-maker
↓
greater chance of decision-maker losing office
↓
responsiveness of decision-maker to citizen dissatisfaction

[1] We are, of course, tracing only the broad outlines of the constitutional-democratic model. A full description of reality would require that this model be greatly elaborated and qualified. For an extensive development of the basic propositions given here see Anthony Downs, *An Economic Theory of Democracy* (New York, Harper, 1957).

theorists. The Peruvian pattern of political bargaining is an intelligible system, a kind of "democracy by violence." This possibility has been overlooked by many theorists who appear to see no middle ground between a peaceful constitutional democracy and anarchy. The tendency has been to treat patterns of violent interaction as "chaotic" (and therefore beyond analysis) or as the foreshadowing of a "revolution." Many scholars have equated, usually implicitly, the persistent use of violence with "the breakdown of the system." This view betrays an undesirable element of ethnocentrism. As we have attempted to show in the case of Peru, the persistent use of violence *is* the system, or at least a very large part of it.

As one might expect, the general model given above for this pattern of "democracy by violence" is not found in reality without imperfections. We have seen that organization is an important requisite for successful activity and that there are barriers of size and cohesion which must be overcome for effective action. Also regional location (in Lima rather than in the provinces) and the disposition to employ violence (blue-collar workers compared with white-collar workers, for example) affect outcomes. Hence, power is not evenly distributed. But similar imperfections are found in the distribution of power in a constitutional democracy: organization size and cohesion; disposition and ability of certain groups to turn out and vote; regional location. These factors greatly influence the outcomes of decisions in a constitutional democracy.

Of course, whether one wishes to call the Peruvian pattern a genuine "democracy" will depend upon the definition he selects for that word. We are not concerned with this semantic problem here. By employing the phrase "democracy by violence" we merely indicate that certain basic features usually associated with democracy are found in the Peruvian system of political bargaining. That the democratic norms of limited tenure of office and responsiveness of the officeholder to citizen demands should be achieved by the mechanisms of civilian violence and military intervention (two very "undemocratic" acts) poses an interesting problem for the political theorist.

OLIGARCHY

The suggestion that, on issues of political bargaining, large numbers of citizens have a voice in decision-making, goes against the popular notion that Peru is controlled by a small oligarchy. The exact nature and extent of the power of this group is never stated clearly, but most of the vague references to the "oligarchy" convey the impression of an extremely influential group. We are tempted to imagine, as one writer puts it, that (in Peru) "the politics have long been under the control of the landowning and commercial aristocracy, supported by officers of the army."[2]

One of the greatest difficulties encountered in dealing with the Peruvian oligarchy lies in determining who the oligarchs are. Although many writers—scholars and journalists alike—employ the word "oligarchy" without hesitation, an explicit operational definition of this term is rarely found. The vagueness surrounding the concept has made it possible for writers to say anything they like about the oligarchy. As an undefined term it tends to be manipulated independently of any data. Follow, for example, these two somewhat contradictory conclusions about the oligarchy under Odría:

> Odría held power for eight years, during which the armed forces increased their customary lion's share of the national budget and the oligarchy was secure in its dominant economic position.[3]

> During most of his tenure in office, Odría had maintained a military dictatorship, cracking down on any and all dissidents. His regime handled certain elements of the oligarchy as cavalierly as it had treated the *apristas*.[4]

Was the oligarchy "secure" or was it "handled . . . cavalierly"? Unlike a scientific disagreement, this inconsistency cannot be resolved because neither writer provides an operational definition of oligarchy.

There are, of course, many possible definitions. One could employ income statistics, occupation, family background, or membership in social clubs. If it is suspected that 20, 40, or 60 families constitute an oligarchy, then a list of the names of these families or their distinguishing characteristics must be provided. It might be

[2] Preston E. James, *Latin America* (3rd ed. New York, Odyssey Press, 1959), p. 202.

[3] Edwin Lieuwin, *Arms and Politics in Latin America* (rev. ed. New York, Frederick A. Praeger, 1961), p. 82.

[4] Robert J. Alexander, "The Army in Politics" in Harold E. Davis, ed., *Government and Politics in Latin America* (New York, The Ronald Press, 1958), p. 159.

argued that some writers have employed the word "oligarchy" to refer to "upper classes" and have not meant to imply anything about political power. But oligarchy is a political term. It refers specifically to the rule of the few. Consequently, the search for an oligarchy is a search for a group that wields the preponderance of political power.

Once the proposed oligarchy has been identified there remains the more formidable problem: does this group rule? In order to be considered an oligarchy a group must be highly influential, controlling the outcomes of practically all important decisions. The methodological problems involved in determining the existence of an oligarchy or power elite which runs politics are impressive. The many logical and empirical problems which face the analyst cannot be dealt with here.[5] At a minimum, however, it appears that in order to test for the existence of an oligarchy we must know the answers to the following questions:

1. Who are the proposed oligarchs? How will they be identified?
2. Where are they influential? What issue-areas or key decisions are they supposed to control?
3. What is the position of this group on the specific subject under study *before* the matter is decided? If the proposed oligarchy is found to be divided or if many other groups support the same position taken by the proposed oligarchy, then the investigator faces serious problems in determining the power of this group.
4. What was the outcome of the particular decision, or collections of decisions studied? Did the proposed oligarchy win?

[5] For an excellent discussion of the methodological problems involved in determining power distribution in political systems see Nelson W. Polsby, *Community Power and Political Theory* (New Haven, Yale University Press, 1963). See also John C. Harsanyi, "Measurement of Social Power, Opportunity Costs and the Theory of Two-Person Bargaining Games," *Behavioral Science,* 7 (1962), 67–80; Raymond E. Wolfinger, "Reputation and Reality in the Study of 'Community Power,'" *American Sociological Review,* 25 (1960), 636–44; Peter H. Rossi, "Community Decision Making," *Administrative Science Quarterly, 1* (1957), 415–43; Herbert Kaufman and Victor Jones, "The Mystery of Power," *Public Administration Review, 14* (1954), 205–12; Daniel Bell, "The Power Elite—Reconsidered," *The American Journal of Sociology, 64* (1958), 238–50; Talcott Parsons, "The Distribution of Power in American Society," *World Politics, 10* (1957), 123–43; Nelson W. Polsby, "Three Problems in the Analysis of Community Power," *American Sociological Review, 24* (1959), 795–803; Peter Bachrach and Morton S. Baratz, "Two Faces of Power," *American Political Science Review, 56* (1962), 947–52. Also see next footnote.

5. What did the proposed oligarchy do to influence the outcome? What resources did it have at its disposal and which were employed?[6]

The data contained in this study make it possible to examine one possible oligarchy theory. Although other conceptions are available, the following definition seems to be one of the more credible alternatives.

1. The proposed oligarchy will be defined as the group of employers and top management personnel. This is a large group, to be sure, but easily identified and usually united on the issues to be considered. To restrict the definition to a smaller subgroup—large employers, for example—would obscure the fact that such a group is usually supported by many other individuals. In any case, it seems obvious that if this group as a whole does not prevail in the issue-area studied, then subgroups within it cannot be said to rule.

2. Expressed union-employer conflicts will be considered as our area of concern. This issue-area is important on two criteria: (A) the number of affected individuals is very large; (B) the outcomes are seen as highly significant by the participants.

3. We find that usually employers are united against the unions, opposing their specific demands on wages and working conditions. The employer position is ascertained from newspaper statements, from paid advertisements by the employers or their ownership federations, and from personal interviews with employers and their representatives.

4. The outcomes of these union-employer conflicts are by no means consistently favorable to employers. Many times (most of the time, in fact) the unions obtained far more than the employers wished to grant. One cannot say that employers were powerless, for sometimes the unions were clearly defeated. Also, the workers seldom obtained all of what they wanted. But the conclusion that employers always win or usually win these disputes is clearly untenable in the light of the data presented in this study.

5. An explanation of the outcomes of these conflicts must rest on

[6] This list has been constructed from analyses and research proposals offered by the following writers: Robert A. Dahl, *Who Governs?* (New Haven, Yale University Press, 1961); Dahl, "A Critique of the Ruling Elite Model," *American Political Science Review*, 52 (1958), 463–69; Dahl, "The Concept of Power," *Behavioral Science*, 2 (1957), 201–15; Nelson W. Polsby, "How to Study Community Power: The Pluralist Alternative," *The Journal of Politics*, 22 (1960), 474–84.

an analysis of the resources available to and employed by each side. Employers have greater social standing and a superior cultural background which enables them to communicate more effectively with government officials. They are much more likely to be personal acquaintances of the Minister of Labor. They tend to be allied with consumers and taxpayers. They may present themselves as fundamental instruments of economic development. They may command publicity. They have money. But often these resources are not fully employed. Many employers may not be greatly concerned with a particular conflict and will remain inactive. Sometimes their arguments are weak or obviously false. Publicity may be denied by some newspapers (*La Tribuna*, for example).

The workers have resources on their side too. They may get free publicity from certain newspapers and from sympathetic congressmen. They may present themselves as underdogs, oppressed and miserable, and therefore worthy of special consideration. In addition to these weapons, the unions have a key resource not available to employers: violence. When this resource is properly mobilized it tends to outweigh any that employers might bring to bear. Arguments about inflation, invoking friendships, and perhaps even bribes would not prevent a substantial union victory when the executive is threatened by violence. Even the lowly agricultural laborers, when they are properly mobilized, win substantial gains using this resource. The ability to employ violence is the trump card in the Peruvian system of political bargaining and it is a card employers do not hold. It is this distribution of resources which explains why the business group does not regularly win conflicts with worker organizations.

Only one of the many possible definitions of oligarchy has been treated above. Given this conception, we conclude that there is no oligarchy in Peru. The group of employers and their immediate representatives, while exercising a modest degree of power in most union-employer conflicts, are by no means dominant. Moreover, since one major issue-area where lower-class groups have a significant impact upon decision-making has been identified, the idea that this oligarchy controls *all* political decisions must also be rejected.

Of course, anyone is free to propose alternative conceptions of oligarchy and different subject matters over which it is supposed to rule. But until systematic presentations exist, it would seem wise to avoid using "oligarchy" or similar "power elite" concepts.

To a large extent the use of such terms has been a substitute for analysis. Politics, instead of being viewed as the product of complex patterns of interactions, is all too often dismissed as a struggle between the "oligarchy" and the "reformers." It is time that this caricature of Peruvian politics is consciously discarded.

THE STRUCTURE OF DECISION-MAKING

The term oligarchy, then, would seem to be inapplicable to the issue-areas dealt with under political bargaining. Even if one proposes as oligarchs the large group of employers and their immediate managers (a somewhat unwieldy oligarchy, to be sure) it appears that this group does not win most of the conflicts. Nevertheless, it is on precisely the issues of political bargaining that Peruvians speak of the oligarchy most frequently. In the newspapers, at the rally or meeting, "oligarchy" is widely used. When Peruvians speak of the oligarchy they do not have in mind the modest conception suggested above. They see a very small group of nasty, selfish individuals who seem bent upon increasing the misery of the people. The self-interest of the oligarchy (which is allegedly followed with terrifying persistence) is held to be incompatible with everything good, including progress, happiness, and justice.

Everyone is against the oligarchy—even those who are supposed to be oligarchs. Luís Miró Quesada, for example, the publisher of *El Comercio*, often accused of being an oligarch, was a most vocal enemy of the oligarchy in the columns of his newspaper. It is perhaps understandable, therefore, that writers should have come to employ the term. How, they apparently reasoned, could millions of Peruvians be deceived? There is, perhaps, an explanation for the widespread use of the term, especially on issues of political bargaining. The explanation lies not in an actual description of the power structure but in the pattern of decision-making and the political phraseology appropriate to it.

In the United States the government is an arena of decision-making. The many diverse groups enter this arena and attempt to extract a favorable result. In Congress, regulatory commissions, the Supreme Court, or branches of the administration, various groups are seen battling each other: employers and workers, integrationists and segregationists, exporters and local industries, urban and rural groups, to name a few. The fragmented nature of the decision-making process provides a multiplicity of points of access so that virtually all groups and their representatives interact *within* the government.

In this inclusive structure of decision-making the diverse competing groups tend to confront their opposition directly. They are not encouraged to speak of an oligarchy because they (and their audience) perceive the size and diversity of the group or groups in opposition. Participants, naturally, seek to employ a political phraseology which is credible given this decision-making structure. They appeal to a higher standard to justify their demands: "the national interest"; "the national defense"; "constitutional rights." Opposing groups are labeled "selfish interests" or "lobbyists." Whenever possible an attempt is made to show that opponents are seeking "unconstitutional" objectives.

With political bargaining one does not find a symmetrical decision-making pattern where all groups confront each other within the structure of government. Instead the government is seen actively protecting one side and being assaulted by the other. The government's position of partisanship is a direct consequence of the extreme centralization of the system. The executive plays such a preponderant role in decision-making that he tends to *be* the government. As a single individual, the president can seldom present himself as a neutral participant. If violence occurs it is his job to react against it. In so doing he automatically allies himself with those groups that oppose or might oppose the demands of the attackers.

Thus the government protects those groups which are unable to employ violence on a particular issue. Usually these groups include employers, consumers, and taxpayers. The assaulting groups are usually workers or students. Professionals (doctors, lawyers) may be found on either side, depending on the issue. Sometimes consumers, represented by worker organizations, are on the assaulting side while retailers and some workers are being protected. The government, insofar as it repels the assaulting groups and resists their full demands, is a partisan. Consequently the attacking side does not confront its real opposition directly; instead it confronts the government.

The phraseology adopted by the participants reflects this arrangement. The attacking groups see the government as an opponent standing in the way of their demands. Their battle-cry is that the government (or more accurately, the executive) is protecting the "oligarchy." In this way they may justify their use of violence against the government itself. Also, by calling the protected groups the "oligarchy," the attackers further obscure the already unclear dimensions of their opposition. They obscure the fact that the groups defended by the executive may be large—often larger than they are. A widely-based attack on the government requires a strong rationale. If the government can be accused of defending the indefensible, of defending a monster-like oligarchy, broad support is more easily enlisted.

The opponents of the attackers, particularly the government officials themselves, attempt to undermine the assault by obscuring the real nature of the opposition forces on the issue. They accuse the assaulting groups of being "communists" or of being inspired by "agitators." Although there is often an element of truth in these charges, the fact remains that real citizen demands are imbedded in nearly all attacks. By labeling the assault as merely the work of agitators (and therefore devoid of real demands), the executive hopes to cut the attacking group away from possible allies.

The use of the terms "oligarchy" and "communist agitators" should therefore be interpreted in the light of the structure of decision-making. The observer will learn little about the existence of an oligarchy or the activities of the communists by listening to talk or reading newspapers. Both terms are political slogans, employed because they suit the needs of the participants.

The utility of viewing violence as a basic component of the Peruvian system of government has been demonstrated. The analyses of the mechanisms of leadership responsibility, of the power distribution, and of the decision-making structure were grounded in a descriptive model of political interaction. This model employed civilian violence and military intervention as central variables.

This study is not an attempt to explore political bargaining as applied to other countries. Our sole concern has been to unravel the elements of this pattern as it applied to the Peruvian labor movement. One does not need to look very deeply, however, to realize that the general pattern of political bargaining is an important system in many other Latin American countries. The literature on Latin American politics contains widespread awareness of the prominence of violence and military intervention. Explanations for this pattern abound, touching on a wide range of factors: Iberian or Latin personality,[7] economic underdevelopment and poverty,[8] illiteracy,[9] the weakness of the middle sectors,"[10] the nature of the class system,[11] the "legitimacy vacuum,"[12] the lack of military "professionalism,"[13] and the role of the Catholic church.[14] This is by no means an exhaustive list but it indicates the interest which scholars have in the problem.[15]

[7] See Lionel Cecil Jane, *Liberty and Despotism in Spanish America* (Oxford, The Clarendon Press, 1929). Jane spoke of a personality which contained the antithetical elements of "liberty" and "efficiency." Several writers have noted "Individualism," including Frederick B. Pike, "Sources of Revolution: Their Impact on Freedom and Reform in Latin America" in Pike, *Freedom and Reform in Latin America* (Notre Dame, University of Notre Dame Press, 1959), p. 43; W. Rex Crawford in "Pathology of Democracy in Latin America: A Symposium," W. Pierson, ed., *American Political Science Review, 44* (1950), 145. See Arthur P. Whitaker, ibid., pp. 105–06 for a brief discussion of the theory of racial intermixing of Lucas Ayrragaray.

[8] One of the earliest proponents of this view was James Bryce, *South America—Observations and Impressions* (New York, Macmillan, 1912), p. 546. See also Sanford A. Mosk, "Pathology . . . Symposium," pp. 129–42. Merle Kling points to economic development as operating through the mechanism of social mobility to produce violence in his article "Toward a Theory of Power and Political Instability in Latin America," *Western Political Quarterly, 9* (1956), 21–35. For a discussion of the "rising expectations" theme see Karl M. Schmitt and David D. Burks, *Evolution or Chaos? Dynamics of Latin American Governments and Politics* (New York, Frederick A. Praeger, 1963), especially pp. 45, 241.

[9] See, for example, Bryce, *South America—Observations and Impressions,* p. 546; and Russell H. Fitzgibbon, "Pathology . . . Symposium," p. 125.

[10] John Johnson, *Political Change in Latin America* (Stanford, Stanford University Press, 1958), pp. 17–19, 92–93, 127, 179, 181.

[11] See George I. Blanksten, *Ecuador: Constitutions and Caudillos* (Berkeley, University of California Press, 1951), especially pp. 169, 174; Blanksten, "Revolutions," in Davis, *Government and Politics in Latin America,* pp. 143, 145.

[12] See Martin C. Needler, *Latin American Politics in Perspective* (Princeton, D. Van Nostrand, 1963), pp. 33–39. This same idea seems to be present in Kalman H. Silvert's discussion of "anti-nationalism" in "The Costs of Anti-Nationalism: Argentina" in Silvert, *Expectant Peoples* (New York, Random House, 1963), pp. 347–72. Fitzgibbon also speaks of the lack of "integration" in Latin American society: "Pathology . . . Symposium," pp. 120–22.

[13] Lieuwin, *Arms and Politics in Latin America,* especially pp. 151–53.

[14] Pike, *Freedom and Reform in Latin America,* p. 33.

[15] Specific discussions of violence in Latin American politics include William S. Stokes, "Violence as a Power Factor in Latin American Politics," *Western Political Quarterly, 5* (1952), 445–68; Gino Germani and K. H. Silvert, "Politics, Social Structure and Military Intervention in Latin America," *European Journal of Sociology, 2* (1961), 62–81; K. H. Silvert, *Reaction and Revolution in Latin America* (New Orleans, The Hauser Press, 1961), pp. 20–25; George I. Blanksten, "The Politics of Latin America" in Gabriel A. Almond and James S. Coleman, *The Politics of the Developing Areas*

Several writers have suggested that military intervention ought to be treated as "normal," given the persistence of this pattern. Pike expresses this view:

> So much a permanent and integral part of Latin American politics is the revolution that to many it appears to be the only important political institution in the Southern Americas during nearly 150 years of independence.[16]

Silvert echos this position:

> If the normal way of rotating the executive in a given country is by revolution, and if there have been a hundred such changes in a century, then it is not being facetious to remark that revolutions are a sign of stability.[17]

In spite of the fact that violence is widely recognized as a prominent phenomenon, scholars have been reluctant to base their analyses upon it. The frequent use of terms such as "instability," "pathology," or "chaos" reveals a pervasive commitment to the American model of constitutional democracy. This bias has encouraged writers on Latin America to inject normative judgments into their discussions of behavior. As a result, we have a large body of opinion on the way people ought to act, but very little knowledge about why they behave as they do.

Our argument, then, is for descriptive as opposed to normative models, for models that explain what does happen, not what ought to happen. This study attempts to construct such a model. There is no need to insist, however, that this construct must apply to all Latin American countries. Our particular conception of political bargaining was designed to explain one prominent pattern of interaction in Peru. It seems that many of the basic features of this system are duplicated in other Latin American countries, and that what has been said will be of some use in understanding political behavior elsewhere. Nevertheless, the wide diversity in political structures in Latin America leads to the belief that patterns of

---

(Princeton, Princeton University Press, 1960), pp. 496–502; Russell H. Fitzgibbon, "Revolutions: Western Hemisphere," *The South Atlantic Quarterly,* 55 (1956), 263–79.

[16] Pike, p. 28.

[17] Silvert, *Reaction and Revolution,* p. 20.

labor relations and political behavior vary considerably.[18] In dealing with any particular country, therefore, the investigator must be alert to this diversity and construct a model based on the reality which lies before him.

[18] For accounts of some of these differences see Robert J. Alexander, *Labor Relations in Argentina, Brazil and Chile* (New York, McGraw-Hill, 1962); Charles A. Page, "Labor's Political Role in Latin America," *The Virginia Quarterly Review, 28* (1952), 481–99.

Toward a Theory of Political Violence: The Case of Rural Colombia

Robert C. Williamson

Violence has generally been associated with revolution, war, or organized crime. The present century has been remarkable for large-scale violence in these three categories. Much of recent mass violence has been a product of guerrilla or undeclared warfare, including struggles of liberation from colonial rule, and conflicts between different power groups. At the broadest base, one might say, a trifle pretentiously, that violence and terror are an erratic by-product of the vast social change toward equalitarianism in the world. Yet this article focuses on a unique process of violence: a variety of civil war, which, since 1948, has annihilated nearly 200,000 people in the backlands of Colombia. Before examining this phenomenon, we shall establish the theoretical context of terror and violence.

Violence can be defined as a severely dysfunctional form of conflict, which in the case of Colombia has been a vendetta between the two political parties, an abortive revolutionary process, and a "blind reaction" to social frustration.[1] Violence is, among other

From Robert C. Williamson, "Toward a Theory of Political Violence: The Case of Rural Colombia," *Western Political Quarterly*, Vol. 18 (March 1965). Reprinted by permission of the University of Utah, copyright owners.

NOTE: The author expresses his gratitude to the Facultad de Sociologia of the National University of Colombia (at which he was a Fulbright lecturer in 1961), and particularly to Dean Orlando Fals Borda and Monsignor Germán Guzmán, who provided much of the material. The author is also indebted to Jerome I. Fischman, Anthony Leeds, and Aristóbulo Pardo who have made suggestions about the manuscript.

[1] For a discussion of violence as a factor in power politics in the traditional Latin American patterns, cf. William S. Stokes, "Violence as a Power Factor in Latin American Politics," *Western Political Quarterly*, 5 (September 1952), 445–68.

things, a cultural artifact, and in the Colombian case, a traditional behavior pattern periodically becoming a cataclysm under certain social pressures. If we accept the Simmel theory[2] that conflict is necessary for group integrity, cohesiveness, and the "boundary maintenance" of the group, the Colombian example pushes the case to the breaking point.

The question may be raised as to what type of society is most likely to produce violence, or in what sociopolitical climate violence is a predictable outcome. According to Kornhauser, violence is associated with mass movements that are non-institutionalized.[3] In our twentieth-century mass society, organized violence has occurred most dramatically under totalitarian governments where formalized and legitimatized channels are a prescribed part of the social system, or at least are available. Regarding transitional or developing nations, a different sociopolitical climate has generally been the case. In recent Colombia, the individual is alienated from the society he has known. In rural areas, the decline of localism and the emergence of a federated social order have posed a difficult problem for both the *campesino* (peasant) and the *llanero* (range cattleman), different as they are. Anomy results from conflicting norms; the relations of the little man to the land and to the proprietor are caught in the web of larger territorial allegiances. Traditional *caudillismo* is lost in party bureaucracy, the national police force, or other large-scale administrative units. Moreover, Bogotá and other cities have encroached on what was once an untrampled landscape. The *campesino* finds his values in confusion.

In developing a theory of violence one inevitably turns to the frustration-aggression hypothesis. It is hardly revolutionary to suggest that in most underdeveloped or transitional areas of the world, a majority of the population may find the status quo unacceptable. How militantly these individuals release their tensions depends on a number of factors, including literacy level, leadership, and access to sanctioned channels for expression of discontent. To a large extent, Colombians have been denied these outlets. Thus, internecine warfare has been the end-result of social, political, and economic frustration as well as of personal *anomie*.

[2] Georg Simmel, *Conflict*, tr. Kurt H. Wolff (Glencoe: Free Press, 1955). Cf. also, Lewis A. Coser, *The Functions of Social Conflict* (Glencoe: Free Press, 1956).
[3] William Kornhauser, *The Politics of Mass Society* (Glencoe: Free Press, 1959), p. 36.

THE BACKGROUND OF *LA VIOLENCIA* IN RURAL COLOMBIA

Colombia has had an unenviable history in the degree of violence even when judged by Latin American standards. However these events have been more in the direction of civil strife than of ruthless dictatorship. In the 1860's and 1870's it is estimated that roughly 80,000 were decimated in warfare, and again in 1899–1902 perhaps 100,000 were eliminated.[4] The present era of rural violence began in 1949 and continued with a lapse at the accession to power of Rojas Pinilla in 1953, increasing again from 1954 to 1958 when the National Front or coalition government was created. It has continued on a reduced scale since that time and is described more adequately as psychopathic banditry than as a political conflict.

This tragic episode arose from a deadlock between the numerically superior Liberal party and the oligarchical, politically entrenched Conservative party. The return of the Liberals to government in 1930, after decades of Conservative rule, resulted in somewhat enlightened social legislation largely under the leadership of Alfonso López. As the progressive advance faltered in the forties, a charismatic revolutionary leader, Jorge Gaitán, received immense popular support. The government returned to the Conservatives largely because of a split in the Liberal party in 1946. The two key Conservative figures, Ospina Pérez and Laureano Gómez, successively provided an increasingly arbitrary rule. On April 9, 1948, the assassination of Gaitán precipitated the famous *bogotazo*, a period of mob rioting, looting, and killing in the capital. While order returned to Bogotá and other cities, political violence became the pattern for much of rural Colombia. Although the Conservative party was not distinct in ideology from the Liberal party, it generally had the support of the military and the Church. At the same time, the Conservatives were a minority party and were perceived by the Liberals as maintaining power by fraudulent means.

---

[4] Everett E. Hagen, *On the Theory of Social Change* (Homewood: Dorsey Press, 1962), pp. 379–80; and Jésus Maria Henao and Gerardo Arrubla, *History of Colombia* (Chapel Hill: U. of N. Carolina Press, 1938), pp. 480–519.

STRAINS IN THE COLOMBIAN
SOCIAL STRUCTURE

Violence in Colombia is unquestionably related to social disloca-
tions, which have their counterparts in other Latin American areas.
Aside from the more than one hundred years of violent struggle
between the two political parties, a number of conflicts or psychological pressures have been and are operating within the social
fabric:

1. *Particularismo* or separatism has precluded a sense of national
unity until recently. Discontinuities include geographic barriers
with consequent regionalism resulting from isolation of many parts
of the country as well as from varying ethnic strains and cultural
traditions. As with most of Latin America, there is a feudalistic
class system and an urban-rural cleavage whereby the rural population and lower segments of the urban population have been denied
certain sanitary and medical services, educational facilities, occupational mobility, and general socioeconomic advance. Also, there are
the cleric and anti-cleric rivalries which are partially reflected in
party loyalties.

2. A major problem for Colombia has been traditionalism and
rigidity in the institutional structure, as, for example, grossly unequal land tenure. Other disproportionate social arrangements would
include the inability of the Church to provide a functional program, failure of the educational system to reform its curriculum or
to expand its services sufficiently, and, most serious, lack of effective
government because of party rivalry and the threat of military
intervention. While Colombia has generally fared better than most
Latin American countries, its government at best has represented a
"populist democracy" rather than a "liberal democracy."[5] The lack
of efficient national administrative machinery has been labeled "ad
hoc federalism" by a former consultant.[6] Under Laureano Gómez
(1950–52) and Rojas Pinilla (1953–57) these problems were ag-
gravated as the country gradually drifted into dictatorship.

---

[5] Kornhauser, *op. cit.*, pp. 130–32.
[6] Lynton K. Caldwell, "Technical Assistance and Administrative Reform
in Colombia," *APSR*, 47 (June 1943), 494–510.

3. The country's economic plight cannot be overemphasized. The level of poverty of both the *minifundista* and the quasi-serf of the *latifundio*, along with the urban worker's dilemma of spiraling inflation in the postwar years have been severely unhealthy symptoms. With increasing geographic mobility and wider communication, the vocalized discontent of the city has affected the countryside and vice versa.

4. At the risk of unwarranted generalizations, the author would posit a hyperemotionality or even psychopathic elements in certain subcultures of Latin America. The high homicide rate of the area is evidence, although we grant that parts of Latin America have a lower rate than certain North American cities. Alcoholic and drug addiction, interpersonal rivalry, and violence are outlets for this "need aggression"[7] triggered by social, political, and economic frustration.

SOME CAUSATIVE LINKS IN
COLOMBIAN VIOLENCE

Despite the general background of unrest combined with certain social situations, economic deprivations, and extreme political rivalry, the question still remains as to why this guerrilla warfare has continued for well over a decade. Among the specific causes are:

(1) *Political and military involvement.* The use of the national police force by the Conservative Government became an irreconcilable fact to the Liberals. Conversely, various police units and army members defected to the support of pro-Gaitán forces during the *bogotazo* and the rural violence of the early fifties. In other words, both sides regarded the conflict as a kind of holy war. To what degree the Communist influence played a role cannot be accurately assessed despite Gómez' easy characterization of his opponents as "Liberal crypto-communist banditry."[8] It is true that extremely liberal contingents were affected by foreign communist ideology and organization—hardly surprising in a socioeconomic order that was not altogether alien from the world described by

---

[7] Hagen, *op. cit.*

[8] Testis Fidelis, *El Basilisco en Acción o Los Crimenes del Bandolerismo* (Medellin: Tipografía Olympia, 1953), pp. 16f.

Karl Marx. However, the battle was mainly fought on the basis of party loyalties irrationally perpetuated by family and village tradition.

(2) *The breakdown of traditional institutions.* There has been in the country a partial shift from the "familistic Gemeinschaft" to the "contractual Gesellschaft."[9] With the gradual dissolution of localism have come a number of changes: cityward migration, initiation of cash economy, appearance of organized labor, and the suggestion of women's rights. These and other innovations were difficult to superimpose on the rural folkways and the rigid patriarchal family institution with its extreme bifurcation of sex roles, sexual and other liberties being permitted the male, while the female is completely subservient. It is significant that the Caribbean or coastal area with its more varied ethnic background and more permissive sexual norms as well as less rigid Catholicism was not especially affected by violence. On the other hand, the more Hispanic central area was less adjustable to changing needs.[10]

(3) *Inadequate socialization.* The psychopathic character of the killing in which whole village populations have been eliminated on both sides poses some problems. To what degree this aggression may be cultural in view of the mélange of Spanish feudalism with indigenous cultures cannot be known. One fact is clear however: leaders of violence were isolated from normal society during their formative years. Many of the participants are parentless children or products of the traditional consensual union. The limited exposure to family life has been further complicated by years of violence and consequently the present day *bandoleros* (bandits) exhibit even more markedly this background. Possibly 90 per cent are illiterate. Moreover, the mass carnage reflects a need to express one's deep hostility to society, a final settling of scores, and suggests

[9] The Gemeinschaft-Gesellschaft continuum has been variously defined as traditionalist-rationalist, sacred-secular. Cf. Talcott Parsons, *The Social System* (Glencoe: Free Press, 1951), pp. 496–520, or Charles P. Loomis and J. Allan Beegle, *Rural Social Systems* (New York: Prentice-Hall, 1950), especially chaps. 1–3. Regarding the application of this concept to transitional nations would be Daniel Lerner, *The Passing of Traditional Society* (Glencoe: Free Press, 1958).

[10] Possibly Colombia was responding by a vendetta or guerrilla warfare to the *anomie* precipitated by the confrontation of old and new, or "traditionalized" and "emancipated" elements of the society, where a decade or two earlier Italy, Germany, and Spain responded to the higher level conflict of the traditionalized and the rationalized by varying expressions of fascism; cf. Talcott Parsons, *Essays in Sociological Theory* (Glencoe: Free Press, 1954), pp. 134–37.

the lack of any adequate superego structure. In other words, the bizarre nature of torture and death demonstrate an extremely low cultural level combined with obscure psychopathic needs.[11]

(4) *Commercial and economic aspects.* The case has been made as much that violence at present is the retention of a quasi-institutionalized habit system. Yet it is not less the result of economic motivation. It is no accident that violence shows an upward spurt during certain agricultural seasons: crop theft is attractive during the semi-annual coffee harvest, and cheap land is available when the occupants are threatened by violence. At present in certain areas the victims are generally those who have failed to pay for protective services against banditry and violence.[12]

THE PATTERN OF VIOLENCE

Statistics reveal the degree to which violence has affected the country. While the larger part of the country has at one time or another been affected, in recent years four *departamentos* have had the most severe losses: Tolima, Caldas, Valle, and Huila. In Tolima, for example, 42 per cent of the roughly 750,000 inhabitants have been forced to migrate from their homes, for most of the decade ending in 1958.[13] Not less than 17,000 were killed of whom 80 per cent were males between fifteen and forty years old.[14] In an intensive study of one refugee-crowded barrio, 37 per cent of the families had lost an average of two close relatives.[15] It may be added that the over-all loss to the country is not as tremendous as often calculated. Instead of the conventional 300,000 figure, it is reasonable to consider a maximum of 180,000 deaths to 1958, with possibly some 20,000 since that date, or a total of between 1 and 2 per cent of the country's population.[16]

[11] Germán Guzmán, Orlando Fals Borda, and Eduardo Umaña, Luna, "La Violencia en Colombia," *Monografías Sociológicas*, No. 12, Volume I (Bogotá: National University, 1962), especially chaps. 5–7.

[12] *Hispanic American Reports*, 16 (May 1963).

[13] Hernando Amaya Sierra, Alfred Wells, and Sergio Restrepo, *La Violencia en el Tolima* (Ibagué: Secretariá de Agricultura, 1958).

[14] *Ibid.*

[15] Roberto Pineda, "El Impacto de la Violencia en el Tolima: El Caso de El Líbano," *Monografías Sociólogicas*, No. 6 (Bogotá: National University, 1960), pp. 16–17.

[16] Guzmán, *op. cit.*, p. 262.

Guzmán points to the determination of *jefes* and their followers on both sides to *no dejar ni la semilla* (leave nothing, not even the seed), or to completely eradicate entire families or villages including even the youngest members.[17] This fanaticism helps to explain the high death rate. However, the above figures are proportionately somewhat below the losses in the United States and Spanish civil wars or in Colombia's previous civil wars. Colombia's population growth was only slightly deterred during these years, roughly a 2.5 per cent natural increase, which might otherwise have been something over 3.5 per cent.

Also the losses would have been higher if the early Rojas Pinilla regime and the *Frente Nacional* had not come into existence reducing party rivalries, and incidentally, making specific efforts to reduce the violence. The continuance of violence is a function of a number of barriers in addition to those mentioned above: rugged terrain, army inefficiency, and the half-heartedness of interest and organization within the national and local power structure to implement means of combating the problem.[18]

INSTITUTIONALIZATION AND SOCIAL ORGANIZATION

One of the more remarkable aspects of the *violencia* has been the elaborate deployment of personnel. During the period 1949 to 1952, the national police and army units carried on the Conservative causes, and again the Conservatives entered into a guerrilla warfare of their own in the Rojas Pinilla period. The complexity of organization and degree of depravity were apparently matched in kind by the Liberals, defending the *Directoria del Partido* (party directorate) in the anticipation of one day returning to power, or at least being represented in the government. Perhaps the most extensive organization on the Liberal front was the guerrilla army that controlled the Eastern Plains in the early fifties.[19] Generally, in theory the guerrilla army was not radically different from conventional military organization in its generally hierarchical char-

---

[17] *Ibid.*, p. 205.

[18] It has been suggested that another factor is underpopulation; cf. Theodore Caplow, "La Violencia," *Columbia University Forum*, 6 (Winter 1963), 45–46. However, an area most affected by violence is also heavily populated, namely, the Quindío in the state of Caldas. Similar areas in Antioquia and Valle are also examples.

[19] A vivid account, among others, is to be found in Eduardo Franco Isaza, *Los Guerrillas del Llano* (Bogotá: Libreria Mundial, 1959).

acter.[20] At the same time, especially with the communist-inspired guerrillas, organization was frequently informal. In the more or less spontaneously initiated movements, loyalty and organization were on a primary group basis, oriented toward the *vereda* (local territorial or governmental unit) and village. On the other hand, a number of guerrilla movements were linked into a large-scale national organization, as with the *Movimiento de Autodefensa Campesina*. Integrating the large-scale organizational structure has been the *comando* or *Estado Mayor*, with the impressive title *Comando General de las Fuerzas Revolucionarios de los Llanos Orientales* (Eastern Plains), which in reality functioned only on paper. But the literature, including some dozen novels of *violencia*, portray the importance of the local *jefe*, the corporal or the lieutenant. Today most of the violence or *bandolerismo* is in the form of gangs with relatively small-scale organization.

In addition to the more familiar military roles, there are specialized roles or groupings; for example the *cuadrilla*, a task force composed of peasants. There are the *observador*, a contact man carefully screening the activities of the local residents; the *señalador* (signaler), often a pre-adolescent who indicates to the band at what hour the victim is most vulnerable; the *aguantador*, the protector who for a fee will hold off the *bandoleros*. Other roles include the arrangement of military stores frequently in the hands of a woman. In some cases, the *jefe's* concubine has been the assistant leader of the gang.[21] Whether the group is large or small the movements of each member had to be managed by the leader, or *pájaro* (bird) as he is more recently labeled—the chieftain without a party attachment.[22] Despite the close tie between leader and follower, punishments were severe and fairly primitive. For the leader as for the follower, the roles were new ones: in several areas the

[20] Organizationally, the *fuerzas guerrilleras* were composed of a hierarchy: (1) the *guerrilla* or *escuadra*, generally led by a *cabo primero* (corporal) and usually numbering three to nine men; (2) *sección*, composed of three to five *guerrillas* under the command of a lieutenant; (3) company, of three to five sections under a captain; (4) *agrupación guerrillera*, five of the *agrupaciones* under the command of a colonel or general. Cf. Guzmán, *op. cit.*, pp. 143–44.

[21] Philip Payne, "Death in the Countryside," *Time*, August 6, 1951, pp. 30–31.

[22] During the Rojas period the Conservative gang leaders were called "Blue Birds" for the party color, but with the continuance of violence the terms (*godos, chulos,* etc.) for Conservative chieftains during the high water mark of violence suggest the dominant devotions to the Liberal side. *Chusmero* has been used by Liberals as the preferred equivalent term of *pájaro*. *Chulavita* (a town in Boyacá) became the term for police officers who in the years 1948–53 made war on the Liberals.

jefes were almost all former farmers who had been deprived of their lands by *violencia*, still others were ex-police lieutenants, a few were former students, and one key figure on the Plains was an ex-teacher.

Beyond the formal and informal organization there has been the *mística*, or a kind of spiritual and ritualistic morale. The trappings included tattooing of the cross for the *Conservadores*, the hammer and sickle for the Communists, often including the name of the *jefe*; a number of romantic and martial songs; an extensive new jargon;[23] and an elaborate folklore, with lengthy newspaper accounts regarding the *pájaro* and his exploits, the name itself conveying considerable imagery: *Mico Blanco* (White Monkey), *Lengua Brava* (Loud Mouth), *El Mosco* (The Fly), *El Vampiro*, *El Condor*, and many others—some affectionate, some aimed at invoking terror. Not least impressive among the rituals were the varieties of mutilation which differed for region or party; for example, *el corte de franela* of Tolima (the "flannel underwear cut").[24]

SOME IMPLICATIONS OF *LA VIOLENCIA*

Upon investigating this history of guerrilla warfare and terror the question remains as to what it contributes to our knowledge of the sociology of violence. For one thing, as a costly civil war, it was relatively unnoticed by world opinion in the years of larger global conflicts. Perhaps this ignorance or indifference is an index to the degree of interest in the world at large to Latin American issues. Also, *violencia* illustrates at least two problems of rural life in certain underdeveloped parts of the world: the relative immunity of the city to this kind of warfare, and the frustration of rural life as a cause of violence. Fracturization of land plots and other problems of tenure, along with erosion and soil exhaustion, all point to the potential dangers in other parts of our hemisphere. Parenthetically, it may be mentioned that the Alliance for Progress is alloting high priority to land reform problems.

Social psychological explanations to the Colombian violence pose a number of problems. Among the peripheral variables is the possible effect of the release of hardened Korean war veterans—

---

[23] Guzmán, *op. cit.*, chap. 8.
[24] *Ibid.*, p. 206.

Colombia being the only Latin American country to participate in that action.[25] This event should be considered in light of Gómez' aversion to communism along with his love of rightist dictatorships. It is just possible that Korean involvement was a means of creating national unity and a distraction from certain domestic problems, including violence itself.[26] Another possible explanation of the crescendo of violence was the release of some hundreds of prisoners during the *bogotazo* in 1948.[27] In reality, most criminals, including *bandoleros*, serve relatively brief terms and this factor cannot be disregarded in understanding violence in a number of Latin American countries. And for many participants constant exposure to violence only served to reinforce this mode of behavior. Socialization was systematically devoted to aggression and sadism over the larger part of a generation, at least for some thousands of males in relevant geographic areas.

Deeper analysis would probably reveal that the "aggression need" in Colombia is particularly strong, not only for economic privation but for the lack of a coherent family structure with adequately warm and stable relationships between family members, whether husband and wife, or parents and children. However, a number of Latin countries might demonstrate this same lack of psychological sophistication in family roles and functions without the history of violence, or of any other objective criterion of behavioral or personality defect. It is beyond the scope of this paper to examine the contribution of Freudian and neo-Freudian theory as to what it can contribute to our understanding of mass violence but the relationship of various categories of frustration, aggression, and sadism are relevant.

A significant aspect of the violence phenomenon has been a "self-impelling process" carried on between party adherents at the community or *vereda* level.[28] Party loyalty which is ascriptive by family and village becomes a major motivation in the individual's life in

[25] Vernon Fluharty, *Dance of the Millions: Military Rule and the Social Revolution in Colombia* (Pittsburgh: U. of Pittsburgh Press, 1957), p. 272.
[26] Orlando Fals Borda, "El Conflicto, La Violencia y La Estructura Social Colombiana," in Guzmán, *op. cit.*, p. 373.
[27] John D. Martz, *Colombia, A Contemporary Political Survey* (Chapel Hill: U. of N. Carolina Press, 1962), p. 117, cites this among various theories of mass violence.
[28] Andrew Pearse, "Factors Conditioning Latent and Open Conflict in Colombian Rural Society," Fifth World Congress of Sociology, Washington, D.C., September 2–8, 1962.

this drive toward revenge. His own anxiety level, fed by environmental frustration, leads to violence as cyclic behavior with snowballing effect. Consequently, although party labels are less meaningful than before the 1958 coalition, the habit system pervades. Its continuance in spite of the rounding-up of *bandoleros* points to a deviant but inherent role within the culture.

Finally, on the problem of causation, we return to cultural and subcultural or regional variables. The deep relation to Spanish institutions always becomes a fulcrum in any discussion of Colombian processes.[29] It is significant that the coastal area with its Caribbean ethnic strains, industrialized plantation system, and milder clericism has been spared violence, as have the southern regions of Colombia, but for different reasons. The area toward Ecuador has had a stabilized culture pattern; even the few Liberals are pro-clerical. Still different are the vast Eastern Plains with their peculiar type of violence based on the restless, individualist cattle peon in rebellion against the landowner. Even within the high violence area of the intensively populated dissected highlands there are regional variations. For instance, the rich Valle province has diffuse, unorganized violence which has incidentally made the refugee center Cali the fastest growing major city of the republic. Although the cities themselves are protected enclaves, population density within the rural areas has no apparent relationship to the rate of violence. There is also the problem of why some areas caught up earlier in the violence culture are no longer so addicted, notably Antioquia and El Chocó. It is realized that some of these generalizations about regional variations are tentative hypotheses requiring further investigation.

CONCLUSIONS

We have chosen the literal translation of *la violencia*, although instead of "violence" the term "civil war" or some other epithet might have been selected. The generality of the term "violence" is well suited to the diffuse events in rural Colombia.[30] For one

---

[29] One writer asks whether the Civil War in Spain and *Violencia* in Colombia might be compared. Herbert Matthews, *New York Times*, April 23, 1951, p. 7.

[30] The Colombian episode also represents the four motives of violence as presented by Wright: (a) "maintenance of law and political authority," as

thing, the process has the usual characteristics of guerrilla warfare: a government deprived of power, the blending of larger organization with local units, a marginal relationship to brigandage, and its use of or predilection for topographic and climatic extremes.[31] Certainly the adroitness is equal to the exploits recorded in the last few centuries of this historic type of warfare. In pillage, burning, and killing it compares with the extremes of the Napoleonic era or of some of the civil or international wars of the last century and a half.[32]

A less secure interpretation of *la violencia* might be considered a major ingredient of social revolution.[33] In the Colombian case, rural violence may be regarded as reaction to the failure of a revolution to come off. The author's own survey, to cite only one source, demonstrated that nearly 90 per cent of university students in Bogotá were desirous of basic social change (*un cambio radical*) and were to some extent reflecting the aspirations of most of their compatriots.[34] However, the elites are in too much disagreement about how this change or revolution is to be effected, and the economic oligarchy is opposed to any marked shift in the status quo. Not least, the lack of a charismatic leader—or of any coherent

---

effective government has not functioned in the country, at least in the regimes of Ospina, Gómez, and Rojas; (2) "self-preservation and retribution," namely, the Liberal party considered itself as forcibly prevented from exercising any national power, in addition to the frustrations of citizens caught in a corrupt police system, not to speak of economic disorientation; (3) both parties, as well as other alignments, were convinced of the "defense of honor and prestige"; (4) of their "promotion of social and political justice"; and (5) the role of "individual impulses and interests" as both leaders and followers have found in the system of violence a means of livelihood, status, and a most appealing means of expressing *machismo*. Cf. Quincy Wright, *A Study of War* (Chicago: U. of Chicago Press, 1942), Vol. 2, p. 1395.

[31] Carleton Beals, "Guerrilla Warfare," *Encyclopedia of Social Science* (New York: Macmillan, 1950), Vol. 7, pp. 197–99.

[32] Quite beyond the limits of the present paper would be a discussion of possible similarities between violence in such events as the Arab-Israeli conflict, the North Africa surge of nationalism, guerrilla warfare in Southeast Asia (including the Huks in the Philippines), and not least, the role of guerrilla warfare in Fidel Castro's accession to power and the aftermath. Cf. among others, Merlo Kling, "Cuba: A Case Study of a Successful Attempt to Seize Political Power by the Application of Unconventional Warfare," *The Annals*, 341 (May 1964), 42–52.

[33] Ralf Dahrendorf, *Class and Class Conflict in Industrial Society* (Stanford: Stanford U. Press, 1959).

[34] Robert C. Williamson, "Some Students' Attitudes and Their Determinants: A Sample of the National University of Colombia," *Monografías Sociológicas*, No. 13 (Bogotá: Universidad Nacional, 1962).

and responsible leadership—would make revolution a difficult matter. Nonetheless, many of the accompanying phenomena of revolution have been present: demographic variations (especially migrations), an alteration of sex norms, family disruption, and other symptoms of social disorganization. Too, history is replete with various peasant rebellions, czarist Russia being particularly noted for this tendency.[35] But a rebellion is not a revolution, although frequently a substitution or a prelude to one.

It is popular to discuss violence or any phenomenon in terms of its latent as well as its manifest functions.[36] The Colombian episode is no exception. The cityward migration has already been mentioned. It would be illuminating to investigate the effects of the participation of the clergy. Economic consequences are visible in the consolidation of land holdings, for one item, and probably in the development of a national economy. A recent causational analysis of the violence points to frustration resulting from the severe ceiling on upward social mobility. Consequently there have emerged new "career" opportunities, not least of which is mobility in the informal military units.[37] The political aspects are hardly less important: subordination of community or regional authority to federal control and integration. The creation of the coalition government was in large part a product of the *violencia*. In other terms, on the latent level the episode has tended to unify the country despite the intense regionalism, stratification, and particularist traditions.

Finally, violence is itself a form of crime as well as being a category of social conflict. In this undeclared war or quasi-revolution both contenders were acting illegally and yet each of the two political parties claimed legitimacy to their violence. To what degree the process of violence has complicated the future social development of Colombia cannot be known. As a matter of fact, the year 1963 saw possibly the worst outbreaks since 1957. However, 1964 appears to mark the capture and end of some of the most important *jefes*.[38] Although the National Front is still operating,

[35] Feliks Gross, *The Seizure of Political Power* (New York: Philosophical Library, 1958, p. 94.

[36] H. L. Nieburg, "Uses of Violence," *Journal of Conflict Resolution*, 7 (March 1963), 43–54.

[37] Camilo Torres Restrepo, "La Violencia y los Cambios Socio-culturales en las Areas Rurales Colombianas," *Memoria del Primer Congreso Nacional de Sociología* (Bogotá: Editorial Iqueima, 1963), pp. 95–152.

[38] *Time*, May 8, 1964, pp. 36–38.

pro-Rojas Pinilla sentiment increased from 3 per cent of the votes cast in the 1962 elections to 15 per cent of the 1964 elections, with the General himself providing verbal threats in the direction of a coup.[39]

The Alliance for Progress at present regards the country as one of the more hopeful prospects in a particularly bleak hemispheric panorama. One hopes that eventually *la violencia* will be merely history. In any case, for the sociologist the period will probably be recorded as one of an abortive revolution, an inchoate, unconventional civil war, and an arena of collective behavior in which mass hysteria and mass homicide became accepted by certain elements of the power structure and by the rural culture on a regional basis.

[39] *New York Times*, March 22, 1964, p. 7.

Part Two

———— ◆•◆ ————

Social Change and Conflict

Latin American societies are not stagnating; they are changing. Urbanization and population growth have been among the most spectacular of these changes, and attention has increasingly been turned to their implications. It seems clear, for example, that social change has, at least to some extent, tended to erode the rural parochialism of an earlier era, encouraging an awareness of the larger national society and increasing demands for political participation. Such is the case in the classic example of Argentina, analyzed in this volume by Gino Germani. At the same time, political participation is not, in itself, the same as political development, and it has long been pointed out that industrialization and a more equitable distribution of economic resources have lagged far behind the growth of cities. Not only in Argentina, but in the rest of the continent as well, we are thus faced with puzzling problems that have yet to be unraveled. Does social change carry with it the inevitability of an explosive confrontation between old and new, or is it possible that at least some aspects of the traditional rural social order will be permanently transferred to the cities? Will increasing national political participation set the foundations for a democratic political order, or will it lead to a hopeless and permanent stalemate which cannot be broken by any of the participants?

The answers to these questions no doubt will vary from country to country and will depend on a broad variety of conditions and circumstances. In all of the countries, however, two factors would seem to be of major importance. One is the behavior of the traditional groups themselves—the way they change internally in response to the process of modernization and the way they adapt to or are alienated from their changing environments. The analyses (by Kenneth F. Johnson and Robert R. Kaufman) of right wing groups in the widely different contexts of Mexico and Chile and the discussion (by Martin C. Needler) of the behavior of Latin American military elites offer at least some beginning for analysis in this area. A second factor is explored in the articles contributed by Norman E. Whitten, Jr. and John Duncan Powell. Here the attention is on the development of new demands themselves, the way they emerge on the local levels of social life and the processes by which they are plugged into political struggle and change at the national level.

The Transition to a Mass
Democracy in Argentina

Gino Germani

1. THE ARGENTINE "PARADOX" AND THE PROBLEM OF ITS EXPLANATION

The political evolution of Argentina can be described as a series of stages or phases, in accordance with a scheme which in general is applicable also to the rest of Latin America. As has been shown in other works[1] this process is part of a more general change, i.e., the transition from some type of traditional structure toward some form of industrial society. In this sense the process of modification of the political structure has points in common with analogous processes occurring in the West in the early industrializing countries. Nevertheless it departs from these in greater or smaller measure depending on the peculiarity of the change within a historical context in each country, on the moment in which the transition is begun (and on the ideological and social climate prevailing at that moment at the international level), on the velocity of the transition itself, and on other factors. In the case of Argentina (and Uruguay and Chile) the transition was more similar to that of the early industrializing countries, the so-called "Western model," than was that which occurred in the other countries of Latin America. Nevertheless it is precisely Argentina which presents certain paradoxical "deviations." And the profound political crisis which has affected the country for more than thirty years constitutes a veritable enigma for those studying the sociology of economic development. When the various countries of Central and South America are compared, Argentina, as is immediately recognized, appears the most "advanced" in the transition. But also in a general international comparison the position of the country is situated in a kind of "middle class" of nations, certainly much above the so-called underdeveloped countries in terms of the social "indicators."[2] An explanation of the political instability that has characterized the country has been attempted in other works, and a preliminary theory has been formulated that specifically links this instability with the transition. But causes of a general order are in no way sufficient for explaining the Argentine "paradox." This essay attempts to draw together other circumstances peculiar to the political evolution of Argentina that might clarify the origins of the present crisis. These factors are numerous, and a complete analysis is beyond the aim of this essay; but, briefly, some factors may be indicated that probably have an essential role in the political process and make the Argentine situation extremely rare, if not unique.

First is the rapidity of the growth of Argentine society. This involved a change of scale occurring in a short period and with a velocity unequaled among the countries in which the transition took place in a "spontaneous" manner (change not induced by planning) and along the lines of the so-called Western model. The Argentine population increased 1000 per cent in 90 years (between 1870 and 1960). Compare this with other countries of rapid growth: in the United States the population increased 400 per cent in 80 years (1870–1950); in Brazil, 600 per cent in 90 years; in Chile, 400 per cent in 110 years.

In the second place, the modernization of essential aspects of social structure also occurred with extraordinary rapidity. The dual pattern, still clearly visible around 1860–70, was succeeded by a multi-class pattern, or more highly differentiated and complex stratification (characteristic of modern societies) some thirty years later. In 1900 the middle class already represented an economic force (especially in the sense of a consumer market), as well as a political one, inasmuch as it constituted one fourth of the population. Further, its concentration in the more "developed" areas (the littoral) gave it economic and political "weight" greater than its numerical proportion. At the same time, an urban proletariat of a modern type had formed, and by the beginning of this century the country was already becoming urbanized. In 1895 more than 24 per cent of the population was living in cities of 20,000 or more inhabitants, and this proportion may be raised to 37 per cent taking as limits urban centers of 2,000 and more. These proportions correspond exactly to countries that are undergoing or have passed through the industrial revolution. Possibly fundamental is the fact that other parts of the structure remained backward. All the provinces and territories away from the littoral region remained underdeveloped in terms of land tenancy, the persistence of a traditional elite, etc. But disequilibria in development are typical of the process and are in no way peculiar to Argentina. Here the really distinctive or very uncommon element was the *rapidity* of the change.

At the same time that the class structure was being modified and the country urbanized, the social structure was becoming *secularized*. Not only physical urban concentration, but also modern modes of life were transforming the behavior of the population. A valid indicator here is the gradual decline of the birth rate, owing to the application of voluntary control, in the urban areas of the littoral—first among the middle strata and later spreading rapidly to the lower strata. This process has placed Argentina (and Uruguay) among the countries exhibiting "industrial" birth rate, although the crude birth rate represents an average between the low rates of the more modern zones and the still high rates of the provinces less affected by the change.

The third factor, the proportion of foreigners in the population, is, indeed, unique. Argentina is probably the only country in the world (except Israel and perhaps Australia) the majority of whose population remained foreign during various decades. Of course, if gross percentages are taken, the foreign proportion of the population, although one of the highest in the world, will not surpass a high of 50 per cent for the whole country and for all age groups. (In Argentina this proportion was always two or three times greater than in the United States.) But the important factor here is the proportion of foreigners in *areas and groups most significant in the life of the nation.* The proportion of foreigners among adult males in the littoral region greatly exceeded the *argentinos* for more than fifty years. As is shown subsequently there were four foreigners for each *argentino* in Buenos Aires and some six for each four in the littoral provinces, including its rural areas.

Another important factor was the sudden cessation of growth that probably occurred in the decade 1920–30 and almost contemporaneously in numerous significant aspects of the social structure. The uninterrupted demographic growth of fifty or sixty years was arrested in 1930 with the elimination of overseas immigration and the drastic reduction in the urban littoral birth rate. Economic growth experienced a similar process, and finally political evolution suffered a setback of incalculable consequences with the forced regression to a "limited participation" democracy and the systematic fraud that followed the Revolution of 1930. The effects of this growth stoppage—especially in the economy—were not clearly perceived until much later, but many indications point to this circumstance as a fundamental feature of the present situation. Obviously this arrest was a result of processes generated much earlier; but when it occurred, it became a new independent factor added to the others at that certain moment, and must, therefore, be distinguished from its own origins.

What did these four factors imply for Argentina—especially when considered as events not isolated but integrated into a system of hypothesis that accounts also for their reciprocal effects? In what manner and measure did the rapid expansion and extraordinary rate of social mobility contribute to the creation of certain features, attitudes, and expectations of the *argentinos*? In what way was this same experience differentiated within the various groups and strata composing society? How did the assimilation of that enormous mass of immigrants take place? And above all, was it assimilation, or was it, rather, syncretism, with the development of new cultural forms, in the anthropological sense? What happened and is happening to the first, second, or third generation of immigrants? What repercussions did the growth stoppage have? When and how was it perceived?

And finally in what way did these four factors—peculiar to the Argentine situation—combine with the general circumstances of development and the transition? There are other factors to be considered, such as the unequal transition between different regions of the country, the massive migration from the interior after 1930, the dependency upon dominant countries, the persistence of traditional structures and its consequences for the political and economic order, and further significant elements—all of which Argentina shares with many Latin American countries and other parts of the world. While not new, these questions have never been answered. Although it is not possible to cover them all here, a summary analysis of the political process is herein presented. [EDITOR'S NOTE: a brief discussion of three breakdowns of Argentine history is omitted here.]

2. INDEPENDENCE AND FAILURE IN ESTABLISHING A NATIONAL STATE OF A MODERN TYPE

Independence was inspired in the ideals of 18th century rationalism and the Enlightenment. Its models were the revolutions of France and, even more, of North America. But if an independent state was constituted out of the old colony, its conversion into a modern state based on the cherished ideals failed. The reasons for this failure may be reduced to two. The first was a structural limitation to the program of reforms which the elite was able to accomplish. This limitation was rooted in the group's own position in the social structure and its nature as a social group. The democracy to which it aspired could be only a liberal democracy, in which the effective exercise of power would be restricted to this very group. Popular participation (necessary for carrying out an independence movement) was impossible in the political sphere as it was in the economic and social. This limitation on the achievement of possible reforms produced an irremedial contradiction between the proclaimed goals and effective practical policy, between ideology and concrete action.

Such a contradiction was reinforced, furthermore, by the second cause of failure: the structure of living established by colonial society and the profound ignorance of it exhibited by the intelligent elite. A glaring example is the civil wars which followed the attainment of independence. After the autocracy resisted, these were interpreted as the result of the conflict between two social classes: the small urban group of the cosmopolitan city, oriented toward Europe (civilization) and the popular masses of the interior, still submerged in colonial society (barbarism). There are three paradoxes to be emphasized in this process. The popular stratum, which submerged itself enthusiastically in the independence movement and fought for it, also represented in its way a democratic, or perhaps even more, an equalitarian beginning. The kind of human being who composed the Creole stratum did not correspond to the image of man subjected to a traditional authority, even though in most aspects of his life he was the standard-bearer of the traditional culture. Because of the peculiarities of his way of life, he was a somewhat anarchic individual: individualistic, loving his personal independence, and disposed to recognize the authority only of those who excelled in the qualities he most admired, e.g., valor and personal skill. The autocratic authority of the *caudillos* was not maintained through a *traditional legitimacy* but through its acceptance on the part of these groups of people who recognized in the leaders their own image and an exaltation of their own values. *Inorganic democracy* it was called (J. L. Romero), and it is probably an acceptable term so long as it is recognized that there also persisted all the remaining attributes of the traditional man: social and ecological isolation, ethnocentrism, religiosity (not exactly the cult religion of the cities), resistance to change, dominance of custom and traditional or "prescribed action,"[3] a subsistence economy and corresponding attitudes related to work and economic activity. Out of these characteristics of Creole man arose the first paradox: the democratic and republican solution to the institutional problem was imposed by the presence and the action of this population that could not accept the monarchical coquetries of the educational elite. But the second paradox has an exactly opposite significance: this Creole stratum started the dominion of the *caudillos*, and in particular of Rosas, and provided a place for a type of autocracy that really consisted simply in the restoration—where possible—of the colonial society and the denial of democracy in a modern sense. There is no doubt that the culture and social structure of Argentina in the years prior to 1850 were very close to the traditional pattern of the colonial period.

The third paradox may be seen in the following: The popular stratum and the *caudillos* represented the triumph of the provinces and of the interior, and an affirmation of the localism of the most limited small community; they were incapable of the ideals of the intelligent minorities of the city, of extending loyalty to what is, in a modern sense, the great national community. However, the real result of the authority exercised by Rosas and by Buenos Aires, the so-called "federal" regime, was an effective authority of *porteño* centralism, i.e., that of Buenos Aires, and ultimately facilitated the process of national organization based on a compromise between centrifugal and centripetal tendencies.

3. TRANSFORMATION OF SOCIAL STRUCTURE

The members of the generation that assumed the task of building Argentina as a modern national state were aware of the contradictions between the simple rationalism of the independent elite and the true nature of colonial society as it was perpetuated through the first half of the 19th century by the autocracy and authority of the *caudillos*. They understood that no political reform would be possible which was not founded on radical changes in the social structure. They were "social realists," and they used the philosophic and sociological ideas of the times to understand the native, national situation, and they arrived at what can be called a true plan, a deliberate action directed toward a substantial modification of Argentine society.

TABLE 1.   THE PROCESS OF URBANIZATION IN ARGENTINA: 1869–1957

Years	Urban population (in centers of 2,000 or more inhabitants) per cent
1869	27
1895	37
1914	53
1947	62
1957	65

The essential measures put into effect for accomplishing this proposition were three: education, foreign immigration, and economic development. In these three points may be summarized the program of the so-called "generation of 1837"—of Sarmiento, Alberdi, Echeverría, and others who formulated it and partially carried it through. But the action of the leaders in this program was no less contradictory than had been that of the earlier elite revolutionaries. They were specifically a part of what later came to be called "the oligarchy," a landholding bourgeoisie, in spite of a liberal motivation and a sincere preoccupation with transforming Argentina into a modern state. Its position in the social structure without doubt provided the main source of contradiction in its efforts toward reform.

In the immigration program the objectives were two: first, "to populate the desert," according to a well-known phrase; second, to change the social character of the population in order to give it those features considered necessary to the development of a modern nation. Fundamentally they tried to substitute for the "traditional" social form a more adequate form, the modern industrial structure. In that period this was viewed as a "racial" change and not as the

effect of the transition from one social structure to another. In the
parlance of the times, they were trying to "bring Europe to
America," to Europeanize the interior population, considered to be
the principal factor in the political instability and economic backwardness.

For this purpose it was necessary above all to "colonize," to
insure the rooting to the land of the European immigrants. Although the rise of urban activities—in industry, services, etc.—was
also desired, there is no doubt that immigration was correctly
oriented "toward the desert." Certainly the population was radically
altered, and, as is shown later, one of the features essential to the
understanding of present-day Argentina is its migratory origin.
The traditional social and economic structure was also transformed
through the emergence of Argentina as one of the world producers
of grain and meat. But the social structure of the rural regions was
not changed as had been hoped. No large, strong agricultural middle
class, rooted in ownership of the land, emerged. Instead of "colonization," what has been termed a colossal land speculation succeeded
in increasing and reinforcing the influence of the *latifundistas.*
When massive immigration began, most land accessible and adapt-
able to cultivation was already held by a few proprietors. In
1914, after the middle period of immigration and with foreigners
composing no less than half the total active population, immigrants
represented only as much as 10 per cent of the owners of landed
property (Table 4). The traditional families had maintained and
substantially increased the *latifundista* regime; in 1947 three fourths
of the land was still concentrated in little more than 20,000 agricultural holdings, less than 6 per cent of the total.[4]

The legal pattern of land use was and continues to be land rental,
or other less favorable forms, and the place of a rural middle class
was occupied in large measure by renters and small proprietors,
highly exposed to all the exigencies of climate and the national
market. Even though some prospered, the low economic condition
of the majority obliged them to move continually in search of better
circumstances and subjected them to all kinds of restrictions. In
still worse condition were the landless peasants, unsalaried workers
exposed to seasonal labor needs, low levels of employment and
low standards of living. One of the principal and undesired effects
of this situation was the concentration of foreigners in the cities and
an extraordinary urban growth.

Clearly massive migration and the rest of the innovations sought
by the elite who directed the "national organization" from the

second half of the last century meant a profound change in the country. But the social structure that arose therefrom also clearly deviated from the ideal of establishing a stable base for a democracy. One of the most consequential deviations was the unfavorable rural structure and population distribution.

To populate the desert was desired, and in a certain sense this was achieved. But the population was concentrated in the cities; and instead of reducing the disequilibrium between the underdevelopment of the interior and the development of the littoral, it was further accentuated. The consequences of this were evident by the middle of the century.

The process of urbanization in Argentina developed in two great phases: the first, 1869 to 1914, was effected by the massive European immigration; the second, corresponding approximately to the period 1930–35 to 1950–55, was sustained by massive internal migrations.[5]

The role of foreigners in the formation of Argentina's urban structure is shown very clearly in Table 2. Not only in cosmopoli-

TABLE 2.   PERCENTAGE OF FOREIGNERS IN THE POPULATION ACCORDING TO THE SIZE OF THE URBAN CENTERS: 1869–1947[6]

Zone	1869	1895	1914	1947
Greater Buenos Aires	47	50	49	26
Other cities of 100,000 or more	9	34	35	15
Urban centers of 50,000 to 99,999	8	18	22	7
Urban centers of 20,000 to 49,999	12	23	26	10
Urban centers of 2,000 to 19,999	7	19	23	10
Urban centers of less than 2,000 and populations outside of urban centers	3	9	14	9

tan Buenos Aires, whose population was 50 per cent foreign between the years 1869 and 1914, but also in the remaining cities this proportion was exceptionally high. Also of significance is the direct correlation between population volumes and proportion of foreigners. Thus in cities of 100,000 and more inhabitants between the years 1895 and 1914 more than one third had been born abroad.

Furthermore, to this urban concentration was added another of regional type. All the large cities were situated in the littoral zone, and in general foreigners naturally located therein. Thus the metro-

politan area of Buenos Aires and the provinces of the littoral always
retained about 90 per cent of the immigrants. This concentration
had profound effects on the social structure and the political life,
particularly when combined with the expansion and transformation of the economic community. By the beginning of the present
century the traditional pattern had been destroyed and replaced by
forms closer to the "modern" model. Also as a result of other
measures aimed at the economic development of the country—
attraction of capital, construction of railroads, legal reforms—the
country became a great grain and meat exporter. New demands of
foreign commerce, needs of the great urban concentrations, and
the increased wealth of the country gave impulse to the first industrial development. Since the last quarter of the century modern
industrial activity has appeared and expanded through the country,
replacing the old surviving artisan forms, and, although continuing
to be centered in agriculture and livestock, already reached a respectable volume of production in the first decade of the present
century. At the same time the popular strata of the old society
—largely rural—are being replaced by an urban proletariat and a
rapidly expanding middle class. Thus the "bipartite" traditional
society (an upper stratum of the landed estate holders versus a low
stratum composed of a majority of the population, with an intermediate stratum of minor importance, usually identified with the
upper stratum) is replaced by a tripartite (upper, middle, and
popular classes) or even multipartite system. The differentiation
between classes, especially in the cities, becomes obscure, and the
structure assumes the image of a continuous series of superposed
ranks in which the transition from one to another becomes difficult
to perceive.

The emergence of a middle-class of sufficient numerical, economic, and social importance for political influence occurred between 1869 and 1895. By the last decade of the nineteenth century
it had become a group of great importance. In evaluating Table 3
it should be kept in mind that the data are concerned for the most
part with an urban middle class, concentrated in the littoral zone.
Its influence was greater in these areas which were playing a central
role in national life. Also it is essential to take into account the
qualitative changes produced by the transition from the traditional
pattern to more modern forms. While the upper class, the traditional families, retained broad control in agriculture until the beginning of the century, the middle class was made up of men who

promoted the new activities, small and average impresarios con-
solidating commercial activity and nascent industry. A smaller rural
middle class, peasants of some prosperity or economic stability, was
also formed. But this was a small group in comparison to the foreign
immigrant masses and the rural native population. Later, particularly after 1910, the middle class owed its growth to the expansion
of its "dependent" sectors: "white collar" workers, employees and
functionaries, professionals and technicians of public and private
bureaucracies. And this successive change in the composition of the
middle class also has its political significance. From the so-called
popular strata rural *peones*, people without a trade, old skilled
artisans, and domestic servants are being transformed into urban

TABLE 3. MIDDLE AND POPULAR OCCUPATIONAL STRATA IN ARGENTINA:
1869–1947[7]

Occupational strata	1869	1895	1914	1947
Middle strata* (*patrones* of business, industry, agriculture, employees, professionals)	11	26	32	40
Popular strata (urban workers, rural laborers, *peones*)	89	74	68	60

* Including a small proportion (around 2 per cent) of the upper class.

workers in industry, commerce, transportation, and services, i.e.,
in activities accomplished in accordance with the typical relations
of modern business enterprise and concentrated in the cities. The
conditions are available for the rise of proletarian movements
which, in the typical pattern of early stages of industrialization and
urbanization, appear as movements of "social protest."

4. END OF DEMOCRACY OF
LIMITED PARTICIPATION
AND INTERVENTION
OF THE MIDDLE
CLASS

The political significance of these changes is well known, involving
the entrance into national life of groups which were differentiated
out of the old traditional strata. The implication was that a func-

tioning democracy, particularly in its most immediate manifestation, universal suffrage, will include such recently formed classes.

Faced with this evident basis for founding a democratic state, the ruling elite did not seem disposed to share power, much less to cede it to the new groups which were being incorporated into the national life. Its goal continued to be a liberal democracy of limited participation by the upper strata of society. Although in many other respects (as already noted) its attitudes were progressive and open to greater participation in national life by the popular strata—such was its position, for example, in education—there were certain limits which were difficult or impossible to transcend in economic and political matters. In the first, it not only was unable to relinquish its monopoly of the land, but it definitely profited from advantages derived from the economic transformation, and often its development measures were oriented more toward its own class interests than toward the national interests. Politically a prolonged struggle, limited only by the amount of public opinion, was necessary for the most progressive elements of that same "oligarchy" to make possible universal suffrage and accede peacefully to the participation in power of the new social groups. The first elections with total participation of the citizenry were realized in 1916 and gave the government to men of the middle class, politically organized in the radical party that appeared three decades earlier.

This date, 1916, can probably be taken as the beginning of mass democracy and the end of limited democracy, taking into account all the reservations attendant upon fixing rigid divisions within such complex social processes. And moreover it was only the beginning of a long process, replete with contradictory alternatives, that is still in development.

The transition from a "limited" democracy to "mass" democracy in Argentina was particularly traumatic. There was, first, the paradoxical situation created by the massive immigration. During thirty or forty years persons born abroad were much more numerous than those born in the country. If one considers the effects of the double concentration—by geography and age—and the proportion of foreigners in those groups most important in political life (adults, males over 20) in the central zones of national activity (the capital and provinces of the littoral), the extraordinary fact is that this proportion reaches between 50 per cent and 70 per cent.

In terms of elections, this meant that precisely where participation in the vote could have greatest importance, between 50 per cent and 70 per cent of the inhabitants were outside its legal exercise. For example, in absolute figures, in 1895, out of 216,000 male inhabitants of the city of Buenos Aires only 42,000 were natives of Argentina (and those naturalized amounted to less than 2 per cent). In the same year in the littoral provinces (Buenos Aires, Santa Fé, Córdoba, La Pampa, Entre Ríos) of over 600,000 adult males, 287,000 would eventually have had the right to vote, as natives. If the further drastic reduction in political participation deriving from the remaining social conditions is considered, the significance of the term "limited democracy" will appear in all its plentitude.[8]

This political marginality of the majority was a constant concern to the leaders of the period, but, as is widely known, the elite maintained toward it a characteristic ambivalence. In reality the functioning of the "limited" democracy gained from this circumstance. In all probability the political effects of the appearance of the middle strata were considerably retarded by the fact of its dominant foreign composition. The failure of the popular classes to form a party capable of representing it politically was very probably due to similar reasons. It is instructive here to analyze the variable proportions of foreigners in some occupational and economic categories (Table 4).

As already noted, landed property remains almost totally in the hands of *argentinos*. This situation contrasts with that of commercial and industrial development. The entrepreneurs of commerce and industry, and the industrial workers are largely foreigners, and this in a proportion above the medium level existing in the total active population. Furthermore, in the popular strata the pre-industrial activities (ancient arts and crafts, domestic service) are held by a native majority, and, of course, native people predominate in the rural population, especially of the interior. The elite firmly retained control of activity in land; the middle class and proletariat were formed in the cities, founded on the massive immigration. As the children of these immigrants became active, and the extraordinary proportion of foreigners diminished, these recently formed classes began to have the possibility of a *direct* influence in political activity.

Here the word *direct* has a particular importance. Effectively these mass majorities, although marginal from the viewpoint of their electoral rights and in large part their own political interests, exercised an indirect gravitational force, although there are no

TABLE 4. PROPORTION OF FOREIGNERS IN DIFFERENT CATEGORIES OF THE
ACTIVE POPULATION: FOREIGNERS PER 100 PERSONS OCCUPIED IN EACH
LISTED CATEGORY: 1895–1914[9]

Strata	Economic and ocupational categories	1895	1914
Some sectors of the middle classes	Owners of landed property*	No data	10
	Entrepreneurs of industry	81	66
	Entrepreneurs of commerce and services	74	74
	Professionals	53	45
	Commercial employees	63	51
	Public employees	30	18
Some sectors of the popular classes	Industrial workers**	60	50
	Domestic servants	25	38
	Laborers in domestic and craft industries	18	27
Total active population		30	47

* Excluding owners in the federal capital.
** Including some employees.

studies and data which might permit it to be evaluated correctly.
At the same time, the popular class nourished—as leader and as
masses—the great protest movements of the first decades of the
century, and the middle stratum provided the human *ambiance*
most propitious for the emergence of the movement that should
have represented the political expression of these groups in national
life.

Thus in Argentina the step from governments of the elite, of a
limited democracy, to governments of the middle class signified the
incorporation of the foreign immigrant masses, or of their children,
into political life. But it is probable that the peculiar composition
of the population and particularly the predominance of foreigners in
the protest movements of the first decades of the century implied a
considerable delay in the formation of adequate political organisms
of the urban proletariat that supported radicalism, the expression of
the middle classes.

It was this party which governed the country for fourteen years

and, until 1930, should have spoken for all the new strata in the
social structure arising in the change from the traditional to the
"modern." But it cannot be said that it complied with this responsibility. It in no way effectively used the power to effect those
alterations in the social structure that might have assured a safer
base for the functioning of democratic institutions and the participation of all social strata without limitations. It did nothing, or
very little, to resolve one of the country's most basic problems, the
agrarian problem. Even though until the end of this period rural
conditions were significantly better than previously—the stability
of the rural population was much greater, so that these years were
ones of minor urban growth—the socioeconomic structure of the
rural regions remained practically unchanged, since the measures
adopted were totally insufficient to the magnitude of the problem.
In regard to the urban proletariat the attitude of radicalism was no
less ambivalent. Although numerous measures for social protection
of labor were adopted, the problem was not only one of a much too
moderate legislation, but also that it often had no practical application. On the other hand in spite of the climate of freedom which
was enjoyed during the period, it cannot be said that the labor
organizations saw much development. Legislation did not explicitly
provide the unions with any legal status, although of course their
activity was permitted by virtue of the general disposition of the
constitution. This lack of recognition, reflecting opinion in the
upper strata and openly against such organizations, increased the
difficulty of their task and provided a very serious obstacle to their
operating as a means of progressive incorporation of the popular
strata into the political life of the nation. It is symptomatic that the
radical parliaments maintained the same repressive legislation created
by the "oligarchy" at the beginning of the century in the face of
the first expansion of labor movements. In 1918 the radical government did not hesitate to resolve the social problem with a bloody
repression of the uprisings originating in the postwar situation.

The high proportion of foreigners during the epoch of the
emergence and first development of labor movements probably
impeded and rendered difficult the formation of a party which
might integrate them within the democratic structure of the country. On the one hand in spite of their numerical and social importance in the population, they had to remain in a marginal position
within the electorate. On the other hand the foreign composition
of the labor movements, together with an internationalistic ideology

which in this epoch was characterizing so strongly the movements of the left, probably contributed to placing such movements in an unfavorable light precisely at the moment when the immigrant offspring was being incorporated and his identification with the new country must have been emerging with particular intensity. It is not necessary to review the undoubtedly nationalistic character (in a democratic sense) of the U.C.R. and its refined "isolationism," particularly during World War I. That which may be produced in Argentina through acquisition of national identity and trans-cendency of the old regional and local loyalties by means of the immigrant offspring continues to have a notable importance, in this and other respects.

Thus if the radical party, in spite of its popular appeal and sup-port, was not capable of politically representing the proletariat, neither were the Socialist party and other leftist organizations—in large measure for the aforementioned reasons. Moreover the former was gradually becoming composed of middle class groups and ended by symbolizing an alternative to radicalism only for the independent electorate.

Finally the fact that large areas of the country remained in under-developed conditions, that the process of progressive incorporation of the inhabitants into national life was realized only in the littoral and highly urbanized zones, while the "interior" remained com-pletely marginal, and that the same occurred in rural sections of the littoral, constituted another disturbing factor of fundamental im-portance for later evolution. In effect it would have been essential for the country's political equilibrium (i.e., with respect to se-curing a representative democracy) that the strengthening of a party of the democratic left, endowed with the support and adherence of the popular sectors, be produced in an ideologically adequate climate, i.e., within the democratic philosophical tradition of the left, such as occurred in the early industrializing countries of Europe.

5. THE GREAT INTERNAL MIGRATIONS AND INTEGRATION OF THE POPULAR STRATA

Such was the situation in 1930 when a repercussion of profound processes (the particular social structure of the country) and most recent events (the world-wide Depression which rudely struck

Argentina's economy) produced military intervention which for the first time in many decades overthrew a constitutional government. This movement, which also was expressing the new international political climate created by the rise of fascism in Europe, fundamentally signified the return of the "oligarchy" displaced from power by the radical majority. But this "return" could not mean a reversion to the past situation and the intent to establish a type of limited democracy in which political participation would be restricted to certain classes. It was to have significance and consequences very different from the apparently analogous exclusive situation of a half century before. The principal measure employed by these groups lacking the electoral support necessary to govern was a systematic fraud, through which, without formally denying the exercise of civil rights, the exercise of these rights and their consequences in the forming of the government were effectively impeded. Freedom of the press and of association were respected, more or less, as were other rights formally sanctioned by the constitution. But the activity of the unions encountered greater and growing difficulties, and this, combined with frustration produced by the systematic manipulation of the popular will in elections, created in a majority a feeling of profound skepticism—skepticism which continued to be influenced by the general crisis of democratic ideologies during the decade of the thirties. Nor were the opposition parties, moreover, at the height of their mission just at the moment when a new stage in the country's socioeconomic development was being enacted.

In effect two convergent processes were produced in Argentina as a repercussion of the new conditions created by the world crisis of 1929: a new and decisive phase of industrialization was begun, and urbanization gained an unusual impetus with the massive migration to the cities from the interior of the country. During the decade 1936–47 the proportion of *argentinos* born in the provinces who moved to the metropolitan zone of Buenos Aires was equal to almost 40 per cent of the natural increase of these same provinces. It was an exodus en masse, by which vast layers of people from the underdeveloped zones—masses until this moment completely outside the bounds of the political life of the country— were established in the large cities and particularly in Buenos Aires.

It seemed to be a process in a certain sense comparable to that of the massive overseas immigration a half century earlier, but with

TABLE 5

POPULATION OF THE METROPOLITAN AREA OF BUENOS AIRES:
COMPOSITION OF INTERNAL AND EXTERNAL MIGRATION: 1869–1957[10]

Years	Total population (thousands)	Immigrants from abroad (% of total population)	Migrants from the interior (% of total population)	Average annual internal migration
1869	230	47	3	
1895	783	50	8	} 8000
1914	2035	49	11	
1936	3430	36	12	
1947	4720	26	29	} 83,000
1957	6370	22	36	96,000

three great differences: first, the rhythm of the earlier was much
slower, since the urban population growth lasted over at least three
decades; second, the masses that exerted political pressure and led
toward effective universal suffrage were not immigrants themselves
(who, being foreigners, were participating only indirectly and
with difficulty in political processes), but their offspring; and
lastly, above all, it was a matter of a rise of the newly formed middle
class, leaving a nascent urban proletariat in a subordinate situation.
These large masses, transplanted in short order to the cities, transformed suddenly from rural *peones*, artisans, or persons with hardships into industrial workers, acquired a political significance
without at the same time finding the institutional channels necessary
for integrating themselves into the normal functioning of the democracy. The repressive policy of the governments from late in
the last century until the beginning of this one, the ambivalence
and relative failure of the governments of the middle class between
1916 and 1930, the severe limitations to the functioning of the
democracy after that date, and the general doubts and skepticism
created by all these experiences coupled with the absence of political parties capable of furnishing adequate expression to the sentiments and necessities of these masses left them in a state of "availability," making them an element inclined to be exploited through
whatever happenstance might offer them some form of participation.

Meanwhile international events also were exerting pressure in a direct manner on Argentina; the expansion of nazism in Europe and its first victories during the first three years of the war precipitated reverberations. A new military intervention in 1943, this time of open totalitarian intent, interrupted the conservative experiment of "democracy limited by means of fraud." But the social structure of Argentina, particularly at this point in the process of forming an urban industrial society, and the kind of masses "available" for utilization as the human basis of a totalitarian movement, were far from lending themselves to a fascist experiment of the classic type, i.e., the Italian or German form. It was necessary to bring about extensive revisions in this system, and *peronismo*, which arose starting from the military revolution, was precisely the expression of the particular conditions created in Argentina through the accumulation of the series of factors, ancient and new, which have been summarized herein. Thus is encountered another of the paradoxes which abound in the history of the country. A movement of the fascist type set off a regime of undoubtedly totalitarian character but endowed with features very different from its European model; it was a type of authoritarianism based on the consent and support of the majority, which for the first time in sixteen years was able to express its wishes in regular elections. This fact is of singular significance, since free elections were becoming transformed into the principal if not the only symbol of democracy and constituted one of the myths most dwelled upon by the opposition democratic parties, particularly the radical, during the conservative regime.

The *peronista* regime, by its origin, the character of its leaders, and the circumstances of its emergence, was called upon to represent only an ersatz political participation of the popular classes. Although the result of a conjunction of very different forces, its fall was possible only through its intrinsic limitations. And the principal one of these was in defending itself: it should have transformed this illusory participation into a real intervention; it needed, in other words, a change of nature, to become truly an expression of the popular classes. This was impossible, and it had to fall in the face of incessant attack by groups of very different orientation and origin. But the process initiated with *peronismo*, and even much earlier with universal suffrage, has remained unfinished; and the problem of the incorporation of all social strata into national political life within a democracy functioning in an effective manner and based on the respect of political and social rights summarizes in itself the history of the present and of the immediate future in Argentina.

NOTES

1. See especially Chapters 5 and 6 of the author's work *Política y sociedad en una época de transición de la sociedad tradicional a la sociedad de masas,* Buenos Aires, Paidós, 1962.

2. This "underdeveloped" stereotype was incorporated in the image of Argentina by its inhabitants relatively recently. It contrasts with the pre-existing image of a rich country, characterized by one of the highest national per capita incomes, as well as by other indices of economic and social advancement. Of course this older image was, at least in part, an ideological deformity, maintained for the support of a specific economic policy and a world-wide view of political and social organization. Those who, from opposite angles, did not share this image denounced the "dependent" character of Argentina's economy and the consequences of this dependency. But in spite of the "poor provinces" of the interior the characterization of Argentina as a socially "backward" country would not be shared even by the critics most "alienated" from the country's ruling social regime. Nevertheless, especially in the last decade, the indiscriminate usage of the category "underdevelopment" has induced many—particularly intellectuals and pseudo-intellectuals of the left (and pseudo-left)—to assimilate *tout court* Argentina's case with that of the ex-colonial countries which are presently beginning the first phases of the transition in Latin America, Asia, or Africa. This image is no less deformed than the former (that of Argentina as a country completely developed economically and advanced socially, subsequently destroyed by "statist" experiments, etc.) and leads one to accept certain ideological and political orientations that are not absolutely viable for a country whose social structure is rather different from those of countries actually in initial phases of the transition. Perhaps it may be worthwhile to record some recent data. In two international typologies concerning economic and social development and based on a large number of economic, demographic, educational, sanitary, and other indicators, Argentina is in an intermediate position, closer to countries of advanced development than to the rest. In a typology prepared by the United Nations, based on a series of socioeconomic indicators relating seventy-four countries, Argentina is in the third category, on a scale of six (cf. United Nations, *Report on the World Social Situation,* New York, 1961, Chapter 3). In another work (for presentation at an international conference at Yale, September, 1963) Professor K. Deutsch places Argentina, among a total of ninety-one countries, in a second category out of a scale of five. The five categories are: Traditional Primitive Societies, Traditional Civilizations, Transitional Societies, Societies in Industrial Revolution, and Societies of High Mass Consumption; in this last category to which pertain the countries of highest economic development there are thirteen nations, great and small (K. Deutsch, *Yale Political Program: Preliminary Report,* March 1963).

3. On the typology "prescribed action vs. elective action" see G. Germani, *op. cit.,* Chapter 2.

4. G. Germani, *Estructura social de la Argentina,* Buenos Aires, Raigal, 1955, Chapter 10.

5. G. Germani, *El proceso de urbanización en la Argentina*, Semanario sobre Urbanización en América Latina, Santiago de Chile, 1959. Mimeographed by United Nations, Economic Commission for Latin America.

6. *Ibid.*

7. Instituto de Sociología, Universidad de Buenos Aires, *Estudios sobre la estratificación social en la Argentina a base de los Censos Nacionales*, 1959. (Unpublished.)

8. The proportion of voters relative to the adult population (20 or more years old) in some presidential elections between 1910 and 1958 was as follows (until and including 1946 only the male population was considered in these computations; for 1958 the female population was also included):

Years	Per cent of voters relative to total population 20 years and older (including foreigners)	Per cent of voters relative to total native argentinos only (naturalized citizens were less than 2 per cent)
1910	9	20
1916	30	64
1928	41	77
1936	48	73
1946	56	83
1958	78	90

(The base of 20 years and older was chosen not in regard to legal arrangements but because this age was considered a departure point beyond which there exists a voting *expectancy*. Also, this procedure was used for international comparisons employing these data, in a work in preparation.)

9. G. Germani, "La asimilación de los inmigrantes en la Argentina," *Revista Interamericana de Ciencias Sociales*, 1961, I, 1–28.

10. G. Germani, *El proceso de urbanización, op. cit.*

Ideological Correlates of Right Wing
Political Alienation in Mexico[*]

Kenneth F. Johnson

Evaluations of single-party democracy in Mexico have yielded a substantial literature from the researches of contemporary scholars.[1] Their primary subjects of treatment have been the institutionalized agents of moderation and compromise that have made Mexico one of Latin America's more stable political systems. In prosecuting these studies, however, only scant attention has been given to political groups outside the officially sanctioned "revolutionary family" of the *Partido Revolucionario Institucional.* The PRI has maintained a virtual monopoly of elective and appointive offices since 1929 and traditionally has been thought of as affiliating to itself the *only* politically relevant groups in Mexico.

Modern Mexican political life has always had its "out groups" and splinter parties. Mostly, they have come and gone, leaving little

From Kenneth F. Johnson, "Ideological Correlates of Right Wing Political Alienation in Mexico," *American Political Science Review,* Vol. LIX (September 1965). Reprinted by permission.

[*] An abbreviated version of this paper was prepared for delivery at the Annual Convention of the Western Political Science Association, March 19, 1965, at Victoria, B. C., Canada. Field work on the project was supported by Rockefeller Foundation funds received via the University of Denver Social Science Foundation.

[1] *Cf.* L. Vincent Padgett, "Mexico's One-Party System: A Re-Evaluation," this REVIEW, Vol. 51 (Dec., 1957) pp. 995–1008; Martin C. Needler, "The Political Development of Mexico," *ibid.,* Vol. 55 (June, 1961), pp. 308–312; Philip B. Taylor, Jr., "The Mexican Elections of 1958: Affirmation of Authoritarianism," *Western Political Quarterly,* Vol. 13 (Sep., 1960), pp. 722–744; Robert E. Scott, *Mexican Government in Transition* (University of Illinois Press, Urbana, 1959); Howard Cline, *Mexico: Revolution to Evolution, 1940–1960* (Oxford University Press, London, 1962); William P. Glade and Charles W. Anderson, *The Political Economy of Mexico* (University of Wisconsin Press, Madison, 1963); David T. Garza, "Factionalism in the Mexican Left: The Frustration of the MLN," *Western Political Quarterly,* Vol. 17 (September, 1964), pp. 447–60.

or no impact upon the political system which they have attempted to influence. Howard Cline has contended that opposition groups in Mexico find it impossible to woo the electorate away from the PRI and thus feel forced to adopt demagoguery and other extreme postures which serve only to reduce their popular appeal.[2] Cline writes further, "in nearly every case, the dissidents return quietly to the PRI ranks, without prejudice or reprisals."[3] The historical accuracy of these contentions goes unquestioned here. Rather, I seek to explore, using modern analytic techniques, the possibility that Mexico is becoming a less rigid single-party authoritarian system, that it may be moving instead toward a cooperative two- or even three-party system surrounded by a number of alienated but relevant satellite groups.

I undertake this with due deference to the works just cited, whose authors have told much of the Mexican story and told it well. In addition, I respond directly to Merle Kling's recent dictum that it is time to "assume the risks of creating and testing hypotheses, formulating generalizations and theories" about the nature of change in contemporary Mexican politics.[4] This cannot be done if potentially relevant "out groups" continue to be neglected. Kling refers to "risks." One is surely the chance that the Mexican "out groups" selected for study are not indeed politically relevant. My criteria for relevance, stated below, are intended to obviate that difficulty. Perhaps a more severe risk is conservative resistance to the very suggestion that groups outside the "revolutionary family" may be gaining political relevance within the Mexican system. But to offer such a suggestion is my prime purpose.

I

When the Mexican Revolution was scarcely one year old, the following challenge was hurled against its leader:

> Mexicans: Consider that the cunning and bad faith of a man are shedding blood in an outrageous manner because of his incapacity to govern . . . we turn arms against him for having betrayed the Revolution . . . (Emiliano Zapata et al., *Plan de Ayala*, 1911, as

[2] Cline, *op. cit.*, p. 168.
[3] *Ibid.*
[4] Merle Kling, "Area Studies and Comparative Politics," *American Behavioral Scientist*, Vol. 8 (September, 1964), p. 10.

quoted in Heriberto Garcia Rivas, *Breve Historia de la Revolución Mexicana*, México, Editorial Diana, 1964, p. 112)

Those words were voiced in outrage over a promised land reform that had not materialized. After a half-century of equally inspiring promises, and of progress along many lines, one still hears words faintly reminiscent of those above.

> Citizens: by means of the vote you can once and for all put an end to the lies, exploitation and fraud of those who would profiteer from the Revolution. With no other arms than your honorable and clean vote, citizens, National Action is confident of victory. (From a speech by José González Torres, presidential candidate of *Partido de Acción Nacional*, as printed in *La Nación*, 17 mayo, 1964, p. 32)

Both expressions are examples of political alienation, but there is an important difference in degree. The one is a call to armed rebellion; the other acknowledges the silent force of popular challenge in an honestly counted vote. Measurement of such contemporary political alienation in Mexico is the immediate task of this paper. Political alienation is one element in a larger theoretic formulation that I have described elsewhere as an analytic approach to the study of stability and instability in the Latin American political culture.[5] In Mexico, political alienation will be understood to mean a specific and identifiable syndrome of ideology and behavior which is manifest in support for, sympathy toward, or participation in political extremism. This, in turn, is defined (for Mexico) as advocacy of violence, advocacy of a conspiratorial interpretation of Mexican political life (including the doctrine that the political system is manipulated by hostile foreign powers or by a treasonable internal cabal), advocacy of turning the government of Mexico or its major subdivisions over to private enterprise or to the Roman Catholic Church, or advocacy of the total abandonment of constitutional government. This definition was designed with right wing alienation in mind but a modified version of it could prove suitable for left wing alienation as well.

Before coming to the present scene, let us look back briefly over the development of right wing ideology in Mexico. One sees it

[5] Kenneth F. Johnson, "Causal Factors in Latin American Political Instability," *Western Political Quarterly*, Vol. 17 (September, 1964), pp. 432–446.

nurtured in the Querétaro Club of 1810 that produced Hidalgo and Allende and in the subsequent rebellions against the *gachupines*. Reactionary ideology thrived during the regimes of Iturbide and Santa Anna, and burst forth in the clerical opposition to Lerdo, Juarez, Ocampo and to the Liberal Constitution of 1857. Ultra-conservative thought was rejuvenated for thirty-five years by the *cientificos* during the *Pax Porfiriana*, and passed thereafter into the hands of the *cristeros* who fought Calles and Vasconcelos who unsuccessfully opposed Ortiz Rubio. Ultimately, it was crystallized in the organized popular reactions to Lázaro Cárdenas's reform era during the 1930's. The latter period is particularly important for this study since it included the genesis of two groups that are of chief concern here.

Especially bitter targets of reactionary attack were Cárdenas's sweeping nationalizations of industry, accelerated distribution of agricultural lands via the usufructory device of *ejidos*, and stricter enforcement of the anti-clerical provisions of the Constitution of 1917. Those who organized against Cárdenas and his political predecessors embraced an ideological outlook that persists in Mexico today and is gaining political relevance. I shall term it "restorationism." Mexico's restorationists are those who would return to the Church its political and financial privileges, to the great families or *abolengo* the land, and to the unhampered forces of the marketplace business and commerce.

They are, to some extent, those whose aspirations for socio-economic advantage are thwarted by restricted access to places of influence within the governing single-party system. In short, the revolutionary machinery has not accommodated itself adequately to the psychological and material requirements of *all* relevant and active political sectors in Mexico. True to the prototype of France's experience following 1789, the Mexican Revolution scored a violent dislocation of the political *status quo*, radically changed the social structure, but preserved seeds of potential unrest by its failure to supplant entirely the reactionary right. Today, Mexico's restorationists have two principal organized forms, *Unión Nacional Sinarquista* and *Partido de Acción Nacional*.[6]

[6] Several lesser groups that have been variously affiliated with PAN and UNS are *Acción Católica Mexicana* (which cannot legally call itself a party because of the constitutional prohibition against use of religious titles in political organization), *Unión Nacional de Padres de Familia,* and *Partido Nacionalista de México*.

The term *sinarquismo* is a corruption of two words, *sin anarquiá*, without anarchy—or in better English, with order. Order, *órden*, as the name of its official journal implies, is the hallmark of *Unión Nacional Sinarquista*. It is an order of Christian democracy, first under God, then under a God-fearing state. UNS members are ardent practicing Roman Catholics, disciplined soldiers of a theocratic faith. The movement was born (according to official doctrine) amid an explosion of enthusiasm, faith, and courage.[7] The basic committee that proclaimed UNS from León, Guanajuato in 1937 consisted of José Antonio Urquiza, José Trueba Olivares, Manuel Zermeño, Juan Ignacio Padilla, Rubén and Guillermo Mendoza Heredia. So intense was the local popular frenzy in response to their declarations that the Governor of Guanajuato, an appointee and puppet for President Cárdenas, drove the committee from his state, whereupon they established offices in Mexico City and began publication of a mimeographed *El Boletín* in an effort to develop a national organization.[8]

Although José Antonio Urquiza is most often called the Founder of UNS, its first national chief to hold working office was José Trueba Olivares who still lives as a retired attorney in his native León. Soon after taking office, Trueba resigned for "economic reasons" and was followed by Manuel Zermeño.

The assassination of José Antonio Urquiza in 1938 was the first of many crises for UNS. Its stepped-up counter-offensive against an alleged Communist design to liquidate it produced a period of ambiguous rioting and bloodshed about the country, which lasted throughout the war years in the 1940's and which the *sinarquistas* stubbornly blame on the political left.[9] The same disorders were

[7] Juan Ignacio Padilla, *El Sinarquismo* (2d ed., Ediciones UNS, México, 1953), p. 25.

[8] *Ibid.*

[9] On July 11, 1939, in Celaya, Guanajuato, a woman *sinarquista*, Teresita Bustos, was murdered while performing in a UNS rally. As a symbolic gesture of unity each outgoing national president of UNS delivers to his successor the flag which she was carrying at the time of her death (*Orden*, 31 de mayo, 1964, p. 2). The ceremony is repeated annually in the main plaza of León, Guanajuato, where the *sinarquistas* hold a mass pilgrimage, normally during March. *Sinarquista* leaders wear armbands bearing a geographic shape of Mexico. They march in a semi-military fashion that has given *sinarquismo* the largely erroneous appearance of being Fascist- or Nazi-oriented. Use of a Hitler-type hand salute reinforces this image. In an earlier work, Howard Cline developed the theme of fascism in *sinarquismo*, *The United States and Mexico* (Harvard University Press, Cambridge, 1953), p. 320. My own experiences in interviewing and knowing UNS members

blamed by the Cárdenas regime on fascist elements within *sinarquismo*.

It is fair to say that the *sinarquistas* did cause a great amount of trouble for Cárdenas and for his successors. But since the labor riots around the time of the 1958 presidential succession (blamed officially on both leftists and rightists), *sinarquismo* has tended to function as a pacific, although not passive, civic opposition.[10] As an ideology that is essentially restorationist, *sinarquismo* finds little likeness between its own image of the ideal state and the political realities of contemporary Mexico.

The second major political group in Mexico that reflects a restorationist ideology is the *Partido de Acción Nacional*. PAN was founded two years later than UNS, as a distinct part of the conservative reaction to Cárdenas. *Sinarquistas* are quick to point out that they antedate PAN and that it was formed out of splinter elements from their own group. Although many *panistas* deny this, enough agree with it to make the contention plausible. Most scholars of Mexican politics have agreed that PAN is the only serious opposition to the official PRI.

PAN emerged as a political party in September, 1939, at a convention held in Mexico City, and claims as its founder Manuel Gómez Morín, an attorney who is still active in the party's national organization. Unlike UNS, PAN has always considered itself a political party and, except in 1940 and 1946, has offered congressional, state, and presidential candidates throughout Mexico. In its appeals, PAN carefully avoids direct attacks upon those institutions which are traditionally *mexicano* and are important symbols of nationhood. Thus the Constitution of 1917 (except for Article 3)

---

indicate that it could be easy to mistake religious vehemence and anti-semitism for a full-scale commitment to Nazi or Fascist doctrine. I take issue with Cline only in suggesting that branding this group as a "fascist type organization" does not give the *sinarquistas* credit for the truly progressive civic spirit which I have known them to demonstrate. See footnote 10, below.

[10] *Sinarquistas* and their sympathizers have been instrumental in a number of civic protest movements throughout Mexico. Three recent examples are: *Asociación Cívica de Usarios de Servicios Públicos de Chihuahua* (formed in 1962 to protest unfair property taxation and public service scandals); *Agrupación de Iniciativa Privada Pro-Morelos* (formed in Cuernavaca during 1962 in protest over fiscal mismanagement of state funds); *Unión Cívica Defensora de los Intereses del Pueblo* (formed in Tepic, Nayarit to protest abuses in meter reading and collection of water charges by the municipal government during 1964).

is upheld as a basis for freedom and equality among Mexicans. PAN charges the PRI with "bastardization" of this great work through administrative abuses of liberty. Principal foci of the PAN attack are the anti-clerical provisions of the Constitution[11] and the extension of state capitalism into the traditionally private sector. Today's *panistas* include the *abolengo,* old established families whose wealth and position have been reduced or threatened, certain of the *nouveaux riches* who aspire to greater places, many of the upwardly mobile middle class who "never quite made it," and an uncertain base of peasants and artisans whose susceptibility to clerical propaganda has placed them within PAN ranks. Philip Taylor correctly observed that PAN claims a heavy female membership.[12] Having never been able to claim more than 12 percent of the officially reported vote in a presidential election, PAN carries the image of a weak and ineffectual alternative to PRI.

II

Few contemporary observers will deny that *Unión Nacional Sinarquista* and *Partido de Acción Nacional* represent bodies of alienated political sentiment. But are they politically relevant and, if so by what criteria? Politically relevant alienation must be of sufficient magnitude to pose a threat (latent, incipient, or actual) to the stability of a political system. The threat can be judged by the adaptive responses it is able to force upon the operative power structure, upon the incumbent custodians of the political *status quo.* Merely to direct frustration and aggression against the state is not enough. The stewards of political power must actually see an organized group as a threat to system stability and condition their behavior to that belief; *i.e.,* they must react adaptively or defensively. Thus a recent study by David Garza points to the low political efficacy of fragmented leftist groups in Mexico that are

[11] Article 3 of the Constitution of 1917 prohibits priests, ministers, and ecclesiastics generally from participating in primary or secondary religious instruction. The Revolutionary regime has interpreted this to include the teaching of religion in public schools as well. Under the López Mateos regime (1958–64) a program of gratuitous distribution of textbooks was initiated by the national government. The *texto único* has preoccupied much of the right-wing attack on officialdom because it deliberately does not mention religion or the name of God.

[12] Taylor, *op. cit.,* p. 741.

associated with the *Movimiento de Liberación Nacional.*[13] It is questionable whether these formations are politically relevant in the Mexican system, since they are not so viewed by the *status quo* regime. In the light of recent events surrounding the 1964 presidential succession, however, there is a strong basis for arguing that Mexican rightist alienates are coming to be viewed as politically relevant.

Elsewhere, I have described in some detail the machinations of political groups during the 1964 presidential campaign.[14] The evidence I have to present in support of the contention that UNS and PAN are viewed as politically relevant by the *status quo* regime may be shortly summarized here. Several months prior to the voting in July, *Unión Nacional Sinarquista* entered into a coalition agreement with a nearly defunct splinter party, the *Partido Nacionalista de México.* The latter, PNM, enjoyed official recognition by the *Secretaría de Gobernación* and was to be placed on the official ballot as a registered opposition party. When word of the UNS-PNM alliance became public, the *Secretaría de Gobernación* cancelled the PNM registration, ostensibly on the ground that the party lacked the legally required membership of 75,000. Confidential sources in PAN, UNS, PNM, and even in PRI itself admitted that the cancellation was a reaction to the threat of a large *sinarquista* vote for PNM candidates for the *Cámara de Diputados.* [A] UNS spokesman claimed it could muster a popular vote somewhat in excess of one million. Under Mexico's new electoral law, this could place up to twenty *sinarquistas*, or their sympathizers, in the Congress.[15] Moreover, I was informed that the original demand for

[13] Garza, *op. cit.*, passim.

[14] See my "Political Alienation in Mexico: A Preliminary Examination of UNS and PAN," *The Rocky Mountain Social Science Journal*, Vol. 2 (May, 1965), pp. 155–63.

[15] The reformed electoral law was a major issue in the campaign and was stressed by PRI candidate Gustavo Díaz Ordaz and incumbent President Adolfo López Mateos as the Revolutionary party's guarantee of an honest and "clean" election (*Novedades*, 12 de junio, 1964, front page). The new law provided a "mixed system" of proportional representation for the *Cámara de Diputados.* A registered party could win either electoral districts or deputies at large known as *diputados de partido*, or both. For deputies at large, the party would have to win at least 2.5 per cent of the total national vote for deputies, a means of eliminating parties which contested in only a few states. Winning the 2.5 per cent vote meant an automatic receipt of five deputy seats. Then, one additional seat would be awarded for each one-half per cent of the national total, up to a limit of twenty seats. PRI, *Primera Reunión Nacional de Programación* (México, 1963), pp. 292–293.

the cancellation came from the national committee of *Acción Nacional* which feared loss of its own "privileged" status as the "official opposition party."[16] This testimony came from highly placed sources in the groups involved, whose confidence I had cultivated over the past several years, and whose testimony could be viewed as reliable.

We may say, therefore, that the incumbent regime's defensive reaction to the threat of a UNS-PNM alliance is an indicator of the potential, if not actual, relevance of that combination in the Mexican system. By coopting PAN as its official opposition, PRI recognized the relevance of that group as well. Maintenance of a favored opposition party may be an instrument for periodic legitimizing of what still remains a single-party democracy. Significantly, and for the first time in post-revolutionary Mexican politics, an opposition candidate publicly admitted honest defeat without disparaging the election and was warmly thanked by the winner for this gesture of "political maturity."[17] This points to an important fact that was independently corroborated in confidential interviews. The upper hierarchy of PAN is no longer as acutely alienated toward the single-party system as it was in recent years.[18]

---

[16] In return for its guaranteed status as an "official opposition," PAN leaders gave its pledge to support the official election returns. As an additional bonus, PAN was guaranteed twenty *diputados de partido,* less those elected from districts. Two *panistas* were declared district winners in Chihuahua and León and the total national vote for PAN candidates was sufficient to guarantee the remaining eighteen deputies. According to informed sources in both PRI and PAN, the official returns of the election were reported honestly but the official regime was prepared to keep its commitment to PAN regardless.

[17] *Novedades,* 11 de julio, 1964, front page. On June 15 the same periodical carried a cartoon whose caption wryly summarized the plight of PAN as follows: "*hay algo peor que no ganar . . . perder, sin fraude.*" [There is something worse than not winning . . . losing without fraud.]

[18] The 1958 presidential campaign period was marked with severely alienated pronouncements by PAN's leadership. Luis H. Alvarez blamed all the ills of Mexico and of the world on the PRI. He cursed his defeat as an enormous fraud leaving strained relations between the two parties. There was certainly a great amount of fraud in the 1958 election, but not enough by itself to have taken the presidency away from Alvarez. However, the election was conducted in a tense atmosphere that involved the murder of one PAN campaign worker and several attacks on Alvarez himself. This writer interviewed Luis H. Alvarez after the election and did not find him to be the demagogue that Taylor pictured him, *op. cit.,* p. 741. The violence of the opposition to his presidential candidacy undoubtedly accounted for much of PAN's extreme alienation in 1958. None of these misfortunes were visited upon José González Torres in 1964, which—in all likelihood due to the

The main body of severely alienated sentiment that can be properly attributed to the Mexican right wing, therefore, continues to be the *sinarquistas* and lower echelon *panistas* who do not see themselves as beneficiaries of deals—"sweetheart contracts," in the terminology of labor relations—such as the recent *rapprochement* of PAN and PRI.

If working relationships exist between PRI and PAN there is little sympathy for them in the lower echelons of *Acción Nacional*. It became patently clear in interviewing *panistas* that many have defected out of disgust for alleged deals between the rival parties, even at the local level. A number of former PAN members were found working in the context of UNS, boycotting the 1964 election, or casting ballots for independent rightist candidates. Repeatedly, I found rank and file PAN members harboring intense resentment and hatred toward developments in their political arena. These restorationists, along with many of their *sinarquista* counterparts, frequently volunteered the belief that violence of 1910 proportions would again be an ultimate necessity in restoring true democracy to Mexico.

On the basis of the preceding observations, it will be the major contention of this paper that *Partido de Acción Nacional* has been partially coopted into the Mexican single-party system and that *Unión Nacional Sinarquista* now serves as the principal catalyst for articulation of alienated restorationist sentiment in Mexico. It is contended further that ideological differences between UNS and PAN are amenable to empirical verification and measurement.

Quantitative techniques for multivariate analysis were utilized in order to examine these contentions and to isolate correlates of political alienation among Mexican rightists. On the basis of the author's previous fieldwork, the state of Guanajuato was selected as a research site. Guanajuato offered the advantage of being rela-

---

rapprochement of PAN and PRI—made the most recent campaign appear much less antagonistic. Significantly, the campaign's only reported violence of serious proportions was directed against the PRI. An attack by stone-throwers on Díaz Ordaz in Chihuahua city (see *Indice*, 7 de abril, 1964, front page) and a frustrated dynamite attempt in Nuevo Casas Grandes (see *La Nación*, 26 de abril, 1964, p. 11) were officially blamed by the regime on the leftist splinter group *Frente Electoral del Pueblo*. One of their leaders, Braulio Maldonado Sández (a former governor of Baja California Norte) was deported as a result of the incident. Similar happenings during the 1958 campaign were blamed exclusively (and in many cases unfairly) on *Acción Nacional* and the *sinarquistas*.

tively compact, with all major urban centers accessible by bus. It is also the symbolic home of *sinarquismo* and a traditional stronghold of the *Partido de Acción Nacional*. The author and a graduate assistant arranged a series of interviews with UNS and PAN leaders in the four principal cities of the state, León, Irapuato, Guanajuato, and Celaya. Their cooperation was secured for purposes of distributing a measuring instrument to key members of each group.

UNS and PAN have an overlapping membership. Because neither group would divulge its total membership list it was impossible to draw two independent samples. Definition of the proper universe for which population parameters would be generalized was handled, therefore, on the basis of an exhaustive sample of what might here be called the "esoteric" members of each group. In practical terms, this meant the basic municipal committees for both UNS and PAN in each of the cities specified above. Between twenty-five and thirty intensive interviews were held with group leaders who in turn promised to distribute the questionnaires to *all* of their municipal committee members. A return of ninety-six per cent was secured by mail and later by personal follow-up. Although the sample is not necessarily adequate for generalization about the total Mexican universe of UNS and PAN members, the results of processing the data using standard tests of significance yield strong inferences that, in all likelihood, do represent Mexico's restorationist ideologues.

Although, as just stated, it was not possible to draw two completely independent samples of UNS and PAN members, the responses were sorted on the basis of answers to question thirty-four which asked the respondent to state which political party or group he preferred to see gain political power during the next five years. This item discriminated the respondents into roughly equal groups, and so provided a basis for statistical comparison. The questionnaire consisted of forty items including standard SES and attitudinal variables together with scalogram items of the Guttman-Himmelstrand type.[19] Most of the correlations were without major

[19] The questionnaire represented this author's second pilot attempt to devise an instrument for attitudinal measurement for use among a specialized Latin American clientele. The scalogram components yielded a coefficient of reproducibility of .63 in the instrumental items but failed to scale at all in the emotive or "High L" items (*cf.* Ulf Himmelstrand, *Social Pressures, Attitudes, and Democratic Processes,* Stockholm, Almquist and Wiksell, 1960). While insufficient to be reported here, these findings did provide insight into the problem of instrument construction in the Spanish vernacular.

statistical significance. Those that achieved significance appear in Table 1.

From these data it is apparent that the *sinarquistas* have a much more instrumental orientation to concrete human problems (such as unemployment) than do the *panistas* in this sample. The UNS respondents seem geared for concrete action while more of the PAN respondents are willing to take refuge in an emotive "resort to principle" approach. The *sinarquistas* are decidedly less optimistic about their future chances for improvement in status. This corroborates the general impression I have gathered in knowing and interviewing members of both groups. PAN members scored much higher on the SES index than did the UNS members. Although the *sinarquista* scores on social gregariousness point toward withdrawal, at least in terms of discussion outside the primary group, it is well to remember that *sinarquismo* is something of a large primary group in itself and it would be possible, therefore, for members to see themselves as operating within esoteric confines. The incidence of *sinarquista*-led pressure movements throughout Mexico that was cited earlier is adequate testimony to the fact that UNS members do not generally feel that they lack political efficacy as a result of their being denied overt participation. Finally, and significantly, the *sinarquistas* took a decidedly jaundiced view of public morality while *panistas* expressed a more laudatory evaluation. This finding lends weight to the contention that *Acción Nacional* is gradually being coopted into the single-party system.

III

The foregoing results of an attitudinal survey in one Mexican state are insufficient to call into question Philip Taylor's assessment in 1958 that Mexico seemed to be a "smoothly running authoritarian regime."[20] The potential threat to the stability of the system that is represented by restorationist ideologues is not at the moment large enough to justify alarm. If PAN is being coopted into the "revolutionary family," other rightist formations may come to be similarly blessed, especially under the conciliatory new regime of Gustavo Díaz Ordaz. Thus we could expect to see an enlarged brotherhood of *revolucionarios* dividing eventually into a smoothly running

[20] Taylor, *op. cit.*, p. 729.

TABLE 1

ALIENATION CORRELATES OF PAN AND UNS MEMBERSHIP

Item	Partido de Acción Nacional (N=45)		Unión Nacional Sinarquista (N=52)		p under H₀ that x≥chi square
	%	N	%	N	
R's participation in organizations that seek to solve such community problems as unemployment					
often	32	15	33	17	
sometimes	27	12	48	25	
rarely or never	41	18	19	10	.05
It's easy to make up my mind about solving the unemployment problem. It's just a matter of principle.*					
agree	28	13	21	11	
undecided	42	19	25	13	
disagree	30	13	54	28	.05
R's optimism as to his own chances for socio-economic mobility					
high	36	16	17	9	
medium	39	18	28	15	
low	25	11	55	28	.01

R's discussion of social and economic problems with persons outside the primary group				
often	35	16	18	9
sometimes	42	19	23	12
rarely or never	23	10	59	31	.001
R's view of change in the morality of Mexican public officials during the past twenty years.†				
improved	27	12	10	5
the same	48	22	21	11
worse	25	11	69	36	.001

* This was one of the Himmelstrand-type items which produced a statistically significant correlation with group partisanship. In an earlier work I suggested the hypothesis that "High L" political actors may be the most acutely alienated toward the political system (*cf.* "Causal Factors in Latin American Political Instability," *op. cit.*) The data above do not at all confirm that hypothesis.

† Admittedly, there is some ambiguity in the second response category for this item. It could be argued that answering "the same" meant "the same old immorality" to the PAN and UNS respondents.

multi-party system. Then, UNS and its leftist counterparts would no longer occupy satellite positions. The probabilities of such a development are difficult to calculate.

The nexus between political alienation and potential instability must not be forgotten, however, and the direction taken by such relevant "out groups" as *Unión Nacional Sinarquista*, either toward or away from integration into the national political life, will be critical for any effort to hypothesize the broad outlines of Mexican political change. Continued right-wing political alienation of the restorationist variety could have serious implications for stability within the Mexican political system.

Mexican restorationists view social conflict as the product of a sinister design engineered by political cabals. Their ideology does not embrace a rationalized concept of human misunderstanding and error. Restorationists feel they are denied both political participation and equality of socio-economic opportunity. Competitive material consumption, which Robert E. Lane found to be a stability factor for American political ideologies,[21] does not operate to reduce ideological polarization in Mexico. In fact, the *sinarquistas* and some *panistas* moralize their demands for status and deference to a degree that encourages polarization and political cleavage. The Mexican restorationist does not "morselize"[22] his conceptual approach to political issues but rather looks beyond the day-after-tomorrow issues in life to an ethereal vision of the perfect future. Estranged from the main thrust of Mexican revolutionary ideology, the restorationist hoists the spectre of his martyred heroes and withdraws his support of the political *status quo*. He expects the system to respond only to his minimal needs of personal security, not to his aspirations for mobility and achievement. Protest movements against established government policies, therefore, are designed more to dramatize evil and injustice than to bring about a constructive redress of grievances.

Is the system just? Indeed not, in the minds of Mexican restorationists. Unintentionally, but poignantly, the spirit of their dilemma was captured by Carlos Fuentes in these lines from *La Muerte de Artemio Cruz:*

> It is a sin, a very grave sin against the Holy Spirit to refuse to receive the gifts of heaven ... everyone should go forth to farm the land, to harvest the crops, to deliver the fruits of the earth to their

[21] Robert E. Lane, *Political Ideology* (Glencoe, 1962) p. 80.
[22] *Ibid.,* pp. 346–363.

legitimate landlord, a christian landlord who pays for the obliga-
tions of his privilege by promptly delivering a tenth to Holy
Mother Church. God punishes disobedience.
—And justice, father?
—Final justice is imparted up there, son.
Do not look for it in this vale of tears.[23]

There can be no felt sense of justice in this life, say the *sinarquistas*, when the political system which governs them is manipulated by one or all of several protean cabals. No one cabal will
do for every occasion. Jews, Masons, Communists, *gringos*, all are
believed to interact concertedly in a voracious web of planned
aggression against the Mexican nation.

The practical implication of this evaluation can be stated briefly.
Conspicuous supporters of the official regime will be, and are,
targets for the wrath of alienated "out groups." Accurately or
not, United States Ambassador Fulton Freeman was quoted as
having endorsed the candidacy of Díaz Ordaz in May, 1964. In a
rare moment of affinity between left and right, the allegation
brought outcries from editors of PAN and UNS publications as
well as from a leading left wing publication (*Política*) with strong
marxist leanings.[24] Ambassador Freeman was likened to former
ambassadors Poinsett and Wilson, two damaging symbols of influence in Mexican-American history. Such an event takes on added
significance if, although momentarily, it forces opposing "out
groups" into a negative coalition of anti-Americanism.

More common are the cases of defensive adaptation by the *status
quo* regime in the face of restorationist pressure. A dramatic example
of this occurred during February, 1963, when the official regime
in San Luis Potosí seized and destroyed the first printing of a
restorationist-oriented book that exposed local government corruption.[25] Later that year, PAN and UNS came out openly together
protesting electoral fraud in the municipal elections of Apaseo el

[23] Carlos Fuentes, *La Muerte de Artemio Cruz* (México, Fondo de Cultura
Económica, 1962), p. 46.
[24] *Política*, 1 junio, 1964, p. 19.
[25] Antonio Estrada M. *La Grieta en el Yugo* (2d ed., México, no publisher
cited, 1963). The first edition was destroyed and the press that produced it
wrecked by the government of San Luis Potosí. The work is a crude tabloid
but contains photographs of documents and detailed accounts of events in
San Luis Potosí which were largely corroborated by independent observers
interviewed by this author.

Grande, Guanajuato.[26] More recently in the same state, *sinarquistas* were jailed after a public protest meeting at Celaya.[27]

Mexico's right wing alienates are not yet ready to launch a violent revolution. But they say that they desire one and are building the social and ideological base for it. Finding no external promise of psychic security in a *gemeinschaft* society of spiritual brotherhood, they take solace in an ideological view that promotes cleavage in the body politic. Excluded from effective involvement in a political system that offers few gestures toward immediate change, the restorationists have constructed an apocalyptic view of eventual salvation and relief. We must place the restorationists at the negative end of the allegiance-alienation continuum. The future of their ideology and behavior, indeed perhaps of political stability in Mexico, will be determined by the direction of change and flexibility in the single-party system.[28]

[26] Based on interviews in Apaseo el Grande and on handbills and other printed propaganda bearing the insignia of both PAN and UNS that are currently in the author's possession.

[27] Based on confidential communications recently received from informants in Celaya. A founder of *Unión Nacional Sinarquista* and currently an important member of its national executive board, Juan Ignacio Padilla, was reportedly kidnapped from a public street in Ensenada, Bcfa., at gunpoint by members of that state's judicial police (see *La Suegra de la Cotorra,* 29 de noviembre, 1964, front page). There is little doubt that harassment of political restorationists continues throughout Mexico.

[28] The only other published effort to measure political attitudes among Mexican rightists is included in the recent work of Gabriel Almond and Sidney Verba, *The Civic Culture* (Princeton University Press, 1963). Almond and Verba did not include UNS within their sample and they do not isolate alienated nuclei within the Mexican system. They do make the interesting broad contention that Mexicans *generally* are more alienated from governmental output than respondents of the other four nations (not Latin American) surveyed in their study (p. 495).

The Chilean Political Right and Agrarian Reform: Resistance and Moderation

Robert R. Kaufman

I. INTRODUCTION

Analysis of the current political battle over agrarian reform in Chile has usually stressed the conflict between those who urge change and those who oppose it. Important as this focus is, it obscures shifts in the position of the agricultural elite that have tended to change the terms of the debate. Whereas in 1958 many defined agrarian reform only as increased aids to production, today most would admit that it means division of large properties as well. In 1960, most would have opposed deferred payments for expropriations, while in 1966 the issue is the number of years the state should have for payment. Even more recently, it was argued that only abandoned or inefficient property should be divided, whereas today what is at stake is the amount of land the efficient landowner should be allowed to keep.

The significance of these changes is subject to debate. Certainly opposition to the reform is bitter, and both legal and extra-legal means of resistance have been employed. Nevertheless, the shifts on the part of the right[1] have kept open lines of communication to

---

From Robert R. Kaufman, *The Chilean Political Right and Agrarian Reform: Resistance and Moderation,* Institute for the Comparative Study of Political Systems (ICOPS), Washington, D.C., 1967. Reprinted by permission.

[1] When the term "right" is used without modifiers, it is intended to mean those sectors of the social system—rural and urban upper-class individuals, families, cliques, interest groups, and political parties—that tend to defend their advantageous position in Chilean society and advocate conservative social and economic policies. The term is not used without some misgiving, since it is precisely a point of the paper that the differences among these elements are as important to a general understanding of Chilean politics, as are the common features. On the other hand, the term, with all of its problems, does reflect a certain reality in Latin American and in Chilean politics.

the reformist Christian Democratic government and may add a stabilizing element to the conflict. The possibility of dealing with the right, without doing fundamental damage to the main points of the new reform bill, may save the government from the difficult alternative of abandoning its agrarian reform entirely or relying solely on the left for support of its general legislative program. At the same time, the shift may save the right from the need to choose between controlling the legislative process or overthrowing it, as the only effective means of self-defense. In short, the nature of resistance to agrarian reform has discouraged a polarization of political forces and the grave threat to social stability that such a development might imply.

When placed within the general context of Latin American politics, it can be seen that these Chilean developments should not be taken for granted. In most Latin American countries, it is the right, not the left, that has posed the most radical and immediate challenge to political and social stability. It has been the right in most cases that has obstructed attempts to engineer social changes that might satisfy, appease, or neutralize potential sources of revolutionary unrest. And the right, more frequently than the left, has led insurgent forces that have challenged or toppled governments dealing with these problems. While the Chilean upper class has been generally felt to be more "flexible" than similar Latin American groups, finally, it has been assumed that it would react fiercely and even violently to proposals for land-tenure reform.

*   *   *   *

This paper seeks to examine, therefore, not only the conflict that is evoked by the right's resistance to agrarian reform legislation, but also the restraints on this conflict. It will argue that the strategies of resistance to agrarian reform proposals that could have led to a broader and more intense type of conflict were considered within various sectors of the Chilean right, but that these strategies were rejected in favor of those which tried to seek areas of agreement with the other side and to limit and isolate the conflict that remained. Secondly, the paper will argue that central to an understanding of this moderation is a factor that clearly distinguishes the Chilean right from most other Latin American elites: in other countries, group interests, family prejudices, or individual idiosyncrasies are brought to bear on the political system either directly or through non-governmental institutions such as the army or the Church. In Chile, conservative views have tended to be filtered through a fairly modern and complex network of parties and interest groups, whose defensive posture with respect to the question of agrarian reform should not obscure the more complex role they played in conciliating diverse groups, in articulating agrarian interests, and in moderating or denying access to disruptive demands before they reached the centers of decision.

II. AGRARIAN REFORM, THE RIGHT, AND THE CHILEAN SOCIAL CONTEXT

To discuss special characteristics—internal to the Chilean right—that have tended to restrain its resistance is not to deny that both the right's resistance and its moderation have depended to a great extent on factors beyond its control. Pressures for land-tenure changes are bound to meet with objections from the classes that are being asked to sacrifice, and the intensity of their resistance will depend on the extent of the sacrifices being asked and the groups that are demanding them. On the other hand, the right's resistance will also depend on the relation between its power and that of the other groups demanding change.

In the case of Chile, these "external" factors have encouraged moderation on the part of the right. Agrarian reform proposals have not inherently meant that the large landowners must be obliterated, and conflict with the groups demanding change has not needed to involve a "fight to the death." Secondly, social, economic, and political developments in Chile have sharply reduced the power of the landed elite and have thus encouraged its relatively peaceful acceptance of the reform. Nevertheless, to an important degree, both in the past and present, moderation has depended on the way the right itself has perceived the threat and defined its options. Much more moderate proposals might have led to a fierce and absolute defense of the status quo, while current changes in the Chilean balance of power have not left the oligarchy without the means to conduct a much more violent resistance than it has.

The Threat of Agrarian Reform

It has frequently been assumed that, whatever other accommodations conservative sectors have made to other changes, agrarian reform challenges a "basic" feature of its interests and cannot be accomplished without a total reduction in its power. The continuing ideological polemic between "progressives" and "reactionaries" throughout Latin America lends strength to the idea that adjustments in the interests of the right that might help to mitigate the conflict are almost impossible.

Arguments for reform thus seem aimed at a total attack on the existing rural-class structure, while opposing arguments seem to allow no room for the possibility of change. Proponents of agrarian reform argue that there is a concentration of agricultural land in the hands of a tiny rural aristocracy, while the right has continued to challenge the very existence of an "uneven" distribution of property.[2]

The proponents of agrarian reform maintain that the power of the landed elite is not only socially unjust, but that it blocks economic progress as well. As bearers of the Latin "feudal" heritage, the rural aristocracy lacks the "capitalistic" inclination to invest its wealth and to rationalize the production of its land. The conservatives, on the other hand, argue that stagnation of agricultural production is due not to the existing land tenure structure but to unwise government policies that have restricted investment in rural infrastructure, denied credit for the import of farm capital, and held agricultural prices artificially low under the political pressure of the urban middle class. Far from being a privileged group, therefore, the landed elite argues that it is a neglected one.

These analyses, finally, seem to lead to mutually exclusive policy proposals: the reformers promise that a breakup of the large estates provides the key to a simultaneous solution of the social, economic, and political evils that plague Latin America. It will redistribute wealth at the same time that it removes inefficient obstacles to production. New rural markets will be opened up for domestic manufacturing. A more efficient farm economy will replace food bought abroad, freeing foreign exchange reserves for capital imports.

Opposed to this, the right has argued that to break up large estates would be to ignore the advantages of scale that have led to larger and larger farms in all parts of the developed world. Attempts

---

[2] Figures from the Chilean Census of 1955 are cited frequently: 37% of the rural proprietors possess only 1% of the arable land, while 7% of the owners possess 65% of the arable land and 78% of the irrigated surface. The conservatives argue that these figures are out of date and incomplete and that they consider the extension, not the value of the land.

to redistribute wealth in this manner will only aggravate the insecurity that has already discouraged production and will insure the intensification of the social problem that it is designed to solve. What is needed is not to persecute the landowners even more, but to induce the government to replace its policy of neglect by price and credit benefits that can create positive incentives to production.

Finally, the proponents of agrarian reform have argued that as the state is the institution that must plan and administer the reform, it is necessary to wrest the machinery of government out of the hands of the elite, to reform archaic administrative structures, and to make the entire apparatus more responsive to the "will of the masses." The conservatives have argued that any such change will bring totalitarianism and a collapse of all democratic values.

This clash of philosophies has helped to promote a "two-camp" idea of Latin American political conflict over the issue of agrarian reform. As problems of defining specific policies and interests grow, however, the sharp differences between "proponents" and "opponents" may become blurred. In the first place, the possibility of agreement on single issues cannot be ruled out, as perceptions of interests and realities change. Proponents of the reform in Chile, for example, have come to accept the idea that price and credit incentives to farmers are an essential feature of over-all policy to increase agricultural production, a point argued for years by the right. A. O. Hirschman, moreover, suggests the possibility that opposing sides may be brought to agreement on concrete reform proposals, despite disagreements on ultimate goals and implications. The right may see a reform as a means of precluding further change, while the left may see it as a step in the direction of even broader ones.[3]

Perhaps more important, however, is the possibility of perceptions that will not end, but contain the conflict between proponents of reform and the right. It is clear, for example, that economic and social objectives of land-tenure change are neither perfectly compatible nor mutually exclusive, as the opposing ideologies claim. Dividing some estates may be good social policy but may have negative repercussions on production. Or, long-term production gains may be offset by short-term costs in political disruption. For a government seeking to retain some control over the process of social change, planning and administering a reform

---

[3] Albert O. Hirschman, *Journeys Toward Progress,* p. 283.

will always involve the necessity of juggling these competing goals, and some important aspects of the status quo will probably be left intact.

For the right, therefore, bargaining may be possible, even with a strongly reformist government, if it seeks to defend its interests by slowing the reform rather than blocking it. Even if the government's primary objective is a more equitable distribution of property, there will be questions about the types of property to be expropriated, how much land is to be left to old proprietors, exceptions to be made for special regions and special types of cultivation, and the treatment to be given to land that is exceptionally well managed.

Even if there is a sweeping "replacement" of the old proprietors, moreover, most reform plans contemplate at least some compensation for expropriated owners. Payment in bonds, rather than cash—which all reformers agree is necessary—involves a considerable sacrifice for land owners in inflationary Latin American economies. But the types of bonds still concern questions that can be negotiated: What period of time should be allowed for payment? In what other economic activities can the owners use these bonds? How should especially efficient owners be compensated? To what extent should consideration of equity for the owner be balanced against the needs and pace of the program?

Finally, even broader questions may arise which may allow for bargaining and compromise between reformers and the right. For example, how are priorities to be established between agrarian reform and other government projects? How much land is it "necessary" to expropriate, how many peasants should be affected by the redistribution of the land, and at what pace should this process be carried out? The right may exert influence in decisions about how the peasants are to be trained, the means to be used in smoothing the transition of ownership, and the resulting structure in the countryside when the process is completed.

This is not to argue that the right will not resist sacrifices or that it will cease to oppose reforms. Even facing a radical change, however, its interests can at least to some extent be negotiable. A crucial factor, however, will always be not only the extent of the sacrifices demanded or the willingness of the reforming groups to bargain, but also the way the right itself perceives the nature of the reform. If it feels that either the program or the government intends to destroy it, its resistance could be quite violent, even if the actual changes proposed are quite mild. On the other hand, groups have learned to live and operate even in the midst of changes that have at first seemed to challenge their very survival.

THE CHILEAN SYSTEM AND RESTRICTIONS ON THE RIGHT

It would be unrealistic, however, to expect that the general culture and values, even of the relatively enlightened Chilean elite, could permit the right to limit its resistance to agrarian reform if its alternatives were not considerably restricted by the broader social and economic system. In fact, the power of the Chilean landed elite has been progressively balanced by the rise of new social and economic groups, and this is a factor that cannot be ignored in an analysis of the right's moderation.

In the first place, pressure for reform has been growing within the urban middle class and the non-Marxist intellectual community; and to a lesser extent even the peasants themselves have been able to make their demands felt. Secondly, the Church, which was a political ally of the right, has reversed its position and joined the call for change. An even more important factor has been the steady erosion of the social and economic power of the landed elite, relative to new industrial and commercial groups that have moved into the upper class. The military, moreover, which is the usual defender of most upper classes, has had a history of neutrality in Chile, and recourse to coups d'état is closed to the right as an immediate alternative of resistance. Finally, the democratic tradition that has been established in Chile inhibits the right from trying to block the constitutional exercise of political power by groups—like the Christian Democrats—that are committed to the realization of agrarian reform.

Although these developments might seem to leave few rational alternatives open to the right besides an attempt to accommodate itself to change, the "objective" restraints on the power of the landed elite have not entirely restricted its capacity to expand its resistance, should it choose to do so. The existence of a large middle class in Chile has never, in itself, proven to be a sufficient counterweight to the veto power of the elite, and in Argentina, an even larger middle class has not been able to prevent a continued pattern of coups d'état led by the army and the oligarchy.

It is not entirely clear, moreover, that the partial displacement of agricultural wealth by new industrial and commercial fortunes has significantly weakened the unity of the upper class and its capacity to resist agrarian reform. Despite the relative decline in the economic power of the rural elite, there are some signs, at least until recently, that its political influence was not diminished. While only 46 per cent of the Liberal Party congressmen owned large rural estates in 1941, for example, this percentage climbed to 62 per cent in 1961.

Important social and economic ties between the rural and urban sectors of the elite also may serve to counteract a tendency for the industrial community to remain neutral in the struggle over agrarian reform. The officers of the leading industrial pressure group, the Society for Industrial Development (SFF), all own large *fundos* (agricultural estates). More important, in 1961, over 56 per cent of the congressmen belonging to the Liberal and Conservative parties had ties to both economic sectors. These ties, of course, could encourage a moderation of the landed elite by facilitating a transfer of its wealth from agricultural to other activities. But the ties also mean that, notwithstanding the decline in its independent control of wealth and prestige, the landed elite has the resources and connections to mobilize other sectors of the oligarchy as allies against reform.

The growing political weakness of the right as a whole, finally, has not left it without the capacity to conduct a more closed defense of its interests or even to deal a powerful blow to the stability of the political order itself. The right, in the first place, began to make concessions during a period in which it still retained considerable influence within the political system. Secondly, despite its currently reduced representation in the Congress, the right still has the political resources to obstruct the legislative process and put a severe internal strain on the government party itself. Finally, the economic and social elements of the oligarchy's power can still be brought to bear as a powerful challenge to the regime's authority, and in such a period of political and economic tension, the tradition that has kept the military out of politics could disintegrate rapidly.

It must be emphasized that such events do not appear likely and that the choice of such options to defend its interests would involve great risks for the Chilean elite. Yet attempts to obstruct or overthrow the political order might not be "irrational," if the elite were to feel that there were even greater risks to its "way of life" involved in accepting the current order. In any case, "rational" choices have often been far from obvious, and the risks of a closed resistance to change, so apparent to the outsider, may not be so clear to the people whose values are threatened.

In short, it has been argued that neither "objective" interests nor "objective" social forces are sufficient explanations for the behavior of the Chilean right. Much must be explained by the right's own perception of these factors and by its own strategic choices. It has to evaluate the implications of tolerating the concessions involved in agrarian reform and the intentions of the government proposing the reform. And it has had to define the limits and possibilities of resistance or accommodation, where to mobilize allies, and on what terms.

POLITICAL INSTITUTIONS AND SOCIAL CONFLICT

While political institutions are correctly assumed to reflect these strategic problems, their role in resolving them is often underestimated or ignored. In the case of Chile, however, the formal rightist organizations have developed goals, procedures, and interests of their own that influence the way they interpret the broader economic and social values of the conservative classes. A degree of autonomy from the pressure of these classes allows the organizations to act not only as agents of representation but also as agents of the political system in conciliating the values of the upper class to the needs of social change.

Particularly striking are the age and number of such agencies. While most right-wing political parties, for example, are based on the personality of a particular leader and are noted only for their ephemeral lives, Chile's two rightist parties—the Liberal and Conservative parties (*Partido Liberal*, or PL, and *Partido Conservador Unido*, or PCU)—have had formal existence for over a century. Similarly, the major interest groups that represent the large landowners and industrialists—the National Society of Agriculture (SNA) and the Society for Industrial Development (SFF)—are the oldest of their kind in Latin America, dating back to 1837 and 1876 respectively. Considerably less developed but of major national significance are two other large agricultural groups—the Consortium of Agricultural Societies of the South (CAS) and the Agricultural Associations of the North. And added to these are a

large number of locally based associations and six producers' associations that group the producers of a single product, such as
wheat, rice, sugar beet, and seeds.

The emphasis on the importance of formal, institutional structures may seem startling to many observers accustomed to stressing
the more informal aspects of the Chilean system. Certainly these
factors should not be ignored. Political life is centered in the small
Santiago society, where members of the elite are bound together
by ties of family and friendship. Many of the groups mentioned
above are relatively loose cliques or "letterhead organizations," and
even the more developed political parties and the SNA are bound
together by important informal ties. Thus, of the total PL and
PCU congressmen in 1961, 45 per cent attended one of three
prestigious secondary schools. And there is no question that considerable power and influence can still be wielded directly through
the use of social standing, wealth, or family connections. Even in
the most developed countries, however, informal influences interact with more institutionalized patterns of behavior; and in Chile
itself there is evidence that the party and pressure-group structures
have increasingly tended to channel and guide the more "traditional" patterns of power within the right. . . .

One indication of this phenomenon can be seen in patterns of
advancement within the two rightist parties. While social status
still remains an essential prerequisite for party power, it has become
increasingly difficult for landowners or industrialists to command
high party offices without first serving apprenticeships at lower
political levels. A study of the backgrounds of 54 PL and PCU
congressmen in 1961 indicates that 47 per cent had first served as
local party leaders. Twenty-nine per cent had served in the party
youth movements, and 14 per cent had been functionaries, either
within the parties themselves, or, through party connections, within
the executive branch of the government. The growth in the importance of these apprenticeships over time should also be noted:
of the PCU congressmen in 1941, 47 per cent had had no previous
political experience as compared with only 13 per cent in 1961.
Similarly, in the PL 46 per cent had jumped directly to Congress
in 1941, while only 12 per cent did the same in 1961.

*   *   *

If within these organizations advancement is dictated by standards of service as well as social standing, official posts themselves

command considerable power and prestige, relative to less formal bases of power outside the organizations. A president of the PCU, PL, or SNA can obtain press coverage or government hearings by virtue of his official position. All have at their disposal organizational machinery that gives them considerable leverage over simpler and more traditional bases of influence. Both the SNA and the SFF, for example, have the services of technical staffs and full-time administrators; and the SNA publishes a well-written and widely read magazine. Both parties have created the post of secretary general to rationalize internal administration.

Finally, the internal complexity of these organizations indicates the capacity of the parties and pressure groups to respond to changing social demands and a set of restraints and limits on the leaders themselves. The SNA, for example, advises its membership on a broad spectrum of problems, ranging from technical matters of production to labor relations. Within the parties, there is a network of sub-units—youth, labor, and technical departments—that can exert pressure on party policy-making. The larger ruling councils of the parties, the SNA and the SFF, meet frequently and with good attendance, exerting broad controls on the leadership.

These patterns of institutional political behavior, of course, are not static, but interact with the social system in which they exist. As the current decline of the parties and the development of the SNA indicate, organizations can gain or lose vitality as they become more or less appropriate to meet the needs of a particular period. Nor does the degree of autonomy of the rightist parties and pressure groups, with their restricted social bases, permit their complete independence from broader economic and social upper-class values.

Nevertheless, institutional objectives of survival and procedural orientations toward coalition, bargaining, and compromise, have provided cues that have led to a more moderate definition of the way these more general economic and social values apply to the specific situations that have confronted the right. In the pre-1964 period, it was the PL and the PCU that narrowed the conflict over agrarian reform by confirming that it was at least a legitimate topic of debate and that some sort of change was acceptable. In the current situation, it has been the SNA that has argued that restrictions on the right's power and the possibility of compromise with the current government point to a strategy of limited resistance. In both periods, the power of these political organizations has served to dissuade or neutralize sectors of the right that have advocated a broader, less moderate interpretation of class interests.

III. FROM OBSTRUCTION TO CONCESSION: THE RIGHT IN POWER

In the presidential period of Jorge Alessandri (1958–64), the subject of agrarian reform was moved from the level of abstract theoretical debate to the more immediate arena of congressional action and legislative decision. While the legal reforms of that period had little direct effect on the land-tenure structure, conservative stands that might have disrupted the more serious efforts of the current government were eliminated, and certain elements of policy continuity were established. By participating in the process, the right abandoned its previous position that any land-tenure changes besides mild colonization efforts were dangerous and that a general law of agrarian reform was unnecessary. More important, it relinquished recourse to important constitutional principles that hitherto had been serious obstacles to effective government action in the field of agrarian reform, a move that has facilitated bargaining and compromise, rather than stalemate, as the major strategy for the defense of conservative interests.

Broad Resistance and Incentives for Moderation

Prior to 1958, the control of the landed elite in the countryside had gone practically unchallenged. A preservation of the rural status quo was an explicit condition on which the right accepted concessions in the urban areas that were demanded by the center-left coalition of the 1940's. Although provisions for the expropriation of abandoned rural property were included in a more general law passed by the center-left government in 1943, even this mild proposal prompted the bitter opposition of the rightist parties, and the provisions were never applied. . . .

Throughout the 1950's, the status quo was defended as if any change whatever would mark the demise of such non-economic values as freedom, property rights, and constitutional government. The advisability of land tenure adjustments for economic or social reasons was also emphatically denied. As the conservative news-paper, *El Mercurio* put it, ". . . The land tenure system does not need any reform whatsoever. What is lacking is a methodical plan of agrilogical reform . . . that might improve the application . . . of technical procedures so that the countryside might produce more."[4] . . .

In any case, the existing legal and constitutional structure assured the frustration of any significant efforts to act in the countryside. The major legal bulwark of the status quo lay in cumbersome expropriation procedures that made acquisition and redistribution of land by the government—even on a moderate scale—a practical impossibility. The Constitution of 1925 provided that any expro-priated property must be paid in cash, unless the owner consented to other terms. The government could take possession of the property, against the will of the owner, only after a long and costly process of litigation, within a judicial branch still in the hands of the conservative classes. And even if these procedures were altered, the government lacked even the most rudimentary institutional machinery to plan and administer such a reform.

Subsequent modification of these legal bulwarks and points of view is usually attributed to events that were external to the Chilean system. In the first place, the Cuban revolution seemed to indicate the urgency of social concessions as a means to preserve more basic elements of the status quo. Secondly, through the Alliance for Progress, the United States officially endorsed the idea of land-tenure changes and held out the incentive of massive eco-nomic aid if such changes were effected. Finally, the economists of the FAO and the Economic Commission for Latin America (ECLA) lent respectability to the idea of agrarian reform and provided technical economic arguments to support their position.

In almost all Latin American countries, these events brought most conservative sectors to pay lip service to the term "agrarian reform," but they rarely produced either legislation or concessions on the basic legal and constitutional principles that land-tenure changes would imply. What led to distinctive results in Chile were factors internal to its political system that created specific political interests in producing an agrarian reform law and a certain im-mediacy to the general notion that some sort of adjustments were necessary.

---

[4] Editorial, *El Mercurio,* Santiago, April 6, 1957, p. 3.

The relatively free system of elections provided a kind of social thermometer to measure discontent and the threat to the status quo.[5] These danger signals had grown increasingly loud since 1952 when the hold of the Conservative Party over the countryside began to be loosened. By 1956 much of the peasant vote shifted to the FRAP, and in 1958 it nearly provided the margin of victory for the FRAP presidential candidate, Salvador Allende. Pressure on the right to adjust its position was increased even more when the center parties—the Radicals and the Christian Democrats—turned in the late fifties and early sixties to agrarian reform as a central feature of their electoral platforms, a move at least partially influenced by the possibility of competing with the FRAP for peasant and urban votes.

The immediate catalyst that led to the right's support of concrete reform legislation was also internal to the political system. The congressional elections of March 1961 marked the first time in their history that the rightist parties had lost joint control of one third of the votes in the Congress. In the Chilean congressional system this marked a real reduction in the right's power to legislate, for after a bill has been passed "in general" by the majorities of both houses, one-third control becomes a crucial figure in determining the specific content of the bill.[6] Prior to 1961, the Alessandri government had gained unconditional legislative support only from the PCU and the PL, and had picked up its congressional majority through the erratic and uncertain cooperation of the Radical Party. The results of the 1961 elections, however, now put a special urgency on the creation of a formal cabinet coalition that would include the PR. Such a move, it was felt, would not only strengthen the hand of the government in the Congress but would also set the

[5] The Communist Party was outlawed for about a decade from the middle forties to the middle fifties. The law did not apply, however, to the Marxist Socialist Party, which continued to function and to gain strength in the period. And the law was enforced only irregularly against the Communist Party itself.

[6] More specifically the one-third vote is important for the following reasons: after a bill is passed "in general" by majority votes of both houses, it passes back and forth between the two houses until disagreements on the specific content of the bill are resolved. The initiating house can "insist" on its version by a simple majority, and if one-third support can be gained in the second house, this version will stand. If this is not successful then a one-third vote in the initiating house will prevent the disputed provisions from becoming part of the law. Finally, the president, through his veto, can *add* provisions to the bill itself, and these will become law if they are supported by one-third of each house.

basis for an electoral alliance that could beat the FRAP in the presidential elections of 1964.

It was within the context of these electoral and congressional pressures that Laws 15020 and 15296—the Alessandri agrarian and constitutional reforms—were passed. The conservative leadership of the PR was anxious to enter the coalition, but a prior commitment from the rightist parties on a program of "structural" reforms was necessary before they could take such a step. The Radical leadership needed a law both to justify the formation of the coalition to the party's left wing and also because a reform law might help win electoral support among the urban middle class and the rural peasants. Their bargaining positions weakened, the PL and the PCU had little choice but to accept the Radicals' conditions. In August 1961, after a few months of sparring, the PR entered the cabinet; and immediately thereafter tripartite commissions were formed by the three government parties to work out the details of the reform legislation. The agrarian-reform bill was passed in 1962 and the constitutional amendment in 1963.

While, of course, there was considerable controversy within the commissions and in the Congress, a more interesting debate occurred simultaneously within the right itself. Within the parties, this debate covered both the issues of the coalition and the broad idea of reform, and the more specific principles of agrarian reform legislation. The debate between the parties and their broader constituencies centered more on the second aspect, and particularly on the question of whether to accept a constitutional amendment that would allow payment in bonds for the expropriations of abandoned or badly cultivated property.

INTRA-PARTY STRUGGLES: THE
PCU, REFORM AND COALITION

Within both rightist parties, considerable pressure had been building for some time for a shift to a more flexible orientation toward the problem of agrarian reform and reform in general. To recuperate from their losses of the early fifties, both the PCU and the PL had attempted to broaden their links to student organizations, to government and party functionaries, and to elements from middle-class occupations, practicing lawyers, trained economists, engineers. These groups, however, began to challenge the leadership of the conservative agricultural and industrial families, and drawing on what they considered to be the ideological traditions of their parties, they argued that neither liberal nor Catholic values limited the role of the parties to a defense of the interests of the economic elite. As rural problems grew more pressing, many of these groups began to argue that the parties must face up to the problem of agrarian reform. The head of the *Caja de Colonización Agrícola* (Agricultural Colonization Fund), an organization established to encourage the settlement of Chile's unpopulated southern regions, urged with the PCU that payment in bonds for agricultural land would solve the *Caja's* financial problems and breathe some life into the nearly defunct institution. Within the Liberal Party, the youth organization maintained that "agrarian reform" must not be confused with aid to current agriculturalists and that it meant instead a lowering of the "high index of property concentration, control over the land and *latifundismo.*"[7]

While these groups had gained ground throughout the fifties, it was not until the elections of 1961 that their influence on party leadership was felt decisively. As the Conservative Party had suffered most in the election, moreover, the prior arguments for reform were not reinforced by the idea that to win back some of the middle and lower-class urban sectors that had supported Alessandri in 1958, the party must be less intractable in facing urban and rural structural changes. In the early spring of 1961, a factional struggle for the presidency of the party arose between the "reformists," headed by Héctor Correa, and the more conservative wing of the party, led by Luis Valdés. In what was considered a rather surprising upset, Correa defeated Luis Valdés in a vote of the General Council, which consists of some five hundred members and is nominally the party's ruling body.

*   *   *

It is difficult to draw a direct relation between this broader factional struggle, however, and the more specific issues of agrarian reform. The battle for the presidency of the PCU involved many other issues of personality, ideology, and broad political strategy that obscured this more specific problem. Thus, for example, many of the backers of Correa were ideological militants who accepted cooperation with the Radicals on many of their substantive proposals for agrarian reform, but at the same time felt that the PR's anti-clerical ideology and apparent political opportunism made a

[7] José Garrido Rojas, "Declaración de la Juventud Liberal," *El Mercurio,* Santiago, October 10, 1961, p. 23.

larger presidential coalition unadvisable. At the same time, among
the supporters of Valdés were men such as Francisco Bulnes and
Sergio Diez. These men were perhaps less committed to the idea
of reform than the supporters of the other faction, but they were
willing to accept concessions, as a step toward a larger presidential
coalition with the PR. While the Correa movement served to
make the PCU more receptive to the general idea of reform, therefore, their victory did not preclude further internal struggle over
the specific issues of land-tenure changes, and the subsequent
decline of their influence within the party did not preclude the
party's willingness to make concessions on these issues.

THE DEFERRED-PAYMENTS DEBATE:
INTRA-PARTY STRUGGLE AND DECISION

While there was considerable controversy both inside and outside
the parties over many of the specific issues of the agrarian-reform
legislation, the most heated battle occurred over the decision to
accept the PR proposals for a constitutional amendment, providing
that expropriations of badly cultivated or abandoned property should
be paid 10 per cent of its value in cash and the balance over a
period of thirty years. It is not surprising that this should have
been the major issue of debate, since without such an amendment
the government would have been required to pay cash for all
expropriations and many of the provisions of Law 15020 would
have been totally inoperative. The struggle can be divided roughly
into two stages: the first was the maneuvering and final decision
to accept deferred payments within the parties themselves, ending
in the fall of 1961; the second stage was the debate within the
broader conservative sector. It began long before the party decisions
were officially made, but it erupted into public debate only after
November 1961, and reached a crucial turning point in a vote
taken within the SNA in January 1962. It subsided more or less
completely when the amendment was sent to Congress in the same
year.

Under the leadership of Correa, the Conservatives had begun to
negotiate with the Liberals and the Radicals within the tripartite
commissions. While there were, of course, consultations with the
executive junta of the party, Correa had hoped to gain a relatively
free hand in the negotiations and had apparently given an informal,
personal commitment that the party would accept deferred pay-

ments. His efforts were frustrated, however, when his opposition within the party unexpectedly forced a negative vote in the ruling junta. Correa denied the validity of the vote and threatened to resign. In an attempt to placate Correa, a committee was appointed to study the issue, but it was packed with men thought to be basically out of sympathy with the amendment. Still feeling himself repudiated, Correa requested a "leave of absence" from his active duties, and actual leadership of the party fell to Bulnes and Diez.

The maneuver that defeated Correa, however, did not mean a defeat for deferred payments within the party. The new leadership still had to face the problem of conciliating the reformist faction and preventing either a party split or large-scale defections. . . .

At the same time, within the special commitee, Bulnes, Diez, and Joaquín Prieto all argued that failure to accept a constitutional reform would mean the failure of a coalition with the Radicals, and even a possible dissolution of the party. The urgency of such a coalition was defended explicitly by Bulnes some years later when, in a report to the party, he stated:

> In the case of our party, we were not only suffering a defeatist cancer. . . . Besides, we were losing faith in our destiny and in our *raison d'être*. Many conservatives already thought that the party could never again exercise any influence in the national destiny, and the weakest were already beginning . . . to abandon a ship that they believed condemned to sink. The only way out of this problem was to form a combination with the PR.[8]

Swayed by these arguments, the special committee voted to accept deferred payments, although it hedged by suggesting that the period of payment be only five years. Bulnes, however, later suggested that the payment time be extended to ten years, and the party finally accepted a term of fifteen years, at the urging of the Radicals.

A parallel process of self-criticism and decision had gone on within the Liberal Party, and although neither the leadership shake-up nor the internal dissension was quite so great as among the Conservatives, the PL was not without its difficulties. By the time the executive council approved deferred payments by a vote

[8] Francisco Bulnes, "Discurso a la Directiva General," *Diario Ilustrado,* Santiago, June 13, 1963, p. 2.

of 22 to 6 in November 1961, three of its most prominent members had resigned from the council in protest. The major pressure for reform was led by the youth organization, and especially by its president, José Garrido, who was later to be made the head of the government agricultural-planning agency. The "trade-union" department of the party, backed essentially by white-collar guild organizations, also argued that the working class should be made to realize that the PL "is not a bulwark of the economic right" and that "impulse must be given to the agrarian reform on the basis of projects already studied by the technical committee of the party."[9] Finally, the new president of the party, Ladislao Errázuriz, while definitely a man of the right, was convinced for many of the same reasons used by Bulnes that deferred payments were essential; and under his leadership there was never any real danger that the PL would refuse to accept such a step.

The Deferred-Payments Debate: The Parties and the Right

The acquiescence of the two rightist parties to Radical demands loosed a torrent of public debate and activity. The most radical center of opposition crystallized around a coalition of the presidents of the national producers' organizations—the National Association of Producers of Wheat, Rice, Seeds, and Sugar Beets. Although they were dominated by large landowners, these groups had long been critical of conservative as well as moderate governments for maintaining agricultural prices at low levels. They felt that the SNA had not dealt strongly enough with this issue and had not given the producers' organizations enough voice in setting the general position of the society. These broader criticisms developed into a more specific challenge to the constitutional reform, and an ad hoc organization calling itself the Agricultural Federation (FEDAGRI) was formed to oppose the measure. Also in opposition, although somewhat less vociferously, was the rival pressure group to the SNA, the Consortium of Agricultural Societies of the South (CAS)—which represented large numbers of central as well as southern farmers. Finally, although the leadership of the SNA hoped to go along with the parties, there was within the ruling council of

[9] Departamento Gremial Liberal, statement in *La Nación,* Santiago, May 7, 1961, p. 13.

the society itself a strong current in favor of rejecting the project. On the other side, the party directorates moved to defend themselves in private conferences and social clubs, and formally within the councils of the SNA itself, where many politicians held leadership positions.

Unlike the intra-party debates, in which congressional and electoral considerations played a central role, arguments in favor of the amendment were now based on three broader points: the amendment was essential to the preservation of the constitutional system; it could be of positive advantage to the interests of the agricultural sector; and the limited nature of the amendment insured that no real damage could be done.

Thus, in the first place, it was argued that the right could no longer defend the present property structure indiscriminately. Land-tenure changes could be legitimately based on a distinction between "efficient" and "inefficient" landowners, as an essential concession to preserve social stability. In a memorandum presented to the SNA, this point was made as follows:

> Nothing will be gained by a fierce defense of all proprietors without exception, since this would indicate . . . a refusal to reform juridical institutions in an evolutionary form, and would create dikes that subsequently would be swept away by prejudice against the whole social structure.[10]

Moreover, one party leader and agronomist, Domingo Godoy, added that the expropriation of abandoned lands would serve two additional objectives: it could raise agricultural production by putting abandoned properties into cultivation, and it could lead to the creation of a new rural middle class with a vested interest in avoiding massive social overturns:

> If through the agrarian reform, we can give access to the land to the most efficient *campesinos* . . . we will have eliminated the . . . criticism that the farmers are not duly exploiting the land. These new proprietors . . . will constitute a middle class of peasants that is indispensable to a greater social stability . . .[11]

[10] "Informe sobre la reforma constitucional," *El Campesino,* official bulletin of the National Society of Agriculture, Vol. XCIV, No. 1, Santiago, January 1962, pp. 9–19.

[11] Domingo Godoy Matte, letter, *Diario Ilustrado,* Santiago, December 12, 1961, p. 2.

The memorandum also pointed out that the reform could be of positive advantage to the interests of efficient proprietors. It was through judicial interpretation, rather than explicit textual injunction, that the constitution currently required cash payment for all expropriations. Although the interpretation was currently unchallenged, even this solid ruling might be reversed, whereas an explicit amendment would leave no doubt as to the firm guarantees for efficiently cultivated land. Moreover, limited and moderate use of deferred payments might be better than progressive taxation, since the latter tool would put a broader and potentially dangerous weapon in the hands of a government determined to revise the property structure. In any case, concluded the memorandum, the passage of the amendment would bring increased foreign aid which could be channeled into agricultural credit, building rural infrastructure, and importing farm capital.[12]

At the same time, special emphasis was given to the limited nature of the amendment. Only badly cultivated or abandoned properties could be paid in bonds. The "normal" farmer might count on cash payment for any expropriation. The amount of payment would be readjusted to compensate for inflation, and any default on payments would require an end to further expropriations. The bonds could be used to cancel any debts that the landowner might have with the government. Finally, expropriated farmers would be able to appeal to the regular courts to protect their interests. The memorandum pointed out that this last provision would be one of the most important protections because:

> One of the dangers that are seen in the reform is that it would permit a *massive* agrarian reform. This cannot happen because the recourse to the Tribunals of Justice . . . will impede a massive agrarian reform by the very limitations of the proceedings.[13]

* * *

As might be expected, the opposition to the reform tended to equate the amendment with the destruction of private property and the basic elements of equity and justice. Beneath these charges, however, lay a shrewd and by no means "unenlightened" analysis of the risks of such a concession to agricultural interests. It was argued that the current threat to the status quo by no means justi-

[12] "Informe sobre la reforma constitucional," *op. cit.,* pp. 9–19.
[13] *Ibid.,* p. 15.

fied such an important concession of principle as deferred payment. Other tools, such as fines, might serve as a sanction for
whatever inefficiency might in fact exist. The CAS, for example,
argued that:

> The aspiration to expropriate a few abandoned or badly cultivated
> lands does not by itself justify a constitutional reform. If these
> lands must be sanctioned, the entire country can support the
> resources necessary for it, as beneficiary of the social peace that
> [this move] is intended to obtain.[14]

The limited provisions of the current amendments, moreover,
would simply raise expectations, without supplying the adequate
mechanisms to satisfy them:

> The people have instinct. It is not easy to fool them. They will
> think, and with reason, that what can be conviction in the left, is
> simple, occasional demogogy in the conservatives and liberals.
> They will continue following their leaders, and with much
> more reason after seeing them triumph, destroying the bastion of
> private property.[15]

Thus, limited though the specific provisions of the amendment
were, acceptance of the reform would unleash a dynamic that
ultimately would be far more dangerous to all proprietors than a
refusal to do anything at all:

> . . . it can be maintained tomorrow that it is as legitimate for a
> payment made in fifteen days to be made in fifteen or one hundred
> and fifty years. . . . The amendment presently projected will not
> permit the realization of what is intended, [and] a way will be
> sought to prolong the terms as much as might be desired, now
> without the need of breaking any solid principle.[16]

Answers were provided by men like Fernando Coloma, a vice
president of the PCU, who held that "a government that had such
purposes . . . could simply dispense with this [constitutional]

---

[14] Consorcio de Asociaciones de Agricultores del Sur, statement, *Diario
Ilustrado,* December 22, 1961, p. 7.

[15] Bulnes Correa, *op. cit.,* p. 3.

[16] Javier Echeverría Alessandri, letter, *Diario Ilustrado,* Santiago, December
27, 1961, p. 3.

'formality' . . ."[17] But to some extent, this reply misses the point of the criticism. From the perspective of 1961, a Radical victory seemed highly likely, or at least a good possibility. The combined percentage for the PL, PCU, and PR had risen from 47.2 per cent in the 1958 presidential elections to 53.2 per cent in the 1961 congressional elections, despite a loss of votes for the two rightist parties. On the other hand, while Allende won 28.9 per cent of the vote in 1958, the FRAP obtained only 22.9 per cent in 1961. One opponent stated in an interview that he thought the *"Frente Democrático* (Democratic Front)—the PR, PCU, PL presidential coalition—would rule for thirty years."[18] The opponents were concerned not about the action of a future FRAP government, but about the effects of the reform on a future Radical administration. Thus, FEDAGRI predicted that:

> All prudence in the application [of the measure] will explode under public pressure, sustained by the fact that the government had requested and obtained the legal arms for deferred payment. As limited as the range of the constitutional reform might be, it creates a precedent that will make its amplification necessary.[19]

There were dangers, of course, that rejection of the constitutional amendment would break up the coalition or cause it to lose the election. These possibilities were not lost on the opponents of the reform, but they argued privately that these were risks worth taking. In the first place, the Radical leadership was as anxious as the right to form a coalition and may well have managed to salvage it without the constitutional reform. Present concessions by the Liberals and Conservatives would not stop the Radicals from imposing further concessions as the price of continuation in the future government coalition, and it seemed pointless to cede a solid legal obstacle in advance of the elections. Secondly, if a FRAP victory was coming in 1964, limited concessions were not likely to be effective in stopping such an event. In short, only if the proponents had calculated more or less exactly the nature of the crisis—neither too early nor too late—would their position be truly protecting agrarian interests. . . .

[17] Fernando Coloma Reyes, letter, *Diario Ilustrado,* Santiago, December 30, 1961, p. 3.
[18] Interview, Santiago, March 3, 1966.
[19] FEDAGRI, statement, *Diario Ilustrado,* Santiago, May 17, 1966.

A month after both parties had agreed to support the amendment, the broader debate reached a turning point within the SNA, where a vote on the issue by the council ended in a tie. While the council's action was hardly a rousing confirmation of party activity, failure to reject the proposal meant, in effect, a victory for its proponents. The SNA officers, who were generally sympathetic with the parties' position, were now free to encourage a further softening of the organization's general stand on reform. More important, the tie prevented the society from siding officially with the FEDAGRI and the CAS, a move that might well have caused the bill to be withdrawn from congressional consideration. With the crisis passed within the SNA, at least some of the groups that had originally opposed the reform were silenced. Others explicitly reversed their positions. Although sporadic public debate continued, the back of the opposition was broken. FEDAGRI was disbanded and most objections ceased after the passage of the measure in 1963.

THE ROLE OF THE PARTIES
AND "CAREER POLITICIANS"

The chronology of the narratives, as well as the outstanding role of such individual party leaders as Bulnes, Errázuriz, and Godoy, indicate the leading role of the parties in the deferred-payment debate. From the bitter accusations of the opponents of the reform, moreover, it can be seen that they seem to share this interpretation, and in a subsequent interview, at least one party leader made the same point from his own perspective:

> The PL and PCU congressmen were not only farmers or industrialists. We had to take into account the political and electoral problems, as well as the technical ones. [The opponents] were concerned only with their occupations, and they didn't see the implications of the problem of an expanded electorate or of external pressures for change.[20]

Also, the flexibility of the various agricultural pressure groups seems directly related to the "politicization" of their leaders. A comparison of the biographies of twenty of the council members of the CAS and 34 of the men on the council of the SNA seems to bear out this idea. On the CAS council, 70 per cent of the members

[20] Interview, Santiago, April 28, 1966.

were without any sort of political experience, as compared to only 35 per cent for the SNA. On the SNA council, on the other hand, 6 per cent had backgrounds as student leaders, 35 per cent had been local leaders, and 21 per cent had been functionaries, while the CAS membership had only 5 per cent, 15 per cent, and 10 per cent in these three categories. Although 32 per cent of the SNA council had sat in the Congress, and 12 per cent were current party leaders, the CAS council had no men in any of these categories. It might be added, finally, that of the seven FEDAGRI organizers whose biographies are available, none had had any party experience.

Biographical studies of the men voting on this issue in the SNA council, moreover, tend to support the initiating role of men who had had active careers within the PL and PCU. Table 1 breaks down the backgrounds of 34 of the 40 men who had participated in the vote. All of the four men sitting in the party executive juntas were in favor of the legislation. The twelve who had been local leaders were divided, but the eight who had been student leaders or functionaries all supported the reform. In contrast, the men without any political training tended toward the conservative side: thirteen of the seventeen men in this category opposed the amendment. It is interesting to note, at the same time, that there were no strong relations between the economic backgrounds and the voting. Only twelve of the twenty agriculturalists without other economic ties opposed the reform, and the fourteen men with "mixed" backgrounds split evenly on the issue. Apparently the possession of diversified economic interests had little impact on the landowners' willingness to accept sacrifices in the agricultural sector itself.

* * *

These figures should not be taken to mean that economic cleavages within the elite are not important, however. The powerful industrial pressure group—the Society for Industrial Development (SFF)—remained neutral in the battle over the constitutional reform, and in general showed a reluctance during this period to be drawn into a position on the agrarian-reform issue.

On the other hand, the leaders of the SFF have always resisted efforts to drive any explicit wedge between the industrial and agricultural communities. One such attempt occurred at a society convention in 1961, when the following resolution was proposed by the Association of Plastics Manufacturers:

TABLE 1

SNA VOTE ON DEFERRED-PAYMENTS AMENDMENT*

POLITICAL BACKGROUND

	Political Apprenticeship								Current Status				
	None	% Support	Student	% Support	Local	% Support	Functionary	% Support	Congress	% Support	Executive Junta	% Support	Total Vote
For	4	27	2	13	6	40	6	40	3	20	4	27	15
Against	13	68	—	—	6	32	—	—	—	—	—	—	19
Total in Each Category	17		2		12		6		3		4		34

ECONOMIC BACKGROUND

	Agriculture						Agriculture—Other				
	Agriculture	% Support	Agriculture & Other	% Support	Total in Agriculture	% Support	Agriculture Commerce Industry	% Support	Agriculture & Professional	% Support	Total Vote
For	8	53	7	47	15	100	5	33	2	13	15
Against	12	63	7	37	19	100	7	37	—	—	19
Total in Each Category	20		14		34		12		2		34

* The list of voters and their positions is taken from the SNA magazine, *El Campesino*, January 1962, Vol. XCIV, No. 1, p. 9. They are: *For*: L. Errázuriz, Fernández L., Fuenzalida, Greve, Godoy M., Hederra, Illanes, Infante, Jory, Larraín C., Larraín V., León N., Lobos, Valdés F. *Against*: Alcalde, Araya, Ardizzoni, Barros B., Bermúdez, Braun, Correa F., Correa M., del Río C., González, Larraín E., Letelier, G. Noguera, R. Noguera, P. Opaso, V. Opaso, Ossa, Schacht, Vial L.

> . . . Chilean industry has transformed and continues evolving its
> social and economic position in response to the growing social
> demands of the masses . . . this does not occur to an equal extent
> in the agricultural sector, where systems subsist that need urgent
> modification. . . . It is convenient for the industrial interests that
> the general opinion of the salaried masses might distinguish be-
> tween these two types of employer attitudes, and that they do not
> confuse the industrial and agricultural entrepreneurs in a single
> combination of interests that might be impeding development.[21]

The day following the publication of this statement, the secretary general of the SFF published a statement emphasizing that the
resolution "referred only to one of the many suggestions presented
to this congress and does not reflect final thought of the gather-
ing."[22] Even a much milder resolution presented to the congress
was considerably watered down by the leadership.

What is more important, however, is that the neutrality of the
SFF did not restrain a tendency to accept the reform, but to reject
it. Unlike the SNA, the leaders of the SFF were not closely tied
to the activity within party structures. Of the thirty biographies
available of men who sat on the council of the society, only five
had had any party experience, only one person had been in Congress, and none of the councillors were currently sitting on the
executive junta of either party. Many of the remaining 25 had
acted within the structure of government: eleven had served in the
Corporation for the Development of Production (CORFO) or as
managers of a state enterprise, and three had served as cabinet
ministers; but this was all outside the frameworks of the formal
party organizations, and a number of councillors had lent support
to "independent" movements that were hostile to and suspicious
of the regular parties. Subsequent interviews with leaders of the
society itself, finally, indicate that they privately opposed the
deferred-payments amendment, and refrained from intervention for
essentially two reasons: they did not want to embarrass Alessandri,
who was an industrialist from within their own ranks, and they
felt that they could not take any action if the agricultural community itself was divided.[23]

These data indicate both the importance and the "spheres of

[21] Jorge Bronfman, statement by the Asociación de Industriales de Plásticos.
Diario Ilustrado, Santiago, June 19, 1961, p. 8.
[22] Guillermo Feliú, Secretary General of the SFF, letter, *Diario Ilustrado.*
Santiago, June 21, 1961, p. 1.
[23] Interview, Santiago, June 13, 1966.

influence" of parties and the "career politicians." The parties provided initiative and leadership that helped to rally the forces for moderation within the right. Although party experience seemed to have a moderating effect on men of all economic sectors, the major impact of the parties as organizations seemed to be within the agricultural community. The close relations with the party structures seemed to have a moderating effect on the SNA, as compared with the CAS and FEDAGRI. The "career politicians" and party leaders provided the arguments in the public debate and the formal margin of votes for the tie within the SNA that helped to soften the definition of interests within the landed elite. At the same time, the parties at least indirectly influenced the relations between the agricultural and non-agricultural sectors of the right, for by heading off the opposition of agriculturalists opposed to the reform, they helped to neutralize potential opposition from the industrial sector as well.

CONCESSIONS AND THE ESTABLISHMENT OF CONTINUITY

The final legislative products that emerged out of this process—Law 15020 and the constitutional amendment—have been subject to strong criticisms from reform-minded Chilean and foreign experts. These criticisms are based on the general point that the legislation is cumbersome and filled with obstacles to the smooth and efficient realization of what is "needed" in the countryside. The conservatism of the constitutional amendment, giving the state only fifteen years to pay out bonds, puts a severe financial limitation on the state's ability to move rapidly in the acquisition of land. In any case, Law 15020, which was passed first, had no provision for deferred payment, and payment could not be made in bonds without the permission of the owner until further enabling legislation was passed.

Moreover, in limiting expropriable land that is payable in bonds only to abandoned and inefficient properties, the state is restricted from touching "average" land that might be needed for redistribution. More important, the definitions of abandoned and inefficient properties are so vague that endless court proceedings are necessary to determine if specific lands actually fall in this category. And while special courts were established to expedite these disputes, appeal to the regular courts insures further juridical snarls that could slow or stop expropriation proceedings.

It is argued further that the Alessandri goal of 5,000 to 7,000 new proprietors a year was far too small to have a real effect on an active rural population of 600,000, and the Alessandri administration fell pitifully short of even these modest goals. The actual number of new proprietors created during 1963 and 1964 only reached several hundred in total. Finally, of these new proprietors, only around 60 per cent were actually peasants, the rest being foremen, agricultural engineers, or even members of the urban middle class.

These criticisms, in short, rest on the idea that the Alessandri reforms are "weak" when compared with other Latin American agrarian-reform laws and when judged in terms of what needs to be done in Chile. Viewed from the perspective of the previous position of the Chilean right and the contemporary position of comparable groups in other Latin American countries, however, the judgment must be different. Law 15020 was written, after all, with the support of the conservative classes when most Latin American governments had not even begun to consider the problem seriously. In those countries where reform bills were written, they were usually passed with the opposition, rather than the support of rightist groups. . . .

Similarly, from a prior position of defense for all proprietors without exception, the parties of the right and the SNA had now restricted their concern to "efficient" landowners, leaving the others to the sanction of expropriation and payments in bonds. While they have not ceased to challenge the economic justifications given for agrarian reform, moreover, they have recognized that putting abandoned lands into cultivation can in fact help to increase agricultural production. And although they still emphasize the tensions between economic and social objectives of an agrarian reform program, they now admit the possibility that with proper safeguards for efficient owners, the objectives of increased production can be balanced against the need for social concessions. The modesty of creating only five to seven thousand new proprietors a year, moreover, should not obscure the facts that in ten years, such a program could make a considerable change in rural property and that it was proposed by a sector of the society that had argued only a few years before that the land-tenure system needed "no change whatsoever." Finally, that special reform legislation was necessary and legitimate at all represents perhaps the most important change in the viewpoint of the right. One Socialist senator was not exaggerating too much when he stated in the Senate that:

If [the issue of agrarian reform] had been raised five years ago, there is no room for the slightest doubt that [the right] would not be debating in such a hurry. Those same sectors would have been here with no less than heated bayonets, disposed to stop the dispatch of a law that even accepted the principle, the idea that it is necessary to make an agrarian reform.[24]

Acceptance of the principle of deferred payments, moreover, was not the only concession "in principle" that was made in the legislation itself: the law, for instance, recognized that under certain conditions even efficiently cultivated property should be subject to expropriation. A farm can be expropriated, for example, if this is necessary to rationalize the tenure and production system for an entire zone of the country, or if the government has financed at least 50 per cent of the irrigation. The concept of *latifundia* is introduced in Law 15020 with the legislative admonition that land over a certain value should be given preference in expropriation, regardless of the state of its cultivation. The need for special courts to expedite the process of acquisition and redistribution is also recognized explicitly, in both Law 15020 and the constitutional amendment. With all the "traps" that render these provisions ineffective, they are frequently referred to by defenders of the current bill as legal precedents, and they represent a considerable shift from the previous position of the groups that accepted them in the old law.

In any case, criticisms of the essential weakness of the bill may be somewhat overdrawn, since the shortcomings of the bill itself are often confused with an apparent lack of will on the part of the Alessandri government to administer the law. In fact, since the advent of the current government, the provisions of Law 15020— with all their faults—have allowed at least a beginning of land redistribution. The two most important institutions in charge of the agrarian reform, the Corporation for Agrarian Reform (CORA) and the Institute for Agricultural Development (INDAP) were granted their legal powers to expropriate, to buy and sell lands, to extend credit, and to administer property under the terms of the old law. The Frei regime inherited these two organizations underfinanced and badly organized, but without additional legislation they have taken the leadership not only in drawing up the current

[24] Salomón Corbalán, speech, *Discursos del Senado de Chile,* 25th Session, July 26, 1962, p. 1920.

bill and administering the current program, but also in rallying and organizing the peasants and mobilizing support for a more extensive reform.

Finally, using Law 15020 during its first year, the Frei regime was able to expropriate—under the abandoned or inefficient clause—over 45 *fundos* and has established over 2,500 families on *asentamientos* (transitional settlements) before the land is given over in definitive ownership to the peasants. While the government still lacks the legislation that might force the owner to accept payment in bonds without a long court struggle, the threat of a new law with much tougher terms has induced many owners to settle out of court with terms favorable to the government. Additional legislation that would streamline the procedures of Law 15020 could, at this point, probably pass the Congress without much difficulty. But this possibility has never been publicly considered by the government, even as a temporary measure, since no doubt it would prefer to wait until the much stronger terms of its own law might allow it to act with even greater efficiency and economy.

IV. FROM CONCESSION TO DEFENSE: THE RIGHT IN OPPOSITION

In spite of the concessions of the Alessandri period and the elements of continuity they established with the policy of the current government, a sharp contrast between the two periods remains. If the old agrarian reform was one of the most conservative of its kind in Latin America, the new bill proposed by the Christian Democrats is one of the most radical. The balance of power within the Chilean system, moreover, has shifted dramatically toward the left, while profound institutional changes have altered the political composition of the right itself. Finally, while some of the general questions of agrarian reform have been settled, potentially disruptive stands are still possible, and important disagreements still exist about the way the current challenge should be handled. Nevertheless, forces within the right have worked to limit the areas of disagreement on agrarian reform even further, to moderate the style of resistance, and to keep the conflict from spilling over into other issues besides the agrarian reform and other arenas of debate besides the political and congressional arena itself.

The Christian Democratic Challenge

The new Christian Democratic government has proposed a sweeping reform in the land-tenure structure, and in its presidential campaign of 1964 it promised to create 100,000 new proprietors by 1970. This goal will probably not be reached, both because of the slowness of the reform legislation and because of financial difficulties that will impede the process of expropriation and settlement. Whether or not the new government actually reaches its goal, however, it is probable that the pace and extent of the change will exceed by a wide margin the action of most other countries in Latin America.

The reform bill that was presented to Congress by the Christian Democratic Party was fully in keeping with these radical plans. Important departures that the new bill has made from Law 15020 are: 1) the size of a property, as well as its state of cultivation, has become an important cause for expropriation, and 2) the expropriation of efficient as well as inefficient holdings is to be paid for partly in bonds. While abandoned or inefficiently managed lands could still be totally expropriated, now even a normally efficient landowner would be legally entitled to keep only eighty "basic" hectares or its equivalent in other parts of the country, and the exceptionally efficient owner might keep only 320 basic hectares. Proprietors who may have tried to escape these limits by dividing their land among sons or relatives since November 1962 were also subject to expropriation.

Properties expropriated for reasons of size would be paid 10 per cent in cash and the balance over 25 years, while other expropriations would be paid at only 1 to 5 per cent in cash and the rest over thirty years. All owners would receive indemnity for the tax valuation, and not the commercial price, of their properties, a provision which could reduce total payment as much as four or five times. Unlike the old constitutional reform, the owner would not be fully compensated for the deterioration that inflation might cause in the real value of his bonds. Instead, the amount of readjustment would vary inversely with the size of the property.

In addition, a number of tough new provisions cut through many of the procedures that had snarled the application of the old law. The CORA was entitled to take immediate possession of the property, without waiting for an affirmative court decision. In cases of expropriations due to size, the CORA was to decide the section of the property that should be reserved for the owner. To expedite the resolution of legal conflicts, two agricultural engineers and one local judge would constitute a special tribunal, and two magistrates from the ordinary courts and one agrarian engineer would compose regional appellate tribunals. No appeal to the regular courts was to be allowed.

Whereas under Alessandri land was simply handed over to new owners in individual parcels, the PDC bill created the legal transition settlement, or *asentamiento*, in which the land was to be jointly administered by CORA and a peasant committee before granting definitive titles of ownership. Although the period normally was to last only two years, it could be extended indefinitely at CORA's discretion, and when the period did end, the peasants themselves would vote whether to divide the land into individual parcels or farm it on a collective, "communitarian" basis. These last two provisions represent perhaps the clearest ideological break with the old regime. Previously, the principle of private, individual property had not been questioned. With the new law the possibility of considerable state control and of giant collective farms was opened up.

To complement these new provisions, a new constitutional amendment was presented that was designed to sweep away many of the obstacles left by the old constitutional amendment. The previous reform had limited the types of property payable in bonds and carefully defined the conditions of payment and the jurisdiction of the courts, but the new amendment left all of these substantive decisions to ordinary legislation. The only constitutional limitations now were matters of form and procedure: expropriations must be only for reasons of public utility, they must be dictated by law, and the owner must receive an indemnity.

It should be noted that there have been frequent attempts by government leaders to assuage the alarm of the landowning classes. The right has been assured that the Christian Democrat ideology is opposed to the concept of class war, that the party is not bent on exterminating all large private estates, and that the object of the reform is not to destroy private property but to extend its benefits. Both the president and the minister of agriculture have reiterated that of the estimated 10,000 large estates, only 3,500 would be affected by the reform. The rights of efficient proprietors are to be respected. Even if the government does reach its goal of new proprietors, moreover, this would affect only one third of the workers currently without property.

Privately, moreover, landowners and industrialists within the PDC have tried to reassure the right even more. Clearly, the limits on size that give the state the right to expropriate land does not mean that all such properties would actually be taken. The government, the right has been told, will use its new legal powers responsibly and prudently, and the actual reform will not be as radical as the law.

Nevertheless, the sweep of the government bills has surprised even the Chilean left, which supports the projects. The spirit of the new government marks an abrupt change from the preceding period, and the will of almost all parts of the ruling party to impose sacrifices on the landowning class is unprecedented. Despite its attempts at reassurance, therefore, the legislative policy and attitudes of the government represent what many sectors of the right feel to be a challenge to their basic values.

Institutional Changes: The Decay of the PCU and the PL

The political environment in which the new reform bills were presented had also changed profoundly. In the countryside, the presidential campaigns and the growth of peasant trade unions raised the expectations of the peasants and the pressures for reform. Within the system as a whole, the most important change, however, was the surge of the PDC to an unprecedented position of predominance within the Congress and the equally unprecedented electoral collapse of the two rightist parties in the elections of March 1965. While the latter parties had been on the defensive for generations and had received a blow by the disintegration of the *Frente Democrático* in 1964,[25] neither the extent of the Christian Democratic victory nor the severity of the rightist defeat was expected. The PDC, with 42 per cent of the vote, won an absolute majority in the Chamber of Deputies and 13 of 45 Senators, while the PCU-PL combination won about 13 per cent of the vote, as compared with over 30 per cent in 1961. In the Chamber, rightist

[25] Federico G. Gil and Charles J. Parrish give a good analysis and account of this election in *The Chilean Presidential Election of September 4, 1964, Part I*, Institute for the Comparative Study of Political Systems, Washington, D.C., 1965. In retrospect, it was clear that the center-right coalition had badly miscalculated the extent of popular disaffection and the impact of new voters on the system.

representation shrank to nine of the 147 deputies, while in the Senate, which was only partially renewed, the right retained only its seven senators who were not up for reelection.[26]

Under the impact of the electoral collapse, the internal complexity that had been developed through the coexistence of various groups and sub-units within the parties turned into tensions that could not be contained within the party structures. The most dramatic example of this occurred within the Liberal Party. The youth organization, supported by several PL congressmen, had long demanded a more advanced party line and a leadership that was more open to the influence of the "progressive" sectors of the party. While PL leaders had made occasional concessions to these demands, the distance between the groups had grown with each party setback suffered in the 1960's, and a showdown was threatened in a general party congress that was scheduled for the spring of 1965. The leaders protected their position simply by refusing to convene the congress, however, and many of the progressive sectors of the party either resigned in disgust or ceased to be militant. Power fell unchallenged into the hands of the more traditional family elements, and the formal party structure that previously had had at least some influence on policy-making gave way to the more shadowy and personal rule of older cliques.

In April 1966, hoping to take better advantage of a Chilean electoral law that penalized smaller political groups, the PCU and the PL formally merged to form the National Party (Partido Nacional, or PN). But the merger seems to have marked their further decline, rather than a resurgence. The smaller and unorganized "independent" followers of Jorge Prat, previously the bitter enemies of the established political parties, have been accepted as allies and

[26] The seats held by the major parties after the 1961 and 1965 elections are as follows:

	Chamber		Senate	
	1961	*1965*	*1961*	*1965*
PCU-PL	45	9	13	7
PR	39	20	13	10
PDC	23	82	4	13
PS-PC	28	33	11	13

THE FRAP has bitterly opposed the PDC on most issues, but supports the agrarian-reform legislation. The PR has split into a pro-FRAP wing, Independents, and a pro-right group. Like the FRAP, it has opposed most of the PDC reforms, but has promised to give the agrarian reform its general support.

granted equal voice and positions of leadership within the new
party. This action has also alienated at least two powerful Liberal
senators who had sympathized with the moderate element of the
party. Many members of the new party itself are privately pessimistic about its chances for success, and others feel that the merger
was a tactical mistake. While the organization and strength of the
new party may grow, most observers would share the opinion of
one ex-Conservative, who termed the fusion a "marriage between
two dead souls."[27]

This, of course, does not mean that since then the career politicians have not been very important in leading the opposition to
agrarian reform. Nor does the right remain totally without bargaining power within the Congress. Despite its overwhelming popular victory, the PDC's total of thirteen senators still leaves the party
two votes shy of the crucial one-third mark in the Senate. On at
least one important occasion, the votes of the right have been
needed to overcome the combined opposition of the PR and the
FRAP and to break the deadlock between the House and the Senate.
Yet the rightist political professionals are acting, both in and out
of the Congress, in more individual roles. While they cooperate in
Congress, they are no longer operating within the constraints set
by coordinated organizations, with their own objectives and incentives.

INSTITUTIONAL CHANGES: THE
DEVELOPMENT OF THE SNA

In the current period, the gap in initiating and articulating refinements in the interests of the agricultural elite has been filled by the
SNA itself. This role, however, was not left to the SNA simply
by the default of the two parties. Changes in the institutional traditions and the directorate of the society also explain the manner in
which it has assumed its position of leadership.

Just as traditional ties of family and friends balanced the more
formal aspects of party procedures, the SNA prior to 1964 had
characteristics that distinguished it from interest groups of many of
the more developed countries and that identified it with the same
loose and informal patterns of traditional power out of which the

[27] Interview, Santiago, April 28, 1966.

parties had grown. Its links to the centers of power had always been much more direct than those of a normal lobby group. Not only did SNA representatives sit formally on many government bodies, but informal relations made positions within the parties, the SNA, and often the government itself, practically interchangeable. It had served both as a forum in which political leaders could garner support for their positions and, in collaboration with the parties, as a "veto group" with almost unchallenged power to block programs deemed repugnant by the leaders.

On less "basic" issues of prices, credits, and taxes, however, there have frequently been frictions between the SNA, the parties, and the government. And on these types of issues, the society had developed a pragmatic style of operation similar to that of many other lobbies. It tried to "get along" with government powers by avoiding unreasonable demands and needlessly antagonistic postures. It sought compromise in cases of disagreement, and marginal defeats were accepted gracefully. Channels of access were sought where the chances to influence government decisions have been most favorable.

During the early 60's, moreover, the society had made organizational changes that gave it more complex functions and allowed it to represent a broader variety of agriculturalists. Many of these changes were made at least partially in response to the FEDAGRI challenge of 1961. Thus, the presidents of the producers' associations have automatically been incorporated into the SNA council and have been granted voting rights. A second vice presidency has been created to serve as a liaison between the leadership and the local organizations. More attention has been given to the development of extension services and technical studies. Finally, the presidency of the SNA has been made a full-time, paid position.

Also in the last few years, the SNA has recruited a small but influential group of younger men into its leadership cadres. These men are usually from the best families, but they belong to a newer generation of professionals and experts and have often been trained in the same universities and classes as the young *técnicos* (experts) that have now filled the ranks of the PDC. They have close ties— either formal or informal—with the rightist parties, but their active services have usually been in interest-group or technical organizations. Although they are supported within the SNA by many of the older *políticos* (politicians), they themselves act more as lobbyists than as politicians, and their power has been based on their professional careers and their technical skills, rather than on local economic bases and party affiliations.

Luis Larraín, the man who was in 1965 to become president of the SNA, is a good example of this type of individual. Larraín, only 38 years old, was director of the Institute of Rural Education, a conservative but effective Church-sponsored organization that has tried to recruit and train peasants for community-leadership positions. He also served as director of the Sheepmen's Association and sat on the board of various cooperatives and guild organizations. In 1960–62 he served as the Chilean delegate to the Latin American Common Market. In 1963 he became a vice president of the SNA, and in 1965, the president.

The election of Frei and the collapse of the rightist parties destroyed the "veto power" of the SNA and opened an unprecedented distance between the society and the government. These previous internal developments, however, helped the SNA to elaborate even further its "interest-group approach," drawing on pre-existing cadres and traditions for a renovation that would allow it to cope with the new challenge. An account of Larraín's rise to the presidency of the organization exemplifies this process.

Shortly after Frei's victory in 1964, Víctor Braun, then president of the society, held a meeting with Hugo Trevelli, the new minister of agriculture, to discuss the new government's program for agrarian reform. While there was apparently little said in the meeting that the PDC had not reiterated many times before, the general proposals so alarmed the old SNA leadership that a strongly worded memorandum was circulated among the membership, harshly criticizing Trevelli, the government, and the reform plans. Relations with the new government, which were already strained, were virtually broken off.[28]

To many members of the SNA council, however, the lack of communication with the government was an intolerable situation, and considerable pressure built up within the organization for the resignation of the old leadership. To placate the various currents within the society, a compromise was the first step attempted. Resignations of the old leadership were to be offered and rejected,

[28] A good article on the memorandum appears in *Ultima Hora,* Santiago, November 6, 1964, p. 3.

and formal control of the society was to be retained in their hands. But at the same time, the actual job of policy-making and lobbying would be left to the first vice president, Luis Larraín.

Even such a compromise arrangement, however, was bound to be only temporary, and many of Larraín's active supporters within the council remain unsatisfied. One such supporter, the editor of the SNA monthly magazine, Aníbal Correa, published an open letter of protest, calling for a more definitive solution to the problem of leadership. While admitting that the old directorate had served its purpose, Correa argued that:

> . . . the times are now different and we, as a pressure group organization, have virtually no communication with the government . . . the current directorate is undoubtedly in a situation in which there is no clear and legitimate possibility of an understanding with the government. We know that [agrarian reform] signifies a profound transformation of the present structures, but in the SNA we have not been able to determine, for lack of contacts and information, in what form this step will be applied or proposed to Congress.[29]

. . . On April 6, the council did completely overhaul its directorate. Not only was Larraín elected president, but the two vice-presidential posts were filled by young men of similar backgrounds. The first, Tomás Voticky, was only 34 years old, a teacher at the Catholic University, and a past president of a producers' organization. The second, Gilberto Fuenzalida, 44 years of age, had been active in student politics, was also a teacher at the Catholic University, and was serving as vice president of the National Association of Wine Growers.

Gestures of conciliation were made both on the part of the government and the society. From the SNA's side, as early as November of the preceding year, Aníbal Correa, in a speech at the agricultural exhibit of Valdivia, stated that:

> . . . the misuse of an internal document of our organization has provoked misunderstandings that we want to dispel, because our fervent desire is to contribute to the creation of full understanding between the trade groups and the government.[30]

[29] Aníbal Correa Ovalle, letter, *La Nación,* Santiago, December 23, 1964, p. 3.

[30] Aníbal Correa Ovalle, speech, *Diario Ilustrado,* Santiago, November 22, 1964, p. 11.

From the beginning of his presidency, Larraín tried to present a progressive and open posture toward the government in press conferences and interviews, and in the serious earthquake of March 1965, he cooperated with the government in urging farmers to take responsibility in rebuilding the damaged homes and facilities of their workers. On its side, the government responded in *La Nación*, the official newspaper, with the following editorial:

> . . . We previously criticized the closed attitude that had been adopted by the past directorate of the SNA toward all dialogue with the Executive . . . the new directorate . . . is free from these past criticisms . . . the point of view of the new directorate reflects an ample understanding of the historic moment in which the country is living. . . . In not opposing these inevitable changes but, on the contrary, collaborating with their execution, the farmers are demonstrating a valuable understanding of national necessities at a critical point . . .[31]

The SNA Strategy

With the presentation of the agrarian-reform bill in November 1965, many of the earlier efforts of cooperation between the government and the SNA gave way to sharp controversy. Yet underlying both the SNA's early posture of rapprochement and its later resistance to the government measures has been a set of assumptions that have been described as follows by one of Larraín's close associates:

> Larraín feels that with a single party controlling both the executive and the Congress, we can do little more than defend ourselves through the strength of our arguments. Our objections must be accompanied by proposals for modifications that are based on the government's own general terms and are designed to attract the people within the government who are willing to listen to us.[32]

Under Larraín's leadership, the SNA had developed a strategy of opposition based on a perception and acceptance of limitations that were imposed by the radical reduction in the right's political strength. This strength must be supplemented by a search for allies

[31] Editorial, *La Nación,* Santiago, June 9, 1965, p. 4.
[32] Interview, Santiago, May 17, 1966.

within the government itself—Christian Democratic landowners, industrialists, and politicians—that might be inclined to listen sympathetically to SNA proposals that were not incompatible with the basic goals of the reform. The society's command of funds and technical information, moreover, could be used to balance its lack of broad popular support and could add considerable force to its arguments within government offices. As a supplement to this approach, the society could use its access to the public media to present its case to the urban middle class, and the bargaining strength left in Congress could be used to provide at least some muscle to its efforts at persuasion.

At the same time, the SNA has argued that it is in the interest of the landowners to restrict the conflict as much as possible to the congressional arena. Landowners should not succumb to fear and insecurity that might lead them to neglect production. On the contrary, attempts should be made to rationalize management and increase investment. There should be strict compliance with all social legislation, and efforts should be made where possible to go beyond this legislation in raising the salaries and living standards of the workers. Labor disputes and falling production will discourage moderates within the government and the middle class, and will encourage more vindictive elements to turn the agrarian reform into a crusade against all members of the rural elite.

In short, the SNA argued that by recognizing its limitations, it (and the right as a whole) could maximize its remaining assets and retain some influence in the process of change. On the other hand, attempts to block the reform by mobilizing economic or political pressure against the government would probably not succeed, would alienate allies within the PDC, and would in the end probably only make the law even more radical.

This general approach has not, of course, precluded SNA efforts to preserve the appearance of a "united front" with non-agricultural sectors of the oligarchy. Thus, for example, it has argued that the new constitutional amendment is a danger to urban as well as rural property, and it has resisted suggestions to "isolate" agriculture by restricting the constitutional reform to rural property alone. In individual instances, moreover, the public statements of the SNA have challenged almost every aspect of the complex bill.

The most constant themes of criticism that the SNA has presented to the government have reflected the characteristics of the moderate strategy described above. These criticisms have centered on the determination and adjudication of the efficient landowners' right of reserve, the definition of "efficiency," the retroactive clause that subjects to expropriation lands divided by the owners since 1962, and the provisions governing the *asentamiento*. Almost all of these issues were raised in a press conference held by Larraín shortly after the presentation of the bill.

In the press conference, Larraín complained that the tables that convert the eighty basic hectares of reserve into their equivalent do not sufficiently "contemplate the agricultural reality or distinguish between the diverse ecological and soil categories." More important, the "bill concedes to CORA the right to locate the reserve of the expropriated proprietor. This implies that he might lose even his home, an extremely hard situation that has not been accepted by any country in the world." Within the special court system, moreover, Larraín pointed out that the accused owner must prove that he is not inefficient, whereas the burden of proof should be placed on CORA as the accuser. The decisions of the special local courts on the right of reserve, finally, could not be appealed, even to the special appellate courts established in the bill.[33]

Another major complaint has been the vagueness and uncertain nature of the clause defining "efficiency." In an interview, Larraín pointed out that a small fraction of the social security laws can exclude an owner from the right to reserve 320 hectares, a punishment hardly fitting the crime. A provision that 80 to 95 per cent of the land must be cultivated, moreover, may not fit the special circumstances of production or of the zone. What is needed, according to Larraín, is a more exhaustive definition of efficiency, through a more objective and detailed point system, based both on productivity and social welfare for the laborers.[34]

A third and perhaps the most heated objection is that "the project makes totally subject to expropriation all land that has been divided after November 1962. . . . This means that an act that was legal under existing law, becomes currently illegal. It is a vindictive disposition that gives retroactivity to the project . . . [and] it introduces a factor of hatred unknown till now in Chilean law."[35]

Serious objections can, of course, be raised to many of these criticisms. The retroactive clause in the project, for example, was

[33] Luis Larraín Marín, press conference, *El Mercurio,* Santiago, December 3, 1965, p. 21.
[34] Luis Larraín Marín, interview, Santiago, March 17, 1966.
[35] Luis Larraín Marín, press conference, *op. cit.,* p. 21.

not designed simply for vengeance against the landowning class but to block private efforts over the past four years to escape legal definitions of "latifundia," without actually changing the social and economic reality that the term implies. Many of the other apparently harsh provisions were also designed to avoid legal obstacles that might be used by the landowners to slow the agrarian reform to a halt, and it can be argued that if these provisions are in some sense "inequitable" for the individual landlord, this is a "cost" that must be balanced against larger considerations of national interest, economic development, and social justice.

Yet the charge that some have made against the SNA—that it is simply trying to stalemate the agrarian reform by subtle legal modifications instead of by a broad frontal attack—is probably false. It is doubtful that many of the modifications requested would really slow the reform as much as many persons fear. Even if some modifications were to create serious legal obstacles, this need not be because they were designed for purposes of obstruction, but because they were proposed within the context of a generally cumbersome legal structure that is accepted by almost all elements in Chilean society. For example, the call for a more precise legal definition of "efficiency" might seem to deprive the government of necessary flexibility in the application of the law. A strong reliance on the Roman system of minutely written legal codes, however, makes Larraín's criticism not only understood but shared by many Chileans who cannot be identified with the right.

Finally, it is quite possible that many of the SNA suggestions could add not only to the equity but also to the efficiency of the agrarian reform. Even the most ardent defenders of the bill admit that a point exists where the gains of granting great legal powers to the government may be outweighed by the costs of falling output caused by lack of security for existing owners. In short, one of the most important aspects of the SNA's criticisms is that they are limited, "reasonable," and well within the range of values and objectives held by persons who "really want agrarian reform."

Even more important than these explicit criticisms of the bill by the SNA are the features that were *not* criticized. No objection has been made, for instance, to payment in bonds for efficient property that is expropriated for causes of size or location. Nor has there been any strong insistence that land be paid for at its commercial value. The idea of limiting the amount of inexpropriable land that can be held by any one proprietor, finally, has not been challenged.

All of these tacit concessions represent considerable advances over the position of the SNA, even since the passage of the old constitutional amendment in 1963. This has been confirmed more explicitly in a private interview with one leading official of the SNA who stated:

> We are not really objecting to the limit of eighty basic hectares. The conditions of payment for what is expropriated is of course important to us. But what we really want is to make sure that the efficient proprietor can keep, with security, the reserve land that is due him under the law.[36]

Finally, it is interesting to note in SNA statements the rarity of inflammatory language and of categorical condemnations of the government. Even on the new and ideological explosive issue of the *asentamiento* and collective farming, for example, the SNA has been cautious. In the press conference quoted above, Larraín objected only to CORA's power to extend the *asentamiento* indefinitely, and he argued that in the case of land farmed "cooperatively" the law gives no protection to rights of the individual peasant or even to the collective, as against the state. These criticisms are identical to those made by the non-Marxist peasant unions themselves, who, like the SNA, fear the potential power of CORA and mistrust the men who direct it. Rather than condemning the *asentamiento* or even collective farming as a whole, however, Larraín criticized only aspects of these provisions. And while these aspects might be "dangerous" or "totalitarian," the basically democratic motives of the current government and the current president are not questioned:

> With this law an agrarian reform can be realized with free citizens, owners of their property, and it also can be made a collectivist reform where the new retainers are slaves of the state. The president has been clear in indicating that his road is the first of those named, but [the possibility] that others, with the same law, might follow the second road puts the agrarian reform bill and the future of the Republic in the darkest shade.[37]

Although the challenges of the current period have put a premium on the public appearance of unity, the strategy of the

[36] Interview, Santiago, March 11, 1966.
[37] Luis Larraín Marín, press conference, *op. cit.*, p. 21.

SNA has been the subject of strong criticism from other groups within the right. The most radical criticisms have come from many of the same elements who had opposed the parties in the earlier debates on deferred payments, while a more complex type of position has been assumed by members of the industrial community and the career politicians themselves.

THE NON-POLITICAL AGRICULTURALISTS

As in the previous debates, the hardest line against the agrarian reform has been taken by leaders of the regional agricultural associations—most notably the CAS—the heads of the producers' associations that had formerly associated with the FEDAGRI, and in general men who had operated outside the organizational framework of the rightist parties. Extensive, informal interviews were held with ten such men. It should be noted that all were from prominent upper-class Chilean families, and that while four of those interviewed do have industrial and commercial connections, all have gained reputations as efficient agricultural entrepreneurs. The lack of political apprenticeships and party positions, however, does not mean that these men have lacked power within the system: two of the ten have served as cabinet ministers and one has held a high post with CORFO, but these have been associated with the anti-party movements of Ibáñez and Jorge Prat, and none of the people interviewed had pursued active careers within the structure of either of the rightist political parties.[38] . . .

But the chief points of disagreement between this group and the SNA seem to be whether further concessions should be made and whether allies within the government were worth cultivating. Thus, several of the persons interviewed felt that the right should take the position that no further legislation was necessary, and unlike the

[38] Notwithstanding their social and economic connections with non-agricultural activities and with the aristocracy, there are some indications that these leaders represent a more militant breed of geographically isolated smaller farmers who lack other economic, social, and political connections. The large German population of the South, for example, supports the CAS and has always remained somewhat separate from the Santiago society. The studies of the Inter-American Committee on Agricultural Development (CIDA) show a heavier concentration of medium size, owner-occupied farms in the southern zone, and at least some evidence of militancy is indicated by press reports of armed southern farmers, ready to resist seizure of their land by force, if necessary.

SNA, almost all refused to accept the idea that size, and not efficiency, should be a criterion for expropriation:

> The SNA position is that we should not make an issue of the 80-hectares maximum, but this is absurd. If a property is inefficient, let it be expropriated. But if it is efficient, it should be left in peace, no matter what its size.[39]

Several members of this group also objected strongly to the SNA tactic of bargaining with the government behind closed doors. A third agriculturalist thus derided both the political parties and the SNA, stating:

> They think they are shrewd puppeteers, and that by pulling strings they can manage politics like a puppet show. Actually, Frei has made vague promises, and then the Christian Democrats have turned around and done what they want about agrarian reform. It is the government that is fooling them [the parties and the SNA] and not the other way around.[40]

As the basis for these criticisms, those interviewed offered three broader challenges to the SNA's role as the major representative of the landowners and to its strategic assumptions about the way this representation should be carried out. First, behind the objections to the lobbying activities of the society, there was evident a basic mistrust of the motives of the institution and of the type of people that it represented. Legal loopholes negotiated into the project would not protect the persons at whom they were aimed. On the contrary, it would be the rich and influential members of the landed class who could use their political and social connections to escape application of the law, while the "real, efficient" farmers would still be left to suffer from arbitrary administrative decisions. The following statement is quite representative of the type of sentiment found among all the persons interviewed:

> The SNA is composed of *políticos*, and not true farmers. They are using land for real estate, not for purposes of production, but they're moderate because they think they will be able to escape the agrarian reform.[41]

[39] Interview, Santiago, June 3, 1966.
[40] Interview, Santiago, March 3, 1966.
[41] Interview, Santiago, March 10, 1966.

Secondly, many felt that the SNA attempts to gain marginal
concessions were pointless, not only because its demands did not
go far enough, but also because few felt that the government could
control the process of massive agrarian reform once it was under-
way. In a point similar to the one used in the deferred-payments
controversy, therefore, they argued that the political dynamics produced by rising expectations within the countryside and the PDC
itself would force the government to ignore whatever restraints
were in fact written into the law. It was argued that:

> . . . legal concessions will probably not make much difference one
> way or the other. The agrarian reform will be realized in fact,
> regardless of what it says in the law. Politically, the Christian
> Democrats must move to the left, because they will be pressured
> to do so by their own radical elements and because they must
> outbid FRAP for popular support.[42]

Finally, against the SNA assumption that "hard-line" resistance
could only lead to a more massive reform, the agriculturalists
argued that without standing firm they would face a peaceful but
certain destruction. Current landowners would be deprived of their
land without full compensation, while collectives would be established in the countryside under the euphemism of "communitarian"
property. Efforts to cultivate friends within the government would
only blur this threat. On the other hand, by charging openly that
there were Marxists within the PDC, and by calling the government program a "totalitarian" threat to liberty and property, they
could rally allies from urban sectors, who until now had been timid
or neutral. Pressure from a united front against the government
might force it either to back down, or to show its "true" color.

The threat to stability implicit in such a move was not entirely
lost on its advocates. Most, however, placed a low priority on such
a value. . . .

Such an approach, moreover, is necessarily "suicidal" only if, like
the SNA, the right were to perceive and accept the limitations imposed by the current political order. While none of the persons
interviewed advocated revolution as an immediate alternative to the
SNA policy of accepting these limitations, certainly behind their
arguments lay the assumption that a united upper class, with its
command of wealth and organization, would have a good chance of

[42] Interview, Santiago, April 1, 1966.

emerging victorious in any breakdown of governmental authority. The links to the military were stated explicitly by one of the persons interviewed:

> We are moving into an institutional crisis, in which eventually the military may have to step in and take over. The real question is whether it would step in on behalf of the right or the left. I think it would be the former.[43]

THE "CAREER POLITICIANS"

Midway between the position of the SNA—led by its small group of "lobbyists"—and the active opposition to this policy by the non-party agriculturalists is the position of the "career politicians." Extensive interviews were also held with ten of these men, whose collective backgrounds are as follows: of the ten, eight had interests in agriculture, four in industry, and four in the professions. All had served some sort of political apprenticeship: eight had been student leaders, two had been local leaders, and five had also served as functionaries. Finally, of the ten, five had been deputies, three had been senators, three others had been presidents of their party, and eight had served on the executive junta of their parties.

Two tactical points in the politicians' approach have tended to separate them from the line of the SNA and to offer a basis of cooperation between the politicians and their former adversaries, the non-party agriculturalists. In the first place, like the non-party group, the politicians favor a broader, more extensive public criticism of the government bill. To the more limited criticisms made by the SNA, for example, a PCU statement added complaints about the length of payment for expropriated properties, the lack of appeal to the regular courts, and the failure to pay at commercial value.[44] Perhaps even more than the non-party group, moreover, the politicians have shown a great fear of the *asentamiento*, because during this time they see the chance for the PDC to establish a massive electoral machine that would guarantee them a permanent base of votes, much as the old *latifundia* system had done for the right itself. . . .

[43] Interview, Santiago, May 23, 1966.
[44] Statement by the Conservative Party about agrarian reform, *Diario de Sesiones del Senado*, 46th Session, December 22, 1965, official publication, Extraordinary Legislature, pp. 7–12.

Furthermore, like their former enemies, many politicians have
argued that the right should not accept the limitations on its power
that is imposed by the political system itself. Lacking the usual
weapons of defense provided by congressional representation,
several felt that the right could not rely solely on interest-group
techniques for a defense of its interests. Other means must be
sought that would allow a more direct pressure on the government:

> The SNA has been acting like a beggar. It has no parliamentary
> strength, no tools. It is pleading for some adjustment to make
> in the bill, saying all the time "we agree to reform." Personally,
> I think they have been in error. What they should do is organize
> a huge publicity campaign, public concentrations, and even
> producers' strikes, to put added pressure on the government.[45]

Despite the narrowing gap between the non-party and party
groups, however, the "career politicians'" attitudes indicated important restraints on their opposition to the current agrarian-reform
proposals. The politicians continued to share many of the assumptions of the SNA approach, and notwithstanding the decay of the
party organizations, they did not—like the non-party group—feel
themselves totally alienated from the government or its program.

Notwithstanding their broad attack on the PDC bill, for example,
the politicians seemed more willing than the non-party groups to
accept the need for further concessions in the position of the right.
All defended the existing legislation that they had supported, not
only as a regrettable part of the reality, but as a positive contribution. Unlike the non-party group, moreover, none of the politicians
was willing to argue that no further legislation was necessary; on
the contrary, several strongly urged further modifications. Furthermore, no one challenged the SNA policy of accepting such basic
features of the bill as the 80-hectares reserve, or the payment in
bonds for the expropriation of efficient properties. Also, it is
interesting to note that in the negotiations over the new constitutional amendment, Francisco Bulnes was even willing to admit that
while the value of the bonds should be readjusted to compensate
for inflation, the readjustment "does not always have to be total,
since this will depend on other factors."[46]

[45] Interview, Santiago, April 20, 1966.
[46] Francisco Bulnes Sanfuentes, "Debate sobre la reforma constitucional,"
Boletín del Senado No. 22021, p. 69.

This more moderate posture, moreover, is due not only to commitments in past legislation but also to broader loyalties apparently not shared by the non-party group—loyalties that tend to tie the politicians closer to the political system. Almost all the politicians spoke of friendship and respect for particular persons within the PDC, and unlike the non-party group, very few were willing to charge that there were "Marxists" in the government. In fact, many of the politicians, in spite of their general opposition to the government, admired many of its individual policy initiatives: several singled out its massive educational reform, and another cited mobilization of the youth. . . .

Finally, unlike the group without party experience, the "career politicians" denied neither the importance of concessions within the bill nor the role of the SNA in negotiating these concessions. All shared the SNA assumption that legal modifications could be of basic importance in moderating the actions of the government, and several reiterated assurances, made by the Christian Democrats themselves, that the government would act with restraint, even within the considerable powers granted it by the law. Others argued that as the PDC leadership reached the financial limits of its program, it would have the responsibility and power to control pressures to go beyond these limits.

The argument for a broader resistance, therefore, did not mean that the politicians belittled the need for bargaining with the government or for using allies within official circles. None of the politicians argued, like the non-party group, that acceptance of the current government implied a peaceful but total destruction. . . . Rightly or wrongly, several politicians felt that a strong categorical challenge to the government bill would be understood by the government, not as the beginning of a total break, but as an initial position that would be moderated by compromise. One Liberal politician thus admitted, when questioned about a particularly bitter public exchange on agrarian reform:

> That is the way our country is. You know, for example, that we Liberals were in the cabinet with the Communists and we had pretty good relations with them, too. One day we can attack the president bitterly, and the next day we can deal with him.[47] . . .

The "career politicians," in short, did not advocate that the SNA strategy be replaced, but that it be supplemented. Like the

[47] Interview, Santiago, April 20, 1966.

non-party group, they criticized Larraín's tactics, but they also supported the general role of the SNA and acquiesced to a formal change in its directorate. And although like the non-party group, they have advocated a more strenuous opposition in principle to the bill, they have shown an active concern for its details as well and have been among the leaders in bargaining for changes that would soften the impact of the law.

THE POSITION OF THE INDUSTRIALISTS

The position of the industrialists is, of course, central to the strategic debate between the agricultural sectors of the elite. In fact, there is considerable division within the former group. Individual members of the industrial and commercial elite have supported the PDC, and several are serving in the cabinet. Others have shown a clear reluctance to be drawn into a struggle that does not affect them directly. The industrial pressure groups have taken no position on the agrarian reform, and their public statements on the constitutional reform are both rare and cautiously worded. The pressure-group leaders have tried to avoid jeopardizing their own contacts with the government, and in a press conference SFF leaders suggested making special and specific exceptions for rural and urban properties subject to reform, while preserving in the constitution the general norm of cash payment for expropriations.[48]

This behavior would seem to indicate that the industrial sector of the elite is, in fact, an uncertain ally of the agricultural community. This supports an assumption implicit in the SNA strategy: although the agricultural sector should avoid being explicitly isolated from other parts of the elite, efforts to win the more active support of the urban upper classes does not warrant steps that risk loss of access to the government. There is some evidence, however, that this assumption is, at least in part, a type of self-fulfilling prophecy: the approach suggested by the non-party groups might in fact serve to mobilize industrial allies, while the moderation of the SNA itself may be one of the restraining factors that encourages their neutrality.

It should be noted that while some individual industrialists sup-

---

[48] SFF, statement, "Conferencia de prensa de la mesa directiva de la Sociedad de Fomento Fabril," June 6, 1966.

port the current regime, others have bitterly opposed it. One former leader of the Alessandri administration, for example, publicly rebuked the current caution of the SFF leaders and strongly opposed both the agrarian and constitutional reforms:

> I understand that I am not the most authorized person to [speak out] but I have waited in vain for others of the private economic sector to do so. Perhaps . . . the fear of seeing their legitimate interests even more greatly affected has led them to maintain silence in the mistaken hope that a complacent, suicidal attitude might drive away the dangers . . .[49]

. . . Going well beyond the attack of the SNA, or even of the parties, on the system of payments for expropriations proposed by the PDC, the letter asks:

> What confidence can citizens have if their goods can be expropriated without exception; if their indemnity can be paid in bonds—that can come to lose all their value—at twenty, thirty, or more years; if claims can be made to tribunals distinct from the regular court system; and if any law whatever can fix the amount of indemnity . . .?[50]

Also, many of the top industrial leaders do have agricultural interests and consider themselves directly affected by the reform. While they have not taken a public stand on the government measures, many have strongly condemned them in private and show an unwillingness to accept even the more limited principles embodied in the past legislation. One industrial leader, for example, argued:

> I don't think there really are any "inefficient" landowners. Usually, if land is not fully exploited it is because government price policy does not permit full cultivation.[51]

Several prominent members of the SFF, moreover, now feel privately that their past neutrality has been a mistake. They regret their failure to oppose the deferred-payments amendment of 1963. More important, they are quite critical of the current SNA em-

[49] Enrique Ortúzar, letter, *El Mercurio,* Santiago, May 29, 1966, p. 43.
[50] *Idem.*
[51] Interview, Santiago, April 4, 1966.

phasis on "efficient proprietors," and argue that a more basic
defense of "private enterprise" is required. Another leader re-
marked in an interview that:

> You can't work by agreeing basically and then trying through
> private negotiations to get minor changes. The thing to do is to
> defend private enterprise, without all these divisions between
> efficient and inefficient proprietors. This is not the real issue.[52]

. . . In short, while there are clearly "internal" factors that restrain
the industrial community from a more active opposition to the
government, one of the most important restraints may also be
"external." Whatever their private inclinations, leaders of the non-
agricultural upper class may feel that their public stand on agrarian
and constitutional reform cannot go beyond the limits set by the
SNA itself.

BARGAINING AND CONCESSIONS

With the industrial groups at least temporarily on the sidelines,
bargaining on the reform bill has been carried out chiefly by the
agricultural societies, while the opposition to the constitutional reform has been led by the politicians. A month before the agrarian-
reform bill was presented to Congress, a Coordinating Committee
of Agricultural Associations was formed by the CAS, the Society
of the North, various powerful local societies, and the SNA itself,
in an effort to present a unified front on the issue of agrarian
reform. From the very beginning, however, controversy broke out
between the SNA and the other constituent organizations over the
approach that should be taken by the committee.

The man chosen to represent the "united front" was Pedro
Enrique Alfonso, a prominent Radical politician and currently a
leader of the northern association. The choice was supported formally within the committee by CAS and the northern association,
and received informal encouragement from many former colleagues
of Alfonso, both within the Radical and the rightist parties. It was
opposed, on the other hand, by the SNA. While the SNA advocated efforts toward increased production and a moderate political

---

[52] Interview, Santiago, June 3, 1966.

line of opposition to the government. Alfonso and the groups he represented advocated sympathy, if not encouragement, for the inclination of farmers to avoid capital investment and to resist the demands of labor. Also emphasized was a hard and vigorous stand of opposition to the reform. Under Alfonso's leadership, therefore, the committee itself became the focal point of challenge to the SNA strategy. Thus, an opening declaration from the committee warned that:

> . . . even in democratic sectors, there exist clear infiltrations of a totalitarian character that [tend] to submit agricultural activity to forms of collective exploitation and absolute state control.[53]

This accusation was soon concentrated into a more specific attack on the Institute of Agricultural Development (INDAP) and on the head of this organization, Jacques Chonchol. "There is," complained the committee, "a real technique of agitation in the countryside promoted by administrative functionaries." This agitation has been carried out by "INDAP and other functionaries who are undoubtedly acting without the knowledge of those who have charge of the overall direction of the government."[54] Charges were also made that Chonchol was an "international agent," a "Marxist," and one of the leading figures in the Cuban revolution who was now seeking to accomplish the same thing in Chile.[55] Relations between the committee and the government deteriorated completely. Government leaders closed ranks in defense against the charges. A series of public assemblies were held on Chonchol's behalf, and there was a bitter exchange of public letters between Alfonso and the president of the PDC, Patricio Aylwin.

The atmosphere was charged further in the months following the introduction of the agrarian reform bill by another event: the rightist senators—in the hope of gaining concessions on the constitutional reform—joined the Radicals and the FRAP in voting against key provisions of the government copper program.

[53] Comando Coordinator de Organizaciones Agrícolas, statement, *El Mercurio*, Santiago, October 21, 1965, p. 27.

[54] *Idem.*

[55] In reality, Chonchol has long been affiliated with the more militant wing of the Christian Democratic Party. He has served as an expert in many international organizations. During a period of service with the United Nations Food and Agriculture Organization (FAO), he was stationed in Cuba as an adviser to the Cuban government on its agrarian-reform program. It was on this activity that the committee based its charges.

This program, if anything, had an even higher priority for the PDC leadership than the agrarian reform itself. By granting tax concessions to existing foreign copper companies, the government hoped to increase their investment and to raise copper output. At the same time, the government hoped to answer calls for nationalization by the alternative of "Chileanization," or acquiring large blocks of stock in a number of key mines. The FRAP, arguing for outright nationalization, had consistently opposed all aspects of the program, not only in Congress, but in the mines themselves, where the leftist unions had organized a series of strikes that paralyzed operations for several months. The Radicals, after supporting the bill in general, began to vote with the FRAP on many of the important specific aspects of the bill.

Thus, the government had counted on the votes of the rightist senators to supply the one-third vote in the Senate necessary to uphold the president's veto. Instead, the senators who had previously given support to the bill reversed their position, opposing provisions that authorized all of the Chileanization program and roughly one half of the investment program. The act opened the rightist parties to bitter government charges of collusion with the left and obstructionism.

Throughout this period, however, contacts between the right and the government on the agrarian-reform bill were maintained through the efforts of the SNA. The president himself spent much of the first week after the presentation of the bill in conference with Larraín and other SNA officials, and the SNA continued to be heard with respect by various other government leaders, both at the congressional and ministerial levels. At the same time, the government reintroduced the crucial copper provisions as riders on another measure that it presented to Congress, and the question of rightist support on these provisions was brought into the negotiations over the constitutional reform by Francisco Bulnes in the Senate.

In spite of these contacts, bargaining with the government proved slow and difficult. Whatever the moderation of the SNA's position, considerable distance remained between what it demanded and what the government was willing to concede. In addition, many left-wing members of the PDC privately shared the FRAP view that the copper companies should be nationalized. They had supported the government program at least partly because they expected a radical agrarian-reform project. Compromise on the agrarian and constitutional reforms as the price for the right's support on copper, therefore, made the government's position difficult with the congressional wing of its own party, and it had to proceed with caution in the negotiations.

By March 1966 the copper program was still blocked in Congress, while the government showed few signs of willingness to make serious concessions on either the constitutional or the agrarian reforms. A meeting of the Coordinating Committee was held to assess the situation, and it was here that the most concerted challenge to Larraín's position was mounted. According to reliable sources, there was "a lot of excited talk about producers' strikes, united fronts, and other extreme measures."[56] The government was seen as totally closed to "constructive suggestions," and it was argued that the negotiations should be broken off and opposition continued from the "outside." At the end of the meeting, over Larraín's protests, it was agreed to reaffirm publicly the extreme criticism made of the government's position. In some of the most provocative language that had been used in the public debate, Alfonso charged at the press conference following the meeting that:

> This is a totalitarian government that represents the will of a single party . . . It is precipitating Chile toward communism and will end in an abyss that will provoke disaster for the country . . . it has created a great political machine, managed by Mr. Trevelli [the minister of agriculture] through CORA . . .[57]

Larraín could not, of course, explicitly state his opposition to such charges without breaking the façade of public unity that was supposed to exist among the agricultural groups. In a symbolic gesture, however, he showed his disagreement by failing to appear at the press conference that Alfonso held along with the presidents of the two other main agricultural societies. More directly, the treasury of the SNA was closed to the committee and, unable to maintain the costs of a substantial campaign of publicity or public meetings, its activities slowed to a halt. As one politician put it quite bluntly, "The committee has run out of funds and is paralyzed."[58]

[56] Interview, Santiago, April 15, 1966.
[57] Pedro Enrique Alfonso, press conference, *El Mercurio*, Santiago, March 26, 1966, p. 25.
[58] Interview, Santiago, May 17, 1966.

By the first of April, direct conversations between the presidents of the two rightist parties and Frei had broken the impasse on the reform bills. The following day, the copper provisions were supported by the right in the Senate, and shortly afterward a series of changes were made in both the constitutional and agrarian reforms.

It is interesting to note the cheapness of the "price" which the rightist senators finally accepted in return for their support on copper. The most important government concessions centered on the constitutional amendment, which was changed to read that indemnities for expropriations must be determined "equitably" and that all tribunals must "judge conforming to law." With these concessions it was now possible for an expropriated owner to make legal protests against particularly harsh terms of payment. The concessions also established overall direction of the special courts by the Supreme Court, opening the door to certain limited appeals to the latter tribunal.

The government, however, could still expropriate at tax value, it could establish a strong system of special courts, and according to Bulnes' own admission, even partial readjustment in the value of the bonds did not constitute an "inequitable" indemnity. It is interesting evidence of the distance that the right had come on this issue, when despite the limits of the government changes, Bulnes could still argue in the Senate that:

> . . . the long campaign . . . to show the government and the PDC the range and effects of the reform . . . have produced results a little late, but positive . . . I am glad . . . that the final result, without being fully satisfactory . . . constitutes a sufficient definition in favor of private property and even a minimum safeguard in cases of expropriation.[59]

In the agrarian-reform bill that passed the Chamber of Deputies, the government also introduced a number of changes. Some were included as part of the "copper deal," while others were sponsored by Christian Democratic cabinet members or congressmen who had shown a concern for moderating some of the harsher aspects of the bill. In any case, it should be noted that these changes have at-

[59] Francisco Bulnes Sanfuentes, speech to Senate, text in *El Mercurio*, Santiago, April 13, 1966, p. 1.

tempted to answer many of the original criticisms made by the SNA.

Thus, as part of the copper deal, the table of land equivalences to the eighty basic hectares which had previously considered only irrigated and non-irrigated land, now added a third category of partially irrigated soil. This gave owners of this type of property a larger right of reserve.

Other changes, which may or may not have been part of the copper negotiations, moreover, also reflected the SNA point of view. Thus, complaints concerning the denial of the right of reserve could now be appealed to the special appellate tribunal, a right not granted in the original bill. Also provisions were added that would allow an expropriated owner to invest his bonds in nationally owned industry and to use them for cancelling debts to the government.

Also, while in the original project it was the CORA that had the power to determine the location of an owner's right of reserve, the bill passed by the Chamber of Deputies allowed the owner to do this. It added the provisions that the reserve must be composed of contiguous territory, it must be equal in quality to that of the soil expropriated, it must include the owner's home and a reasonable proportion of his capital investments, and it must be susceptible to rational cultivation. Also, it was now the CORA, and not the owner, that would have to appeal this decision to the special courts.

Finally, the retroactive provisions of the original bill, which had provoked Larraín's bitter criticism, were now considerably modified. While originally, properties divided after November 1962 were subject to expropriation if they were not worked personally by their owner, now only properties divided since November 1965—the date of the current bill's presentation to Congress— would be expropriable.

Conflict has not ended with these bargains between the government and the rightist political groups. The constitutional reform has passed both houses of the Congress, but as of this writing the agrarian-reform bill has passed only the Chamber of Deputies and must still go through the Senate and to the President for his approval. Bargains made at one point in this complex process may be unmade at others, both by the government and the right. After winning rightist support for the copper reforms in the Senate, the

PDC modified the constitutional reform in the Chamber with the proviso that rural property would be subject to expropriation at its tax value and in bonds of up to thirty years. The rightist parties have charged that this special clause discriminates against land-owners. The SNA, moreover, while admitting that the "agrarian-reform bill [now] includes the rectification of many of the innumerable points that were objected to when the bill was in-troduced," has also gone on to demand further modifications.[60] Many of the non-party group continue to belittle the concessions already made by the government. The bitterest part of the con-troversy, however, seems at least temporarily to have subsided. The change in atmosphere was so evident, that as early as May, the weekly news magazine *Ercilla* commented that:

> The attacks . . . have lessened in their heat . . . The [Co-ordinating Committee] has made a truce in the duel of insertions that it made with the government . . . the SNA itself has adopted a more lenient attitude with respect to what officials say or do.[61]

The SNA and the Containment of Conflict

New issues will be raised as the reform moves more directly into the countryside itself, and the resistance of the right will certainly continue. Under the leadership of the SNA, however, there is evidence that the right will continue to move toward a strategy of restricting rather than broadening disputes. In this way interests may be defended at the administrative level, and conflict may be kept to manageable limits in which bargaining and compromise are still possible.

The society has already shown some indications of being willing to accept not simply legislative but "real" sacrifices on the part of the landowning class. SNA representatives on the CORA council opposed only one of the 162 expropriations agreed on by the council.[62]

The SNA has also chosen to recognize and stress other features of the government's agrarian policy, besides land-tenure change,

---

[60] Sociedad Nacional de Agricultura, statement, *El Mercurio,* Santiago, April 13, 1966, p. 1.

[61] José Pablo López, "Reforma agraria sin macetero," *Ercilla,* No. 1,615, May 18, 1966, p. 6.

[62] *Ibid.,* p. 6.

that are designed to help current farmers. As the government has moved to promote higher prices for agricultural commodities, for example, the society has responded with public praise:

> The recent decision of the government on the readjustment of the price of milk constitutes one of the most serious efforts . . . in many years to overcome one of the factors that weighs most negatively in the development of milk production.[63]

The agrarian-reform battle, moreover, has been carried out within a social context which contains other disputes between the right and the government, but the SNA has attempted to keep these issues separate from the agrarian reform itself. The rise of new agricultural unions, for example, may change the rural social structure even more radically than land-tenure changes. While the SNA has opposed legislation restricting the firing of workers, it has tried to cooperate with the government in its administrative effort to discourage dismissals of union leaders. Conversations between the SNA and non-Marxist unions, finally, indicate the beginning of efforts to accept the unions as part of the new rural status quo.

In short, the SNA has shown signs of moving toward an interpretation of "reality" that does not end at the limits of land-tenure changes. Whatever the outcome of agrarian reform, other problems and possibilities will remain for both the current landed class and the SNA itself. An *El Campesino* editorial entitled "A New Stage in Our Task" discussed the policy directions. The editorial point out that:

> Those who believe that the Agrarian Reform Law will close the door to agricultural problems for good or bad are wrong. The future will bring many surprises.[64]

The editorial criticizes both the limitations of the society's past activities and the lack of a productive energy among the farmers themselves, and it projects its own general role as follows:

---

[63] Sociedad Nacional de Agricultura, official statement, *La Nación,* Santiago, May 12, 1966, p. 2.

[64] Editorial, "New Stage in our Task," *El Campesino,* official bulletin of the National Society of Agriculture, Vol. XCVIII, No. 4, Santiago, April 1966, p. 15.

The SNA is engaged in giving impulse to a change in attitude and method. It is for this reason that our concern is not only concentrated on improvements in the agrarian-reform bill but also is designed . . . to incite farmers to assume an advanced and clear position, conscious of their duties to the rest of the rural collectivity.[65]

More specifically, the editorial discusses an expanded role for the SNA in its extension services, in promotion of better means of production, and in the initiation of profit-sharing schemes to reduce tensions between the rural social classes:

We want to mark the beginning of a new stage; the organization of our agriculture on modern technological bases, made by the entrepreneurs themselves, who will also have as a goal the incorporation . . . of the workers themselves in a system of profit-sharing. There is only one way that agriculture can avoid in the future the repetition of today's confusion: that is to prove to the country that the entrepreneur is the most qualified to make the land produce more.[66]

V. CONCLUSION

The role of the rightist parties and the SNA calls into question some conventional ideas about the politics of agrarian reform that are based on the problems created by the right's resistance. Because the right resists reform, it is assumed that while it has power, it will attempt to sabotage and stalemate reform programs. The stalemate can only be broken by an elimination of the right's political influence. With the execution of the reform, conflict will end, both in the political system and the social environment, through the destruction of the group that caused the conflict in the first place. Thus, one noted economist argues:

The essential thing is to destroy the old political structure and to replace it with a new order based in an equality of rights and responsibility. If such a change takes place, automatically there will flow—in a type of chain-reaction—successive waves of changes in social and cultural values and in national and individual objectives.

[65] *Ibid.*, p. 14.
[66] *Ibid.*, p. 15.

. . . What is required is that a group decidedly opposed to the feudal elite might have the initiative, the authority, the imagination, and the time to diffuse and implant new productive techniques.[67]

The Chilean case indicates that, at least in certain respects, this analysis must be refined and modified if it is to explain the accomplishment of reform within the context of social and political stability.

"Reform" should not be seen as one action, which at a single moment, transforms the social and political structure of the country. In Chile, if there is a transformation, it will more likely be a process over time, with ebbs and flows of activity, controversy, and bargaining. Even if the "feudal elite" were eliminated from positions of power, moreover, conflict would not be ended. Different groups would still have different objectives and priorities that would have to be balanced and compromised.

The events in Chile point to the possibility that the landowners might also participate in this process, along with the other groups. And even more important, their participation might be an important factor in determining their past and future moderation. Certainly in the initial part of the controversy, the emphasis on "overpowering" the right in order to break the stalemate has probably obscured important elements of persuasion that have also played a role. Only toward the end of the reform process will the right cease to be in an economic and social position that might allow it to challenge the authority of the PDC. In the meantime, it must be dealt with one way or the other.

THE RIGHTIST PARTIES AND THE SNA AS AGENTS OF CONCILIATION

Central to an understanding of the relation between the right's participation and its moderation is the way its influence has been channeled into the Chilean political system. In the different periods, the parties and the SNA have not only represented the landowners, but they have also conciliated this potentially radical social group to political developments that threaten its existence. They have in-

[67] Edmundo Flores, *Tratado de economía agrícola*, Mexico-Buenos Aires, 1961.

fluenced the right's perception of its options by promoting the idea that change is "inevitable," and they have defined the interests of the landed elite so that they can be defended within, rather than against, the reform process. They have acted as buffers between broad conservative values, on the one hand, and the need for reform on the other.

This does not mean that the parties and the SNA have "betrayed" the interests of the landed class or that they have reached agreement with other political groups that challenge the right. On the contrary, their political influence has been on behalf of the right and has probably added elements of resistance and conflict on congressional and administrative levels. But at the same time, this type of behavior has probably dampened or precluded controversy at broader levels that might, in the long run, have been even more dangerous to the efforts of the system to respond to social demands. Their role, in short, has been one of helping the political system to manage conflict, rather than to resolve it.

In the Alessandri period, the influence of the rightist parties served to slow the impact of groups more strongly committed to a radical reform, and their control over the machinery of government had its costs in terms of the weakness of the reform legislation and of its actual application in the countryside. By responding to electoral and congressional pressures, however, the PL and PCU helped to narrow the conflict over agrarian reform as well. They promoted the idea that land-tenure changes need not be intolerable and that the subject was a legitimate topic for political debate. The influence of the parties, moreover, was a central feature in inducing the right as a whole to accept the general principles of reform. Legislation would be accepted, because it was to be administered by groups that the right, as a whole, felt it could trust.

More important, the past action of the parties may have facilitated "splitting the difference" now that the PDC finally has come to power. The right can criticize the harsh terms of the new deferred-payments plan, for example, but it can no longer object to the principle of deferred payments itself. Bargaining would have existed, no doubt, even if there had been no previous legislation. By making its original position closer to the center of the debate, however, the right's representatives have been able to settle closer to the PDC's original terms, with less fear of recrimination from their own bases for "selling out."

In the current period, the SNA has tried to make the reform

bill more conservative, and it has had some success. But leaders of the SNA have also argued that the organization can be most effective if it moderates its objections and exploits channels of access to the PDC government. In following this strategy, it has narrowed the conflict even further. It accepted many of the provisions of the PDC bill—such as the 80 hectares limit—that go considerably farther than the provisions of the first bill. It has sought to emphasize areas of agreement with the government—such as on price policy—that cut across the conflict on agrarian reform. It has tried to keep disagreement on other issues from being dragged into the reform controversy by "policing" its own constituents. It has thus urged compliance with social laws and the rationalization of production, and it has avoided sweeping attacks on the government or its reform project.

The existence of organizations that perceived and responded to cues leading to a limitation of the conflict were important restraints on a counter-tendency toward an intensification of social and political controversy over agrarian reform. The influence of the parties and the SNA helped to restrict the rise of individual leaders and ad hoc organizations that sought to cut off relations with the other side and to present objections in terms that discouraged compromise. The interviews with these persons suggested that many were more or less aware that their positions threatened a continuation of regular political processes. Certainly, they gave less priority to questions of political advantage than did the parties and the SNA. Nevertheless, the implications of their position need not have been fully clear to them. Many within the right may have supported stronger terms of resistance without perceiving the possibility that reactions from the government might, in turn, have necessitated still stronger terms of resistance from their side. In short, without political organizations with interests in limiting the conflict, it might have developed an inner-dynamic of its own that would have moved toward escalation.[68]

[68] James S. Coleman, in *Community Conflict,* presents a model of conflict escalation in small communities that bears important similarities to tendencies evident in the Chilean agrarian-reform dispute. The most important changes in *issues* are: a) from specific disagreements to more general ones, b) elaboration into new and different disagreements, and c) a final shift from disagreement to direct antagonism. The changes in the *social organization* of the community are as follows: the polarization of social relations as the controversy intensifies, as the participants cut off relations with those who are not on their side, and elaborate relations with those who are; the formation

The Institutional Autonomy of the Rightist Parties and the SNA

The capacity of the rightist parties and the SNA to play this role was, to an important extent, due to internal features of their organizations that allowed them a certain autonomy from and influence over the broader social and economic values of the Chilean landed class.[69] The interests of the organization were considerations that the members took into account, even while they were engaged in defending themselves and their friends from the challenge of agrarian reform. Organizational patterns of behavior gave the institutions the capacity to influence the way that the broader values were defined within the upper class as a whole: the parties and the SNA could convince some groups that they were doing a "good job" on their behalf, and they could restrict the pressures from outside groups that did not accept their role.

The evidence suggests that experience in party or interest-groups activities gave the members a different perspective from that of persons with similar social backgrounds or economic interests who did not share these experiences. Since the advancement of the former group depended, in part, on service to the organization, it is plausible that loyalty to the organization's interest would influence the way the members responded to social and economic controversies. Thus, in spite of family and economic backgrounds that gave them the inclination to reject deferred payments, many party leaders accepted the concession for the sake of party advantage. The "career politicians" have had their impact on the SNA as

---

of partisan organizations and the emergence of new, often extremist, partisan leaders to wage the war more efficiently; and the mobilization of existing community organization on one side or the other. (p. 13)

[69] Samuel P. Huntington, in "Political Development and Political Decay," *World Politics*, Vol. XVII, No. 3 (April 1965), pp. 386–431, suggests that the degree of development or "institutionalization" of an organization is indicated by the elaboration of four characteristics: 1) an organization becomes more developed as it moves from *rigidity* to *adaptability*—as it takes on new functions to replace old ones, 2) as it moves from *simplicity* to *complexity*, an organization will be more capable of making these functional changes, 3) as an organization moves from *subordination* to other spheres of behavior to *autonomy*, it will be more able to resist the pressures of outside groups and be capable of moderating and restricting changes that threaten its existence, 4) finally, an organization will be more institutionalized as it moves from *disunity* to *coherence*—as it develops the capacity to reach an internal consensus and to close ranks on new groups.

well, and newer leadership cadres—whose power has been more closely related to jobs within the society itself—have also developed a sensitivity to the problem of the SNA's survival.

The multiplicity of groups and functions within the rightist parties and the SNA has allowed them a certain flexibility in responding to the pressure of any one group or to the need to fill any one function. Thus, for example, in the first period, the recruitment of groups with professional occupations and the influence of youth, labor, and technical departments exerted pressure on the more conservative party leadership to accept many of the concessions demanded by the Radicals. In both the PL and PCU moreover, the existence of these groups allowed at least a partial renewal of the leadership itself.

In the SNA, an increase in the importance of lobbying on prices, of moderating labor disputes, and of extending technical aid decreased the chances that the life of the organization might end with defeats or compromises on agrarian-reform issues. By emphasizing other aspects of agricultural interests, organization leaders may also have influenced the perception of other segments of the agricultural community that they could also survive current changes. With its extended functions, moreover, also came an elaboration of internal organization. The formal incorporation of local and producers' associations into the SNA decreased the dependence of the leadership on the views of any one segment of the agricultural community and gave the society more authority to speak for the community as a whole.

Moreover, both the rightist parties and the SNA showed considerable oganizational coherence—the capacity to resolve internal conflicts by established institutional procedures. This has increased the power of the organizations, both relative to other political groups and relative to their own bases. The early commitment on deferred payments gave the parties bargaining strength not only within the tripartite commissions, but also in the presentation of their case to broader agricultural groups. Formal and informal links to the SNA proved to be resources that the parties could use in influencing and persuading SNA members. Other groups, less closely connected to the parties were presented with a *fait accompli* and could no longer mobilize the resources necessary to block the reform.

In the current period, the resolution of the problem of leadership within the SNA allowed a relatively small group to speak with authority for the organization. Dissidents within its ranks have been silenced. Control of technical facilities and information has given the SNA directorate considerable influence in shaping both government decisions and the thinking of its members. Manipulation of wealth and prestige has given the leadership the capacity to neutralize the industrial community and to restrict the broader challenges from the CAS and the Coordinating Committee.

These characteristics of organizational behavior can develop or disappear as they interact with the larger political system and the social environment itself. Changes in the rightist parties and the SNA in the two periods indicate a constant interplay between their moderation, their influence on government decisions, their internal organization, and their capacity to command the support of their constituents. The SNA has based its current strategy on the idea that the government can still be influenced in important ways. Without doubt, its capacity to retain the support of the agricultural community will depend to a great extent both on its continued internal development and on its actual capacity to produce some sorts of "results."

At the same time, rightist party lines toward agrarian reform have become less moderate, relative to the SNA's, as party organization and the ability to exert pressure on the government have weakened. The alienation of more progressive sectors within the parties has reduced the restraints on the more conservative elements. Groups previously antagonistic to party goals and orientations have risen rapidly within the ranks of the newly formed National Party. Party leaders respond to the loss of more conventional congressional tools of bargaining by advocating the substitution of broader, more dangerous ones.

THE RIGHTIST PARTIES AND THE SNA: DIVERGING RESPONSES TO CHANGE

None of the above is meant to challenge the basic truth of the notion that new reforming political groups must rise to power, if reform is to be successful in appeasing other social sectors that might also challenge the stability of the system. The Radicals were the initiators of the old reform law, because the declining congressional and electoral strength of the rightist parties left them no choice but to accept Radical leadership. The stronger current efforts toward reform are due to an even more complete displacement of the rightist parties by the PDC. There is no doubt that the Christian Democrats' current job of legislating and administering changes has been made considerably easier by the sharp reduction in the right's congressional and administrative strength.

What the analysis does suggest, however, is that even while the right's social and economic power has been challenged and its grip on the political system has been loosened, an important stabilizing feature in the operation of the Chilean system has been the retention of some institutional channels through which the right could defend itself at the governmental level. The key to the future restraint on conflict may also depend to a considerable extent on this factor. With the growth of other social demands, however, the challenge to stability may also increase. As these new groups move into positions of governmental power, it may become more difficult for the right to be "felt" in government decisions without at the same time unduly clogging the governmental machinery. And as the rightist organizations move farther from control over the political system, they may themselves lose the incentive and the means to moderate the interests of the right.

The changing responses of the rightist parties and the SNA to the decline of their political power offers an opportunity for speculation about which type of institution may best meet these conflicting needs in the future. When the parties thought they could arrest the decline in their political strength by forming part of a winning coalition, they were willing to moderate their economic positions on agrarian reform in order to pick up support from more reform-minded groups. As these chances decreased and they moved toward an "out" position, they began to emphasize differences and obscure points of agreement with the party in power. The SNA has acted differently: its position has tended to become more moderate as it has moved farther from the center of power. In the Alessandri period, it acted as a proud and powerful veto group, which the government parties had to appease and restrain. With the rise of the PDC to power, the SNA began to rely more on elements of persuasion than on pressure to win modifications in the reform.

Thus, while the right-wing parties and the SNA share common features of organization and are oriented toward the same social bases, there are also important differences. The parties are related to the political system through the electoral mechanism. They compete directly with other parties for control of the government, and they depend for their strength on their capacity to command large blocks of votes. The SNA, as an "interest group," responds to access that is available in other parties and within the administration. They depend for their strength, not only on broad popular support, but also on their control of information and their prestige with important decisionmakers. Of course, in reality, the rightist parties have "lobbied" other political groups, and electoral results and the composition of the Congress have always been important to the SNA. But to an important extent, as institutional types, the parties and the SNA have responded to different incentives within the system. They have mobilized the resources of the right in different ways, and they have used different tools to influence Chilean political decisions. These differences may be increasingly important in the changing Chilean context.

In early periods of change, the rightist parties served the important function of filtering and refining the interests of the "dominant class." The progressive breakdown in traditional social ties between classes may now make this role more difficult. Rightist politicians can no longer use upper-class wealth and status to win large numbers of votes from the lower and middle classes, without at the same time abandoning their basic conservative orientation. And a small nucleus of supporters may no longer be sufficient to make the rightist parties an effective political force in the Congress. In any case, as the demands of new groups become louder and stronger, party efforts to force bargaining at the congressional level may be too clumsy and obstructive to allow them to conciliate the interests of the right with those of the new groups.

As control of the government has passed more directly into the hands of parties that represent these new groups, however, the refinements of the rightist parties may no longer be necessary. As an interest group, on the other hand, the SNA may be better suited to use the resources remaining to the landed class in a way that can protect its economic interest without jeopardizing the general program of agrarian reform. The SNA can direct technical skills, wealth and organization toward a more subtle type of influence than that used by the parties. It need not challenge directly the other political groups that base their power on broad electoral strength. It can influence decision-making on the administrative as well as on the congressional level. And it can give the right the means to defend its interests that are more compatible with the "modernization" of both the social and political systems.

Political Development and Military
Intervention in Latin America

————— ◆•◆ —————

Martin C. Needler

It is noteworthy that the recent spate of writings in the field of
"political development" has shown a pronounced tendency to
omit consideration of Latin America. Thus the "communications"
and "bureaucracy" volumes in the SSRC political development
series[1] are totally innocent of Latin America data, as is an excellent
recent treatment of—of all things!—the political behavior of the
military in developing areas.[2]

The Latin Americanists, for their part, have largely stressed
those key features of the area's politics which have long remained
constant—executive predominance, military intervention, and the
influence of the peculiarities of Hispanic culture. At the same time,
it is clear that the social changes usually collectively termed
"modernization"—urbanization, technological borrowing, and the
development of mass communications grids—together with their
political correlate, the expansion of the political community to
include hitherto excluded social elements, are proceeding in Latin
America too.[3] Accordingly, it becomes desirable to reexamine the

From Martin C. Needler, "Political Development and Military Intervention
in Latin America," *American Political Science Review,* LX (September 1966),
pp. 616–626. Reprinted by permission.

[1] Lucian W. Pye (ed.), *Communications and Political Development* (Prince-
ton: Princeton University Press, 1963); and Joseph La Palombara (ed.),
Bureaucracy and Political Development. (Princeton: Princeton University
Press, 1963).

[2] Morris Janowitz, *The Military in the Political Development of New Nations* (Chicago: University of Chicago Press, 1964).

[3] Karl W. Deutsch, "Social Mobilization and Political Development," this
REVIEW, 55 (September, 1961), 493–514; Bruce M. Russett *et al. World Handbook of Social and Political Indicators* (New Haven: Yale University Press,
1964), esp. pp. 294–298.

"statics" of Latin American politics in the light of the "dynamics" of the processes of political development and social mobilization.[4]

The present article attempts this reexamination with respect to the most characteristic feature of Latin American politics, the coup d'état and the establishment of a de facto military government.[5]

A priori, mutually contradictory theses about the relations of the military coup to social development can be constructed—and indeed the literature on the subject abounds in such contradictory theses, evidence to support each of which is always available.[6] These hypotheses focus on whether military intervention in politics, represented most typically by the extra-constitutional seizure of power, is (a) increasing or decreasing, and (b) occurring primarily with the object of promoting socio-economic change or of resisting it. Their starting points are the changes assumed to be going forward in the armed forces—the growth of professionalism, recruitment from a wider range of the population, greater influence from the United States, etc.

Now if evidence can be cited on either side of a proposition

[4] Two exceptions to the general lack of attempts to relate static and dynamic factors in a systematic way are the very fine article by Gino Germani and Kalman H. Silvert entitled "Politics, Social Structure, and Military Intervention in Latin America," *European Journal of Sociology,* 2 (1961), 62–81; and Karl M. Schmitt and David Burks, *Evolution or Chaos: Dynamics of Latin American Government and Politics* (New York: Praeger, 1963).

[5] This article forms part of a larger work currently in progress. I wish to thank the Horace H. Rackham Graduate School of the University of Michigan for the Faculty Summer Research Fellowship which enabled me to begin work on this subject, and the Harvard Center for International Affairs for the appointment as Research Associate which is enabling me to bring it to completion. I also wish to express my gratitude to Walter C. Soderlund, a doctoral candidate at the University of Michigan, whose research is reflected in the statistical data reported here.

[6] A series of such pairs of mutually contradictory hypotheses drawn from the literature is neatly formulated by Lyle N. McAlister in his contribution to John J. Johnson (ed.), *Continuity and Change in Latin America* (Stanford: Stanford University Press, 1964), pp. 158–159. Some authors point out the evidence that various mutually opposed tendencies exist without attempting to subsume them in some general formulation. This is Johnson's own approach: see his *The Military and Society in Latin America* (Stanford: Stanford University Press, 1964), Introduction and Chapter IX; and also that of Irving Horowitz, "United States Policy and the Latin American Military Establishment," *The Correspondent,* Autumn 1964. Lieuwen reconciles opposing tendencies by means of positing cycles in which a set of trends in one direction is succeeded by a countervailing set; see his *Arms and Politics in Latin America,* rev. ed., (New York: Praeger, 1961), esp. Chapter V.

about developmental tendencies, it is clearly necessary to quantify these items of evidence along a time dimension; what is needed, accordingly, are empirical data giving the change in the frequencies of the occurrence of each of the contrasting possibilities over time.

The empirical questions we want answered, therefore, are:

(1) Since the breakdown of early twentieth-century stability began the current period of change in Latin America, have coups d'état become more or less frequent?

(2) What changes have been occurring in the function of the coup in relation to changes taking place in the larger society?

(3) What are the effects of changes in the Latin American military on the form, structure, and timing of the coup d'état, and what political significance do these effects have?

INCIDENCE OF COUPS D'ÉTAT

One must first eschew the hopeless task of trying to account for coups d'état that were not successful. The categories of coups that were aborted, suppressed, or abandoned melt into each other and into a host of other non-coup phenomena so as to defy accounting. At the same time, of course, since coups are after all illegal, they are matured under conditions of secrecy which make it inevitable that the unsuccessful projects for coups which become known about represent a highly biased sample. At the same time, an unsuccessful coup attempt may be the work of one or two atypical people; its occurrence does not necessarily say anything about the state of the polity as a whole, as does a successful coup.

During the thirty-year period 1935–1964, there were 56 successful changes of government by extra-constitutional means in the twenty independent countries of Latin America. The frequency of their occurrence was as shown in Table 1.

That is, the number of successful coups normally fluctuates between one and three per year. The clearly exceptional period was that from 1938 to 1942, during which only a single coup took place.

The first explanation which suggests itself is that these were years of recuperation from depression in which economic conditions were improving and the performance of government was

TABLE 1.   FREQUENCY OF SUCCESSFUL COUPS D'ETAT IN LATIN AMERICA,
BY YEAR, 1935–1964

1935	1	1945	2	1955	2
1936	3	1946	2	1956	2
1937	3	1947	1	1957	1
1938	0	1948	4	1958	1
1939	0	1949	4	1959	1
1940	0	1950	1	1960	1
1941	1	1951	2	1961	2
1942	0	1952	2	1962	2
1943	2	1953	1	1963	4
1944	6	1954	3	1964	2

likely to be regarded as satisfactory.[7] One would then hypothesize
that a successful coup or revolt is less likely when economic conditions are improving.

A very rough test of this hypothesis can be made on the basis of
figures for annual changes in real per capita product given in the
UN Statistical Yearbooks for the 1947–1963 period.

It should be borne in mind, here and at subsequent points, that
statistical data from Latin America leave much to be desired. It
should also be noted that the data are not complete. However, data
are available, for most of the years during that period, for ten
countries in which coups d'etat occurred.

During 1947–63, it is possible to assert, real per capita income
figures for these countries showed a rise over the previous year's
figure 87 times, a drop 39 times, and remained the same ten times.
(These figures cannot be assumed to be typical of Latin America
as a whole, it should be noted, since it is precisely the countries
whose economies are likely not to be improving which do not
report reliable economic statistics.) If coups d'etat occurred without relation to the state of the economy, one would then expect at
least twice as many coups to have occurred in years which showed
improvement as in those which showed deterioration, since there
were more than twice as many "improvement years" as "deterioration years." However, that is not the case. Of the fifteen coups

[7] Edwin Lieuwen discusses the relation between the depression and military
intervention in "Militarism and Politics in Latin America," in John J. Johnson
(ed.), *The Role of the Military in Underdeveloped Countries* (Princeton:
Princeton University Press, 1962).

occurring during years for which the economic data are available, seven took place during years which showed an improvement, seven during years of deterioration, and one when no change was reported. The incomplete nature of the evidence should be stressed; in future years more complete calculations will doubtless be possible; other factors, not now identifiable, may be partly responsible; but the available data are consistent with the hypothesis postulated, that the overthrow of a government is more likely when economic conditions worsen.[8]

It seems reasonable, accordingly, to regard the years of low coup activity from 1938 to 1942 as due to the economic recovery of that period. Since 1949, a very slight secular trend in the reduction of the frequency of coups may be discernible. Since economic conditions are generally improving, although irregularly, this too might be expected on the basis of the same premise. Yet it should be remembered that variation in economic conditions can be held responsible for only a part of the variation in the frequency of coups as, the data discussed above also show.

COUPS D'ÉTAT AND SOCIAL
AND POLITICAL CHANGE

We turn now to the question of changes in the function of the coup in relation to social and political change. This question is extremely awkward to get at, since the origins of coups are often obscure, and the intentions of those staging them mixed. The author nevertheless believes it sound to explain the coup functionally rather than genetically, or in terms of factors external to the military rather than of internal characteristics of the military establishment, because of several considerations.

First, a military coup is not made by the military alone. Almost invariably, the conspirators are in touch with civilian politicians and respond to their advice, counting on their assistance in justifying the coup to public opinion and helping to run the country afterwards. This relationship not infrequently takes the form of

[8] It should not be thought that economic conditions always worsen as a result of a coup. At least as commonly, in the writer's experience, conditions improve as business confidence shows an upsurge after a coup, which normally occurs without appreciable economic dislocation and typically removes a government regarded as incompetent.

a coup only reluctantly staged by the military at the insistence of
civilian politicians, who appeal to the officers' patriotism, the historic role of the army in saving the country at its hour of need—
of which national history doubtless affords many examples—and so
on.[9] The chairman of one military junta which had outstayed its
welcome spoke bitterly of some of its latter-day detractors "who
used to cry at the doors of the barracks asking that the constitutional government be removed and even used to complain about
the apathy of the military who did not want to act."[10]

Second, among the various conspirators, with their varying
orientations and objectives, the position of those who can most
count on outside support, whose own objectives are most in har-
mony with the aims of major outside forces, will be strengthened.

Third, the autonomy of the military decision to intervene may
further be reduced by the fact that the political situation to which
the military respond has been "engineered" by outside groups
desiring intervention so as to trigger military predispositions in that
direction. It is not unknown, for example, for Right-wing activists
to fake "Communist" terrorist attempts in order to help create an
atmosphere conducive to military intervention.[11]

If the military coup is thus frequently called into play by the
workings of the political system, what is its function in relation to
social and economic change? Clearly, its purpose must increasingly
be to thwart such change. This is so because the point of the coup
is to prevent from happening what, it is assumed, would happen in
its absence.[12]

[9] McAlister argues in favor of this "revisionist" approach, which regards
military intervention as chiefly a response to functional imperatives rather
than as an expression of willful selfishness, in "Changing Concepts of the
Role of the Military in Latin America," *The Annals* (July 1965), pp. 90–92.

[10] Admiral Ramón Castro Jijón, quoted in the *Diario Las Américas* (Miami),
May 28, 1964. For a detailed account of the creation of an interventionist
frame of mind on the part of the military, see Chapter V of my *Anatomy
of a Coup d'Etat: Ecuador, 1963*. Johnson gives an example from Brazil of
public incitement of the military to revolt by civilians on p. 124 of his *The
Role of the Military in Developing Societies*. Finer discusses the interventionist
mood in Chapter 5 of *The Man on Horseback*.

[11] For one such case of which the author has personal knowledge, see
Anatomy of a Coup d'Etat: Ecuador, 1963, p. 19.

[12] This is also Lieuwen's view: "On the balance, the armed forces have
been a force for the preservation of the *status quo;* their political interven-
tion has generally signed, as it does today, a conservative action. . . ." Edwin
Lieuwen, "The Military: A Force for Continuity or Change," in John
TePaske and Sydney N. Fisher (eds.), *Explosive Forces in Latin America*
(Columbus: Ohio State University Press, 1964), p. 77.

Since social mobilization is proceeding, that is, constitutional presidents are likely to be responsive to social classes of progressively lower status, as these enter the political arena by moving to the city or otherwise become mobilized. The policies of each successive constitutional president are thus likely, on balance, to constitute a greater threat to the status quo than those of his predecessor. This may be interpreted to the military by those trying to secure their intervention as a threat to the personal interests of military officers in the economy at large, as a challenge to the military in its role of preserver of domestic order, or, most likely, as a long-term threat to the special status and privileges, and even the continued existence, of the military institution.[13]

It thus seems probable that as social and economic development take place:

(1) military intervention increasingly takes the form of an attempt by the possessing classes to maintain the status quo;

(2) military intervention is increasingly directed against legally elected presidents heading constitutional regimes;

(3) interventions increasingly occur to forestall the election and inauguration of reforming presidents; and

(4) popular resistance to military intervention increases, resulting in greater likelihood that a military coup will lead to open fighting.

An analysis of the 56 successful insurrections[14] which occurred in the 20 countries of Latin America during the thirty-year period 1935–1964 appears to confirm each of these hypotheses, and thus

[13] It is the conclusion of Lieuwen's insightful *Generals Vs. Presidents* (New York: Praeger, 1964), pp. 101–107, that the last factor mentioned has been the crucial one in the recent coups.

[14] Successful insurrections took place during the period in Argentina: June 1943, February 1944, September 1955, and March 1962;

Bolivia: May 1936, July 1937, December 1943, July 1946, May 1951, April 1952, and November 1964;

Brazil: October 1945, August 1954, November 1955, and April 1964;

Colombia: June 1953 and May 1957;

Costa Rica: March 1948;

Cuba: March 1952 and January 1959;

Dominican Republic: September 1963;

Ecuador: August 1935, October 1937, May 1944, August 1947, November 1961, and July 1963;

El Salvador: May 1944, October 1944, December 1948, October 1960, and January 1961;

to substantiate the argument made above. Table 2 gives the numbers and percentages of insurrections during each of the three decades of the period in which:

(1) The reformation of the social and economic status quo was clearly a goal of the conspiratorial group; this shows a decrease.

(2) A low level of violence (essentially a bloodless coup without streetfighting or other popular involvement) was maintained; this also decreases.

(3) Constitutional, rather than de facto governments were overthrown; this shows an increase.

(4) The insurrection occurred during the 12 months prior to a scheduled presidential election, or in the four months immediately following; this likewise increased.

DYNAMICS OF COUPS D'ÉTAT

Even if it be granted that the major determinants of the occurrence of a successful coup lie in the functioning of the total political system rather than in the internal dynamics of the military institution, those dynamics are of significance in such questions as the timing of the coup, and become especially important in determining the directions followed after the coup is successful and its leaders installed in government positions.

An examination of this problem must start from an appreciation of the fact that officers of the armed forces are not dominated by a single political viewpoint, but hold a variety of political orientations. The correlates of these political orientations in personal characteristics have not as yet been systematically evaluated and weighed for the Latin American military, along the lines of Morris Janowitz's *The Professional Soldier*.[15] However, available evidence suggests that on top of a primary set of conditioning factors such as those

---

Guatemala: July 1944, October 1944, June 1954, and March 1963;
Haiti: January 1946, May 1950, and December 1956;
Honduras: October 1956 and October 1963;
Nicaragua: June 1936;
Panama: October 1941, November 1949, and May 1951;
Paraguay: February 1936, August 1937, June 1948, January 1949, September 1949, May 1954;
Peru: October 1949 and July 1962;
Venezuela: October 1945, November 1948, and January 1958.

[15] Morris Janowitz, *The Professional Soldier* (New York: Free Press, 1964).

which the American voting studies indicate are significant in party preference—that is, family tradition, social and economic level, and ethnic or other particularistic identification—is imposed a second set of factors peculiar to the military profession: rank, branch of service, occupational specialty, and career pattern. In a situation in which a coup d'état becomes a possibility, ranking military officers are called on to develop policy positions on the question of the continuance in office of the president. The position each officer assumes will have two components, one based on attitudes towards the president's personal abilities, his programs, and the arrangements he is making for the succession; the other, partially independent of the first, reflecting the officer's views on the question of military intervention in polities in general.

TABLE 2.   STATISTICS OF SUCCESSFUL INSURRECTIONS, BY DECADES, 1935–1964

	1935–1944		*1945–1954*		*1955–1964*	
	No.	*%*	*No.*	*%*	*No.*	*%*
Total	16	100	22	100	18	100
(1) Reformist	8	50	5	23	3	17
(2) Low in Violence	13	81	15	68	6	33
(3) Overthrew Constitutional Governments	2	12	7	32	9	50
(4) Around Election Time	2	12	7	32	10	56

The changes which have been taking place in Latin American armed forces in recent years suggest that the variety of political views represented within the military services has been on the increase, as the social origins from which officers are drawn have become less upper-class,[16] as the range of military technical specialties has been extended, and as the sheer size of military establishments has increased.[17] At the same time the increasing complexity

[16] Medina Echevarría states flatly that the officers seizing power today "come, practically without exception, from hard-working middle-class families"; José Medina Echevarría and Benjamin Higgins, *Social Aspects of Economic Development in Latin America* (UNESCO: Paris, 1963), vol. II, p. 88.

[17] The evidence for these developments is summarized by Edwin Lieuwen in Chapter 5 of *Arms and Politics in Latin America,* rev. ed. (New York: Praeger, 1961), pp. 122–153. If one thought solely in terms of these factors,

of the governmental apparatus and the steady expansion of the proportion of the population which participates in politics, together with the technical improvement in the means of communication, have meant that a military coup needs itself to be more complex, to be more carefully planned, and to involve more people if it is to be successful. Because of heightened popular involvement in politics, a coup is also more likely to lead to open fighting, rather than being accepted passively by an indifferent population. Given the range of political orientations within the military services, then, the task of the organizer of a successful coup d'état is thus to build up a coalition of officers of a size and character adequate to execute the successful coup. The prime mover or movers in organizing the coup must therefore be engaged over a period of time in the process of building a coalition which will eventually exceed, in size and "weight,"[18] the minimum necessary to insure success.

The originators of the conspiracy and the first to join it are those most opposed to the president and his policies, while other officers of different political orientations and a greater commitment to constitutional procedures have higher thresholds to interventionism. However, as time goes on, these thresholds will be reached for many officers as the tendency of the president's policies becomes clearer, as the country's situation, seen from their point of view, worsens, or as the succession problems becomes more acute with the approach of the end of the president's term.

It is of course possible that as time goes on the changes which take place in the situation are such as to reduce the degree of hostility to the president on the part of the organizers of the conspiracy, which may then disintegrate. It seems clear, however, that a successful coup would show a curve of support within the ranks of the military, rising over time and beginning with the original instigator of the plot, who represents the most extreme opposition to the president. The development of the curve of military support for the coup is likely to be exponential as the end

---

as some authors do, regarding military political activity exclusively as being "pushed" by pressures internal to the military, rather than being also "pulled" by the demands of the total political situation, then it would be logical to expect these changes to result in greater professionalism and technicism, reducing military involvement in politics, and in greater sympathy with the lower classes, rendering such involvement more progressive in orientation. Although several authors have assumed viewpoints of this type, they do not appear substantiated by the evidence cited above.

[18] The concept of "weight" is discussed below.

of the president's term approaches. Under normal conditions the president prepares to hand over power to a successor of his own party or orientation, sometimes using not only his personal influence but also extra-legal techniques to guarantee the succession. This raises the prospect of another four or six years of the same policies; yet the trepidation of those who oppose them necessarily increases. The heir-apparent is in part an unknown quantity, which is disquieting; his previous public service will normally have taken place as a member of the president's cabinet, in which his own views necessarily had to be subordinated to those of his chief.

If there is a chance that the heir-apparent would be defeated in the elections, the conspirators may await their outcome before striking. If he is indeed defeated, the need for conspiracy disappears; if he is elected, it then becomes necessary to strike before his inauguration, since his actual occupancy of the presidency would enable him to consolidate his power. Yet it is risky to wait until after the elections, which will mobilize his supporters and which may give him a strong mandate and thus strengthen his position with domestic and foreign opinion.

Thus, for these reasons also, the likelihood of a coup d'état could be expected to increase as a president's term wears on, reaching its high point prior to a scheduled election but remaining high until the inauguration of a new president, this tendency becoming more marked over time, in response not only to the accelerating social mobilization of the masses but also to the increases in the size, technical differentiation, and range of social origins of the officer corps.

Within the group of conspirators, then, a series of thresholds to interventionism is present, the lowest being that of the instigator (or group of instigators) of the plot, the highest being that of the last man (or group) to join in the coup before it is launched. The position of this hypothetical last adherent to the conspiracy is interesting to consider. If one recalls that the success of the coup is predicated on the formation of a decisive coalition to support it, then it is clear that the last adherent or set of adherents to the movement provided the critical margin of support, not just in its size, but especially in its "weight."

The importance of this hypothetical "swing man" in the situation, that is, may be due to any one of a series of factors—his personal influence within the armed forces; his prestige among the public; and/or his critical position in the command structure of the armed forces. It then becomes probable that because of his higher rank, greater prestige, and crucial importance for the coup, the "swing man" is placed at the head of the provisional government that emerges after the revolt is successful—as provisional president, as chairman of the ruling military junta, or as minister of the armed forces behind the façade of a civilian provisional government.[19]

An interesting and paradoxical situation is thus created. The "swing man" becomes the leading figure in the new government; yet he is the person who was least committed to the objectives of the coup, whose threshold to intervention was the highest of all the conspirators, and who was a last-minute addition to the conspiracy perhaps out of sympathy with, or not even aware of, the more fundamental aims of the group that hatched the original plan. Indeed, a situation can actually be created in which the head of the new government actually sympathized with the aims of the conspiracy not at all, but joined it at the last minute only to avoid pitting brother officers against each other, possibly precipitating a civil war.

These characteristics of the "swing man" can perhaps be made clearer by an illustration. A classical occupant of the role of "swing man" has been Marshal Castelo Branco of Brazil. A *New York Times* reporter described his position in the 1964 coup as follows:

"General Humberto de Alencar Castelo Branco has been called a 'general's general.' He rose to his present post of Army Chief of Staff after a long professional career in which he gained the high respect of his fellow officers but remained virtually unknown to the general public . . .

"In the present crisis, the soft-spoken general first played the role of the reluctant dragon in refusing to join the developing movement against President João Goulart. His scruples were the same as those of many other Brazilian officers: The Brazilian Army has a tradition of protecting legality and the Constitution, and General Castelo Branco was not eager to become involved in a coup against a constitutional President.

"But the general became convinced that the continuation of the Goulart regime would lead Brazil to chaos and possibly a sharp shift toward the extreme left. He then drafted a position paper,

[19] This set of dynamics is of course not peculiar to Latin America. Classic occupants of the role of "swing man," with local variations, have been Naguib in Egypt, Gürsel in Turkey, Aguiyi-Ironsi in Nigeria—or even de Gaulle in France.

the 'Castelo Branco analysis' that became the justification for the army's support of last week's rebellion.

"Such is the respect enjoyed by the short, stocky, bull-necked general, that his analysis served as the turning point in the hesitations of many commanders in the crisis over Mr. Goulart."[20]

Clearly, in this kind of situation ample material exists for a conflict to emerge within the new provisional government. The conflict develops along the following lines. The erstwhile "swing man," now, let us say, president of the provisional junta, regards the objectives of the coup as realized with the overthrow of the former president and begins to make preparations to return the country to constitutional normality and to hold elections. The original instigator of the coup and the group around him, on the other hand, resist this tendency and instead urge the necessity for the military to keep power for a longer period, to purge all sympathizers with the deposed president completely from public life, to outlaw his party indefinitely, and to restructure political life to make it impossible for the tendency which he represents again to come to power.

During the recent period the basic situation described above has been reproduced in reality most faithfully in Argentina, Brazil, and Peru, and with local variations in Guatemala, Ecuador, the Dominican Republic, and Honduras.

In Argentina this basic set of dynamics has played itself out again and again since the overthrow of Perón in 1955, the irreconcilable anti-Perón forces being known as the *colorados*, or "reds," whose most characteristic figure is Admiral Isaac Rojas.[21]

Due to the more amorphous character of politics in Brazil, the same basic situation crystallized more slowly. The opposition between the military irreconcilables and the heirs of Getúlio Vargas has nevertheless been waged intermittently for 10 years. The coup staged to prevent the inauguration of Kubitschek and Goulart in 1955 was unsuccessful; the coup designed to prevent the inaugura-

---

[20] "Man in the News," *New York Times,* April 6, 1964. Typographic errors in the original have been corrected.

[21] See Arthur Whitaker, *Argentine Upheaval* (New York: Praeger, 1956); Lieuwen, *Generals vs. Presidents,* pp. 10–25; James W. Rowe, *The Argentine Elections of 1963: An Analysis,* (Washington: Institute for the Comparative Study of Political Systems, n.d.), pp. 11–18; Peter G. Snow, "Parties and Politics in Argentina: The Elections of 1962 and 1963," *Midwest Journal of Political Science,* 9 (February, 1965), 1–36.

tion of Goulart as President in 1962 succeeded merely in having the powers of the presidency temporarily curtailed; only with the overthrow of Goulart in 1964 was the military anti-Getulista movement fully successful. After the successful revolt of 1964, the pattern described above became operative in its purest form, with conflict developing between the prestigious "swing man," Marshal Castelo Branco, metamorphosed into Provisional President, and the *linha dura*, the "hard line" of the irreconcilable military opposition to the heirs of Vargas.[22]

A similar process took place in Peru following the coup d'état of 1962. For 30 years the commanding officers of the armed forces had resisted the assumption of power by the revolutionary APRA movement, despite the fact that it commanded a majority, or at least a plurality, of the votes during the entire period. The party had begun in the 'twenties and 'thirties as a revolutionary Marxoid group, strongly anti-Yankee and prepared to use violence. During the 30-odd years of its sojourn in the wilderness, however, the party leadership, and especially the party's founder, Víctor Raúl Haya de la Torre, had "evolved" to a more moderate position of which anti-communism was the central principle. At the same time, in the search for a respectability which would allay the misgivings of the military about the party, APRA's major tactician, Ramiro Prialé, led the party into alliance with increasingly more conservative forces, culminating shortly after the 1962 presidential election in an entente with the forces of General Manuel Odría. This was clearly the ultimate stage of the party's evolution, since Odría was a former military dictator who had outlawed and persecuted the party during his period of office, and who had run his election campaign in 1962 on a militantly anti-APRA platform. Haya had gathered more votes than any of the other candidates in the presidential elections of 1962, although only a handful more than Fernando Belaúnde and fewer than the one-third of the vote necessary to prevent the election's being decided by Congress. However, the new Congress, due to the vagaries of the electoral system, heavily over-represented the APRA. Immediately following the election, the coup was staged, the leaders of the armed forces implausibly charging that the electoral results were vitiated by widespread fraud. In an unsuccessful last-minute attempt to avert the coup,

---

[22] See *Generals vs. Presidents,* pp. 69–85; and Phyllis Peterson, "Brazil: Institutionalized Confusion," in Martin C. Needler (ed.), *Political Systems of Latin America* (Princeton: Van Nostrand, 1964), pp. 473–477.

the APRA leadership announced that its congressional votes would go to General Odría in a self-sacrificing attempt to break the impasse and avert the breakdown of constitutional procedures.

This situation made possible the emergence of a more muted version of the split which occurred in the Argentine and Brazilian cases. The ranking officer of the military junta, General Ricardo Pérez Godoy, was willing to return the country to constitutionality on the basis of the APRA offer to have its congressmen vote for Odría. The two key younger members of the junta, Generals Lindley López and Vargas Prada, who had personal and family ties to Belaúnde, opposed this solution, which would enable the APRA to exact concessions, for example in the shape of posts in an Odría administration. Pérez Godoy was accordingly forced to resign and the reconstituted junta presided, during 1963, over elections in which, because of the withdrawal of two minor candidates, Belaúnde was successful.[23]

It appears overwhelmingly likely that as time goes on and popular participation in the processes of politics becomes greater, the Peruvian type of situation, in which over as long a period as necessary the popular choice is kept out of the presidency by repeated military intervention, will become increasingly common. As was suggested above, the pattern has extended itself to Argentina and Brazil already. Honduran politics seem to be moving in the same direction as the army has become increasingly committed against the Liberal party; the Guatemalan military staged their coup in 1964 to prevent the return to power of Juan José Arévalo; and the Dominican armed forces have clearly attempted to assume a similar position relative to Juan Bosch and the Dominican Revolutionary Party.

The logic of this type of situation suggests that the conflict between the most popular individual or party on the one hand, and the military irreconcilables on the other, tends to go on for some time, rather than being resolved by a single coup. This occurs for two reasons. In the military junta which forms after a coup, first of all, the irreconcilables normally are in a superior strategic position. The more moderate "swing man," whose prestige has entitled him to the chairmanship of the junta, may wish to restore constitutional processes as soon as possible. If this is likely to lead to the

[23] See *General vs. Presidents*, pp. 26–36; and M. C. Needler, "Peru Since the *Coup d'Etat*," *The World Today*, February, 1963.

coming to power of the individual or tendency originally vetoed by the coup, however, the position of the junta president becomes untenable. Although he occupies the position with most authority and he may have placed close associates in the cabinet, theirs are not the key posts under showdown conditions: the key posts belong to those in direct command of troops, that is, the minister of the armed forces, the three service commanders, and even the commanders in the field. Because of this lack of congruence between the positions of authority when affairs are moving smoothly and the positions of power when a split develops, it is normally easier in such a situation to stage a coup d'état than to prevent one.[24] The odds are therefore that the irreconcilables will be able to prevent the return to constitutionality for an extended period if this should seem likely to favor the archenemy.

Once military elements have vetoed the popular leader and his party, moreover, the hostility between the two becomes self-perpetuating and self-reinforcing, since those who participated in the original coup have reason to believe they will forfeit at least their careers, and perhaps more, if the outlawed party should ever gain power. As one Dominican colonel put it after the coup of 1963 when he was asked his attitude towards a return of Juan Bosch: "If Bosch ever comes back, he will throw me into jail so deep I will never find my way out." Because of this set of circumstances the restoration of constitutional procedures becomes extremely difficult: unless the distribution of voter sentiment changes drastically it is only too likely that the person or party which secured a majority in the last election would do as well in the next one. A temporary return to constitutionality may be possible on the basis of rigged or restricted elections, as has been the case in Argentina. Nevertheless, the Argentine political problem is not permanently solved. Given the persistence of the military irreconcilables and their point of view, the only permanent resolution of the problem lies in: (1) the definitive removal from the political scene of the vetoed leader by death or his renunciation of politics; (2) a shift in the distribution of popular opinion to the disadvantage of the vetoed party; or (3) the party's gaining respectability by drastic modification of its program or tactics. In Latin America, the third

---

[24] In one variant of this situation, the provisional president may save his own personal position by switching sides at the last minute and adopting the program of the "hard liners," if the forces they can marshal seem decisive. This tactic was adopted by Castelo Branco in early 1966.

alternative seems a formal possibility only, since the irreconcilables may simply refuse to believe that the shift towards respectability is genuine. Thus the military veto against the APRA was still applied in 1962, despite the party's evolution to a moderate Center or even Right-of-Center position. If the political problem has in fact been resolved in Peru—and this is not yet clear—it has been by way of the second alternative, in that the APRA may have been driven permanently below a third of the vote by a combination of disaffection from the Left as the party's leadership has grown more conservative, and the permanent establishment in popular favor of Belaúnde's *Acción Popular*. Elsewhere a similar result may be achieved, at least temporarily, by the expansion or contraction of the electorate to shift the balance of forces against the vetoed political movement—by giving the vote to resident aliens, for example, or by taking it away from illiterates.

CONCLUSIONS

This examination of the internal logic of the Latin American coup d'état in the circumstances of the current phase of history has so far led to three conclusions. First, the overthrow of a government is more likely when economic conditions are deteriorating. Second: as the military services have become larger and more various in the social origins of their officers, as military occupational specializations have become more differentiated and more highly professionalized, and as elections have become representative of the sentiments of a wider range of the population, coups d'état have tended increasingly to occur in the period immediately prior to a presidential election and the subsequent inauguration, to be conservative in policy orientation, to be directed against constitutional governments, and to be accompanied by violence. Third: the tendency has emerged for conflict to develop, following a coup d'état, between a more fundamentalist "hard line," and a "soft line" that shows greater readiness to restore constitutional procedures and is normally represented by officers of higher rank, occupying positions of greater prestige in the provisional government.

It is possible to draw a further conclusion, with policy implications for the United States, from this analysis. There has long existed a difference of opinion among students of U.S. foreign policy as to both the desirability and the feasibility of attempting to discourage military seizures of power in Latin America. The desirability argument is outside our present province,[25] but it is possible for us now to add something on the feasibility question—that is, how successful United States attempts to discourage military coups can be.

The failure of the United States to recognize a provisional government issuing from an extra-constitutional seizure of power, plus the imposition of other mild sanctions such as the suspension of military and economic aid, is of different effects to countries differently situated. The smaller countries whose economies are more dependent on actions of the United States—Bolivia, plus the countries of Central America and the Caribbean—are more susceptible to United States pressures than the larger South American countries. Nevertheless, examples can be cited of military coups which have taken place despite clear United States opposition, even in countries in the Caribbean area. These have been regarded as indicating that American opposition to such coups is ineffectual. The coup which took place in Peru in 1962, and the 1963 coups in Honduras and the Dominican Republic, for example, took place in the face of strong and explicit American opposition.

It still seems premature to conclude that American opposition to the military seizure of power is bound to be ineffectual, however. One problem here is methodological, since it is not possible to enumerate the coups d'état that did *not* take place (although in two countries where American influence is heavy and which have known a history of military seizures of power, Venezuela and Panama, the constitutional succession has in recent years been unbroken while other countries of the area were experiencing violent changes of government). If the analysis made above is correct, however, the success of a coup d'état depends, especially where the military services are large and highly differentiated, on the adherence to the coup in its later stages of officers least committed to its goals, less inclined to military intervention, and with more prestige and a higher position at stake. Since the success of the coup thus may well depend on its being joined by relatively few officers with a relatively weak commitment to its goals, it seems overwhelmingly likely that *any* deterrent to intervention—such as the suspension of military aid, or a credible threat not to recognize

[25] I have discussed it in "United States Recognition Policy and the Peruvian Case," *Inter-American Economic Affairs* (Spring, 1963).

the new government—while not sufficient to deter the hard-core organizers of the coup, may nevertheless be sufficient to tip the scales against intervention for the crucial "swing man," or for the small group occupying the same tactical position, and thus may cause the coup to be abandoned, or to be launched without adequate support and thus to prove abortive.

In the coup situation, accordingly, even the mildest deterrent threat, such as a firmly stated non-recognition policy on the part of the United States, may still be effective, because of the pre-coup balance of forces.

Light can also be thrown on the general problem raised in the opening section of the article, that of the relation between the constant features of Latin American politics and developmental trends, by an examination of the varying incidence over time of the characteristic military dictatorship in the area.

Here observers have tended to divide into the optimists, who perceive the evolutionary forces at work in the area as tending in a democratic direction, and the cynics, who take an attitude of "plus ça change . . . ." The incidence of military dictatorships in the area seems to support the views first of one group, then of the other. A few years after Tad Szulc published his *Twilight of the Tyrants*,[26] which celebrates the replacement of dictators by democratic regimes, Edwin Lieuwen can write a *Generals vs. Presidents*, which analyzes the reverse phenomenon.

The relation of cyclical and evolutionary patterns on this point can best be demonstrated by a graph. Figure 1 plots the number of unequivocally dictatorial regimes[27] in power during at least six months of each year over the period of the last 30 years during which evolutionary changes have clearly been occurring.[28]

Conclusions of great interest can be drawn. Clearly, the factors which produce military dictatorships seem in part cyclical. At the same time, the cyclical pattern reproduces itself around a clearly

[26] (New York: Holt, Rinehart and Winston, 1959).

[27] To be considered "dictatorial," a government:

(1) Had to be not an avowedly provisional regime holding office for 36 months or less;

(2) Had to come to power, or remain in power after the conclusion of the constitutionally prescribed term of office, by means other than a free and competitive election; or rule in clear disregard of constitutionally guaranteed liberties.

[28] The idea of approaching the problem in this fashion was suggested to the author by Ronald Schneider's article "The U. S. in Latin America" in *Current History* for January, 1965.

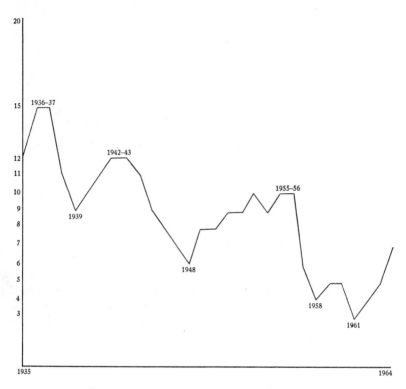

Fɪɢ. 1. Number of dictatorial governments in power in Latin America,
by year, 1935–1964.

descending trend line, so that each successive peak in the number
of dictatorships existing contemporaneously is lower than the last:
in 1936–37, there were fifteen dictatorships; in 1942–43, there were
twelve; in 1955–56, there were ten. Similarly, successively lower
levels of dictatorship are reached at each low point of the cycle: in
1939, nine dictatorships; in 1948, six; in 1961, three.

The conclusion seems inescapable that, in this respect as in the
others examined, while Latin American politics has certain abiding
characteristics which produce its distinctive features, these are being
progressively modified under the influence of forces of an evolutionary character.

Power Structure and Sociocultural Change in Latin American Communities*

Norman E. Whitten, Jr.

Throughout Latin America communities are changing and something does the changing. That something can be termed "power." Before defining power more explicitly the following quotation is offered to introduce a type case of a community in transition:

> In 1920 Chan Kom, like other folk societies, was composed of people all very similar in appearance, habit, and view of life. Like other such communities too, it conducted its affairs chiefly by the exercise of those diffuse controls which depend on personal relationships and are expressed in conversation, gesture, and ceremony. It was a community of people who had little to do with outsiders. The whole village was a single neighborhood made up of intermarried families. These statements could also be made of Chan Kom in 1931, with the additional statement that by that time, when the community was first studied, a simple but more formal structure of government, in the offices appropriate to a village recognized by the state and federal government, had been added. Then, in the following 17 years, many events occurred which might be expected to modify the simplicity of the social organiza-

From N. E. Whitten, "Power Structure and Socio-Cultural Change in Latin American Communities," *Social Forces,* Vol. 43, (March, 1965). Reprinted by permission.

* The author is deeply indebted to Professor Charles J. Erasmus for stimulating his interest in studying Latin American communities for the purpose of making inductive generalizations. This paper has benefited considerably from two critical readings by Dr. Erasmus. Professor John Gulick is also to be acknowledged for incisively commenting on an early version of the paper and for whetting the writer's interest in relationships between power structure and sociocultural change.

This investigation was supported by a Public Health Service Fellowship (14,333) from the National Institute of Mental Health, Public Health Service.

tion and of the mechanisms of social control: a growth in population; a great increase in communication, transportation, and commerce; and the achievement of the political status of a "free municipality."[1]

In order to systematically examine relationships between power structure and sociocultural change in Latin American communities, we shall explore the proposition that the critical link between national and local sociocultural systems lies in the degree of compatibility of the local and national power structures. Our basic hypothesis is:

As community power becomes increasingly rationalized, the local sociocultural system will become less parochial and increasingly similar to the national system.

Power is defined as the ability to influence activities;[2] ". . . its vigor presages further changes."[3] By community power we mean those resources which are used for influence in a given locality. *Rational* refers to the systematic centralized arrangement, secularization, and impersonalization of the ability to influence activities.[4]

Schermerhorn suggests reasons for focusing upon power:

For some years, sociologists have tended to think of society as a configuration or system kept in partial balance either by the reciprocal nature of social interaction . . . or by patterns of maintenance similar to those of an organism. . . . In either case the

[1] Robert Redfield, *A Village that Chose Progress: Chan Kom Revisited* (Phoenix ed.; Chicago: The University of Chicago Press, 1962, first published, 1950), p. 67.

[2] Max Weber, *From Max Weber: Essays in Sociology,* H. H. Gerth and C. Wright Mills trans. (New York: Oxford University Press, 1958), p. 184. For elaborate discussions cf., Bertrand Russell, *Power: A New Social Analysis* (London: Unwin Books, George Allen and Unwin Ltd.), and Harold D. Lasswell and Abraham Kaplan, *Power and Society: A Framework for Political Inquiry* (New Haven: Yale University Press, 1963), pp. 74–102.

[3] Richard A. Schermerhorn, *Society and Power* (New York: Random House, 1961), p. 13.

[4] This definition of 'rational' corresponds to the usages of Weber in Weber, *op. cit.,* pp. 51 and 293, and Schermerhorn, *op. cit.,* p. 7. 'Rational' is used in the sense of being the opposite of 'traditional.' We do not mean to denote, connote or imply anything about the psychological state of 'rational behavior.'

stability is taken as the point of departure and change is explained as the series of internal adjustments or readjustments by which social order is maintained. The study of power, however, reverses the emphasis by assuming that change is the starting point and the order or equilibrium is a by-product of the ceaseless quest for power by individuals, groups and institutions, and nations.[5]

In the October, 1961 issue of *Economic Development and Cultural Change*, a very provocative article by John H. Kunkel raises similar general issues regarding conditions of economic development and cultural change in Mexican villages. Central to the thesis of Kunkel's paper in his statement:

> If the economic role of contact in a community—or the degree of economic autonomy—determines the degree of consistency of social organization of village and of the nation, then social change in peasant communities cannot be considered apart from economic development.[6]

The case of Chan Kom leads us to question that primacy of the thesis propounded by Kunkel:

> . . . economic changes which bind the community to the nation effect changes in the social and cultural elements of the village, so that these elements become consistent with those of the nation; these changes, in turn, pave the way for the further economic development of both units.[7]

The simple assertion that economic change, like change in any sphere of sociocultural activity, produces changes in other areas is not at all in question. However, Kunkel presents his argument in terms of critical linkage. He argues that the link between the local sociocultural system and the national system is the economic one.[8]

We contend that, though Kunkel articulates the necessary condi-

---

[5] Schermerhorn, *Society and Power, op. cit.*, pp. 13–14.
[6] John H. Kunkel, "Economic Autonomy and Social Change in Mexican Villages," *Economic Development and Cultural Change*, 10:1 (1961), p. 63.
[7] *Ibid.*, p. 53.
[8] Kunkel, *loc. cit.*

tions of community incorporation into the national socioeconomic system, he does not delineate the sufficient conditions. We shall attempt to supplement, not attack, Kunkel's hypotheses by approaching the same general problem of community-nation relationships from a somewhat different direction. We will not recheck Kunkel's data and analysis of Mexican villages. Rather, this paper draws from a broad, though not particularly large, sample of Latin American communities. The size of the sample is directly related to the usefulness of data for our purposes found in various Latin American community studies.

Some evidence that sociocultural elements have certain direct, systematic linkages to power structure is pointed out by Redfield in his book, *A Village That Chose Progress*. By introducing two of his examples, we hope to show that relationships between power structure and sociocultural elements are not simple coincidence. For example, regarding settlement patterns, Redfield writes:

> Tradition associates authority and political dominance with this Spanish form of town. If the surrounding pueblos and *rancherias* were to accept Chan Kom as the seat of their government, Chan Kom not only must have buildings in which to hold its public meetings and its legal proceedings but must have the impressive appearance of the proper seat of such authority.[9]

Again, using our type case [Chan Kom] to supplement Kunkel's hypothesis, it is profitable to note that, rather than new economically sponsored wants, "a desire of the leaders of Chan Kom expressed early in the course of their political efforts 'to make a town' was the wish to bring music to Chan Kom."[10]

To systematically analyze such relationships as they exist in Latin America we have set up a *Power Structure Index* and a *Culture Element Index*. These will be discussed below along with the limitations inherent in each. The congruence of the two indices will be presented in tabular form and then discussed in terms of both direct and indirect (non-tabular) support for the hypothesis.

After discussing the indices, the sample, and the findings, attention will turn to the construction of a model of sociocultural change and power structure in Latin American communities.

[9] Redfield, *op. cit.*, pp. 27–30.
[10] *Ibid.*, p. 48.

THE INDICES, THE SAMPLE, AND THE FINDINGS

The Power Structure Index

Delineation of the components of the *Power Structure Index* involved the selection of variables which can be found in many Latin American community studies. The variables are phrased in terms of tendency toward rationality. Where the tendency is in this direction the variable in a given community is assigned a positive symbol indicated by an X. Where it is in the other direction, or has not yet begun to change, a negative (—) symbol is assigned. Some of the variables are phrased in more than one way to allow us to collate data which are congruent, but not identical, in their original monographic presentation. The five variables are:

1. The local political-government system (system of social control) is in some way oriented toward influencing national policies on behalf of the community or on behalf of certain members of the community and uses rational means to effect its influence. A rational power structure is utilized to maintain or change community culture in the face of national policy.

2. The local political-government system (system of social control) is not dependent for efficient functioning upon a religious institution. It does not require religious or supernatural backing. Ascension to office by a community member is not dependent on prior religious prominence.

3. Political officials and administrators are paid and there is a financial ranking of offices.

4. Individuals with competence in national activities have more political strength (more power) than those without. They have more social prestige.

5. There are voluntary non-religious associations with political impact.

The limitations are obvious:

A. No weights have been assigned to the various variables.

B. In some cases (e.g., early Chan Kom and Cantel) it is difficult to make a decision because the variables are at the turning point. However, such problems, though perhaps obscuring quantification, actually aid the construction of a dynamic model.

THE CULTURE ELEMENT INDEX

Since the province of the anthropologist is culture, it might be expected that the establishment of a simple culture element index applicable to all community studies would be an easy matter. Unfortunately, it turned out to be very difficult to select a culture element index which would subsume data from many community studies. The elements finally used in analysis are phrased in terms of national culture.

Like the *Power Structure Index*, some components are phrased in more than one way. Where an element in a given community tends toward the national form, it is assigned a positive symbol (X) and where it does not, it is assigned a negative one (—). The *Culture Element Index* represents the percentage of positive elements to total culture elements presented in the monographs. It is derived by the formula:

$$\text{Culture Element Index} = \frac{\text{positive elements}}{\text{total elements}} \times 100$$

The variables are:

1. People habitually dress in western clothes.

2. The religious institution follows international tradition. There is a minimum of parochialization.

3. People play national games and enjoy national, secular, recreation forms.

4. The national language is commonly used.

5. Literacy exists, at least in the upper segments.

6. Definitions of success follow rational economic lines. "Conspicuous giving"[11] is minimal.

7. "Invidious sanctions"[12] are not important mechanisms of social control. There is a minimum of "indirect coping behavior"[13] or magical forms of coercion in interpersonal affairs.

8. The number of "socially activated kin"[14] in economic activities is minimal. Normally, economic functions are performed individually, or through the nuclear family.

---

[11] Charles J. Erasmus, *Man Takes Control* (Minneapolis: University of Minnesota Press, 1961), pp. 101–134.

[12] *Ibid.*, p. 85.

[13] John J. Honigmann, *The World of Man* (New York: Harper & Bros., 1959), pp. 624–632.

[14] Roger D. Peranio, "Descent, Descent Line and Descent Group in Cognitive Systems," *Proceedings of the 1961 Annual Spring Meeting of the American Ethnological Society* (Seattle: 1961), p. 95.

9. House types and community settlement patterns tend to follow national patterns.

10. In general, status tends to be more achieved than ascribed. This implies a more flexible class structure.

The limitations are:

A. No weights have been assigned to the various variables.

B. The categories are very broad; as such they function primarily to indicate tendencies.

C. It is sometimes difficult to make a decision as to how to score a category in a given community. Where the writer of a monograph indicated a trend, we followed his judgment.

THE SAMPLE

Table 1 presents the data collated from 17 communities, two of which (Chan Kom and Tepoztlán) are used twice due to fortunate restudies.[15] The communities, listed in column one, represent sam-

[15] The following 17 community studies form the basis of this study: Aritama—Gerardo and Alicia Reichel-Dolmatoff, *The People of Aritama: The Cultural Personality of a Colombian Mestizo Village* (London: Rutledge & Kegan Paul, 1961). Buzios Island—Emilio Willems in cooperation with Giocônda Mussolini, *Buzios Island, A Caiçara Community in Southern Brazil* (Seattle: University of Washington Press, American Ethnological Society pub. 20, 1952). Cañamelar—Sydney Mintz, "Cañamelar: The Subculture of a Rural Sugar Plantation Proletariat," in Julian Steward (ed.), *The People of Puerto Rico: A Study in Social Anthropology* (Urbana: University of Illinois Press, 1956), pp. 314–417. Cantel—Manning Nash, *Machine Age Maya* (American Anthropological Association Memoir No. 87, 1958). Chan Kom—Robert Redfield, *A Village that Chose Progress: Chan Kom Revisited* (Phoenix ed.; Chicago: The University of Chicago Press, 1962, first published, 1950); Robert Redfield and Alfonso Villa Rojas, *Chan Kom, A Maya Village* (Phoenix ed.; Chicago: The University of Chicago Press, 1962, first published by the Carnegie Institution of Washington, 1934). Chichicastenango—Ruth Bunzel, *Chichicastenango, A Guatemalan Village* (Seattle: University of Washington Press, American Ethnological Society Publication, 22, 1952). Muquiyauyo— Richard N. Adams, *A Community in the Andes: Problems and Progress in Muquiyauyo* (Seattle: University of Washington Press, American Ethnological Society, unnumbered series, 1959). Nayón—Ralph L. Beals, "Acculturation, Economics and Social Change in an Ecuadorean Village," in Sol Tax (ed.), *Acculturation in the Americas* (Chicago: The University of Chicago Press, 1952), Vol. 2. Nocorá—Elena Padilla Seda, "Nocorá: The Subculture of Workers on a Government-Owned Sugar Plantation," in Julian Steward (ed.), *The People of Puerto Rico . . .* , op. cit., pp. 265–313. Peguche—Elsie Clews Parsons, *Peguche, A Study of Andean Indians* (Chicago: The University of Chicago Press, 1945). Potam—Edward H. Spicer, *Potam: A Yaqui Village in Sonora* (American Anthropologist Memoir No. 77, 1954). San José—Eric

ples from many areas of Latin America: Puerto Rico (4), Mexico (3), Guatemala (2), Colombia (2), Ecuador (3), Peru (1), Brazil (1), and Paraguay (1). Column two contains the total number of traits found in the monograph, and the third column gives the *Culture Element Index*, the percentage of positive, i.e., national, to total elements. The communities are arranged in descending order of national culture content.

The relationship of the power structure variables to the *Culture Element Index* can be seen under the five columns of the *Power Structure Index*.

THE FINDINGS

The findings of this survey indicate a correlation between our two indices. The hypothesis, is, then, at least in part, supported by the tabular representation of relationship. We must now ask whether an emerging rational power structure is indeed *crucial* to the development of national culture elements.

In the segment of the table including the communities with a *culture element index* of between 70 and 100 (nine communities in all), eight have 100 percent of the power elements discernable from the monographs and only one lacks one. From this it would appear that a rational power structure does precede 100 percent development of national culture elements. Some interesting facets of sociocultural change in these communities may be noted here. For example, Nayón, an Ecuadorian Indian community just outside

---

Wolf, "San José Subculture of a 'traditional' Coffee Municipality," in Julian Steward (ed.), *The People of Puerto Rico* . . . , *op. cit.*, pp. 171–265. San Lorenzo—Norman E. Whitten, Jr., *An Analysis of Social Structure and Change: Profile of a Northwest Ecuadorian Town* (unpublished Ph.D. dissertation, University of North Carolina; Ann Arbor, University Microfilms, 1964). Saucio—Orlando Fals-Borda, *Peasant Society in the Colombian Andes: A Sociological Study of Saucio* (Gainesville: University of Florida Press, 1955). Tabara—Robert Manners, "Tabara: Subcultures of a Tobacco and Mixed Crops Municipality," in Julian Steward (ed.), *The People of Puerto Rico* . . . , *op. cit.*, pp. 93–170. Tepoztlán—Oscar Lewis, *Life in a Mexican Village: Tepoztlán Restudied* (Urbana: University of Illinois Press, 1951); Oscar Lewis, "Medicine and Politics in a Mexican Village," in Benjamin D. Paul (ed.), *Health, Culture and Community* (New York: Russell Sage Foundation, 1955), pp. 403–434; Oscar Lewis, *Tepoztlán: Village in Mexico* (New York: Henry Holt and Company, 1960); Robert Redfield, *Tepoztlán: A Mexican Village* (Chicago: The University of Chicago Press, 1930). Tobati —Elman and Helen Service, *Tobati: Paraguayan Town* (Chicago: The University of Chicago Press, 1954).

TABLE 1

Communities	Number of Traits	Culture Element Index	Power Structure Index				
			1	2	3	4	5
Muquiyauyo	9	100	x	x	x	x	x
Nayón	7	100	x	x	x	?	?
Chan Kom (1948)	10	90	x	x	x	x	x
Tabara	10	90	x	x	x	x	x
Cañamelar	9	77	x	x	x	x	x
Tobati	9	77	—	x	x	x	x
San Lorenzo	8	75	x	x	x	x	x
Nocorá	10	70	x	x	x	x	x
Tepoztlán (1940's)	10	70	x	x	x	x	x
Aritama	10	50–60[a]	—	—	x	—	x
Cantel	7	48	x[b]	—	?	—	x
San José	10	40	—	x	x	—	—
Buzios Island	9	33	—	—	—	—	—
Tepoztlán (1926–27)	10	30	—	—	x	—	—
Peguche	9	22	—	—	—	—	—
Saucio	10	20	—	x	x	—	—
Chichicastenango	10	20	x	—	x	—	—
Potam	7	14	—	—	x[b]	—	—
Chan Kom (1931)	10	10	x[b]	x[b]	x[b]	—	—

[a] Split between two orientations.
[b] Just beginning to change in the direction indicated.

of Quito, ". . . is almost completely by-passing the Mestizo culture . . . ."[16] Regarding Muquiyauyo, we find that:

> . . . for perhaps the first time in Peruvian history (and in much of Latin America) a small, agriculturally oriented community developed a political administration which was designed for and adjusted to the needs of a specific town population.[17]

Power is San Lorenzo is summarized as follows:

> . . . it can be asserted that the structure moved toward increasing rationalization while at the same time expanding traditional ways of getting things done . . . rationalization of the structure effectively connects the west Ecuadorian community and the greater Ecuadorian society, while the traditional aspects of the structure get things done within the community. Rationalization is a community-nation link, while traditionalism is an intracommunity means of noncoercive social control and social manipulation.[18]

Tobati lacks one power trait. Its power seems locally oriented. It does not function conjunctively with the national system so as to benefit the town. Rather, it follows the caudillo pattern.[19] In the caudillo pattern the structure functions to further individual rather than group acquisition of power. Rational means are used to exploit the community through graft. The caudillo pattern usurps a rational structure to further unsanctioned, personal power.

The communities manifesting a *Culture Element Index* of less than 70 show a less clear relationship between the two indices. In order to fully explore our hypothesis we shall set forth appropriate features of these communities before constructing a model of sociocultural change and power structure. The communities to be discussed include, in the order in which they will be considered, Chan Kom (1931), Potam, Chichicastenango, Saucio, Peguche, Tepoztlán (1926–27), Buzios Island, San José, Cantel and Aritama.

---

[16] Ralph L. Beals, "Acculturation, Economics and Social Change in an Ecuadorian Village," in Sol Tax (ed.), *Acculturation in the Americas,* (Chicago: The University of Chicago Press, 1952), Vol. 2, p. 73. By Mestizo culture he refers to that complex of traits delineated by John Gillin, "Mestizo America," in Ralph Linton (ed.), *Most of the World* (New York: Columbia University Press, 1947), pp. 156–211.

[17] Adams, *A Community in the Andes* . . . , *op. cit.,* p. 49.

[18] Whitten, *An Analysis of Social Structure* . . . , *op. cit.,* p. 314.

[19] Service and Service, *Tobati* . . . , *op. cit.,* pp. 290–291. For a full analysis of this pattern in Ecuador, see George I. Blanksten, *Ecuador: Constitutions and Caudillos* (Berkeley: University of California Press, 1951).

Chan Kom. "Chan Kom, primitive though it is in many respects, formed a public policy to change itself and thereafter bent its efforts to bring about this change."[20] A glance at the table will show that, although in 1931 Chan Kom was characterized by a 60 percent rational power structure, the only national culture element was slight literacy among the elite.[21] Redfield is more eloquent: "The years 1930–1931 marked the apogee of the spirit of progress."[22] The spirit of progress, then, *was first marked in political life.* It subsequently was felt in the economic sphere and spread throughout the sociocultural system. That rapid change did indeed take place is well illustrated in the restudy of 1948.

Redfield is careful to demonstrate that a more radical ethos prevailed while the political system was in a state of change and that conservative values were reasserted when the change had taken place. "The radicalism that prevailed 17 years ago is forgotten or ignored."[23] Interestingly enough, Adams, too, finds this a characteristic of Muquiyauyo.[24]

Potam is a true "closed corporate community."[25] Its power structure is oriented toward maintaining a schism between national Mexican and local folk culture by remaining removed from the local Mexican municipal government.[26]

Chichicastenango. In Chichicastenango the *Culture Element Index* manifests a low of 20 percent but the *Power Structure Index* contains two rational variables of power. The two elements indicating rationality are: (1) the power structure is oriented toward manipulating those political aspects conjoining town and union, and (2) officials are paid.

In explaining the existence of these variables in Chichicastenango we gain an insight into why the culture elements tend away from

[20] Redfield, *op. cit.,* p. 23.
[21] *Ibid.,* p. 31.
[22] *Ibid.,* p. 113.
[23] *Ibid.,* pp. 113–14.
[24] Adams, *op. cit.,* p. 105.
[25] The concept of a "closed corporate community" type is that developed by Eric Wolf. See his "Types of Latin American Peasantry: A Preliminary Discussion," *American Anthropologist,* 57: 3 (1955), pp. 452–471; and "Closed Corporate Peasant Communities in Mesoamerica and Central Java," *Southwestern Journal of Anthropology,* 13 (1957), pp. 1–18.
[26] Spicer, *Potam . . . , op. cit.,* p. 110.

the national types. First, and most importantly, the power structure functions to keep the national culture *out* and maintains indigenous culture elements.[27] Though officials are paid, those functioning on the Indian community level must pay out more than
they earn.[28]

Chichicastenango is characterized by patterns antithetical to those
developing in Chan Kom in 1931. For example, the combination of
individual wealth plus an ignorance of Spanish, plus a record of
service to the parochialized Catholic church is the principal vehicle
to the attainment of power.[29] The quasi-rationality of Chichicastenango power structure seems to stem from the fact that superim-
posed upon the Indian system is a mestizo system governed by a
national bureaucratic structure. The Indian system articulates with
the imposed structure in a manner which utilizes elements of the
rational structure to maintain its own sociocultural configuration
by keeping national influences out. It, like Potam, is an excellent
example of the closed corporate community type.

Our hypothesis is not contradicted by the superficial inconsistency in the two indices. It is actually supported in that we can
now see the difference between a community manipulating an
imposed rational power structure and one actually developing
one; the difference is precisely the difference between Chan Kom
and Chichicastenango: a difference between openness and closure.

Saucio. Like Chichicastenango the rational components in
Saucio are not an evidence of movement toward the establishment
of a rational power structure and national culture but rather may
indicate an attempt to maintain elements of folk culture.[30] Though
politics has become the focal point for the struggle for existence in
Saucio, political goals are not impersonal but rather personal as
manifested in an orientation toward vengeance.[31]

Another facet of the community dynamics of Saucio, not well-
documented in the other studies, is the emigration taking place.
There has been a steady population decrease since 1938 due to
emigration.[32] In our model we shall discuss the role that population
factors play in the development of the community.

[27] Bunzel, *Chichicastenango* . . . , *op. cit.,* pp. 12–13.
[28] *Ibid.,* pp. 186–189.
[29] *Ibid.,* pp. 67–69, 77, 89–91, 186–189.
[30] Fals-Borda, *Peasant Society in the Colombian Andes* . . . , *op. cit.,* p. 241.
[31] *Ibid.,* p. 210.
[32] *Ibid.,* pp. 58–63.

Peguche.   About Peguche, there is little to say. It fits perfectly into the category of closed corporate, or folk oriented community.

Tepoztlán.   Tepoztlán fitted the closed community type when Redfield first studied it in 1926–27. By the time Oscar Lewis made his famous restudy, Tepoztlán, like Chan Kom, had rationalized its power structure and undergone concomitant sociocultural change in the direction of acquiring national elements.[33]

Buzios Island.   The community on Buzios Island offers data more interesting to dwell upon. There are no rational elements in the power structure. The culture on the whole is folk oriented—the exception being the elements of economic behavior. We find that success is defined along rational economic lines and that there is a minimal number of socially activated kin[34] functioning in economic activities.[35] The economy on the island, though primitive, is nevertheless oriented toward the national success values. Significantly, for our analysis, the individuals most motivated toward rational economic activities are emigrating toward areas presumably characterized by a more rational power structure.[36]

San José.   San José, one of the four Puerto Rican communities studied in conjunction with the insular research conducted by Julian Steward, *et al.*,[37] is characterized by a 40 percent national culture. Unlike Tabara, Cañamelar and Nocorá, it lagged in the development of a rational power structure. The power structure of San José was just beginning to rationalize at the time of the study. The reasons given for this process was that Muños Marín went out to the common people and met them in their folk element. "The political behavior of the party leader conforms to cultural norms with which the country people are familiar in the local context of barrio life; . . ."[38]

The developing power structure, unlike Chan Kom's, came about by first conforming to the folk oriented rural way of life. The

[33] Lewis, *Life in a Mexican Village* . . . , *op. cit.*; "Medicine and Politics . . . ," *op. cit.*; *Tepoztlán* . . . , *op. cit.*

[34] Peranio, "Descent, Descent Line . . . , *loc. cit.*

[35] Willems, *Buzios Island* . . . , *op. cit.*, pp. 1–9, 25, 43–55, 61–63, 74–75.

[36] *Ibid.*, pp. 55, 58.

[37] Wolf, "San José: . . . ," in Julian Steward, *The People of Puerto Rico* . . . , *op. cit.*

[38] *Ibid.*, p. 212.

structure itself was personalized in the figure of Muños Marín.
Whether there is an actual trend in San José toward rational power
structure and national sociocultural elements cannot be determined.
For our purposes, it is sufficient to note that sociocultural change
in San José has lagged behind the general development of community life in Puerto Rico and to suggest that the reason may lie
in the fact that the mass of people are stringently cut off from the
power wielders (hacienda owners); or better, were, until the recent
activities of Muños Marín. San José dwellers have been unable to
attain the national culture elements due to the oppressive power
structure imposed upon them by those few individuals above.[39] The
limited degree of incorporation into the national sociocultural
system developing at the time of the study was a function of an
aspirant national political figure acting in accord with symbols of
folk culture.

Cantel.   In Cantel, a Mayan village, we find a most provocative
example of a community into which a new mode of production has
been introduced. The new mode caused little sociocultural change
until a rational power structure was introduced from quite another
source.[40] The economic development of the town, rather than
affecting political, religious and ceremonial life, actually accommodated itself to the existing configuration.[41] However, when the
power structure did begin to rationalize the culture began to be
seriously affected.

> . . . the entry of the local union into politics, the control of the
> election mechanisms, the ignoring of principles, the slighting of
> religious offices, the overriding of the principles of age and public
> service as criteria for high office and bases for respect resulted in a
> civil-religious hierarchy that was badly undermined. This was the
> major institutional change in Cantel during the entire history of
> the factor in that community.[42]

In Cantel we see that though economic development has important indirect effects, *these effects upon the community must await
the development of a rational power structure.* We can say then,

[39] *Ibid.* pp. 212–213.
[40] For economics see Nash, *Machine Age Maya. op. cit.,* p. 23; political
change and its effects is given in *ibid.,* pp. 103, 105, 109.
[41] *Ibid.,* pp. 1, 38, 71.
[42] *Ibid.,* p. 106.

with more authority on the basis of this evidence, that political development certainly seems to be a crucial variable in the linkage between local and national culture.

Nash submits:

> I do not think it [the civic-religious hierarchy] will ever return to the integral structure it used to be, but rather that it will continue to be secularized and the point of political contention.[43]

And to this we would add that the sociocultural system should rapidly change allowing for autonomy of economics and religion, freeing consumption patterns from religiously defined needs, thereby permitting an expansion of material needs.

Aritama. We come finally to the consideration of Aritama. Here sociocultural change has taken place without change in the power structure and the need for a rational structure is strongly felt:

> In the late thirties and early forties of the present century, a new period of change made itself felt in the village. This time changes were brought about mainly by improved communications and the necessity for making use of them, under the pressure of new needs.[44]

> It is felt by all members of the community that there should be a government-appointed authority and a set of laws and rules to regulate 'pa' que respeten' (so people will maintain respectful behavior), . . . This does not mean that people feel the need for a paternalistic authority from which guidance, advice, and 'progress' are to be expected. What is expected from the representatives of the government is 'justice' in the settlement of a few quite specific conflicts.[45]

The lack of a rational community power structure to control and channel the developing national culture seems to be related to the increasingly strong magical element in political affairs. Even local politicians use magic to attempt to influence national political developments.[46]

All in all, economic change has had a strong effect on the way

---

[43] *Ibid.*
[44] Reichel-Dolmatoff, *The People of Aritama* . . . , *op. cit.*, p. 455.
[45] *Ibid.*, p. 457.
[46] *Ibid.*, p. 403.

of life in Aritama. But its effect has been one of disruption. Countervailing trends such as the development of magic as an agent of
social control and the felt need for a rational power structure still
support our initial hypothesis. Aritama is in some ways like Saucio;
although politics is becoming increasingly important, it is nevertheless personal, an organ through which personal vengeance is taken
out on the nation for disrupting the folk existence.[47]

Our hypothesis that a rational power structure is crucial for the
development of national culture elements within a Latin American
community appears to be supported. Tabular support is evident in
all communities with 70 percent or more of the national culture
elements. Of these, the most direct evidence is found in Nayón,
Muquiyauyo and San Lorenzo. Of the communities tending more
toward folk culture elements, Chan Kom (1931), Buzios Island,
Cantel and Aritama all point strongly toward the development of a
rational power structure at the community level as the crucial
variable of sociocultural change.

SOCIOCULTURAL CHANGE IN LATIN
AMERICA: AN ANALYTIC MODEL

Having satisfied our hypothesis we will attempt to use the data
herein derived to inductively set up a model of sociocultural
change in Latin American communities.

Figures I and II represent our findings. Figure I represents our
conception of the broad framework of the folk oriented or closed
corporate community. Three major systems, prestige, religious-
magic, and economic, are weighted about equally in terms of their
function in the way of life of the collectivity. The religious-magic
system seems more central in terms of framing the core values.
The religious-magic system is a major impediment to sociocultural
change. Power is diffuse through all systems. The diagram is more
symmetrical, implying slower change.

Figure II represents an attempt to illustrate the essential changes
taking place when a community takes on characteristics of the
nation. Economics assumes a central position and the prestige system articulates more strongly to the economic one. A rational centralized power structure binds the community together permitting
expansion in the economic sphere and decreasing the influence in

[47] *Ibid.*

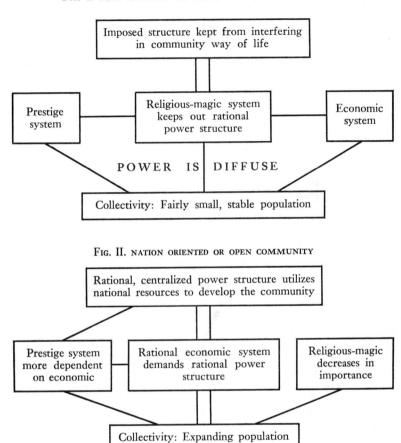

Fig. I. FOLK ORIENTED OR CLOSED CORPORATE COMMUNITY

Imposed structure kept from interfering in community way of life

Prestige system

Religious-magic system keeps out rational power structure

Economic system

POWER IS DIFFUSE

Collectivity: Fairly small, stable population

Fig. II. NATION ORIENTED OR OPEN COMMUNITY

Rational, centralized power structure utilizes national resources to develop the community

Prestige system more dependent on economic

Rational economic system demands rational power structure

Religious-magic decreases in importance

Collectivity: Expanding population

the religious-magic area of activity. The rational power structure directly conjoins with the nation so that the future of the community becomes increasingly that of the nation as a whole. The asymmetry in the diagram illustrates the speed-up in sociocultural change that is so much a characteristic of modern open communities in the world today. As change, always a constant in any structure, accelerates, cohesive agents tend to become more and more a part of a rational power structure; and the vigor of this structure presages further change.[48]

[48] Schermerhorn, *Society and Power, op. cit.*, p. 13.

An important factor leading to change in contemporary Latin American communities is rising population pressure. With the advent of modern methods of health and sanitation, Latin America is currently in the "'demographic gap."[49] Death rates are falling and fertility has not yet begun to drop significantly. Petersen states that "The population of most Latin American countries can be expected to increase by three percent per year, which means a doubling each 23 years."[50]

Rising population pressure creates community problems on two levels. First of all, as Kunkel points out,[51] subsistence agriculture cannot sustain an increasing population unless there is unlimited land onto which people can continuously move. Secondly, and more pertinent to our analysis, as community scale increases, the manner in which cooperation is to be effected among a greater number of individuals with divers aspirations, personalities, and so forth, becomes more complex. Complexity is best handled in a rational manner.[52]

The establishment of a rational power structure taps a broader sociocultural source—the nation. It can be postulated that people oriented toward the national socioculture and away from the folk context of life tend to emigrate toward areas developing a rational power structure while those folk oriented individuals in a community are the ones tending to remain. In this article evidence from Buzios Island and Saucio directly support such a postulate.

Given refined hypotheses along lines suggested above, intensive community studies of value orientations, power structure and sociocultural dynamics could be combined with data from recent Latin American censuses. Since change is going on throughout Latin America and since Latin American nations are indeed initiating censuses using modern techniques, new community studies should contribute much toward the development of a systematic theory of power structure and sociocultural change.

[49] Rupert B. Vance, "The Demographic Gap: Dilemma of Modernization Programs," *Milbank Memorial Fund: Approaches to Problems of High Fertility in Agrarian Societies* (New York: Milbank Memorial Fund, 1952), p. 51.
[50] William Petersen, *Population* (New York: The Macmillan Co., 1961), p. 467.
[51] Kunkel, "Economic Autonomy and Social Change . . . ," *op. cit.*
[52] Cf., Godfrey and Monica Wilson, *The Analysis of Social Change: Based on Observations in Central Africa* (Cambridge: University Press, 1954).

Agrarian Reform or Agrarian Revolution in Venezuela?

John Duncan Powell

In Latin America—still basically a region of peasants despite an astounding rate of urban growth—issues of reform or revolution often focus on *agrarian* reform, or *agrarian* revolution. To be sure, the Agrarian Question is not the most salient in each of the development situations in Latin America. But it is the most salient in some of the region's most important nations—Brazil, Chile, Peru, Colombia, for example—and it is of critical, if secondary, importance in the rest.

The Agrarian Question in Latin America is composed of two elements: the Land Question and the Peasant Question. A great deal of controversy is evident in past and current literature concerning the relative importance of each of these elements, the former concerned principally with the production of needed foodstuffs, and the latter with the social and political welfare of the human beings who happen to be peasant producers.[1] In such an atmosphere, the choice is often misunderstood, or at least artificially posed, as policy choices *between* food production *and* peasant welfare, as if the two, which can be abstractly entangled for analytic purposes, could be disentangled in the real world. But man and land in Latin America, as elsewhere, exist in a complex relationship of interdependence, or specific type of ecology—and an adequate analysis of an agrarian problem, and subsequently of an agrarian reform, must take a specific ecotype into account.[2]

---

[1] An analysis of the European version of this controversy, which was basically Marxist versus Populist in nature, is found in David Mitrany, *Marx Against the Peasant* (Chapel Hill: University of North Carolina Press, 1951). From this source, I borrowed the European—and, incidentally, Latin American—style of capitalizing references to the Agrarian Question and its components.

[2] Eric Wolf, in *Peasants* (Englewood Cliffs: Prentice-Hall, Inc., 1966), presents a detailed descriptive analysis of world peasant ecotypes. Among the

The three best-known and most-studied agrarian reforms in Latin America are the three which accompanied the only widely acknowledged cases of "genuine" social revolution in the area: Mexico, Bolivia, and Cuba.[3] In this chapter, I am going to take, for heuristic purposes, the position that the surface events which scholars have focussed on as comprising these "revolutions"— namely, the flow of political events and personalities on the national level—are less true indicators of revolution or reform than the changes which have or have not occurred in the rural areas of these countries under the label of agrarian reform programs. And by a detailed examination of the Venezuelan agrarian reform process, I hope to show that an agrarian revolution can occur without the cataclysmic, drastic changes in the political system through massive violence that we think of as genuine revolution. This I mean to do by illustrating that reform or revolution can be defined adequately only by carefully defining the concrete level-of-analysis with which one is dealing.

In order to clarify what I mean, but without going into detail, I would like to suggest that while a revolution has occurred in Mexico at the level of the nation-state, that revolution has not yet reached the mass of the peasantry, despite the well-known agrarian reform program of Mexico.[4] I would suggest that while the Bolivian Revolution seems to have failed at the level of the nation-state, it continues to be a concrete reality in the world of the Bolivian peasant—though the Bolivian agrarian reform program has not solved the Land Question, it has solved the Peasant Question. Finally, I will suggest, that while no generally acknowledged revolution has occurred in Venezuela on the level of the nation-state,

---

paleotechnic types he discusses: swidden; sectorial fallowing; short-term fallowing; permanent cultivation (hydraulic); and permanent cultivation of favored plots (infield-outfield system). The neotechnic types analyzed neatly by Wolf are specialized horticulture; dairy farming; mixed farming (balanced livestock and crop raising); and crops of the tropics. Each of these systems differs according to the use of land and labor factors, and consequently in the social effects accruing to landlord and peasant.

[3] Cole Blasier of The University of Pittsburgh has written a fine review article, "Studies of Social Revolution: Origins in Mexico, Bolivia, and Cuba," *Latin American Research Review,* Vol. II, No. 3, which illustrates the levels-of-analysis problem in the literature.

[4] See, for instance, several pointed articles in Stanley R. Ross, editor, *Is the Mexican Revolution Dead?* (New York: Alfred A. Knopf, 1966); but especially Moises Gonzales Navarro, "Mexico: The Lop-Sided Revolution," in *Obstacles to Change in Latin America* (London: Oxford University Press, 1965), edited by Claudio Veliz.

one has occurred at the level of the rural masses.[5] I hope thereby to demonstrate the need for a precise definition of the level-of-analysis with which one is dealing when attempting to judge the question: Reform or revolution?

THE AGRARIAN QUESTION IN LATIN AMERICA

It has been suggested that this issue, in Latin America as elsewhere, consists of two components: land and man—or, precisely, land and labor. Land without labor produces no sustenance for mankind. Labor is both a necessary *and* sufficient condition to render sustenance from the earth, albeit at a primitive level, without inputs of capital and management. Therein lies the nexus of the Agrarian Question: the need to apply labor to land in order to make it produce.

In the process of the Conquest, the *encomienda* system provided the means for the primitive accumulation of land and its corollary labor force in monopolistic form. Andrew Pearse describes the *encomienda* system as a political form of "indirect rule" of the indigenous populations of Latin America by the Spanish crown, through the reward of land grants to *conquistadores* and other loyal subjects, "delegating to them the substance of seigneurial power, with rights to exact compulsory labour (*servicios personales*) and tribute from the Indian populations entrusted to them."[6] The *encomienda* system was transformed into a private property system by the end of the sixteenth century, but labor tribute from Indians not living on such properties could still be levied through the institution of the *repartimiento*. From these earliest forms of agricultural exploitation have evolved the more recent forms of plantations, latifundia, and other land tenure systems. It seems, then, if

[5] The issue in Venezuela is often obscured by various usages of the terms revolution and reform. President Betancourt was fond of referring to his "revolution through evolution"; the National Agrarian Institute published a book entitled *Agrarian Reform in Venezuela: A Revolution Within the Law* (Caracas: IAN, 1964); and, of course, the popularized version of the Betancourt years by Robert Alexander is entitled *The Venezuelan Democratic Revolution* (New Brunswick: Rutgers University Press, 1964). None of these sources argues that a revolution—in the classical sense as defined, say, by Chalmers Johnson in his *Revolutionary Change* (Boston: Little, Brown & Company, 1966)—in fact occurred at the level of national political events.

[6] Andrew Pearse, "Agrarian Change Trends in Latin America," *Latin American Research Review,* Vol. I, No. 3.

we may be permitted to paraphrase Proudhon, that the historical origin of both property *and* labor was theft in much of Spanish America.[7]

The evolution of this primitive, pre-capitalist system into its more recent forms is neatly summed up by Pearse:

> Thus various historical forms cover a basic pattern of pre-capitalist relations which may be expressed in the following terms: In the national or colonial society there exists a landed elite. The exercise of power along with the enjoyment of prestige and all its trappings are means to this status, as well as results of it. Both the power and the prestige can be maintained *directly* by the acquisition of labour power and its application to the land *without* deep involvement in market relations. Applied to land, labour produces minerals, foodstuffs, building materials, skins, fibres, meat, etc. Skilled labour transforms these for the table, or into houses, utensils, clothes, works of art. Similarly, manpower can be organized as porters, flunkeys, canal-diggers, roadmakers, *capangas*, militia, and finally voters. Deficiencies are supplied by marketing surpluses and buying the required goods on the local market or by importation. Thus, ability to get and to hold labour matched the getting and holding of land as pillars of society, but the forms taken by the land-labour institutions have passed through various stages: 1) the corporal ransom was replaced by 2) the imposition of labour as a duty on a legally defined social stratum and enforced by state power, and by 3) African slavery; 4) the republican period is marked by the use of coercive state power against potential labourers by means of the legal contrivance of debt; 5) the monopolistic occupation of lands and the consequent exclusion of an adequate quantity of peasants from independent subsistence; and finally by 6) the buying of labour from the landless or land-poor peasant, in a buyer's market.[8]

What emerged out of this historical process was a pattern of land concentration and a system of labor exploitation based in large part on service-tenancy and payments-in-kind for seasonal labor. Basically, the peasant population had been squeezed off of the land in order to structure a certain type of labor situation—an over-abundant supply without bargaining power. The key factor in this

---

[7] For a discussion of Proudhon's theory of property—which actually came out in favor of private ownership, but controlled returns—see Aime Berthold, *Proudhon et la Propriete* (Paris: Biblio. Socialiste Internationale, 1910), cited by Mitrany, *op cit.*

[8] "Agrarian Change Trends," *op. cit.*, pp. 49–50.

development has been the *isolation* of these rural sub-systems from the larger social and political systems of the nation-state. Owing as much to geographical factors and the weakness of the reach of the nation-state as to an organized system of local power by rural landlords, the landlord monopolized the occupation of linkage points with the economy, polity, and society. It is this distinctive combination of local autonomy (most of the goods and services consumed by the resident labor force were provided on the local property through the landlord) and limited market linkages, monopolized by the landlord, which characterizes the classic latifundia, or hacienda.[9]

The consequence of this situation comprises the Peasant Question. Beyond the obvious and well-known correlates of poverty, ignorance, squalid housing, and disease which latifundia denote, lies the larger question of Who governs? Agrarian reform literature abounds with proof of the fact that the reach of the state is problematic within the confines of the often (even today) isolated latifundia—so that national legislation concerning rural labor conditions, wages, and other legally defined rights are simply not enforceable. Nor are regulations concerning the conditions of tenancy and usury. In fact, incredible as it may seem to North American readers, instances have actually been recorded of neo-feudal service obligations due as "homage" to the person of the landlord still being exacted today![10]

The Peasant Question, however, transcends the existence of latifundia. Even where land is utilized in modern capitalistic form, such as on export-oriented plantation operations, and even when communities of small-holders exist beyond the boundaries of latifundia holdings, the social relationships between mass and elite generated through the evolution of land-man systems in Latin American history have proven durable. They continue to exist in most parts of Latin America today in vestigial form—even in the most modern sectors of agricultural production.

[9] The "classical" *hacienda* system is described in nice detail by Frank Tannenbaum in "Toward an Appreciation of Latin America," *The United States and Latin America* (Englewood Cliffs: Prentice-Hall, Inc., 1963), second edition, pp. 32–41. Herbert Matthews edited the volume.

[10] Cited in Pearse, *op. cit.,* p. 53, from the series of careful field studies conducted by the Inter-American Agricultural Development Committee. For a preliminary report on their seven-country study, with detailed references to the individual country reports, see Solon Barraclough and Arthur Domike, "Agrarian Structure in Seven Latin American Countries," *Land Economics,* Vol. XLII, No. 4.

The classic latifundia is more efficient in the exploitation of labor than it is in the exploitation of land. This is the kernel of the Land Question in Latin America. Holders of latifundia fail to furnish the inputs of capital and management skills needed to produce significant quantities of agricultural products to meet the consumption requirements of their fellow nationals. It is characteristic of the economies of Latin America that highly capitalized and well-managed plantations are what has been aptly described as "enclave economies"—producing in response to the international market, not the domestic market, with which they often have little or no connection and upon which they often have little or no impact.[11] The plantation economies of Latin America, in other words, are subsidiaries of great consumer's markets—primarily in the United States—and are highly peripheral to the domestic economies in which they happen to be located. Thus one notes the phenomenon of the dependence of the Latin American economies on foreign exchange generated by the export of primary agricultural products—and the expenditure of much of that exchange on the importation of foodstuffs!

The Agrarian Question, then, wears two faces: land, and how to utilize it more productively than it is currently being utilized; and labor, and how to free it from a system of unjust exploitation. It is within this context that the issue of agrarian reform must be considered. If the classic latifundia situation no longer applies to the majority of the pasant population, the labor relationships which it epitomizes do. Landless peasants, of course, do seek and find seasonal labor on land holdings of all kinds, and enter therein into the kinds of asymmetrical relationships suggested above. It is well known that a majority of smallholders are also compelled to engage in the seasonal sale of their labor.[12] A composite picture of the pattern of land concentration and the numbers of peasants involved in more-or-less direct relationships in the agricultural economies of several important Latin American countries today is suggested in the following Table.

[11] See the discussion of Charles W. Anderson on "The Four Economies of Latin America," in his excellent *Politics and Economic Change in Latin America* (Princeton: Van Nostrand Co., Inc., 1967), pp. 49–53.

[12] See the various studies cited in the Inter-American Agricultural Committee report by Barraclough, *op. cit.*; and the chapters by Wagley and Adams in *Continuity and Change in Latin America* (Stanford: Stanford University Press, 1964).

PERCENTILE DISTRIBUTION BY COUNTRIES AND LAND-STATUS GROUPS

Country	Of No. of Agricultural Families			Of Extension of Land Used		Of Value of Agricultural Production	
	Estate* operators	Landless	Small-holders	Estate operators	Small-holders	Estate operators	Small-holders
Argentina	5.2	36.3	58.5	51.9	38.1	42.4	57.6
Brazil	14.6	61.9	23.5	93.5	6.5	78.7	21.3
Chile	9.5	49.7	40.8	92.6	7.4	80.0	20.0
Colombia	5.0	24.7	70.3	72.8	27.2	47.8	52.2
Ecuador	2.4	34.5	63.1	64.4	35.6	40.7	59.3
Guatemala	1.6	27.0	71.4	72.3	27.7	56.4	43.6

Source: Andrew Pearse, "Agrarian Change Trends in Latin America," op. cit., p. 62.
* "Estate" includes plantations and a variety of holdings known locally as *fundaciones, estancias, engenhos, usinas, fazendas, haciendas* and, generically, *latifundia.*

These data are based on a series of careful empirical studies conducted by the Inter-American Agricultural Development Committee. The upshot of the studies was that the land tenure system—the way in which land is held and utilized in the archaic rural sectors of Latin America—comprises the primary obstacle to the overall development of these countries. This is so, one of the senior scholars associated with the studies has argued, because:

1) *economically*, land tenure patterns restrain the rationalization of land-use, labor, and the introduction of efficient technology, and hence hold back productivity. Equally, consumption and agricultural investment are held back.

2) *socially*, land tenure patterns are the main prop of a rigid stratification system in which power and prestige are derived from the possession of land and not from achievement of it, and in which social ascension is difficult and motivation to achieve is limited.

3) *culturally*, the dependent classes and ethnic groups associated with the traditional patterns of land tenure have come to incorporate in their sub-cultures protective traits which also operate to prevent change.

4) *politically*, present land tenure patterns concentrate both institutional and arbitrary power in the hands of those who control land, and exclude from political participation and representation the class of primary producers, so that public services and institutions serve narrow private and regional interests rather than broad societal interests.[13]

Thus it seems that the solution of the Agrarian Question in Latin America, whether by means of an agrarian reform or by violent social revolution in the classic pattern of Mexico, Bolivia, and Cuba, clearly implies a revolutionary change in the land-labor status of the peasantry. The question we must now examine is whether such a revolution can occur through an agrarian reform *without* an accompanying social revolution at the level of the nation-state.

[13] Andrew C. Pearse, "Land Tenure, Social Structure and 'Development' in Latin America," a paper mimeographed and distributed by the Land Tenure Center, University of Wisconsin, Madison, Wisconsin (no date).

THE VENEZUELAN AGRARIAN REFORM

The land tenure system in Venezuela developed in the general historical pattern which has been described above. However, certain differences in circumstances distinguish the Venezuelan case. There were no large Indian populations residing in this region at the time of the Conquest; consequently, the system of tied land-labor exploitation which occurred elsewhere in the Caribbean was much less in evidence in Venezuela. Later, the importation of African slaves aided in the establishment of a modest plantation economy, producing sugar, cocoa and coffee. Another mainstay of the early Venezuelan agricultural economy was the cattle industry, centered in the *llanos*, the rain plains of the upper Orinoco River system.[14]

Coupled with the civil wars of the nineteenth century, which divided and decimated the rural elite, the generally undeveloped agricultural economy of Venezuela produced a relatively weak latifundia system. That is, the system was neither highly organized to exploit the peasant labor force for commercial agricultural purposes, nor was it highly unified in its social exploitation of the peasantry through the political process. The essential pattern described above, however, held true for Venezuela—political and economic power were associated with land ownership, and the peasantry was an exploited class in society. This pattern culminated in the regime of Juan Vicente Gomez, dictatorial ruler of Venezuela from 1908 to 1935, who in his time became the single largest latifundista in the nation's history.[15]

By the end of the Gomez regime, the pattern of land ownership and use in Venezuela paralleled the classic situation described by Pearce in the last section: a few owners with massive quantities of land; a number of holders of very small plots; and the mass of the population, being landless, dependent on owners for access to farm-

[14] For the historic origins of the Venezuelan economy, see Moreno A. Arellano, *Origines de la Economia Venezolana* (Mejico, D.F.: 1947), and the overview presented in Pompeyo Rios, "Desarrollo Economico de Venezuela Desde 1830 Hasta 1920," *Revista de la Facultad de Agronomia*, Vol. III, No. 3, 1964.

[15] The properties of Gomez were so extensive in the rural areas that they were declared the *Bienes Restituidos* (the Restored Properties of the state) and a special government agency was created for their care and disposition. See John D. Powell, "The Politics of Agrarian Reform in Venezuela: History, System, and Process" (Ph.D. dissertation, University of Wisconsin, 1966).

ing opportunities. This pattern, illustrated in the following facts, suggests the relative power situation of the rural elite and the rural mass:

> 4.4% of rural property owners controlled 78% of the agricultural area.
> 95.6% of rural property owners controlled 22% of the area.
> 10.6% of rural dwellers classified as campesinos owned land.
> 89.4% of the campesinos worked on the land of other persons.[16]

Property and power have an obvious relationship to economic well-being. The Venezuelan peasantry, being essentially a landless class—or at best a class of aspiring *minifundistas*—has for some time been at or near the bottom of the economic ladder.[17] The litany of socio-economic woes is familiar to the student of rural Latin America—low incomes (less than $150 annually as late as the mid-1950's), unsanitary housing, a battery of gastrointestinal diseases, high infant mortality rates—in fine, a life that is solitary, brutish, and short.[18]

What I have just described as a rather static situation will probably serve as a fairly accurate historical description of the central facts of rural life in Venezuela. Beginning about 1915, however, and accelerating thereafter, certain forces for change began to develop which were to prove the undoing of the neoclassic latifunda system in the country. The landowning class was first affected by the loss of Venezuela's primary coffee market, Germany, following the blockade of World War I. Post-war inflation and the disastrous depression of the 1930's served to make this marketing loss a semi-permanent one. Market losses overseas spread to other agricultural export sectors as well, due to the world depression. Perhaps more important in the long run was the growth of the petroleum industry (beginning about 1920) as the most dynamic factor in the Venezuelan economy, gradually attracting to itself investments and entrepreneurial talents which might otherwise have remained spread throughout the economy, including the agricultural sector. At any

---

[16] See the work of Luis Troconis Guerrero, *La Cuestion Agraria en la Historia Nacional* (Caracas: Editorial Arte, 1962), for the more-or-less official *Accion Democratica* interpretation. The data, taken from the 1937 Agricultural Census, are cited on page 142.

[17] International Bank for Reconstruction and Development, *The Economic Development of Venezuela* (Baltimore: The John Hopkins Press, 1961).

[18] Some detail on these matters is found in my dissertation, *op. cit.*, in the first chapter.

rate, beginning in the 1920's, the Venezuelan agricultural economy entered a period of stagnation as exports began to slip; gradually, its contribution to the national economy declined.[19]

Landowners reacted to these adverse developments in two distinct ways, each of them of great importance for the ripening of conditions for an agrarian reform. Those who were active performers in the agricultural economy, especially in the export sector, reacted by pressuring the Gomez government, as early as 1924, for the creation of a battery of agricultural service programs, such as credit facilities, to ease their problems. The government responded by creating the *Banco Agricola y Pecuria* in 1928, later expanding the magnitude and scope of its operations to cover most cash crops, domestic as well as export. Further, it experimented during the 1930's and early 1940's with a variety of exchange-subsidy programs designed to enhance and invigorate agricultural exports.[20] In addition to pressing for such programs, the landlords responded in a second distinctive and critically important way: they began to squeeze the peasant users of their land and water, as a way of adjusting to a deteriorating situation.

The reactions of the landowning class had three important—but largely unintended, I am sure—consequences which were to create favorable conditions for a later agrarian reform. We have already stated that neither government programs, nor squeezing the peasant users of their resources succeeded in reviving the agricultural economy, which continued its decline into the early 1960's. What did result was the following. First, the government's favorable response to landlord pressures led to the creation of a number of institutions and administrative specialists concerned with agricultural problems. These bureaucratic instruments were later to be useful in the pursuit of a drastic agrarian reform program. Second, the credit program of the Agricultural and Livestock Bank required the owner to mortgage his property to obtain his credits. In view of the continuing world depression throughout the 1930's, and the domestic problems of agriculture even after that time, a number of foreclosures occurred, so that by the time of the first attempt at

[19] An excellent analysis of these events is found in Ramon Fernandez y Fernandez, *Reforma Agraria en Venezuela* (Caracas: Tip. Vargas, 1948), especially pp. 230–236 for the decline of agriculture.

[20] For details, see my dissertation, and the Ministerio de Agricultura y Cria, *La Colonizacion Agricola en Venezuela: 1830–1957* (Caracas: MAC, 1959).

agrarian reform in 1945, the Agricultural Bank held almost 800,000 acres of arable land. This land, plus many of the former Gomez properties (which had reverted to the state following his death) provided the government with a responsive capacity to demands for access to land. Finally, the squeezing of the peasantry resulted, not in maintaining the status quo of the landlord, but in its destruction, since the resistance of the peasantry, increasingly expressed in conflict, and often violent conflict, became organized during the same period.[21]

The organization of the peasantry contains the answer to the riddle of "agrarian reform or agrarian revolution in Venezuela?" Beginning early in 1936, following the death of Gomez and the first stirrings of mass political organization in Venezuelan history, the peasantry was organized into *sindicatos agricolas*—agrarian syndicates—which included not only rural wage laborers, but *minifundistas*, tenants, sharecroppers, and squatters. While legal recognition of the syndicates proceeded with painful slowness under Gomez' two successors, Lopez Contreras (1936–1940) and Medina Angarita (1941–1945), it has been estimated that by the time of the 1945 coup, approximately 500 of these groups were in the process of formation, and from 100,000 to 200,000 peasants were involved.[22] The question is, By whom, and for what purpose, were the peasants being organized?[23]

The answer to this rhetorical question is that the Venezuelan peasantry was organized by political party builders seeking a mass base, and committed to an agrarian reform in the interest of the rural masses. The resulting functional wedding satisfied the needs of both partners—in the political party system, the peasantry found representation and access to important decision-making processes which could affect their lot; in the peasant masses, the political party system found a dependable base of electoral support. The political party which monopolized the first stages of peasant organization was *Accion Democratica* (AD), first in its embryonic form as part

[21] Powell, Politics of the Agrarian Reform, *op. cit.*
[22] *Ibid.*
[23] The question rests on the assumption that some one, or some group "outside" the peasantry was the precipitating factor in the organizational process. For a general and comparative discussion of "outside" leadership in peasant movements, see Henry A. Landsberger, editor, *Peasant Movements in Latin America* (Ithaca: Cornell University Press, 1968). My chapter, entitled "The Peasant Union Movement in Venezuela," discusses the particulars of this case.

of *ORVE*, beginning in 1936, then as the *Partido Democratio Nacional* (PDN) from 1937–1941, and from then on as the well-known party of the democratic left, AD.[24]

Beginning in 1936 under the leadership of Romulo Betancourt himself, a network of politico-syndical organizers—approximately two hundred men, concentrated in the central states of Venezuela—began organizing the peasantry. For the peasants and for *Accion Democratica*, the opportunity for radical action, and changes in social and economic relationships in agriculture and elsewhere in the society occurred with the participation of AD in the successful, militarily sponsored reform coup of October 18, 1945.[25] With Betancourt and other AD leaders as the civilian powers in the resulting *Junta Revolucionaria*, radical changes soon began to occur in the rural areas. The argument that a revolution has occurred in rural Venezuela rests on these changes and their consequences, in the absence of generally recognized and accepted revolutionary events at the level of the nation state.

In brief, the case for a *de facto* revolution—Albert Hirschman called similar developments in Colombia a "revolution by stealth"—rests on the following analysis.[26] In the historic development of Latin America, rights-in-property drastically outweighed other human rights such as those vested in labor, particularly in agriculture. The man who owned land and water resources enjoyed the power, backed by the state, of arbitrary control of those resources. For example, in a typical community of one hundred persons, one landowner would control as much as three-quarters of the land and water resources. Which of the other ninety-nine persons would have access to those resources, and under what conditions, was decided by the landlord, limited only by the customary patterns of land and labor exploitation sanctioned by active state support. The pernicious consequences of this life-and-death power to grant or not grant access to the land, I suggested earlier, are the crux of the Peasant Problem. It was this power—arbitrary private control of land resources—that the peasant union movement, through its al-

[24] For a careful, detailed study of the general developments of these political movements, see John D. Martz, *Accion Democratica: Evolution of a Modern Political Party in Venezuela* (Princeton University Press, 1966).

[25] The coup is covered in considerable detail by Martz, *ibid.*, and in Edwin Lieuwen, *Arms and Politics in Latin America* (New York: Praeger, 1961).

[26] Albert O. Hirschman, *Journeys Toward Progress* (New York: Twentieth Century Fund, 1963).

liance with its partner-in-government, *Accion Democratica*, drastically altered and transferred to another group in rural society. Thus, a revolution—defined as the relatively sudden, drastic transfer of power from one social class to another—occurred in rural Venezuela from 1946 to 1947.

The first evidence of this impending revolution occurred a few days after the coup of October 18, 1945, at a meeting convoked by Romulo Betancourt, civilian President of the mixed civil-military *Junta Revolucionaria*, for the purpose of establishing policy guidelines and procedures for the various state officials of the new regime. At this meeting, the following pertinent steps were taken in light of the Peasant Problem:

1. The right of arbitrary eviction by landlords was suspended by decree.
2. State officials were empowered to sit as parties in the establishment and enforcement of rental agreements and tenant contracts between peasants and landowners, and to mediate "immediate and equitable readjustments" in existing relationships.
3. State officials were to study the possibility of leasing government-owned lands to peasants, and were to encourage private owners of unexploited lands to rent them to peasant users "to the end of . . . experiencing an agrarian reform."

The report on Land Policies closed with the note that "This procedure on the part of the Regional Governments responds to the firm policy of the *Junta* of satisfying the inescapable necessity, for reasons of increased production and social justice, of granting land to the man who works it."[27]

These first tentative steps by AD to wedge state power into the relationships between their campesino allies and the rural landlords were quickly followed by more systematic efforts, indicative of a well-planned intent to accomplish an agrarian reform. Less than one month after the coup, a Land Commission was established within the Technical Institute for Immigration and Colonization (ITIC), the government's agency for recruiting and establishing European agricultural colonists. The new Land Commission became the central administrative structure for leasing governmental lands—such

---

[27] Cited in Romulo Betancourt, *Trayectoria Democratica de Una Revolucion* (Caracas: Imp. Nacional, 1948), p. 175.

as the ex-Gomez properties, and the Agricultural Bank's pool of foreclosed farms—to Venezuelan peasants, and also became a party to the leasing of private lands to peasant users. In May, 1946, a Credit Department, funded with 10 million Bolivares, was established in ITIC to support the new land recipients. By the time the AD regime was overthrown in 1948, approximately 80,000 peasants had been placed on some 400,000 acres of arable land and provided with credits for its exploitation.[28]

Thus, the power of the state was being wielded to place peasants on land, a power that had always been arbitrarily controlled by private ownership. But the initial stages of this *de-facto* land reform utilized government lands for the most part, since private owners were uncooperative in the leasing of unused resources to peasants. This limitation was overcome, and the power of rural landownership finally and completely broken, by the Decree of Rural Property Rentals, passed by the AD-dominated Constituent Assembly in March, 1947, and formally decreed by *Junta* President Betancourt on March 6. The Decree, which created a system of Agrarian Commissions, *required* the leasing of unused arable lands— whether public or private—to peasant users, at rates established as "reasonable" by the Commissions. The Commissions were also empowered to fine uncooperative landowners.[29]

The same *de facto* administrative processes of the state which stripped the power from rural landlords invested it in local leaders of the agrarian syndicates. Land grants by the Land Commission of ITIC were given as a matter of policy in response to petitions by the local syndicates. Thus, syndicate leaders recruiting new members had something concrete to offer, and already established syndicate leaders were able to pay for past loyalties. Also, under the ITIC credit program, a local syndicate leader sat as a member of the three-man administrative boards which actually passed out the credits at the community level. More important, the Agrarian Commissions which were created by the Rural Rentals Decree consisted of five members, one of whom represented the landlords, and another of whom represented the agrarian syndicates. If the landlord wished to appeal the dictates of the Commission, however, he could only appeal to a three man Board, composed of the agrarian syndicate representative (allied with AD), a representative of the

[28] The details of these events are found in Chapter 5 of my dissertation.
[29] *Ibid.*

state (AD) authorities, and a representative of the Ministry of Agriculture of the (AD) national government. Thus a revolution on the land was accomplished in some 500 rural communities during the 1945–1948 period. It did not reach every rural community; it was not marked by apocalyptic violence and murder; but it did rapidly transfer real socioeconomic and political power from landowners to peasant representatives. A pattern for the curtailment of private property rights and for representation of peasant interests by the state was established, which, despite a period of counter-revolution under Perez Jimenez from 1948–1958, still holds true to this day. Before going on to a more detailed investigation of how the system of peasant representation functions at present, we must briefly take note of that counter-revolution and of the more highly publicized agrarian reform program which has occurred under democratic governments since 1958.

By the time of the military coup of November 24, 1948, the elected regime of AD President Romulo Gallegos had passed an Agrarian Reform Law which, at least in its preliminary versions, had explicitly sought to ratify the *de facto* role of the local agrarian syndicate leader in the land-grant process. The final version of the Law, while not formally stipulating the powers of local syndicate leaders, left the question of their participation open in an envisaged process of general transformation in agriculture. Briefly, the Law sought to establish both a class of landed small farmers, buttressed by credit and other state services, and a system of worker-participation in the management of large commercial farm operations, private and public alike. The general idea was to legalize and extend the informal system of agrarian reform which had developed during the AD governance. This system, however, was ruptured following the coup: the land grant program of ITIC was immediately suspended, as was the credit program for peasant syndicates; the Decree of Rural Property Rentals, of course, was null and void following the downfall of its sponsoring government; and within a short time of assuming power, the *Junta Militar* decreed the dissolution of the entire Venezuelan Federation of Labor (CTV), including the national network of agrarian syndicates which had been the primary vehicle through which AD governments had channeled reform benefits.[30]

[30] *Ibid.*, Chapter 6.

The detailed story of the emergence of Colonel Marcos Perez Jimenez as the undisputed military dictator of Venezuela is well known and chronicled elsewhere.[31] In general, political and labor leaders, those affiliated with AD in particular, were harassed, arrested, tortured, assassinated, and exiled during the 1948–1958 counter-revolution. While local leaders of the peasant union movement were less susceptible to this suppression than their urban counterparts, the powers which they had been granted under the AD system were stripped from them. Some land and some of the old powers of landowning were recaptured by private owners, and most of the 80,000 peasants who had been granted access to land under the 1945–1948 revolution were evicted.[32] Mass peasant suppression, however, was not undertaken during the Perez Jimenez regime, and the reversal was not complete. And so it was that the system of empowering local peasant leaders vis-a-vis local landowners was suspended, but not destroyed; agrarian syndicate leaders and members were removed from influence, farmlands, and power, but not eliminated physically. They worked in the clandestine resistance movement for the day when they were once again to be granted access to all of these things.

That day came during the winter of 1957–1958, with the overthrow of Perez Jimenez and the establishment of a caretaker military *Junta*. With the flight of Perez Jimenez on January 23, 1958, a state of general agitation and unrest seized the rural areas. Land invasions—as many as 500 individual properties were taken—occurred in all parts of the country, in many instances on lands which had been given to peasants during the 1945–1948 period, and from which they had been later evicted. Most, if not all, of these invasions were organized by the peasant unions, which had survived the Perez Jimenez regime underground, and, perversely, may even have been strengthened by the experience.[33]

With the election, in December, 1958, of Romulo Betancourt as President, and with the subsequent formation of a coalition government, the ground was laid for the preparation of a new Agrarian Reform Law, similar in thrust to the AD-sponsored 1948 legislation. The new law, however, which was promulgated in March, 1960, was the product of an elaborate process of consultation and

[31] See Martz, *Accion Democratica, op. cit.*
[32] Powell, Politics, *op. cit.*, Chapter 6.
[33] *Ibid.*

negotiation with all of the major political and economic interest groups affected by the prospective agrarian reform; as a multi-partisan effort, it enjoyed smooth sailing through the legislature and, subsequently, in the necessary annual funding of its administrative instrumentalities.

Since 1960, Venezuela has carried out what it widely regarded to be the most significant, non-violent agrarian reform in Latin American history. Some 100,000 peasant families have been placed, as provisional owners, on some 5,000,000 acres of land—one-half from private sources and one-half from governmental holdings—in some 700 consolidated settlements, or *asentimientos*. As in the 1945–1948 period, the peasant syndicate movement has played a central role in the process of initiating and administering this process. This role, which is concrete evidence of the Venezuelan rural revolution, can now be examined in some detail.

THE PEASANT FEDERATION OF VENEZUELA

By the end of 1967, the *Federacion Campesina de Venezuela* (FCV) consisted of approximately 300,000 members organized into over 3,000 local syndicates, leagues, and associations. First affiliated with the Venezuelan Confederation of Workers (CTV) in 1947, and suppressed along with its parent organization in early 1949, the FCV was reestablished as a national labor federation in 1959, after the downfall of Perez Jimenez. Under the Labor Code, the FCV represents agricultural laborers, smallholders, tenants, sharecroppers, and squatters in their dealings, not only with landowners, but more importantly, with all levels of government in matters affecting the welfare of its membership.

Originally dominated exclusively by *Accion Democratica*, the FCV has been a multi-partisan organization since its post-Perez Jimenez renascence. Since 1958, the Social Christian Party (COPEI) has participated actively in its councils, and from 1958–1960, and 1964 to the present, the *Union Republicana Democratica* (URD) has been a part of the FCV. Influence and offices are divided among the parties in a ratio comparable to the number of peasant members affiliated with each party—currently about 65 percent AD, 30 percent COPEI, and 5 percent URD.

The supreme institutional authority of the FCV is vested in the Campesino Congress, held every few years. The First Congress, in

1959, adopted the internal statutes which more or less defined the FCV's organizational forms and activities until a new set was adopted at the Third Congress, early in 1967. The Second Campesino Congress, held in 1962, was devoted mainly to a political struggle to purge radical leftist leadership from the peasant movement.[34] Each Congress, which is convoked following a series of local and state elections of officials and delegates, elects the members of the National Executive Committee (CEN), the *de facto* ruling body of the FCV which governs until it organizes the next Campesino Congress. There are other organizational forms incorporated into the FCV, but the Congress and the National Executive Committee are the only significant ones in terms of internal control and power. Currently, the National Executive Committee consists of: a president (AD); first vice-president (COPEI); second vice-president (URD); secretary general (AD); secretaries of organization (COPEI), agrarian affairs (AD), finance (AD), Indian affairs (URD), agricultural centers and cooperatives (AD), labor affairs (COPEI), education (AD), international affairs (AD), and press and publications (AD), plus an alternate named by each political party to fill in for absent officers in the conduct of their National Executive Committee duties.[35]

The regional organizations, or *Seccionales*, coincide with state boundaries for the most part, and they, like the locals, are organized in a manner comparable to the National Executive Committee, but with far fewer offices—normally there will be a secretary general or president, secretaries of organization, finance, and claims, and an agrarian secretary.

The major function of the FCV at all levels is brokerage—the personal representation of membership before local, state, and national governmental institutions, especially those concerned with the agrarian reform program. For example, approximately 90 percent of the more than 700 agrarian reform settlements (*asentimientos*) were established by the National Agrarian Institute as the result of petitions from local *syndicatos*, processed upward, and pressed by the state and national officials of the FCV. Similarly, obtaining campesino credits from the Agricultural and Livestock Bank is one of the primary functions of local FCV leaders, who fill out and

[34] *Ibid.* For the story of the "purgees," see Ramon Quijada, *Reforma Agraria en Venezuela* (Caracas: Editorial Arte, 1963).
[35] From interviews with various officials at the *Tercer Congreso Campesino,* held at Los Caracas, Venezuela, in February, 1967.

process the applications of their often illiterate followers. This pattern is followed down the line of governmental services in the rural areas—housing, road construction, agricultural extension services, and so forth.

Local, state, and national leaders are able to process membership demands because of their structural access to the decision-making machinery of government. This access is both indirect—through office-holding in the political parties constituting the coalition governments—and direct, by virtue of statutory representation for FCV officials in the governing bodies and advisory boards of all the major governmental agencies with agrarian reform responsibilities. Direct access is also gained in the legislative domain. Among the FCV leaders interviewed, 15.2 percent of local leaders had been elected or appointed to local governmental offices, and 39.1 percent of state FCV officials had held similar public positions. Among the twenty-four national leaders interviewed, five had been (or were at the time of interview) elected members of their respective State Legislative Assemblies, and two national AD leaders, one COPEI leader, and one URD leader were members of the National Chamber of Deputies at the time of interview.[36] It is through this network of linkages with political parties and the executive and legislative branches of government at all levels that the FCV leadership pursues its brokerage functions.

An important, but secondary, set of functions of the FCV concerns internal membership services. Included are a number of Peasant Vocational Schools and other leadership and membership

---

[36] During the summer of 1964, interviews were conducted with all national officials and several state officials of the FCV. From December, 1965, through May, 1966, additional national and state leaders were interviewed, for a total of 24 national leaders (the population of office-holders from 1964–1966), 23 state leaders (a 20 percent—but accidental—sample). During this period, with the assistance of John R. Mathiason of MIT and the CENDES-CIDA agrarian reform evaluation team, I conducted a national survey of randomly-selected local leaders of the FCV, for a total of 118 usable interviews. This data will be presented in some detail in a forthcoming monograph, tentatively entitled *Peasant Mobilization and Agrarian Reform in Venezuela*. Mathiason has written up his work in "The Venezuela Campesino: Perspectives on Change," in *The Politics of Change in Venezuela* (Cambridge: MIT Press, 1967), edited by Frank Bonilla and Jose A. Silva Michelena; and in his Ph.D. dissertation (MIT, 1968), "The Political Mobilization of the Venezuelan Campesino." Without Mathiason's generous cooperation, my own survey work would have been impossible. Similarly, I am indebted to the Land Tenure Center and CIDA for financial assistance in the field work.

training programs; an agricultural machinery purchasing agency (SUCAM); an FCV-owned and operated rice processing plant (INDUCAM); and the tentative establishment of a series of farmers' markets for direct membership sales in major urban areas (MERCAM).

The basic arrangement of the alliance between the peasant union movement and the political party system is that, in return for the delivery of goods and services—specifically the agrarian reform program—the FCV delivers the votes of its membership on election day. This is the other face of brokerage. While no precise measurement has been made of FCV membership voting, the practice of delivering the local rural vote clearly makes an impact on the national political scene. AD and COPEI are the two most successful vote-getting parties in the Venezuelan system, and since 1958, more than one-half of the total national votes of each party has comes from its organized peasant arm.[37] In the 1963 election, votes from rural areas (less than 1,000 population) correlated *.65* (at the .001 level of significance) with AD votes, and .76 (.000 level of significance) with votes for COPEI.[38] This seems to support the proposition that, in a nation which is highly urbanized—almost 70 percent of the population live in areas of 5,000 or more—the two most popular political parties are solidly based in the rural areas, and that the *Federacion Campesina* is the core of this base of support.

CONCLUSION

At the outset of this chapter, referring to Mexico, Bolivia, and Cuba, I stated that I would take, "for heuristic purposes, the position that the surface events which scholars have focussed upon as comprising these revolutions—namely, the flow of political events and personalities on the national level—are less true indicators of revolution or reform than the changes which have or have not occurred in the rural areas of these countries under the label of agrarian reform programs." I took this position because of dissatisfaction, with definitions and usage of terms like "revolution,"

---

[37] Peter P. Lord, "The Peasantry as an Emerging Political Factor in Mexico, Bolivia, and Venezuela," Land Tenure Center Research Report No. 35, 1965 (mimeo.).
[38] Powell, Politics, *op. cit.*

and with the lack of empirical studies that analyze the concrete impact of dramatic national policies on the lives of the majority of the population of Latin America, the peasantry.

An attempt was made, through a generalized presentation of research conducted in Venezuela, to argue that a revolution (defined as "the relatively sudden, drastic transfer of power from one social class to another") occurred in rural Venezuela in the 1946–1947 period; and that despite a period of counter-revolution from 1948–1958, a transfer of power over land-access and use from local landlords to local peasant leaders has been consolidated since 1958 through a program of agrarian reform. This was not done to join issue on definitions of "revolution" or "reform," but to try to show that what passes for reform at the level of the nation-state may have revolutionary consequences at the level of the peasant masses. In short, I am arguing for empirical studies of public policies within clearly defined contexts.[39]

Most of the scholarly literature on Venezuela, and certainly the popularized versions of it, stress the democratic reforms initiated under President Betancourt beginning in 1959.[40] This has obscured the fact that such programs as agrarian reform were in reality the culmination of long-standing organizational efforts in the rural areas, and that the pattern of breaking landlord power and its transfer to peasant leaders occurred much earlier. Thus, to a significant degree, the agrarian reform program carried out under the 1960 law ratified and attempted to rationally influence what was already occurring in fact in rural Venezuela—the coming to power of a new class of peasant representatives. The great accomplishment of Romulo Betancourt, therefore, was not the guiding of the Agrarian Reform Law through the Congress and into application in the countryside, but the role which he played in the prior "revolution by stealth"—the mobilization of the peasantry into effective political participation.

At a more general level of analysis, what I have tried to show is the sequence and interaction of events at the local and national levels, thereby approaching the issue of agrarian revolution or

[39] The provocative posture on the Agrarian Question earlier in this chapter, presented as a corrective, is open to criticism on this very point. It does seem, however, that as empirical field work on land tenure relationships in Latin America—such as the CIDA studies—accumulates, there is a solid basis for an outlook of moral outrage at the lot of the peasant.

[40] Such as Robert Alexander, *The Venezuelan Democratic Revolution,* op. cit.

agrarian reform. What occurred in Venezuela may be quite germane to the situations in Brazil, Chile, Peru, and Colombia. The Venezuelan experience suggests that prior organizational efforts may be necessary for the building of a political base capable of supporting agrarian reform passage and enforcement, and the nature and extent of this prior effort may decisively influence the nature and extent of the agrarian reform program itself. Once an alliance is built, one must operate within its context.

The sequence of events necessary for a relatively nonviolent agrarian reform—or revolution—to reach the rural masses of Latin America, as suggested by the Venezuelan case, seems to be as follows. There exists a concrete set of circumstances under which the peasantry is related to land and landowners—and these circumstances are closely related to the productivity and standard of living of the masses. In most Latin American countries, the political elites have so far been unwilling, or unable to alter these circumstances significantly. Drastic changes may occur, however, if two related events are brought to pass: the formation of a political alliance between local peasant leaders and national political leaders aspiring to break into the arena of public power; and the subsequent success of this alliance in actually gaining national governmental power. History would suggest, however, that even in a case like that of Venezuela, in which the peasantry seems to have made the right kind of alliance and to have achieved a revolutionary improvement in status, it may be a short-lived accomplishment. The fate of the interwar peasant parties in Eastern Europe, and of the peasantry in "successful" peasant revolutions offers evidence that political gains by the peasantry, organized or not, are likely to be precarious.[41] In the particular case of Venezuela, most of the conditions seem to favor a relatively permanent gain in the socioeconomic and political status of the peasantry—but there are several critical problems which cast doubt on this seeming permanence.

The problems of the Venezuelan peasantry, perversely, spring from the same factor which brought it the gains made thus far—its alliance with the political party system, particularly with *Accion Democratica*. In fine, the position of the peasantry depends on the fortunes of its political ally. In general terms, this may mean, for instance, that to forestall reactionary coups, a reformist party may

[41] See David Mitrany, *Marx Against the Peasant, op. cit.*, and for a more widely-based discussion, Barrington Moore, Jr., *Social Origins of Dictatorship and Democracy* (Boston: Beacon Press, 1966).

have to moderate the pace of the "pay-offs" to its electoral clientele. This in fact has occurred in Venezuela, but the organized peasantry has in general seemed to prefer the half-a-loaf of well planned and coordinated agrarian reform to immediate and total revolutionary land redistribution. More serious yet may be internal problems in the political party which threaten its electoral effectiveness. The 1967–1968 crisis in AD, for example, may well spell the end of that party's electoral dominance in Venezuela—and in the event that AD is defeated in the 1968 elections, the consequences for its peasant allies are likely to be negative. A third critical problem for the preservation of the Venezuelan peasantry's revolutionary improvement in status is the growing power of a newly invigorated rural class of entrepreneurs, which has been declared by the leadership of the *Federacion Campesina* to be the present "enemy" of the peasant class, replacing the now defunct *latifundistas*.[42] The new class of agricultural entrepreneurs, moving to meet the still-critical national needs for agricultural products, comes into direct competition with the peasant union movement in its drive for land grants, credits, farm machinery, hybrid seeds, marketing opportunities, and the like.

Whether the agrarian revolution accomplished in rural Venezuela will be permanent remains to be seen. And if, under almost ideal historic circumstances, the most noted democratic agrarian reform in Latin America fails in its ultimate purpose of liberating the peasant masses from the tyranny of the land, what hope is there for the peasants in the rest of the hemisphere?

---

[42] Armando Gonzales, President of the *Federacion Campesina de Venezuela*, address delivered at the *Tercer Congreso Campesino*.

Part Three

———— •◦• ————

Reform and Revolution

We have grouped the preceding writers under headings that do not directly evoke the terms "reform" and "revolution." Yet questions concerning these phenomena thread through the earlier discussion. Some years ago, both forms of change were considered inevitable, the only question being which would occur first. At least some of the articles presented have implicitly raised the more sobering possibility that neither is likely in many countries of Latin America. In some cases the "wave of the future" might conceivably be perpetual instability; in others, a process that falls in subtle and complex ways between the two great poles of reform and revolution. The writers in this section add to the dialogue by raising three additional issues: What are the conditions of social and political revolutions? What difficulties confront a reformist government, once it has won the initial struggle for political power? What is the relative efficacy of a reformist or revolutionary strategy? From different points of view, the contributions by Federico G. Gil and Regis Debray address themselves to the first issue. The study of reform management in Chile raises the second, and the article by Charles Anderson confronts the third.

Antecedents of the Cuban Revolution

Federico G. Gil

I

The true story of the Cuban Revolution in all its meaning cannot be written for some years and even then it will be no easy task. This is an event that will undoubtedly concern many historians for a long time to come, for as it has been said: "The Cuban Revolution has shaken the Western Hemisphere the way the French Revolution shook Europe." Regardless of the fate of the Castro regime, one thing is certain—Latin America will never be the same again. So complex is the Cuban phenomenon within its strictly Cuban aspects that it cannot be understood without considering some historical elements in its background. These have to be explained, not to excuse what has taken place, but simply in order to understand it. The purpose of this article is to analyze the historical circumstances bearing significantly upon the great social upheaval which began January 1, 1959, in the neighbor republic. Therefore, no attempt will be made here to deal with the course of events which later drove Cuba into Communist hands. That story, so full of complexities and contradictions, cannot yet be written.

Throughout its fifty-seven years of republican life, there never existed in Cuba a true democracy. The pathological condition of the island's democracy arose chiefly from difficulties in Cuba's historical heritage and the temperament of the people, the lack of civic training, various economic weaknesses, and the apathy and absenteeism of the most capable and best qualified of the citizenry. As a result of these factors, politics fell into the hands of the corrupt and the

From Federico Gil, "Antecedents of the Cuban Revolution," *Centennial Review of Arts and Science,* Vol. VI (Summer 1962). Reprinted by permission.

inept. Two great evils have consistently plagued Cuba's political history: electoral fraud and administrative corruption. Since the founding of the republic in 1902, the country never had a single government free of graft and immorality.

After what seemed to be a good beginning under its first president, Tomás Estrada Palma (1902–1906), Cuba had its first revolution following an election characterized by fraud. Estrada Palma, appealing to the Platt Amendment, under the threat of which Cuba lived for thirty-two years, called for United States intervention. There followed the administration of Charles E. Magoon as governor from 1906 to 1909, a period about which there are widely differing judgments concerning the efficiency and honesty of the regime. The restoration of Cuban government under the presidency of José Miguel Gómez (1909–1913) witnessed increased venality and new lows in political morality. Putting into practice a phase generally attributed to him, *"el tiburón se baña, pero salpica"* (literally, "the shark bathes himself, but he also splashes"), he allowed his friends and supporters to grow fat at the expense of the Cuban treasury. His successor, Mario García Menocal (1913–1921) was equally ready to encourage the steadily increasing political corruption. His re-election, achieved by what were by now well-established, fraudulent practices, caused a revolt and a brief United States military intervention. The next president, Alfredo Zayas (1921–1925), while serving two masters like his predecessors, the Cuban people and the United States, further frustrated the hopes for honest and competent government as politics sank to a new low. This unhappy state of affairs continued under the presidency of Gerardo Machado (1925–1933) who was elected in 1924. After a brief attempt to moralize Cuban political life through the movement known as the *Regeneración* and the adoption of some measures designed to correct the dangerous one-sided character of an economy based on sugar production, Machado, in time, embarked upon a policy of extravagant public works, undertook new and profitable raids against the treasury, dispensed handsome favors to his friends in the form of concessions and contracts, and built an effective personal political machine. At the same time, as a consequence of the world depression and the fall of the sugar market, the Cuban people were in the midst of widespread unemployment and poverty, yet administrative graft still flourished. The graft involved in the construction of the Central Highway is said to have been thirty million dollars. Twenty millions were squandered on a new capitol of which only eight million were actually spent in construction. In 1928, after rigging the constitution, Machado was re-elected by what was known as *cooperativismo* (an alliance of all existing political parties). By this time, opposition to his regime, spearheaded by University students, had grown strong and determined. Machado then coupled graft with terror. Censorship, persecutions, and torture and murder of student and labor leaders proved ineffective against the wave of discontent and hatred against the dictatorship, and the regime finally collapsed when a general strike and an army revolt forced the "Butcher of Las Villas," as Machado was often called, to flee the country on August 12, 1933.

The revolutionary wave which swept away the dictatorship was originally set in motion by the generalized sentiment of national indignation against the invalidation of suffrage and the general political irresponsibility. In the course of its development, however, this feeling of national revulsion acquired all the characteristics of a more far-reaching program of economic, political, and social reform. The "Revolution," as it became known, although amorphous and lacking ideological substance, was clearly aimed at a radical transformation of all phases of national life.

The fall of Machado marked the end of the old oligarchy of professional politicians and the beginning of a new era of reform. The "generation of 1930," comprising the young students and professional men who led the successful movement against Machado, made its entry into politics. The bid of this generation for political power was to some extent satisfied in the subsequent period, for the only parties able to win national elections without resorting to fraud were those organized by members of this group. Their demands conflicted with the claims of professional politicians and veterans of the war for independence who had enjoyed a practical monopoly of power. The "generation of 1930," professing genuine economic, political, and social revolution, challenged the continued elite status of the veteran group while placing much of the blame for the political evils upon it. In the course of the struggle, the political influence of the veteran *caudillos*, such as Menocal, Mendieta, and others, substantially faded. The fall of Machado marked in another significant way the passing of an era. After having finally learned the futility of interventionist practices, the United States, acting in consistency with the newly adopted Good Neighbor Policy, abrogated the Platt Amendment in 1934.

The post revolutionary period was long and turbulent. Although achieving a remarkable record of accomplishments in economic development and social justice, "the generation of 1930" was later to be discredited by administrative ineptitude and tolerance of personal dishonesty. Its progressive contamination may be seen in the *auténtico* administrations of Grau San Martín (1944–1948) and Prío Socarrás (1948–1952), and the absolute disregard of civil liberties and constitutional forms during the Batista regimes.

II

After 1933, Cuban politics focused upon two figures who emerged from the revolutionary process. One was a civilian, the physician Ramón Grau San Martín, destined to be the leader of the so-called "Authentic Revolution." The other, a young sergeant, Fulgencio Batista, rose from poverty to the position of strong-man and president-maker, becoming the symbol and guarantor of stability and public order against revolutionary excesses. After starting at a brisk pace, during the "pentarchy" government (September 4–10, 1933), the revolution took further steps forward during the provisional presidency of Grau San Martín (September 10, 1933-January 17, 1934), and then came almost to a standstill. The refusal of the United States to recognize Grau San Martín was an important factor in the fall of his government. Concerned with the dangers inherent in social revolution and its impact on U. S. vested interests in the island, American policy was aimed at preservation of the *status quo*. Sumner Welles and later Jefferson Caffery, as personal representatives of President Roosevelt, played a major role in bringing the revolution to a halt. From then on, the revolution became chiefly political, not social and economic. One cannot help but wonder whether or not events in Cuba would have taken a different course, if the United States at that time had favored needed social and economic changes in Latin America as it is doing now. It is valid to pose such a question, for in some respects, the Cuban phenomenon of the 1950's was simply the reincarnation of the revolutionary process interrupted in the 1930's. Set in motion again, this process was to lead, in our time, to disastrous consequences in Cuban-American relations. Also, this time, the revolution was to become chiefly social and economic, not political.

Gradually, Batista, the one-time sergeant, emerged as the arbiter of Cuba's destiny. Until 1940, he ruled through puppet presidents, seven in all, among whom Carlos Mendieta (January, 1934-December, 1936), Miguel Mariano Gómez (1936), and Federico Laredo Brú (1936–1940) were the chief incumbents. Without ever disowning the revolutionary creed, Batista veered to a more conservative course, thus bringing recognition from the United States and the support of foreign investors and the great vested interests. He ruled sternly from behind the presidential chair with the backing of the army until 1940 when he officially assumed the chief executive's office, securing election with the support of a coalition of parties which included the political machines which had once dominated Cuban politics and supported dictator Machado.

For seven years, the constitutional basis of the Cuban government had remained irregular, but on October 10, 1940, a new constitution was adopted. Many of the provisions of this constitution represented radical departures from tradition and reflected the interest in social reform. Despite all the vicissitudes of the post-revolutionary period, the new basic law was clearly the fruit of the "Revolution," reflecting the influence of all those who advocated political, economic, and social changes. It was thought at the time that, at least, the trials and tribulations of the preceding decade had not all been in vain.

Meanwhile, the repository of the ideals of the revolution of 1933 had become the PRC or Cuban Revolutionary Party (*Auténtico*), founded in 1934 as a number of revolutionary organizations combined forces. The PRC played a leading role in drafting the Constitution of 1940, and was to win the presidency in 1944 and 1948. Its program featured economic and political nationalism and social justice while committing the PRC to fundamental reforms. It favored government control of the sugar industry, the establishment of a Tribunal of Accounts and a National Bank, a budget law, tax reforms, a civil service system, creation of a merchant marine, the expansion of education, etc. It also emphasized probity in administration. Under the colorful leadership of Dr. Grau San Martín, who gained immense popularity as the Batista regime became more and more corrupt in the midst of a new bonanza brought about by steady sugar prices, the PRC gained power through a sweeping electoral victory in 1944. It remained in office until the military coup of 1952. In 1948, although somewhat weaker than in 1944, the PRC's candidate Carlos Prío Socarrás handily won the election.

During its two terms in power, the PRC carried out a consid-

erable part of its program with some success. It was a firm exponent
of political democracy and it maintained scrupulous respect for
civil liberties. It established a well-designed policy of stabilization
of the price of sugar and of better distribution of the wealth
derived from this product; it sought to reduce the dangers of a
one-crop economy, gave impulse to a social security system, and
generously financed a vast educational program. During the Prío
Socarrás administration, important institutional reforms were undertaken and the Tribunal of Accounts and the National Bank were
established. On the other hand, the PRC failed to achieve important measures it had promised, chiefly, agrarian reform. More
importantly, far from responding to the popular clamor for honest
and efficient government, the PRC immersed itself in graft and
corruption on a scale surpassed only in recent years by Batista's
second regime. The public became thoroughly disillusioned and
bitter, and Grau San Martín was generally charged with the crime
of perpetrating a cynical fraud upon the Cuban people through
failure to implement and practice the very principles which he
professed. The *Auténticos* had come to power with the most
enthusiastic public support and with the high hopes of the people
that it would accomplish the long-desired social reforms and a
"purification" of governmental practices. These hopes came to
naught after the *Auténticos* enjoyed two terms in possession of the
presidency.

This situation was partly responsible for the rise of a new and
powerful organization, the Party of the Cuban People (*Ortodoxo*),
an offshoot of the PRC in 1946. By 1951, this party had become a
formidable political force under the dynamic leadership of Eduardo
Chibás who now became the standard-bearer of the campaign
for honest government. The party program of "economic independence, political liberty, and social justice" included also an insistence on keeping the party free from political pacts. Much
prestige had been lost by the PRC because of its disposition to ally
itself with some of the old traditional political groups. Observers
agree that, despite the absence of Chibás, who committed suicide
in 1951, had the election of 1952 not been prevented by the military
coup, the *Ortodoxos* would have readily won that contest.

However, as this election approached, the political balance sheet
showed a substantial margin on the credit side of the ledger: since
1940, the electoral processes, although not altogether free from
marring vices, had been generally fair and honest. Batista himself

had permitted an honest election in 1944 and had accepted with grace the victory of his archrival Grau San Martín over his own candidate. The *Auténticos'* victory in 1948 had been a clean one. Under such conditions there were grounds for hoping that, under the pressure of an electorate which had steadily grown more alert and articulate, and with the effectiveness of suffrage relatively assured, the return of morality in public office could eventually be attained. The best evidence that Cuba was an emergent democracy existed in the fact that the fullest freedom of expression and criticism was afforded the individual. Nevertheless, large segments of the population still longed for fundamental reforms of various institutions, and the bankrupt leadership had caused great disillusionment. Cuban public opinion desperately desired the "Revolution"—"to mean, at least, a fundamental departure from the venality, corruption, and fraud so characteristic of Cuban colonial and republican politics." This was demonstrated by the enthusiasm which Eduardo Chibás aroused by his passionate campaign for rectitude and integrity. And along with this went the conviction that these goals could be attained by democratic means. Meanwhile the country, in spite of thievery in public office and periodic looting of the treasury, had gone economically forward by leaps and bounds in a process of development only short of spectacular. There existed a strong organized labor movement, and some progress had been achieved toward social justice.

On March 10, 1952, eighty days before the scheduled elections, Batista, again a presidential candidate but without prospects of success, turned the clock back by his garrison revolt. This was the first, and in a sense, the greatest of his many crimes. What had come to be inconceivable in the minds of Cubans, namely, the settling of political contests by bayonets, suddenly became a frightful reality. Batista's only justification for his act was the woeful state into which public administration had fallen and the prevalence of political gangsterism. He obviously counted heavily upon public approval of what he was to do. The *Ortodoxos* had heaped such vilification upon the Prío Socarrás regime that Batista believed the people would welcome a change, even by violent means. Thus, although criticisms of Prío's regime were certainly well-founded, the highly charged emotional temper of Cuban politics which led the *Ortodoxo* opposition to excessive abuses, contributed to undermine not only the administration but the institutional order as well. Responsibility for the debacle was also to fall in part upon the shoulders of President Prío Socarrás whose inexplicable weakness in vacillating for hours before taking decisive action also contributed to the success of the coup. A close associate of Prío and prominent member of his government told me in 1952 of the astounding spectacle of the president sunk in a chair in an apparent stupor while telephones rang ceaselessly and delegations from political organizations and citizen groups flooded into his office. He was seemingly powerless from shock and helpless to react to the situation. The telephone calls were from chiefs of garrisons from all over the country seeking instructions (they had not yet gone over to Batista's side), and the delegations pouring into the palace were offering to take up arms.

Public opinion was dazed and a sensation of temporary paralysis invaded the entire nation. The usurping government interpreted this as acquiescence and Batista conceived the hope that it would be possible for him to consolidate his position rapidly by rebuilding his political machine, and, with an *ad hoc* electoral system, give legality to his government. This would be in line with the thinking of Batista, since those who know him well state that he is not a man of extremes, and only recurs to excesses when forced to do so. He has never achieved the one thing he has always wanted most, popularity. His failure can be traced in part to political circumstances, to his insatiable greed for wealth and power, and also to the methods he used to further his political career. This contention is well supported by the obvious vacillations between respect for legality and arbitrariness which characterized his rule.

However, public opinion reacted unfavorably to these events. In keeping with tradition, the University students soon assumed the vanguard of the opposition forces. Their ranks were swelled by the *Ortodoxo* and *Auténtico* parties in an attitude of passive resistance with some attempts at conspiratorial activity. It is not within the scope of this article to trace the events which finally led to the outbreak of a full-fledged revolution, but it may be well to summarize some of the major incidents in this process.

After restoring the Constitution of 1940, in response to public pressure, Batista decided to hold elections on November 3, 1953. Far from giving guarantees for the holding of such a contest, he imposed the Draconian legislation known as the *Ley de Orden Público*. On the eve of the elections the atmosphere of violence and coercion forced the withdrawal of the only candidate opposing Batista, Dr. Grau San Martín. So scandalous were these elections that even some of the partisans of Batista, whose personal ambitions had been thwarted, denounced them as a farce. The net result of the event was an increase of general agitation followed by a repression on the part of the government. The regime resorted to the creation of an unscrupulous and complex police apparatus employing a variety of violent methods and the jails filled rapidly with political prisoners. The opposition remained disunited and the two main political parties (*Ortodoxo* and *Auténtico*) were rent asunder by internal fragmentation.

III

The first open gesture of revolt was the desperate and suicidal attack against the Moncada Barracks in Santiago de Cuba, on July 26, 1953. This attack was led by Fidel Castro, a former student leader, who had joined the ranks of the *Ortodoxo* Party only to abandon it later as he became convinced that open rebellion was the only solution to the Cuban situation. The failure of the Moncada attack and the brutal repression that followed it shook the country. The passionate plea for freedom made by Castro at his trial added fuel to the revolutionary fervor. A sentence of 15 years in prison for Castro came to an end in May, 1955, with a general amnesty. A few months after the attack in 1953, another civilian attempt at storming a military barracks was undertaken in the raid on the Goicuría Barracks in Matanzas, this time by partisans of Prío Socarrás. The failure of these attempts and the severe repression that followed them gave rise to a general demand for peace. Efforts at compromise and the search for a peaceful solution were made first by the Sociedad de Amigos de la República, a group of distinguished citizens, and later by the Bloque de Prensa, composed of representatives of the press. Both efforts resulted in failure. All other attempts to bring the matter to the field of negotiation rather than that of civil war bore no fruit due to increasingly deep feelings of hatred and resentment. The opposition demanded the resignation of Batista and the establishment of a "neutral" government as a preliminary step to any peaceful formula.

The historic landing of Castro with 81 other youths on the coast of Oriente Province occurred on December 2, 1956. Only a dozen escaped to seek refuge in the wilderness of the Sierra Maestra mountains. This group was to grow into the rebel army which ultimately defeated the dictatorship. While the insurrection was spreading in Oriente, an attack on the presidential palace in Havana took place in 1957. The attempt, perpetrated by a group of the Revolutionary Directorate, another revolutionary organization, came close to succeeding in assassinating Batista. The brutal revenge taken by the regime, in the form of murder and torture applied indiscriminately to all opponents of Batista, terrorized the population.

By January, 1958, a revolutionary mood was widespread all over the island. Supposedly in response to indirect pressure from the United States, the Batista regime restored the constitutional guarantees with the consequent lifting of censorship. This resulted in a gigantic barrage of attacks against the government through all media of communication, and in the public exposure of the many atrocities committed by the government forces in the preceding months. Public feeling against the government was exacerbated, reaching a new pitch of intensity. For the first time, reports of rebel activities in Oriente were made public. Striking changes of opinion and attitudes among certain segments of the population could be noted and compared with those existing in 1957. At that time substantial elements of the upper and upper-middle classes had not been in favor of Batista but neither had they been openly on the side of the rebellion. In 1958, on the contrary, it could be observed that Castro had gained strong support among these groups. Businessmen, Americans included, were admitting that the situation as it then stood could not continue and that Batista would have to go. By March 1, the fall of the government seemed imminent. The island was flooded by rebel leaflets and other propaganda designed to arouse the people to a nation-wide revolt. While tension was mounting, an attempt at reconciliation was instigated by the Catholic Church hierarchy; again, it resulted in failure. Shortly thereafter, Batista once more revoked constitutional guarantees and declared a state of siege. To stifle the general strike called by Castro, Batista decreed the most drastic measures ever known in the history of the country. The strike called for April 9 was crushed in a matter of hours by brutal methods. The general feeling of dismay at the failure of the strike was mixed with a strong sentiment of horror at the bloody measures resorted to by the dictatorship. The situation developed into a temporary military stalemate. The rebel forces continued in control of large areas of the provinces of Santa Clara and Oriente, and by then con-

sisted of well-organized, efficient, and well-trained men in considerable numbers. Several government offensives to destroy the
rebel forces floundered.

Meanwhile, elections were again set for November 3, 1958. The
four government parties which formed the Progressive National
Coalition (Acción Progresista, Partido Liberal, Partido Demócrata,
and Unión Radical) began an active campaign on behalf of Batista's
personal choice as president, ex-Prime Minister Andrés Rivero
Agüero. There were three other avowed candidates for the presidency: Grau San Martín, supported by a small faction of the PRC;
Carlos Márquez Sterling, backed by the Partido del Pueblo Libre;
and an obscure newspaperman, Alberto Salas Amaro, nominated
by Unión Cubana Party, an insignificant faction. The elections
generated little true public interest. Obviously, with all civil rights
suspended, no legal apparatus in existence, the judicial system
reduced to a mockery, and groups of gangsters roaming the
countryside, the atmosphere was not propitious to the holding of an
electoral contest. Nevertheless the elections took place as scheduled
and the victory went to Batista's choice. If possible, this balloting
was even more farcical than the elections of 1953, and the percentage of voters was the lowest ever registered. Less than two months
later, in the face of outstanding rebel military victories, the Batista
dictatorship crumbled. Following Batista's departure, efforts to arrange for a caretaker government and to preserve the trappings of
"legality" failed when the Rebel Army refused to recognize the
authority of Carlos M. Piedra, senior justice of the Supreme Court,
appointed by army chief General Cantillo, and declared its intention
of continuing the war. It was only a matter of hours before the
rebel-organized government headed by Dr. Manuel Urrutia was in
complete control of the country.

The success of the 26th of July Movement can be explained
only by the national feeling of revulsion for existing political habits,
a feeling which had reached nearly universal proportions. A Cuban
historian, Ramiro Guerra, issued a prophetic warning some years
ago. Referring to electoral malpractices and immorality, he wrote:
"There exists in this situation a general sentiment of indignation
and public shame which is assuming a very dangerous character.
At any period when grave economic or political difficulties are confronted by some administration, the fuel is there to start a revolutionary commotion of incalculable consequences. . . . I believe that
Cuba is approaching by long strides a profound transformation of

its public customs." Another keen commentator expressed it this way: "As long as this state of affairs persists, as long as impunity prevails, often sanctioned by the government itself, civic life will lack the protection of the law, and public morals will lack the cornerstone upon which they can solidly rest."

The astonishment of many observers at the unprecedented revolutionary fervor of the Cuban people in the early months of 1959 might be chiefly attributed to their failure to appraise, in its true dimension, the popular sentiment for a change in public customs. Many have pointed out in the past, as an encouraging factor, the capacity of Cubans for self-analysis and self-criticism. In spite of the attitude and behavior of politicians, the majority of Cubans, although recognizing that all governments suffer, in some degree, from graft and corruption, have always rejected the notion that these practices should become the norm of political behavior, and that those responsible for criminal acts should go unpunished. The marvel is that this ideal persisted in the face of so many frustrations. The belief of the overwhelming majority which enthusiastically welcomed in 1959 the triumph of the new "Revolution" was that the time had come when political leaders could no longer ignore the persistent desire for a moral political climate.

IV

In many respects, the 26th of July Movement was the direct heir of the "Revolution" of 1933. Its program was not too different from the original planks of the PRC or the postulates of the *Ortodoxos* of Eduardo Chibás. Like the ideologies of these two parties; it featured political democracy, political and economic nationalism, agrarian reform, industrialization, social security, and education. There existed, however, some significant facets of the new "Revolution" which, from the beginning, set it in a somewhat different context than that of the 1933 movement. For some time references have been made in Cuba to the "generation of 1950," meaning by it the group of young and rising men who supposedly were exerting presure for political influence in direct clash with the claims of those who enjoyed power from 1933 to this date, members of the "generation of 1930," who are still relatively young and able to participate in politics. This new "generation of 1950," which Fidel Castro and his guerrilla fighters allegedly represented condemned those, who, in their words, had profaned the "Revolution" with repugnant crimes and scandalous graft, and had defrauded the people and demoralized the nation. This group cried out for "genuine" revolution and for a drastic and prompt removal of the political cancers which have plagued the country since its inception.

Consideration of the "generation of 1950" leads us into one of the apparently unique characteristics of the 26th of July Movement, namely, the curiously ethical, moralistic, almost puritanical over-tones with which the movement was pervaded. Its existence was demonstrated by the known events of the two-year war—the testimony of Americans kidnapped by the rebels, the humane treatment of prisoners despite the torturing and killings inflicted on them by government troops, the way supplies requisitioned from peasants and storekeepers were duly paid for, and the strict dis-cipline and morality reported to have existed in all rebel camps. Additional evidence of the movement's emphasis on morals was later furnished by the exemplary behavior of rebel troops during the occupation of the cities, their successful efforts to prevent looting and disorder, and the quick but gentle manner in which public order was restored. The significance of these factors lies in their apparently great popular appeal, in their salutory effect of shaking the rather widespread cynicism among Cubans toward their leaders, and in their kindling the embers of a political crusade in which each citizen saw himself as an active participant in the task of reor-ganizing the country. There was no question that a renovation of the political personnel as well as a rectification of political mores in Cuba had, of necessity, to be preceded by the development of civic consciousness and responsibility, and the eradication of the national tendency toward lack of discipline. There was no doubt either that large segments of the population had not yet developed a sense of personal initiative or of responsibility to work coopera-tively to achieve solution of national problems, of which they were not necessarily unaware. If this sense was to be developed, most Cubans agreed that it was necessary to restore, first of all, public confidence in the competence and morality of those responsible for government. Thus, the moralistic spirit of the 26th of July Movement was not only desirable but indispensable if it was to attain its goals of political and social reform.

A second feature of the new "Revolution" was the greater im-portance it proposed to give to the provinces. Cuba, like many other Latin American countries, had always tended to concentrate all power and influence in the great and rapidly expanding urban centers, and especially in the capital city, to the detriment of the "interior," as the rest of the country is generally called by Cubans. Historically, Havana has been the all-powerful administrative center since colonial days. As industry developed, it too had generally concentrated in the capital. Since the middle classes are predominantly urban and their largest segments are found there, these classes have traditionally favored national policies which promoted the growth of the capital and assigned to it a disproportionately large share of public revenues. The provinces in many respects have been artificial institutions, serving as political and administrative agencies of the central government rather than as agencies to represent local interests. Thus, the nature of the governmental structure, minimizing local autonomy and initiative, represented one of the main difficulties in translating intentions and self-criticism into action for improvement. As for municipal home rule, despite the autonomy granted to the cities, and the extensive powers granted to the municipalities in the Constitution of 1940, in practice the interests favoring centralization had always prevailed. The small degree of decentralization which has been permitted had tended to be administrative rather than political. The 26th of July Movement, in contrast with the "Revolution" of 1933, was not born in the capital, but in the eastern province of Oriente, cradle of the wars for emancipation and depositary of noble traditions of liberty. Santiago, its capital, of all the cities in Cuba, was destined to suffer the brunt of the civil war, and its population became the most frequently victimized by bloody measures of repression, gaining for itself in the process the name of the "martyr city." It was in recognition of its heroic role that Fidel Castro, following victory, proclaimed it provisional capital of the republic.

Spokesmen for the 26th of July Movement constantly emphasized, during the course of the struggle, the need for giving justice to the provinces, criticizing strongly the fact that hitherto, power, wealth, and income had been concentrated in Havana. Since his forces took control of the government, Castro often expressed the desire that governmental power and income be more decentralized and representative. Going beyond mere recognition of the greater role played in the revolution by the population of the provinces, both rural and urban, in contrast to the relatively minor contribution made by the capital, plans presumably contemplated decentralized control of some essential economic activities by basing the Ministry of Mines in Oriente Province, the tobacco authority in Pinar del Rio, the control of sugar in the center and east, and that of cattle in Camagüey. In addition, there seemed to exist a determination to implement effectively the constitutional provisions hitherto disregarded so as to attain a greater administrative decentralization and a fairer distribution of income, a long-sought-after political goal opposed with success in the past by the capital's influential interests.

A third, and perhaps the most distinctive feature of the 26th of July Movement was its emphasis on agrarian reform, and the decision on the part of its leaders to push forward, against all obstacles, the breaking up of large estates. Castro has said that land redistribution was the basis of the "Revolution" and that it would ultimately benefit about 200,000 families throughout the island. Cuba is a country of paradox. It is blessed by nature with the optimum climate and soil to provide in abundance almost any food crops, and yet the vast majority of the Cuban rural population is impoverished, ill-fed, ill-housed, and poorly clothed. Less than 0.1 per cent of Cuban farms contain one-fifth of all agricultural land, and 8 per cent of the farms comprise seventy per cent of the land. Small farmers have an insignificant share of the land. Those with farms under 63 acres constitute 70 per cent of all operators and own only 11 per cent of the land. 18 per cent of the two million hectares of cultivated land belongs to those who work it, the rest being tilled under forms of tenancy.

The large plantation, however, was a comparatively recent phenomenon in Cuba. In contrast to other Latin American countries, the *latifundio* system was relatively unimportant in colonial Cuba, and there was originally a fairly wide distribution of land. While at one time vast areas of the island were included within large circular *haciendas*, many of these properties were communally owned. The communal *haciendas* were later subdivided with the introduction of a new land-use pattern necessitated by the development of sugar cane and tobacco. However, throughout these stages, a comparatively broad basis of land ownership always prevailed, and Cuba counted a large rural population, rooted in land which they owned and exploited personally. With the expansion of the sugar industry, sparked by the slave uprising in Haiti in 1789, and later stimulated by technical developments such as steam power and railroads, the appearance of the sugar *latifundia* radically

changed the island's land-tenure pattern. In order to assure themselves of an ample supply of cane for the mills, sugar companies
acquired immense tracts of land.

It must be remembered that the change of Cuba from colonial
to independent status coincided with the last stage of development
of economic capitalism which featured mass production, financial
concentration and combination of economic interests with international branches, and colonial imperialism. National and international cartels began to flourish in the 1880's and, after the island's
independence, found a favorable environment in which to operate.
Increases of production and exports, as well as financial and technical
expansion were, in general, achieved at the expense of the small
farmers and operators. Powerful sugar companies purchased land
in some cases, and in others obtained control by one-sided legal
suits or by taking advantage of the prevailing corruption in government. The industry passed largely from the hands of the individuals to those of large corporations, many of which were
foreign-owned. The result was that the land in Cuba, once widely
distributed among its inhabitants, became concentrated in the
present century in the hands of a few, and at the same time the
country was committed to the instability of a one-crop economy
dependent upon foreign consumption.

It was not, however, until after the world depression of 1930
had brought disaster to the Cuban economy that agitation for
agrarian reform began. The strong desire for changes in the land
system was manifested in the revolutionary thought of 1933.
During the period following Machado's overthrow, a policy of governmental intervention and control of the sugar industry, which
had a timid start in 1926, began to emerge, and a long series of
governmental actions, designed to protect the small farmer and the
worker, were adopted. An important highlight in the development
of this policy was the adoption of the *Ley de Coordinación
Azucarera* of 1937 and its subsequent modifications, which prescribed in minute detail the rights and obligations of all the factors
(producers, laborers, and mills) participating in the sugar industry.
A few years later, the Constitution of 1940 included provisions
which forbade large landholdings and regulated the acquisition
and possession of land by foreign individuals and companies. Thus,
since 1933, a great deal had been accomplished on the way to a
more rational planning of sugar production and a fairer distribution of its income. The social, political, and economic position of

the agricultural worker had vastly improved in the last decades but still, this betterment was largely confined to the sugar mill workers, approximately 450,000 persons. The rest of the peasantry benefited only insignificantly from the voluminous labor and social legislation enacted since 1933; no adequate reform of the land-tenure system was ever attempted, and constitutional provisions to this end remained a dead letter. The sugar industry still controlled about one and a half million hectares of lands in reserve which were not actually under cultivation.

Another factor which bore upon agricultural problems was the economic dependence of Cuba on the United States, determined chiefly by the geographical proximity of the vast American sugar consumer demand. This often placed Cuba in a weak bargaining position because of the threat or reality of overproduction. Cuban sugar had to compete with United States growers who enjoyed tariff protection, and yet costs of production were becoming gradually more nearly equal. The several periods of "boom and bust" typical of the industry tended to squeeze out all but the largest producers, with the consequent decrease in the number of mills accompanied by an increase in the area from which each mill received its cane. It was estimated that U. S. investors accounted for 60 per cent of the billion dollars invested in the industry. Economic dependency upon the United States engendered strong feelings of national pride and led many Cubans to want to liberate themselves from what is referred to as economic colonialism. This desire was linked to the popular demand for agrarian reform.

With one-third of all arable land devoted to sugar cane, it does not seem feasible, nonetheless, for Cuba, in the near future, to alter the conditions which have linked its economic future to the fortunes of the sugar industry. After all, Cuba's optimum conditions for the production of sugar could support a trebling of present output were it not for artificial restrictions imposed by other countries. Most Cubans are agreed that agrarian reform does not necessarily mean abandoning sugar. There were great expanses of land not in use which could be distributed among the landless, and devoted to supplying the country with some of the products imported, such as rice, beans, and vegetables.

Finally, another distinctive feature of the 26th of July Movement was its complete identification with its leader Fidel Castro. This heavily charismatic or personalistic rather than institutional leadership gave the movement much of its course and character.

It was always reported, while the Cuban rebellion was in progress, that the plans of the 26th of July Movement for the country's future were uncertain and vague. It was also said that because of Castro's ability to capture the imagination of thousands of men and women who never knew him personally, the appeal of the movement was in his personality, not in his program. Its success, therefore, largely depended upon one man, Fidel Castro. The extraordinary circumstances of his accession to power, almost inevitably also made the revolutionary government into a government run by one man. How was the dilemma of a man and a movement committed to freedom and human dignity to be resolved? In the words of a distinguished Argentine writer, Alberdi: "Tyranny cannot live unless personified in one man, but liberty perishes as soon as it is embodied in one leader."

Subsequent events in Cuba have amply demonstrated the wisdom of Alberdi's dictum.

Revolution in the Revolution?

Regis Debray

How is a vanguard party formed? Can the Party, under existing Latin American conditions, create the popular army, or is it up to the popular army to create the vanguard? Which is the nucleus of which?

For reasons beyond their control, many Latin American Communist Parties made a false start, 30 or 40 years ago, thus creating a complicated situation. But parties are never anything but instruments of class struggle. Where the instrument no longer serves its purpose, should the class struggle come to a halt or should new instruments be forged?* A childish question: no one can make such a decision. The class struggle, especially in Latin America today, can be curbed, eroded, deflected, but it cannot be stopped. The people devise their own vanguards, making do with what is available, and the duty of revolutionaries is to hasten this development. But the development of what, precisely?

We are witnessing today, here and there, strange reversals. Che Guevara wrote that the guerrilla movement is not an end in itself, nor is it a glorious adventure; it is merely a means to an end: the conquest of political power. But, lo and behold, guerrilla forces were serving many other purposes: a form of pressure on bourgeois governments; a factor in political horse-trading; a trump card to be

* Our description does not apply to countries where the absence of a serious struggle for power has so far permitted political organizations to escape such tensions.

played in case of need—such were the objectives with which certain leaderships were attempting to saddle their military instrumentalities. The revolutionary method was being utilized for reformist ends.* Then, after a period of marking time, the guerrillas turned away from and rejected these goals imposed from outside and assumed their own political leadership. To become reconciled with itself, the guerrilla force set itself up as a political leadership, which was the only way to resolve the contradictions and to develop militarily. Let it be noted that no part of the guerrilla movement has attempted to organize a new party; it seeks rather to wipe out doctrinal or party divisions among its own combatants. The unifying factors are the war and its immediate political objectives. The guerrilla movement begins by creating unity within itself around the most urgent military tasks, which have already become political tasks, a unity of non-party elements and of all the parties represented among the *guerrilleros*. The most decisive political choice is membership in the guerrilla forces, in the Armed Forces of Liberation. Thus gradually this small army creates rank-and-file unity among all parties, as it grows and wins its first victories. Eventually, the future People's Army will beget the party of which it is to be, theoretically, the instrument: essentially the party is the army.

Did not the Cuban Revolution experience this same paradox? It has been said with dismay that the party, the usual instrument for the seizure of power, was developed *after* the conquest of power. But no, it already existed in embryo—in the form of the Rebel Army. Fidel, its commander in chief, was already an unofficial party leader by early 1959. A foreign journalist in Cuba was astonished one day to see many Communist leaders in battledress; he had thought that battle-dress and pistols belonged to the folklore of the Revolution, that they were really a kind of martial affectation. Poor man! It was not an affectation, it was the history of the Revolution itself appearing before his eyes, and most certainly the future history of America. Just as the name of socialism was formally applied to the revolution after a year of socialist practice, the name of the party came into use three years after the proletarian party had begun to exist in uniform. In Cuba it was not the party that was the directive nucleus of the popular army,

* See "Política y Guerrillas," by Fernández y Zanetti, in *El Caimán Barbudo*, No. 8, Havana.

as it had been in Vietnam according to Giap; the Rebel Army was the leading nucleus of the party, the nucleus that created it. The first party leaders were created on July 26, 1953, at Moncada. The party is the same age as the revolution; it will be fourteen on July 26, 1967. Moncada was the nucleus of the Rebel Army, which was in turn the nucleus of the party. Around this nucleus, and only because it already had its own political-military leadership, other political forces have been able to assemble and unite, forming what is today the Community Party of Cuba, of which both the base and the head continue to be made up of comrades from the guerrilla army.

The Latin American revolution and its vanguard, the Cuban revolution, have thus made a decisive contribution to international revolutionary experience and to Marxism-Leninism.

Under certain conditions, the political and the military are not separate, but form one organic whole, consisting of the people's army, whose nucleus is the guerrilla army. The vanguard party can exist in the form of the guerrilla foco itself. The guerrilla force is the party in embryo.

This is the staggering novelty introduced by the Cuban Revolution.

It is indeed a contribution. One could of course consider this an exceptional situation, the product of a unique combination of circumstances, without further significance. On the contrary, recent developments in countries that are in the vanguard of the armed struggle on the continent confirm and reinforce it. It is reinforced because, whereas the ideology of the Cuban Rebel Army was not Marxist, the ideology of the new guerrilla commands is clearly so, just as the revolution which is their goal is clearly socialist and proletarian. It is precisely because their line is so clear and their determination so unalterable that they have had to separate themselves, at a certain point, from the existing vanguard parties and propose (as in Guatemala) or impose (as in Venezuela) their own political, ideological, and organizational ideas as the foundation of any possible agreement, on a take-it-or-leave-it basis. In sum, it was necessary in both cases to discontinue all organic dependence on political parties and to replace these enfeebled political vanguards. In other words, they had to reach the point at which the Cuban Revolution started.

Thus ends a divorce of several decades' duration between Marxist theory and revolutionary practice. As tentative and tenuous as the reconciliation may appear, it is the guerrilla movement—master of its own political leadership—that embodies it, this handful of men "with no other alternative but death or victory, at moments when death was a concept a thousand times more real, and victory a myth that only a revolutionary can dream of." (Che) These men may die, but others will replace them. Risks must be taken. The union of theory and practice is not an inevitability but a battle, and no battle is won in advance. If this union is not achieved there, it will not be achieved anywhere.

The guerrilla force, if it genuinely seeks total political warfare cannot in the long run tolerate any fundamental duality of functions or powers. Che Guevara carries the idea of unity so far that he proposes that the military and political leaders who lead insurrectional struggles in America be "united, if possible, in one person." But whether it is an individual, as with Fidel, or collective, the important thing is that the leadership be homogeneous, political and military simultaneously. Career soldiers can, in the process of the people's war, become political leaders (Luis Turcios, for example, had he lived); militant political leaders can become military leaders, learning the art of war by making it (Douglas Bravo, for example).

In any case, it is necesary that they be able to make it. *A guerrilla force cannot develop on the military level if it does not become a political vanguard.* As long as it does not work out its own line, as long as it remains a pressure group or a device for creating a political diversion, it is fruitlessly marking time, however successful its partial actions may be. How can it take the initiative? On what will it build its morale? Do we perhaps believe that it will go "too far" if it is allowed to become the catalyst for popular aspirations and energies, which will *ipso facto* transform it into a directive force? Precisely because it is a mass struggle—the most radical of all—the guerrilla movement, if it is to triumph *militarily*, must *politically* assemble around it the majority of the exploited classes. Victory is impossible without their active and organized participation, since it is the general strike or generalized urban insurrection that will give the coup de grâce to the régime and will defeat its final maneuvers—a last-minute coup d'état, a new junta, elections—by extending the struggle throughout the country. But in order to reach that point, must there not be a long and patient effort by the mountain forces to coordinate all forms of struggle, eventually to coordinate action by the militia with that of the regular forces, to coordinate rearguard sabotage by the suburban guerrillas with operations carried out by the principal guerrilla group? And, beyond the armed struggle, must there not be an effort to play an ever larger role in the country's civilian life? Whence the importance of a radio transmitter at the disposition of the guerrilla forces. The radio permits headquarters to establish daily contact with the population residing outside the zone of operations. Thus the latter can receive political instructions and orientation which, as military successes increase, find an ever-increasing echo. In Cuba *Radio Rebelde*, which began transmitting in 1958, was frequently utilized by Fidel, and confirmed the role of the Rebel Army's General Staff as the directive force of the revolutionary movement. Increasingly, everyone—from Catholics to Communists—looked to the Sierra, tuned in to get reliable news, to know "what to do" and "where the action is." Clandestinity became public. As revolutionary methods and goals became more radical, so did the people. After Batista's fight, Fidel broadcast his denunciation of the maneuvers for a coup d'état in the capital, thus depriving the ruling class in a matter of minutes of its last card, and sealing the ultimate victory. Even before victory, the radio broke through government censorship on military operations, a censorship such as prevails today in all embattled countries. It is by means of radio that the guerrillas force the doors of truth and open them wide to the entire populace, especially if they follow the ethical precepts that guided *Radio Rebelde*—never broadcast inaccurate news, never conceal a defeat, never exaggerate a victory. In short, radio produces a qualitative change in the guerrilla movement. This explains the muffled or open resistance which certain party leaders offer today to the guerrilla movement's use of this propaganda medium.

Thus, in order for the small motor really to set the big motor of the masses into motion, without which its activity will remain limited, it must first be recognized by the masses as their only interpreter and guide, under penalty of dividing and weakening the people's strength. In order to bring about this recognition, the guerrillas must assume all the functions of political and military authority. Any guerrilla movement in Latin America that wishes to pursue the people's war to the end, transforming itself if necessary into a regular army and beginning a war of movement and positions, must become the unchallenged political vanguard, with the essential elements of its leadership being incorporated in the military command.

How can this "heresy" be justified? What gives the guerrilla movement the right to claim this political responsibility as its own and for itself alone?

The answer is: that class alliance which it alone can achieve, the alliance that will take and administer power, the alliance whose interests are those of socialism—the alliance between workers and peasants. The guerrilla army is a confirmation in action of this alliance; it is the personification of it. When the guerrilla army assumes the prerogatives of political leadership, it is responding to its class content and anticipating tomorrow's dangers. It alone can guarantee that the people's power will not be perverted after victory. If it does not assume the functions of political leadership during the course of emancipation itself, it will not be able to assume them when the war is over. And the bourgeoisie, with all necessary imperialist support, will surely take advantage of the situation. We have only to observe the difficulties in which Algeria finds itself today, because of yesterday's division between the internal fighters and their government outside the country. There is no better example of the risks implicit in the separation of military and political functions when there is no Marxist vanguard party. Thus it it the revolutionary civil war that strengthens the historic agencies of the new society. Lenin, in his last notes, wrote that "the civil war has *welded* together the working class and the peasantry, and this is the *guarantee of an invincible strength.*"*

In the mountains, then, workers, peasants, and intellectuals meet for the first time. Their integration is not so easy at the beginning. Just as there are divisions into classes elsewhere, groups can arise even in the midst of an encampment. The peasants, especially if they are of Indian origin, stay to themselves and speak their own language (Quechua or Cakchiquel), among themselves. The others, those who know how to write and speak well, spontaneously create their own circle. Mistrust, timidity, custom, have to be gradually vanquished by means of untiring political work, in which the leaders set the example. These men all have something to learn from each other, beginning with their differences. Since they must all adapt themselves to the same conditions of life, and since they are all participating in the same undertaking, they adapt to each other. Slowly the shared existence, the combats, the hardships endured

* Draft of a speech (not delivered) for the Tenth Congress of Russian Soviets, December 1922. Lenin's emphasis.

together, weld an alliance having the simple force of friendship. Furthermore the first law of guerrilla life is that no one survives it alone. The group's interest is the interest of each one, and vice versa. To live and conquer is to live and conquer all together. If a single combatant lags behind a marching column, it affects the speed and security of the entire column. In the rear is the enemy: impossible to leave the comrade behind or send him home. It is up to everyone, then, to share the burden, lighten his knapsack or cartridge-case, and help him all the way. Under these conditions class egoism does not long endure. Petty bourgeois psychology melts like snow under the summer sun, undermining the ideology of the same stratum. Where else could such an encounter, such an alliance, take place? By the same token, the only conceivable line for a guerrilla group to adopt is the "mass line"; it can live only with their support, in daily contact with them. Bureaucratic faint-heartedness becomes irrelevant. Is this not the best education for a future socialist leader or cadre? Revolutionaries make revolutionary civil wars; but to an even greater extent it is revolutionary civil war that makes revolutionaries.

Lenin wrote: "The civil war has educated and tempered (Denikin and the others are good *teachers*; they have taught well; *all our best militants have been in the army*)."*

The best teacher of Marxism-Leninism is the enemy, in face-to-face confrontation during the people's war. Study and apprenticeship are necessary but not decisive. There are no academy-trained cadres. One cannot claim to train revolutionary cadres in theoretical schools detached from instructional work and common combat experiences. To think otherwise would be justifiable naïveté in Western Europe; elsewhere it is unpardonable nonsense.

The guerrilla group's exercise of, or commitment to establish, a political leadership is even more clearly revealed when it organizes its first liberated zone. It then tries out and tests tomorrow's revolutionary measures (as on the Second Front in Oriente): agrarian reform, peasant congresses, levying of taxes, revolutionary tribunals, the discipline of collective life. The liberated zone becomes the prototype and the model for the future state, its administrators the models for future leaders of state. Who but a popular armed force can carry through such socialist "rehearsals"?

The worker-peasant alliance often finds its connecting link in a

---

* *Ibid.* Lenin's emphasis.

group of revolutionaries of bourgeois extraction, from which a
substantial part of the guerrilla command is recruited. Even if today
this tendency is decreasing, because of the extreme polarization of
social classes, it is far from having been eliminated.

Such is the law of "equivalent-substitutions" in countries that
have been colonized even to a limited extent: one finds that a
working class of restricted size or under the influence of a reformist
trade union aristocracy, and an isolated and humiliated peasantry,
are willing to accept this group, of bourgeois origin, as their
political leadership. In the course of the struggle which awakens
and mobilizes them, a kind of provisional delegation of powers is
produced.* Inversely, in order to assume this function, this historic
vicarship, and in order not to usurp a role to which they have only
a provisional title, this progressive petty bourgeoisie must, to use
Amilcar Cabral's phrase, "commit suicide as a class in order to be
restored to life as revolutionary workers, totally identified with the
deepest aspirations of their people." The most favorable time and
place for this suicide is with the guerrillas, during guerrilla action:
here, the small initial groups from the cities have their first daily
contact with rural realities, little by little adjust themselves to its
demands, and begin to understand from the inside the aspirations of
their people; they cast aside political verbosity and make of these
aspirations their program of action. Where better than in the
guerrilla army could this shedding of skin and this resurrection
take place?

Here the political word is abruptly made flesh. The revolutionary
ideal emerges from the gray shadow of formula and acquires substance in the full light of day. This transubstantiation comes as a
surprise, and when those who have experienced it want to describe
it—in China, in Vietnam, in Cuba, in many places—they resort not
to words but to exclamations.

> The renovating spirit, the longing for collective excellence, the
> awareness of a higher destiny are in full flower and can develop
> considerably further. We had heard of these things, which had a
> flavor of verbal abstraction, and we accepted their beautiful mean-
> ing, but now we are living it, we are experiencing it in every
> sense, and it is truly unique. We have seen its incredible develop-
> ment in this Sierra, which is our small universe. Here the word

* On this subject see "Tercer Mundo e Ideología," by Rachid, in *El
Caimán Barbudo,* No. 2 (Havana).

"people," which is so often utilized in a vague and confused sense, becomes a living, wonderful and dazzling reality. *Now* I know who the people are: I see them in that invincible force that surrounds us everywhere, I see them in the bands of 30 or 40 men, lighting their way with lanterns, who descend the muddy slopes at two or three in the morning, with 30 kilos on their backs, in order to supply us with food. Who has organized them so wonderfully? Where did they acquire so much ability, astuteness, courage, self-sacrifice? No one knows! It is almost a mystery! They organize themselves all alone, spontaneously! When weary animals drop to the ground, unable to go further, men appear from all directions and carry the goods. Force cannot defeat them. It would be necessary to kill them all, to the last peasant, and that is impossible; this, the dictatorship cannot do; the people are aware of it and are daily more aware of their own growing strength.*

All these factors, operating together, gave shape to a strange band which was made to appear picturesque by certain photographs and which, because of our stupidity, impressed us only through the attire and long beards of its members. These are the militants of our time, not martyrs, not functionaries, but fighters. Neither creatures of an apparatus nor potentates: at this stage, they themselves are the apparatus. Aggressive men, especially in retreat. Resolute and responsible, each of them knowing the meaning and goal of this armed class struggle through its leaders, fighters like themselves whom they see daily carrying the same packs on their backs, suffering the same blistered feet and the same thirst during a march. The blasé will smile at this vision à la Rousseau. We need not point out here that it is not love of nature nor the pursuits of happiness which brought them to the mountain, but the awareness of a historic necessity. Power is seized and held in the capital, but the road that leads the exploited to it must pass through the countryside. Need we recall that war and military discipline are characterized by rigors unknown to the *Social Contract?* This is even truer for guerrilla armies than for regular armies. Today some of these groups have disappeared before assuming a vanguard role, having retreated or suffered liquidation. In a struggle of this kind,

---

* From Fidel Castro's last letter to Frank País, written in the Sierra Maestra, July 21, 1957. The same wonderment is expressed today in the letters of Turcios, Douglas Bravo, Camilo Torres, and others. Of course this does not mean that it is easy to obtain peasant support immediately; but when it is obtained, it performs wonders. Fidel wrote the letter after eight months in the Sierra and after having escaped betrayal by several peasants.

which involves such grave risks and is still only in the process of taking its first faltering steps, such defeats are normal. Other groups, the most important ones operating in countries whose history proves their importance for all Latin America—Venezuela, Guatemala, Colombia—have established themselves and are moving ahead. It is there, in such countries as these, that history is on the march today. Tomorrow other countries will join and supersede them in the vanguard role.

Has it been noted that nearly all of these guerrilla movements neither have nor want political commissars? The majority of the fighters come from Communist ranks. These are the first socialist guerrilla forces that have not adopted the system of political commissars, a system which does not appear to correspond to the Latin American reality.

If what we have said makes any sense at all, this absence of specialists in political affairs has the effect of sanctioning the absence of specialists in military affairs. The people's army is its own political authority. The *guerrilleros* play both roles, indivisibly. Its commanders are political instructors for the fighters, its political instructors are its commanders.

Let us sum up. Not to understand perfectly the theoretical and historical novelty of this situation is to open the way to dangerous errors at the very core of the armed struggle. To consider the existing party as different from and superior to the new type of party that grows along with the guerrilla force leads logically to two attitudes.

(1) *The guerrilla force should be subordinated to the party.* The system of political commissars is a consequence of this subordination. It implies that the guerrilla army is incapable of leading itself and that it must be guided from outside; that is, it presupposes the existence of a leader, someone who can bring revolutionary orientation from a previously existing vanguard. This hypothesis, unfortunately, does not correspond to reality.

(2) *The guerrilla force should be an imitation of the party.* In other words, the popular army should be built on the traditional party model. We have observed one effect of this system in the preference given to organizational matters over operational tasks, in the belief that the organism can create the function. Another consequence is seen in the meetings of fighters—imitations of cell meetings. This "democratist" method would seem to be to democracy among the *guerrilleros* what parliament is to socialist

democracy (or pop art is to populart art): more than uprooting and transplanting a basically alien form, it is a dangerous graft. Naturally, meetings for political and ideological discussion among the combatants must be encouraged and fostered. But there are decisions that belong to the command, which presumably possesses clear and sound judgment in the military and disciplinary domain. To organize meetings at every turn leads the fighters to lose confidence in the command and, ultimately, in themselves; conscious discipline is relaxed; discord and dissension are spread among the troops; a substantial part of their military effectiveness is sacrificed. We learn from accounts of the war in Spain that Republican fighters sometimes discussed official orders at the height of a battle, refusing to attack a certain position or fall back at a given moment, holding meetings on questions of tactics while under enemy fire. We know the results only too well. In Cuba this method, occasionally adopted at the beginning of the war, led to confusion and desertions from the guerrilla group on the occasion of a public trial which almost cost the life of a highly respected captain, whose gun had gone off accidentally and killed a comrade. One could cite many other similar experiences.

A new situation calls for new methods. That is to say, we must guard against adopting forms of action, whether from error or tradition, which are inappropriate to this new content.

We can now resolve the initial dilemma. In the long run, certain regions of America, for dialectical reasons, will not need to choose between a vanguard party and a popular army. But for the moment there is a historically based *order of tasks. The people's army will be the nucleus of the party, not vice versa.* The guerrilla force is the political vanguard *in nuce* and from its development a real party can arise.

That is why the guerrilla force must be developed if the political vanguard is to be developed.

That is why, at the present juncture, *the principal stress must be laid on the development of guerrilla warfare and not on the strengthening of existing parties or the creation of new parties.*

That is why *insurrectional activity is today the number one political activity.*

Chilean Christian Democracy: Lessons in the Politics of Reform Management

Arpad von Lazar and Luis Quiros Varela

"Pero en este pais todos estan de acuerdo en la idea general. Sin embargo, cuando llega el momento de pedir un sacrificio en concreto, nadie quiere hacerlo. Esto ocurre en todos los planos."
(Eduardo Frei M.)
"El deber de todo revolucionario es hacer la revolucion."
(Fidel Castro)

When in 1964 the candidate of the Chilean Christian Democratic Party (*Partido Democratacristiano*—PDC), Eduardo Frei Montalva, won an overwhelming mandate to the presidency, many were eager and quick to announce this as a bright and shining light pointing toward an opening in the muddle and despair of Latin American politics. Chile's Christian Democrats offered reforms that were drastic in scope and a revolution that maintained the dignity of man through reasoning rather than through bloodshed. Frei soon became the champion of the free world, representing the embodiment of democratic principles and development. He enjoys the support and acclaim of friends, from the Christian Democrats of Western Europe to the White House, as well as the suspicion and hatred of his foes on the left and the right.

But where does reality lie? This article does not pretend to give an answer for such an ambiguous question. What follows is neither a history nor a description of the Christian Democratic Party or of

From Arpad von Lazar and Luis Quiros Varela, "Chilean Christian Democracy: Lessons in the Politics of Reform Management," *Inter-American Economic Affairs,* XXI (Spring 1968), pp. 51–72. Reprinted by permission. Research for this paper has been done in Chile during 1966 and 1967 with the help of a grant from the Social Science Research Council. The authors wish to express gratitude to W. George Wheelwright, field director of the International Development Foundation in Santiago de Chile, for his invaluable suggestions and criticism.

President Frei's administration. It is rather an essay on the ambiguities of manipulating the forces of change in a developmental setting,
an essay on conflicts that arise and their resolution. Thus the discussion centers around an analysis and outline of the manipulative
aspects of socioeconomic and political changes as observed within
the Chilean setting. While avoiding the overextension of characteristics and making a claim for general applicability or validity, this
essay posits that some basic hypotheses should be of relevance in
terms of the overall Latin American developmental setting, regardless of geographic location and specific national characteristics. The
discussion of the topic is divided into three major parts: first, the
characteristics of reform management; second, dynamics of reform
management; and third, the timetable of reform management.

I. CHARACTERISTICS OF REFORM MANAGEMENT

Just as social change and reform are a matter of conflict, adjustment
and conflict resolution within a given society, so the manipulation
and management of these phenomena are also a matter of a continuous, on-going process. Undoubtedly significant political changes,
such as the 1964 presidential election in Chile, can drastically initiate
new departures; still, reform management remains largely a matter
of day-to-day resolution of conflicts.[1] In other words, at times it
might be very difficult to perceive that *anything* does happen, while
below the surface actual changes are being incorporated or rejected.[2]

In such a political setting as present-day Chile, one could forward
the notion that the management of social reforms (meaning the
selection, implementation, and evaluation of these projects) is a
matter of concern solely for the political decision-makers, that is,
the governing Christian Democratic Party. Yet the fact is that
while the formal act of governing is largely a one-party affair, the
management of social reforms involves all the other political par-

---

[1] For a thorough analysis of the 1964 Chilean presidential elections see
Federico G. Gil and Charles J. Parrish, *The Chilean Presidential Elections of
September 4, 1964* (Washington: ICOPS, 1965), and also Federico G. Gil's
recent work, *The Political System of Chile* (Boston: Houghton Mifflin, 1966),
which offers an excellent description of the Chilean political panorama.
[2] See Oswaldo Sunkel, "Change and Frustration in Chile" in Claudio Veliz,
Obstacles to Change in Latin America (London: Oxford University Press,
1965), 116–144.

ties and indeed the entire political system. Chile is a highly politicized country with an articulate and easy-to-mobilize urban population that comprises nearly sixty percent of the total population of the country. The country also has a well-developed, vociferous, and often over-agitated communication network, and one of the highest educational standards in Latin America. These factors make the mobilization of urban elements in terms of their susceptibility to reform projects extraordinarily high.

But the features which best describe the reform management context are those which are characteristic in terms of the functioning of the entire Chilean political system. There are four dominant realities. First, the existence of a working multi-party system is accepted by all of the political forces and parties of the country with the possible exception of fragmented dissenters from the extreme left.[3] Second, the "rules of the game" prevail and are accepted by all. This means essentially that all political parties and a majority of Chileans accept the parliamentary representative system and the basic give-and-take premise of interest manipulation and representation. Third, an overwhelming majority (if not all) of Chileans accept the proposition that socioeconomic reforms are necessary if Chile is to develop, even though among various groups they differ widely over the methods, style and content of these reforms. Fourth, and finally, both interparty conflict on the national level and intraparty conflict in the form of fractionalism are frequently played out with discourse which takes as its terms the interpretation of socioeconomic reforms.[4]

Thus, for the PDC and the present government the proper presentation and implementation of reforms is a matter of political and ideological survival. It is a matter of political survival because the government has staked its existence and its distinctiveness on its claim that it can manage social reforms without societal disintegration and bloodshed. It is a matter of ideological survival because the party's entire value and belief system is centered around the idea of "change and humanism." The two levels of pragmatic politics

[3] These groups would essentially include *pekinista* and trotskyite splinter groups of peripheral significance. Their disavowal of the official communist or socialist line and their extreme-revolutionary stance does only hinder their efforts to gain popular support, with the possible exception of a few educational institutions, such as the *Instituto de Pedagogia* in Santiago.

[4] As it will be shown, both the PDC on the one hand and the Socialist Party and the Radical Party on the other, have experienced internal splits and dissension during 1967. The PDC confronts a crisis of *liderazgo,* the socialists and the radicals a conflict of basic political orientation. Significantly the communists remained as the major united observers of these events.

and ideology meet in the government and the PDC's efforts to claim both monopoly over the successful management of reforms and *uniqueness* for its justification.[5]

But one cannot overlook the fact that the PDC has never been in power before. The relative "youth" of the party often helps to create an image of dynamism and great fervor, but on the other hand, it also betrays the fact that the PDC is a novice at trying to live with and accommodate itself to the give-and-take and the ambiguities of Chilean politics. After the 1964 elections, expectations for implementing far-reaching economic, social and political reforms appeared as a *leitmotiv* in party politics. This was natural since the PDC, as an upstart reformist party, had to show results within a relatively short time-span, and considerable political dangers ranged against the government from all sides of the political spectrum. The PDC was so embattled that by 1967 tendencies for favoring a high degree of societal uniformity and a kind of one-part dominant structure emerged among some elements within the party —probably as the direct result of the frustrations created by the "rules of the game."

For the leftist opposition, *Frente de Accion Popular* (FRAP), the coalition of communists and socialists, an at least superficial participation in the process of reform management demands that it maintain contact with grass-root sentiments and seek to promote a revolutionary image while committing itself only to a minimum degree of responsibility. In any political setting where an essentially noncommunist and non-Marxist political force has preempted the field of social revolutionary reforms usually claimed by the traditional parties of the revolutionary left, there is very little else the left can do but support, with criticism, these projects.[6] An all-out opposition to reform plans would mean electoral disaster for these parties, for when reform projects are translated into pragmatic and visible changes on the local level, these changes (e.g., installing of drinking water facilities in a *poblacion*) cannot be criticized, much less opposed. Indeed, if in a political system the parties of the tradi-

[5] For an official but naturally highly politicized and propagandized presentation of the PDC government's position, the pages of the government daily, *La Nacion*, offer an insight. In addition the *Boletin PDC*, an official party monthly, and *Ediciones Rebeldes*, the voice of the PDC youth, should be mentioned.

[6] The below comments are based upon impressions gained from a series of interviews between the authors and several of the leading personalities of the Chilean left wing communists and socialists whose identities have to remain anonymous. The interviews took place during 1966 in Santiago de Chile.

tional revolutionary left do accept the "rules of the game" that are dictated by parliamentarianism, the only remaining leverage of opposition is to point out the *shortcomings*, the *slowness*, or the *failure* of the reform management efforts of the government, and to build their position from this vantage point and *not* from that of total opposition to reforms.[7] An interesting aspect of the political calisthenics that the left has been performing is to be found in the reversal of the roles and image of a "revolutionary party" between the communists and the socialists. Under the pressure of the PDC's push for social reforms, the communists adopted a rather conservative position characterized by an overall support for PDC reforms but spiced with strong criticism, attempts to prod the PDC into more leftist and potentially internally embarrassing positions, and efforts to pinpoint the failures of the government's efforts. But the Communist Party clearly refuses at this point either to present an all-out opposition to reforms or to take a more revolutionary position. Meanwhile, the socialists, under the same pressures, adopted a more militant and aggressive stand, probably with some idea of counterbalancing their communist partners' past effectiveness in attracting revolutionary elements.

On the whole, however, the revolutionary left is characterized by a position of trying to hold on to the already established strongholds, expanding on such grass-root levels as the *campo*, and generally running alongside events, trying to capitalize on the mistakes and shortcomings of the government.[8]

---

[7] As a matter of fact, the Communist Party of Chile has experienced frictions and tensions in its relations with the socialists, its political partners in FRAP, because of its basically cautious and "conservative" approach in opposing or obstructing the government's economic and social program. The July and August 1966 issues of *El Siglo*, the central organ of the Communist Party of Chile, and the socialist daily *Ultima Hora* gave vent to these frictions within the FRAP. The July 1967 split within the ranks of the socialists, expressed through the personal conflict of former presidential candidate and presently Senate President Salvador Allende and Senator Raul Ampuero, also reflect a conflict in interpreting the role of opposition versus PDC reform policies. See July 1967 issues of "Revista Noticiosa Semanal" of *El Mercurio* (Santiago).

[8] To a certain degree the left not only tries to "run along the sidelines" but also is active, especially in the *campo*, in trying to intensify grassroots recruitment and agitation. Such activities are manifest in work among *campesinos* especially in the *asentamientos*, a form of cooperative-collective farm structures, where they have a clear-cut lead over the efforts of the PDC and the government. In several interviews, FRAP leaders emphasized to this author their determination to "hit hard" on selective basis and manifest more "wait and see" attitudes on the overall front.

So far as the right wing of the political spectrum is concerned, its position is one attempting to salvage or preserve some of its traditional vested interests and power in face of a social revolutionary setting. Pure political power, as is the case in Chile, has slipped from their hands. However, lingering economic influence and power combined with a traditional social importance, articulateness, and ability to manipulate situations still give these traditional sectors more than average influence.[9] In the face of outright reforms, their method is to object noisily on the surface and adapt quietly in practice. Since they basically oppose certain social reform plans, such as agrarian reform in Chile, they have given up efforts to obtain the support of certain groups, e.g., *campesinos* and urban labor. By manipulating economic problems, pinpointing shortcomings of the government, and using some emotional issues such as nationalism, they tend to manipulate and build a base around the urban middle class and even segments of the urban *lumpenproletariat*. For purposes of propaganda and image building, the right will superficially accept and pay lip service to a number of reform projects, excepting those where it thinks it has neither the capability to alter the course of events nor the willingness to accept any compromise. As a whole the position of the right is a "holding operation" that is based upon the assumption—and hope—that the reform plans will bring about further economic hardships, and that the urban sector will remain the predominant element in the country's politics.[10]

II. THE DYNAMICS OF REFORM MANAGEMENT

For a political party or movement that has confronted a socio-economic and political setting in which the implementation of reforms is an objective and subjective necessity, the presentation of these reform plans becomes a matter of combining political skills, flexibility and beliefs with a certain degree of demagoguery. The major question is, "How shall we implement reforms?" Generally, for a governing party or one that is aspiring to obtain the govern-

[9] See the perceptive study of Robert Kaufman, "The Chilean Political Right and Agrarian Reform: Resistance and Moderation" (Washington: Institute for the Comparative Study of Political Systems, 1967).

[10] The author is indebted to Jorge Prat E., lawyer and Chilean politician, for articulating and outlining the position of what one might call the "nationalistic-right wing" of Chilean politics in two lengthy personal interviews.

mental power, as was the PDC in Chile immediately before and
since the 1964 elections, the entire process will begin with an appeal
to rather popularistic images of reform policies. The PDC got off
to a very dynamic start by promising changes of revolutionary
character, maximizing the projected benefits of these changes, and
minimizing their social consequences in terms of conflicts and the
"price" various groups of society might have to pay. At this initial
stage there is also a heavy reliance upon stressing the need for a
revolutionary mentality, expressed mostly in terms of militancy,
unquestioned acceptance of party directives, and adherence to party
ideology.[11] If this early stage is also one in which the party has to
exert a maximum effort actually to gain power, then the degree of
unity and the extent to which conflicting trends within the party
might be swept under the rug will be high. There will be a general
agreement on goals and long-range objectives, however generally,
without a definition of short-range tactics or methods of implementation. Even the long-range goals will be generally expressed in
vague and imprecise terms so that the maximum number of diversely
oriented people will be able to accept them. Of course, at this stage
of development keeping "ultimate" goals sufficiently vague can also
be functional because it can enable the decision-makers to adapt to
environmental changes in time. On the other hand, this vagueness
also draws and accommodates the initial participation of people who
undoubtedly will desert once social conflicts emerge as the direct
result of reform policies.

On the whole, for a reform-oriented, sufficiently democratic and
modestly demagogic political force, such as the PDC in Chile, the
manipulation of the social environment at the *initial* stages of reform
policy is a relatively easy task. It is easy because the groups the
PDC has to manipulate are susceptible to the acceptance of the

[11] The matter of "adherence" to ideology is becoming an increasingly complicated matter as the PDC goes on offering a battle ground for contrasting
ideological trends within the party itself. On the general level all these
conflicts are associated with the interpretation of the relationship of party
and governmental apparatus and the nature of society that is to be built
through the governmental efforts of the PDC. For the latest definition of the
above see the so-called "Plan Chonchol" approved at the recent meeting of
the National Council (*Junta Nacional*) of the PDC, "Proposiciones para una
accion politica en el periodo 1967–70 de una via no capitalista de desarrollo,"
reprinted in *PEC, Politica, Economia, Cultura,* No. 239, July 28, 1967. This
plan was drawn up by a working commission under the chairmanship of
Jacques Chonchol by a group consisting of Tomas Reyes, Luis Maira, Vicente
Sota, Julio Silva, Carlos Massad, Pedro Felipe Ramirez.

projected policies of the party to a very high degree, even if for a diversity of conflicting reasons. It is easy to manipulate those who were frightened or are frightened of the spectre of a social revolution that threatens them with social annihilation. This is the fear of the middle class of a communist-marxist political take-over. The middle class can and generally will accommodate reforms so long as these reforms suggest a basic acceptance of 1) a form of parliamentarianism through which they still think that they will be able to exert maximum political influence, and 2) a form of economic liberalism mixed with state intervention but still offering a sufficient leeway for private enterprise. In other words, the middle class accepts reforms, and has more or less accepted them in Chile, as a price that has to be paid to avoid more drastic changes.

As the PDC's experience suggests, it is also easy to manipulate those who have rather limited and superficial class identification combined with high pro-authoritarian tendencies, such as is the case with the urban *lumpenproletariat*—people like hotel employees, street vendors, newspaper sellers, shoeshine boys, and even people in relatively stable positions such as taxi drivers. These urban elements have a high propensity to accept appealing changes which involve a modest price.[12] They also are the ones who tend to accept the image and appeal of personalistic dynamic leaders sufficiently demagogic for their "quick solution, easy answer" value systems. They are the ones who are the loudest at the rallies, the ones who are the easiest to be swayed by promises, but of course the first ones who will desert once performance is required.[13]

[12] See Sunkel, *op. cit.*, and Anibal Pinto, "Political Aspects of Economic Development in Latin America," *ibid.*, pp. 9–46.

[13] The April 2, 1967, municipal elections offered an interesting example of the behavior of these less committed groups. The results of the election showed big gains for both the left and right at the expense of the PDC!

PDC	36.5% of the total valid vote
Radical Party	16.5%
Communist Party	15.0%
National Party	14.6%
Socialist Party	14.2%
PADENA	2.5%
Abstention	25.1%

Some of the significant "desertions" occurred in districts with heavy *lumpenproletarian* elements. At the same time the heavy abstention rate suggests that the low-motivated and the essentially non-involved voter—consisting largely of the *lumpenproletariat* women voters and *pobladores* (slum dwellers)—a group that represented a significant mainstay for the PDC in

Another sector that is potentially easy to manipulate consists of those elements that have been essentially characterized in the past by political non-involvement, the politically non-mobilized element of the population, such as the *campesinos*. The real social significance of the 1964 elections was not the mere fact of the PDC victory, but much rather the fact that the Chilean *campesino* has been for the first time mobilized for political action and thus also laid open for political competition.[14] Now the PDC managed to tie up this sector initially, due to its highly appealing electoral promises, i.e., offering land and a chance for a more decent life through agrarian reform. This initial advantage and appeal has been further augmented by the very fact that the government has the power to offer, to give and deliver, whereas the political opposition actually has to survive on more modest holding operations that are essentially in the realm of criticism. Still, this sector also manifests a high degree of instability in terms of commitment, a condition characteristic of rural sectors that basically want to satisfy their economic needs yet basically distrust urban political forces and politicians. Also, the *campesino* can be an element that can identify more deeply with *personalismo* than with a party or an abstract ideology.

Hence, to recapitulate, the general pattern of the dynamics of reform management characterized by a fast "takeoff" with the projection of appealing images and stressing of a revolutionary mentality, and with a sense of vagueness in terms of implementation, can be functional to a certain degree. There will be a projection of a relatively high price that has to be paid for the fulfillment of these tasks which could and probably would be minimized with compromise and in time. However, this initial projection of relatively high prices is really not taken terribly seriously by those readily manipulable social groups enumerated above.[15] The middle class will not

---

the past, decided that the elections were just not "significant enough" and thus denied its support from the PDC in the form of abstention. It should also be considered that the month of March is the time for tax payments in Chile and this combined with the fact that the middle and lower-middle classes have to carry the heaviest financial burden for the reform policies of the PDC, might have indicated the reason for the switch of these groups away from the PDC largely to the radicals.

[14] Actually, some state that the integration of the *campesino* in political life began with the election of President Carlos Ybanez (September 1952) but really gained impetus during the Alessandri administration (1958–64). See Federico Gil, *op. cit.,* pp. 231 ff.

[15] There may be an interesting problem emerging here, a problem that is essentially the creation of the FRAP. Through its criticism and pressures

take it seriously because it will have a faith in its ability to force compromises. The *lumpenproletariat* will not take it seriously because basically it is not interested in performance since it is not a socially committed group and exists on the margin of social responsibility. As far as the *campesinos* are concerned, they can only win from the entire process and thus this "price projection" is irrelevant for their case. But because goals are set relatively high, initial results of reforms will be slow on all fronts while expectations remain very high or indeed escalate. We intend to illustrate this through the following case studies.

When Frei came into office, the Chilean economy had already been experiencing years of inflation and stagnation, notwithstanding the efforts of the previous two administrations to spur stability and economic growth. The PDC platform as well as the FRAP's was based mainly on a structural approach to economic development and proposed a series of economic policies to be implemented by a new regime. In this way, the PDC was attempting to deal at once with interlocked economic and social obstacles. Among all the specific policies proposed, three of them deserve special attention in terms of the changes they mean for the Chilean system: the "chileanization" of the copper industry, the agrarian reform, and the *Promocion Popular* in the field of social action.

These economic and social reform policies of the PDC government have to be analyzed within the framework of consensus on parliamentary democracy. Although there is agreement on the ultimate goals, controversy and conflict are rampant when hard core and deep transforming economic measures are to be initiated by the political system. Thus, the nature of the polity determines

---

the FRAP might force the PDC to "over-commit" itself as a response to the challenge of the left opposition. This "over-commitment" might carry the PDC considerably beyond the limitations of its capability and power to deliver. The debate that has emerged within the PDC about the before-mentioned "Plan Chonchol" reflects the ambiguity that the inner circle of Frei has about the acceleration of the demands and promises of "Revolucion en Libertad." Some of these conflicts came to a head at the January 7, 1968 meeting of the National Council of the PDC in Peñaflor. While never openly mentioned, the basic argument raging between the "moderate" President Frei and the more left-leaning PDC leadership centered around the speed and nature of reforms, as demanded in the "Plan Chonchol." In this encounter Frei maintained the "moderate upper-hand" at the price of forcing the resignation of the left-wing from the party leadership after a 274 to 207 vote of confidence in favor of the President's position. But for all matters, the internal tug-of-war continues with the same intensity and also the danger of "over-commitment."

the process and the outcome of such economic measures. This is most important given the evolutionary character of the Chilean political system which has allowed the acceptance of political demands; the integration of new groups, and the adoption of economic and social legislation together with the creation of administrative structures, all of which give the government (*Estado*) a very significant role in the developmental process of the nation.

The PDC found itself with a diversified and efficient bureaucracy and highly legitimized institutions such as the *Corporacion de Fomento* and affiliated enterprises such as ENAP (oil), ENDESA (electricity), YANSA (sugar) together with some newer ones, such as the *Corporacion de la Reforma Agraria* (CORA) and INDAP (*Instituto de Desarrollo Agropecuario*), created during the Alessandri administration. These provided a basic mechanism to implement the first steps of *Revolucion en Libertad* while the new legislation was passed by Congress. Moreover, the broad powers of the President in the economic and financial fields, plus his international prestige, could easily channel the resources of the State or get foreign aid to start his program.

Subsequent experience demonstrated, however, that the highly attractive program of the PDC was just a statement of goals which had to be adapted to the political and economic circumstances of the country. The renegotiation of the external debt and the project for the Chileanization of copper were the first steps taken. The agrarian reform project was delayed for over a year. The *Promocion Popular* began its tasks almost immediately, but as of 1967 no official recognition has been granted due to the political opposition it has met.

The Chileanization of copper marks a significant departure from the traditional approach to foreign investments in Chile.[16] The State, by associating itself with the foreign companies, owners of mineral resources, will participate and control the production and commercialization of products and will encourage new investment in mining, as well as in the expansion of subsidiary activities like refining plants, and chemical industry.[17] The shared management

---

[16] In a recent publication of the Chilean Embassy in Washington it is shown that including copper and nitrate exporters, the Chilean Government owns 48.7% of the top 10 enterprises, 46.4% of the top 20, and 43.2% of the top 30. See Embassy of Chile, *Statistical Profile of Chile*, Washington, D.C., 1967 (mimeo) p. 59.

[17] Raul Sanz, *Chile y el Cobre*, (Santiago: Departamento del Cobre, 1965), Also, Economic Commission for Latin America, New York: UN (1966): pp. 227 and 259 ff.

proposal sounded feasible in its economic and international aspects, because the program would have meant the recovery of the Chilean share of the world market that had been declining since the early fifties. However, on the level of national politics the project has met the rejection of the left and also met objections from the right and the radicals. The left will settle for nothing less than nationalization of foreign-owned investments. The right also wants nationalization, but for different reasons: since the birth of the Alliance for Progress the traditional allies of the United States have assumed a superficial reform orientation while cursing the U.S. for fomenting unrest by supporting social and economic reforms. The radicals, although not totally opposed, appeared reluctant to accept the "Chileanization" project because they expected they could affect the outcome of negotiations by using their power in the Senate.

Congress approved the copper bill in two stages: in the first stage, from November, 1964 and May, 1965, total opposition broke out and the government used the project as a weapon to blast the opposition for its ineffectiveness and selfishness during the congressional elections of March, 1965. This propagandistic use of copper policy paid off in the elections but at the cost of a delay in its approval. The delay continued in the new Congress even with the PDC in control of the lower Chamber. Finally, however, it was approved without much change at the end of 1966. The first agreement was signed in March, 1967. The unprecedented rise of the price of copper during 1966 and the first months of 1967 helped the government to finance the other programs, but by April the price was leveling off, and the government was facing new deficitary budgets, the slowdown of public works, and cutbacks in some social programs.

The Agrarian Reform project was presented a year after the PDC rule, though the Party and the government had claimed that the plan had been ready in September 1964. No other project of the regime created such widespread public discussion. Part of the reason was that the reform of the land tenure system—and thus the law of property—required the reform of the Constitution. Also, the project's execution was to be "fast, drastic and massive," in the words of one of its authors, Jacques Chonchol.[18] The project proposed to give land to 100,000 peasants between 1964 and 1970. It established a series of causes for expropriation that went beyond

---

[18] Jacques Chonchol, "El Porque de la Reforma Agraria" in Oscar Delgado (ed.). *Reformas Agrarias en America Latina* (Mexico: Fondo de Cultura Economica 1965), p. 119.

Law 15020, approved by former President Jorge Alessandri. The
size of the plot, irrigation facilities, and social conditions of the
inquilinos were added to "inefficient exploitation" as criteria for
determining the expropriation. Furthermore, the reform established
different modes and schedules of payment for expropriated land.
The project contemplated three types of settlement for new owners:
the privately-owned family plots, the cooperative settlement, and
the *asentamiento* association between the peasants and CORA.
Under this latter arrangement, the *campesino* would work the land
for a period of three years. After that period, this arrangement could
be renewed if CORA approved it.[19]

When the Senate refused to approve Frei's constitutional reform,[20] Frei was forced to take up the proposal of Socialist Senator
Raul Ampuero to deal with the property clause separately.[20a] This
proposal had been strongly opposed by the PDC leadership and congressmen, and months of lengthy discussions ensued before it was
finally approved. The agrarian reform project stayed even longer
under the scrutiny of the Senate. The shrewd manipulation of
radicals, the right and the FRAP accounted for the delay: the
radicals tried to soften the conditions set by the PDC holding the
balance; the right denounced the project as inefficient, dangerous
and not feasible;[21] and, finally the left supported the project but
tried to press for a stronger bill in order to outbid the PDC. Outside
Congress, the landowners' associations and the newly-formed peasant unions fought a battle, the one accusing the government of
being revolutionary, the other accusing it of going too slow. The
first major extensive strikes on the part of the *inquilinos* (tenant
farmers) began to take place, supported by the Leftist parties or
backed by the PDC. Meanwhile, under the control of the PDC,

[19] *Proyecto de Ley de "Reforma Agraria"* (Santiago: Imprenta del Servicio
de Prisiones 1965).

[20] The Constitutional Reform of Frei proposed the modification of the
constitutional guarantee of private property, the strengthening of the economic powers of the president, the extension of the plebiscite to any case of
disagreement between the executive and the legislature and the reform of
the present system of local government.

[20a] During August 1967, Senator Ampuero was expelled from the Socialist
Party and formed the new *Partido Socialista Popular,* a Titoist brand of
socialist party stressing national solutions and preoccupation with Chilean
problems. Cf. *La Tarde,* September 5, 1967.

[21] On the position of the right on agrarian reform, see Kaufman, *op. cit.
passim.* The official position of the Communist Party was stated in a series of
articles appearing in *Principios,* Cuarta Epoca, Ano XXVII, No. 112 (March
and April of 1966).

INDAP, headed by Chonchol, made strong efforts to organize rural labor unions. This climate of unrest had enough influence on the Senate, and the agrarian reform became law finally in July of 1967, after some minor alterations and a veto by the President. Law 15020 provided a mechanism for the government to implement the agrarian reform. It then remained for the government to demonstrate its ability to carry out its campaign promises. In the first two and a half years it has been able to redistribute 461 farms (*fundos y haciendas*) with a total of 1.36 million hectares, of which 479,000 correspond to 96 *asentamientos* comprised of more than five thousand families.[22] This record is more substantial than for any comparable period between 1928 and 1963.

With Chileanization of the copper and the agrarian reform project, the difficulties met by the PDC in implementing economic aspects of its social reform program are typified. The nature of both policies necessarily had to produce cleavages because of either vested interests or ideological concerns. However, opposition groups were not the only ones contributing to the slow pace of reform. The PDC and the government were implicated as well. First, it appears that the projects were not sufficiently studied in terms of their economic implications. This is more true of the agrarian reform than of the copper policy. Criticism came from groups that ordinarily would have been aligned with the government.[23] The inclination on the part of the PDC to brand, over mass media, the opposition as enemies of the program resulted only in a deepening of cleavages. Moreover, the government's unwillingness to negotiate issues in Congress or with the political parties of the opposition forced the latter to resort to extreme inflexibility. Frei said repeatedly that he would not negotiate his program, and this encouraged the PR and FRAP to intensify the pressure in the Senate. In turn, the lack of leadership in the Congressional representation of the PDC, which had bred an indiscipline within the party, resulted in inefficient passage of the bills. All of these have resulted in slow-

---

[22] *Mensaje Presidencial 1967* (Santiago: Imprenta del Servicio de Impresiones 1967). Under the colonization program of the government on fiscal lands between 1929 and 1963, and between 1963–1964, only 1,068,567 hectares were distributed.

[23] CIDA, *Chile, Tenecia de la Tierra y Desarrollo Socio-Economico del Sector Agricola* (Santiago: Hispano-Suisa 1966). See, also, Jorge Rogers S., *Dos Caminos para la Reforma Agraria, 1945–1965* (Santiago, 1966); and Gonzalo Arroyo, S. M., "Reform Agraria en Chile" in *Mensaje*, No. 146 (January-February 1966), p. 29.

ness and open contradictions between the goals of the executive and the action of the majority in the Chamber. Thus, final decisions have had to be made by the President through the use of his veto power.

In the field of social reform policies, education and health have been the greatest concerns of Frei. The appropriate budgets and achievements have been bigger than those of past governments. The major instrument for these policies has been the *Promocion Popular*. *Promocion Popular* (Popular Promotion) could be defined as a process to integrate the marginal man into the social life of the country by building intermediate structures, composed and managed by the people themselves, and directed by the government.[24] Initially, it seemed that this was going to be an effort to improve the living conditions of the slum dwellers, conditions characterized by illiteracy, illness, poor housing, extremely low incomes, high rates of crime and low degree of participation, all of which define the concept of marginality (*marginalidad*). Later on, this concept was extended to include the formation of labor unions and agrarian unions. In 1966 the government attempted to create a formal institution out of the *Consejeria de Promocion Popular*, which has functioned only at the level of the Presidency since Congress has denied it legal recognition. For several reasons it is most difficult to assess the significance and the achievements of *Promocion Popular*.

First, the diffuseness of goals formulated during the presidential campaign as an appeal to the lower income groups of the urban areas had to become a matter of policy through the give-and-take of compromise once the PDC was in power. Secondly, the program appeared as partisan and the PDC did not like to commit itself to such a course of action in an all-out fashion. Third, the paternalistic approach of the *promotores* (field workers) produced a lack of confidence among the slum dwellers and several conflicts developed due to the lack of communication between the agency and the *poblador*. By the same token, if a project proved successful, *Promocion Popular* publicized it as its own success, failing to recognize the efforts of the people. Fourth, the PDC has tried to use the *Consejeria* as a political tool and, therefore, it has aroused the suspicion of both the *pobladores* and the left. The efforts of the com-

[24] *Mensaje Presidencial 1967* see pages 483–491. These elements have been adapted from *Mensajes Presidenciales* 1966 and 1967; *Revolucion en Libertad* (Santiago: October 1965).

munists have been quite successful in organizing cells in the slums by showing their support and paying close attention to the particular problems of the people. In some other cases, the communists have been successful in infiltrating the organizations set up by *Promocion Popular* and pressing from within for more action and demonstrating the ineffectiveness of the program.

All of these elements have resulted in violent opposition to the establishment of *Promocion Popular* as a government agency. The PDC itself has shown that it doubts whether it should continue to push forward with the project. If anything, the program has had dual effect: it has awakened the *pobladores* to new possibilities, while not creating an identification with the PDC.

III. TIMETABLE OF REFORM MANAGEMENT

As seen above, the response of the various societal groups to the process of reform management varies according to the degree and nature of their involvement. The main concern centers, first, around the degree to which vested interests (economic interests in the *campo*, interests of industry and commerce and generally the urban middle class) are willing to accommodate and accept changes; and second, the degree to which the masses (e.g. low income groups, industrial labor and the *campesinos*) will formulate demands along the line of governmental thinking and action. Thus, the element of timing combined with the dimensions of projecting and implementing socioeconomic reforms appears as determinant. We plan to examine in terms of this projection process image-building on the national and international level, while our discussion of implementation will deal with some of the specifics of limitations imposed by the structure and functioning of the Chilean political system itself.

The primary characteristic of the projection process is rather self-evidently the presentation of reform plans and programs in general broad terms that lack details and clearcut explanations of methods of implementation. This feature is a direct result of political necessities that burden most young reform-oriented non-Marxist governments. Whatever general specificity might exist in projection it will usually refer to (1) projects of great emotional impact (spectacular projects that can be easily popularized but have limited long-range significance), or (2) projects that are or have been popularly accepted as an integral part of a reform orientation such as, for example, agrarian reform (in other words, projects that enjoy a wide popular acceptance in terms of their basic promise but not necessarily their detailed implementation).

The second characteristic of the projection process is the stressing of a revolutionary character of reforms and changes by presenting these in such terms that they appear to be offering maximum rewards for maximum efforts but with a minimum degree of sacrifice. Naturally, this feature will enable an initial and rather emotionally oriented identification with a political movement or party such as was the case with the PDC before the 1964 elections.[25] In the long run, of course, it is much more clear that the extent of rewards will be moderated and the sacrifices, through these conflicts, will be more manifest.

Experience of the PDC in Chile suggests that the presentation of alternatives either on the extreme left or on the right can serve as another important characteristic of the projection process. The PDC maximized the alternatives in extreme and negative terms by pointing to social stagnation on the one hand or the prospect of the authoritarianism of the communist-Marxist solution on the other as being the only other options available. Naturally in this setting the PDC placed itself conveniently between these left and right extremes on the political continuum into a position that was sufficiently revolutionary, reform-oriented, and leftist to be clearly disassociated from the center or right-of-center and sufficiently respectable in its values and ideology to be looked upon by the same center and right-of-center as "one of their own."

The fourth characteristic is the constant appeal for national unity and cohesion and a tendency to decry the lack of solidarity and adherence to reform policies.[26]

[25] The so-called "Plan Frei," widely heralded before the 1964 presidential elections offered the image of a governmental strategy for development that implied careful planning, capability for the realization of these plans and the availability of funds for their financing. See, *Plan Frei* (Santiago: Edit. del Pacifico, 1963) and *Revolucion en Libertad; Resumen Informativo de Un Ano de Gobierno* (Santiago: *La Nacion*, 1965).

[26] The PDC and the Frei government constantly refer to the need for national unity and societal collaboration in the solution of developmental tasks. Obviously, national unity does have its functional aspects in rallying the people for performance but it also has its pitfalls if not properly manipulated. Shortly before the April 1967 municipal elections the PDC leadership decided to convert the elections into an affirmative act of popular acclamation for the policies of the Frei government by turning it into a plebiscite. As the elections neared, the PDC propaganda apparatus increasingly chose to utilize the "yes-no" alternative argument, meaning that all votes against the PDC are

As did the PDC in Chile, reform-oriented political parties and movements tend to present themselves as "saviours of the nation" and often project themselves as the only viable alternative for national development. While national unity is emphasized, internal party unity itself receives plenty of attention under the same collective set of arguments. In this sense, within the party, and also to a lesser degree on the national level, there is often a constant emphasis upon the adherence to the basic tenets of ideology. Thus Christian Democrats before and shortly after the 1964 elections wanted not only that people vote for them and support them but also that they believe in what the Christian Democrats were talking about. Naturally if the latter is a criterion for the acceptance of "true believers" then the party itself has to face up to a flooding of its ranks by ideological opportunists, people who make themselves a part of the reform process not because of their capabilities but because of their swift and parroting acceptance of the basic tenets of dogma.[27]

Also the PDC is forced to discover those "built-in" limitations of a traditional society of which the more "conservative" and battle-hardened parties of the left and of the right were only too well aware. These built-in limitations include a whole range of problems from a set of personal values and attitudes to institutional arrangements of the most complicated sort but are related to the concern with societal and national unity. Because people's habits are hard to change, their work and professional customs, their view of institutions and their approach to conflict resolution in every-day life will also be difficult to alter. Even more significant in Chile is the fact that Chilean urban society, as pointed out before, a substantial part of the population, is basically "middle class" in its values and aspirations. And this middle class orientation strongly suggests a

---

votes against development, the future of Chile, the national interest—indeed, treason! While in this specific instance the plebiscite policy was the direct result of some strategy failure based upon misleading survey indicators (See Luis Hernandez Parker, "Chile se Municipalizo en tres fuerzas parejas," [Santiago: *Desfile*], April 4, 1967), the general trend is a persistent one.

[27] For example in Antofagasta, in the northern mining district, the PDC has come to realize that the "flooding" of the party organization is in direct correlation to the rise in expectations of new or potential party members for job opportunities. In Antofagasta, according to the local party leadership, during 1965 and the first part of 1966 there has been a tremendous influx of jobless *pobladores*, who joined or tried to join the party with the full expectation of a better job, or a job *per se*.

compulsive rejection of innovations that tend to upset or alter already well-established channels of peer relations and methods of peddling influence and obtaining and utilizing information. Undoubtedly the PDC is trying to change some of these deeply imbedded values by drastic and highly artificial sets of administrative decisions such as the *jornada unica* (the unified work-day, without the traditional mid-day *siesta*), restrictions upon serving liquor at certain hours, enforced work discipline, etc. But at the same time the PDC itself is mellowing and learning about the technique of compromise, or perhaps in other words it is being "corrupted" without the negative implications of the term.

Image-building on the international level has somewhat different connotations than the same process on the internal level. While the PDC's example might be an appropriate demonstration of the cleavages existing between the projection of an appealing image and the manipulative maintenance of this image within the Chilean political system itself, a slightly brighter picture emerges on the international scene. On this level, as President Frei's example suggests, it is much more easy to project an image of innovation and dynamic reform orientation. The very fact that the PDC *is* in government only reinforces this appeal.

One of the much-discussed and appraised political developments in the Latin America of the past decade has been the emergence of Christian Democracy as an apparent important alternative to the marxist version of social reform and development. The 1964 victory of Frei was presented indeed as the first step toward the implementation of the promises of Christian Democracy on the national level and thereby offering a model for hemisphere-wide application. In the eyes of the Chilean PDC leadership, being a Christian Democrat is much more than merely being a Chilean Christian Democrat. The constant emphasis on the idea of *confraternidad latina* helps to create the image of Christian Democracy not only being a dynamic alternative to the "capitalist" or Marxist paths of development but also appearing as the *latino* version of modernization on an international scale.[28] And, finally, one should not overlook that the re-

---

[28] Frei's travels in Europe and in Latin America, the general treatment of Chile in the international press and Chile's role in the process of Latin American integration are telling examples of this phenomenon. At the Fifth World Congress of Christian Democratic parties held in Lima during April 1966 the Chilean delegation played a key role in setting the tone and pace of discussions. It must have been an enormously satisfying experience for the

wards of international popularity are much higher than the projected or actual achievements would warrant: the image of the PDC is totally associated—indeed, expressed—in terms of the vast popularity of President Frei. To manipulate this in the external environment is relatively easy: there are no votes to be gained or lost as there are in the case of the Chilean voter. The relative importance of this international image is in maintaining a sense of pride and identification with the party's efforts on the national level and a posture of success on the international one. The function of the two is to reinforce each other.

The example of Chile suggests that the management of socio-economic reforms is a difficult, slow and many-pronged process. Once the excitement and the halo of political victories wear off, the day-to-day management and resolution of conflicts assume primary importance. Performance—the indicator of change and development—is dependent upon both capabilities and time. But time is the resource that is most scarce. Unfortunately, "delayed gratification" is acceptable only for a few; people want results and rewards immediately and the notion that rewards will have to be "reinvested" into the system is not a popular one.

But changes do occur. They occur whether or not the government wants them, plans for them, and helps to bring them about! If nothing else, Chile has experienced during the last two years a definite trend toward the redistribution of income and the involvement of new groups in the political life on the national and local level. In this sense reform management is a tedious, undefined and exasperating process of manipulating social, economic and political forces in an essentially traditional environment. It is tedious because there are no short answers and quick solutions to problems that are the result of years of stagnation and inferiority. It is an undefined process because goals and means are often dependent

---

PDC delegation, headed, by Senator Patricio Aylwin, to note that they were treated as the representatives of a movement that plays the role of a "punta de lanza" (spearhead) in spreading the Christian Democratic version to development. In international terms the movement (meaning both the PDC in Chile and the hemisphere-wide application of PDC ideology) is defined as reformist-revolutionary but hostile to Marxism, which is considered a different form of imperialism. It is *independentista* in refusing to accept the predominance of the United States in hemispheric affairs. There is a reliance on cautious "Third Road" policies, essentially pro-Western in value orientations but at the same time committed to the cause of developing nations, minimizing the relevance of the Cold War conflict to the problems of developing countries.

Reform and Revolution

upon the whims of political life, capabilities and resources. It is exasperating because it is a process that also demands conciliation and compromise. And ultimately the dichotomy between reform and revolution also remains unresolved, while the prize of inertia looms ever greater. As Regis Debray warns: "This encounter is simply rational. In a given historic situation there may be a thousand ways to speak of the revolution; but there must be one necessary concordance among all those who have resolved to make it."[29]

[29] Regis Debray, *Revolucion dans la revolution?* (Paris: Libraire Francois Maspero, 1967).

The Creation of Responsible Demands

Charles W. Anderson

It is perfectly clear that the Latin American nation-state is far from perfect as an instrument of economic and social change. There is no nation on this continent in which even the basic services expected of any modern government—education, water, roads, law enforcement, justice—are available to all citizens. Despite significant advances in economic development in many countries in the postwar period, one can point to few substantive gains in the state's capacity to fulfill its social responsibilities.

The role of government as instrument of change is central to most contemporary political ideology and development theory. Almost every piece of advice or advocacy that has been written on the problem contains urgent, imperative language concerning what the state must do to stimulate development in Latin America.

Two assumptions complicate this literature of advocacy. The first is that the problem is essentially one of political leadership, that if the "right people" could come to power, the problem would be solved. However, the state is not an independent variable in the equation of change. Its capacity to act is limited by the very conditions which it is urged to overcome. How the resources and powers of the state are used certainly depends on the attitudes and zeal of political leaders, but it also depends on what citizens demand of these leaders, and what they are willing to do on their own responsibility to complement and complete the impetus for change that the state provides. There is a vicious circle of political stagnation that is every bit as enigmatic as the vicious circle of economic underdevelopment that Myrdal and others have described.

From Charles W. Anderson, *Politics and Economic Change in Latin America*, (Princeton: D. Van Nostrand Company, Inc., 1967) pp. 367–381. Reprinted by permission.

A second problematic assumption of the literature of development is that politics is largely an "obstacle" to change. Once the "problem" of development has been defined through ideology or economic analysis, and the "solutions" prescribed, one must overcome those "political impediments" that prevent specific recommendations from being carried out. The objective of the political analyst should be to find ways of reorienting the institutions of the political order so that the "right" policies are effected.

From a strictly political point of view, there is no "right" approach to development. The goals of change, and the processes by which change is to be wrought, are contingent upon the aspirations and desires of a particular people. But this definition contains its own enigma. In imperfectly representative societies, where a large part of the population is fundamentally unaware of the alternative choices of modernization and their implications, how are the aspirations and desires of a people to be ascertained? To remark that the aspirations of a specific elite in a developing nation may not be congruent with those of the advanced Western nations is important, but what is more at issue is the extent to which the objectives of that elite are congruent with those of the rest of that society.

As we have noted, the classic political systems of Latin America have not been unrepresentative, but under-representative. Governments of all ideological complexions have taken into account those forces in the society that were interested in and capable of entering the political process. The tradition of Latin American statesmanship has been less rigid and doctrinaire, and far more pragmatic than is generally assumed. But such political pragmatism has been practiced within limited confines. Historically, only a small part of the population has been taken into account in the making of public decisions.

Economic development and representativeness are of course intimately related. We have long assumed that the increased representativeness of governments—the establishment of pluralistic, democratic societies—depends on economic development. Far less frequently recognized is that economic development itself may depend on the establishment of more representative political systems.

It is this intimate interdependence of representation and development that has caused the idea of "revolution" to have a peculiar appeal for many segments of Latin American society, and for many political forces in other developing regions as well. As it is the frustration of the mass of the people that hinders development, so the direction of the energies of the mass of the population through a government sympathetic with their desires can dynamize a nation for development.

The notion of revolution is an everyday concept of politics in Latin America. One should be careful to distinguish the various implications of the term. For some, revolution implies Communistic society, for others, simply a more dynamic government. For some, revolution connotes a millennial vision of a harmonious social order, and for others it refers to quite specific and practical reforms.

However, to assert that development in Latin America requires "revolutionary change" is not to have said very much. In fact, to postulate revolution as a precondition of development is somewhat to beg the question. If in fact revolutionary aspirations are not present, there is very little that constituted authorities can do to effect a revolutionary program. On the other hand, if aspirations for basic change are present and insistent, there is little that a single social institution can do to prevent change from taking place.

What is at issue, then, is how one invests in motivation to change. The cost of such motivation is always high, in terms of time, personnel, and economic resources. To make a revolution is a most expensive process, requiring patience, fervor, dedication, and energy.

One may invest these motivational resources in incitement to rebellion against the established order. This is a most difficult task, particularly in societies where a large part of the population has traditionally lived apart from national society and political engagement. By definition, the full coercive power of the established order will be mounted against such activity. To urge a people to rebellion and civil warfare in a traditional society is a task of political socialization. Particularly in the realm of peasant agriculture, it is a most unnatural activity, requiring sacrifice and a striking shift in values and motivations. Historically, incitement to rebellion has seemed most plausible among those already uprooted, already in the process of change, among those who have lost their ties to existing institutions and feel alienated and alone.

Furthermore, to socialize a people to the political role of rebellion has certain long-range consequences for the new order. After power has been won, the new leaders must cope with the forces they have unleashed. Violence has been encouraged as a power capability within the political process. For both the victors and the vanquished, its legitimacy has been enhanced. Furthermore, to instigate to rebellion may require promised rewards well beyond the capacity of any government.

An alternative investment in revolutionary motivation occurs after a coup has placed in power a government committed to total change. Here the full coercive capacity of the state, as well as existing loyalties to the state as a symbol of the society, may be employed in changing the patterns of values, motivations, and aspiration present in the society.

This is the objective of "mobilization societies," Communist and non-Communist, in our day. With a leadership cadre inspired by a vision of change, with the coercive and motivational resources necessary to galvanize a society to the specific tasks required to implement the design for change, development may occur quite swiftly.

However, the enactment of revolutionary socio-economic change cannot be dated from the day of political victory. There is a significant time lag in every revolution. From the point of successful insurrection, if all goes well, a decade or longer may be required to destroy the old order, endure the inevitable tumult and disorder of opposition, counter-revolution, and initial inexperience of the victorious forces, and complete the investment in motivation, reconstruction, integration, of a new way of life. Thus, we have noted that Bolivia required ten years to organize and effect the land distribution phase of its agrarian reform, and Mexico endured more than a decade of crisis before constructive change took hold. A similar process would seem to be at work in the Cuban Revolution.

Furthermore, mobilization regimes must be to some extent wasteful. Since they have declared the old order to be the enemy, they must do without, or substitute for, the productive services that the old order generated. And their need and capacity to eliminate dissidence from the political order makes them liable to massive error in development policy. Perceiving criticism as disloyalty and opposition, they do without the important advance checks on the soundness of public policy that "weaker" governments enjoy. The grand design for change must be universally affirmed. It is not subject to improvement in whole or in detail by the critical and interested judgment of those who are to be affected by it. Policy can only be tested through implementation. Revision is only possible after resources have been committed.

To make a revolution requires the investment of substantial resources, of patience, organization, and energy. It requires the dedicated allegiance of large numbers of people. More than anything else, it requires time. These motivational resources, required for revolution, may be invested in incitement to rebellion, or in the mobilization of a society after control of the state has been achieved. However, they may also be invested in other ways.

Such resources might be invested in mass-based democratic parties, whose objective is to require that interests presently on the fringes of political life be taken into account in the making of development policy. Such parties can change the equilibrium of power within the society, requiring the investment of public resources and powers in those sectors of the society most disadvantaged by the existing structure of political forces. If such parties are effectively organized at the local level, they can serve to make more precise and subtle the decision-maker's comprehension of the demands and aspirations, the possibilities and limitations, of the society which the development program is to affect. And the democratic party, as a by-product of its role in winning mass consent, becomes an agent of culture change, its organizational efforts bringing new aspirations, values, and a new awareness of the larger national community. Its message also contains cues to the role of the citizen in democratic society.

The motivational resources of revolution might also be invested in democratic labor organization. As we have noted, the most carefully drafted and supervised programs of labor regulation are only imperfectly effective unless workers are capable of asserting their own legal interests, and unless such associations exist to inform workers of their rights and the means of obtaining them. Furthermore, the political needs of labor are not satisfied by the single, revolutionary reform. Constant representation of workers' interests, both before employers and before public agencies, is required if anything is to come of the grandiloquent enactment of the rights of labor, and if the development process is to correct for inequalities in the distribution of wealth and advantage as it goes along.

As an alternative to revolution, political militancy might be invested in the formation of peasant syndicates and associations. Most agrarian reform programs in Latin America are drafted with virtually no feedback from those affected concerning the successes and failures of the program. In the absence of any form of peasant representation, agrarian policy must be made under conditions of acute ignorance. And even the most skillfully drafted agrarian reform is apt to bog down in frustration and confusion if it is to be carried out among a rural population unorganized and inert.

The tools of modern statecraft are usually most effective when used to direct and enhance activities generated in the society itself. It is usually both expensive and inefficient for the state to assume the overhead cost of motivation. Investment in "self-help" programs is apt to have an eventual effect on the developmental role of government. The immediate objective of a cooperative or a community development project may be to market a product, pool machinery, or establish a credit union. However, as the program comes to life, it quickly becomes apparent that public action is essential to perfect the private effort. As such local programs organize to "lobby" for their specific interests, they affect the distribution of political power within the system, and provide information to policy-makers on the interests of sectors of the population only imperfectly represented in the political process.

Mass parties, peasant leagues, trade unions, cooperatives, and community development programs are forms of association that pertain particularly to that premodern sector that has been most notoriously under-represented in decision-making in Latin America. However, it should be noted that effective development policy depends as well on an adequate and continuing confrontation with those interests contained within the modern sector of society. Although rudimentary forms of association in the modern enclave are present in most Latin American nations, they are on the whole imperfect both as agencies of representation and as sources of policy-making information. To emphasize the organization of the premodern sector does not connote ideological bias. Rather, it seems likely that the development of existing interest associations will best be achieved through competition—by confrontation in policy-making forums with more vital agencies of mass organization, where rival interests are required to justify their positions in terms of the developmental goal, and through plausible arguments concerning their situation and the effect of proposed policies on that position.

The case is often made that democratic process is inappropriate to societies undertaking rapid development, that such nations require forceful, decisive government to mobilize for the tasks of change. However, it may be that democratic process is peculiarly appropriate to the requirements of development in Latin America at this point in the ongoing process of socio-economic change in that region.

It should be noted that this case is not based on the inherent superiority of the values of the Western democratic tradition. Personally, I do believe that the dignity of the individual does imply at least the obligation to consult with those whose lives are to be fundamentally restructured through major programs of public action. However, this is not the basis of the argument. Rather, we are dealing with a strictly technical question in development theory, the relative efficiency of various types of political process in making and implementing major development policy decisions.

First, only within a pluralistic framework of competitive representation can the decision-maker be adequately apprised of the alternatives available to him, and obtain information sufficient for intelligent choice among these alternatives. It has long been a canon of development theory that the emergent nations cannot afford to waste resources, but must deploy them skillfully so that they have maximum impact on the process of change and growth. However, in markedly under-representative political systems, where the decision-maker remains unaware of the interests and intentions of those who will be affected by public decisions, policy formulation tends to be blunt and gross. The policy-maker is unable to anticipate resistances, conflicts, and unexpected consequences of his actions. Rather, the total approach to development is put into effect, its imperfections to become known only through disappointment and waste, its correction possible only through massive, and still uninformed, revision, or the deployment of coercion to "make" the program work.

Second, only through a complex process of representations is the decision-maker *required* to take the broader intricacy of this society into account in the choices he makes. Unless the groups that are to be affected by public decisions can also affect the conditions of political survival, they are apt to be disregarded in the making of public policy, as the decision-maker operates with those forces that most urgently require his attention. Democratic process does not make decision-making easier, but more adequate. If the interjection of the power of the people into the political process were all that was required for a successful policy revolution, the monolithic revolutionary party would be a perfectly adequate vehicle of change. However, the formulation of efficient development policy requires a more precise interpretation of what is in fact at issue in the society. It requires a presentation of the diversity, the conflicts, the problems, that actually do prevail. The mass party may project popular power into the political arena in the most compelling way, and provide refreshing policy alternatives. But unless it is supplemented by the more precise forms of functional and constituency representation, it is as liable to massive error or vacillating futility as the "oligarchic" apparatus of decision it replaced.

Third, development requires an understanding of the complementarity of social functions, of the complex interdependence of the nation that would develop. The developmental task includes economic integration, "nation-building," and the enhanced stability and legitimacy of national political institutions. To a certain extent, the educational function that enables specific groups and interests to see their goals in relation to the interdependence of forces in national social and economic systems can be performed by political ideology. We have noted the emergence of what must be described as a "public philosophy" of the nation in development in some Latin American nations. We have noted the contribution of "structuralist" theories of economic development in clarifying the relationship of exchange in various sectors of the economy. Throughout the region, one can observe increased accord on the goals of the development process, though conflict is bitter and acrimonious over the selection of means appropriate to these objectives. However, the process of meshing a society for development is ultimately contingent on the existence of forums for the orderly confrontation of rival interests, and the desire of these interests to use these forums to construct public policy. Only in the confrontation of the various forces present in the society, under conditions that presuppose conciliation and common endeavor, can development as a national task become an operational norm of political activity.

Fourth, only through the confrontation of the various sectors of the society in the formulation of public policy can private performance and public policy be adequately interwoven in an approach to the developmental problem. Within the classic, loosely-structured political systems of Latin America, there has been little willingness for rival interests to engage in negotiation. Rather, the task of finding a satisfactory policy format has been left almost entirely to political leaders who, with little information from, and less assumption of responsibility for the outcome on the part of the critical political forces in the society, must almost intuitively devise a policy stance on which to base their chances for political survival. Having abdicated any collective responsibility for the program of the state, the critical power contenders have no real stake in the survival of any government. They stand ready to withdraw their support for any government that seems less than totally committed to their objectives.

The separation of state from society, the assumption that the state acts on behalf of, but without the participation of, the critical forces in the society, is a tradition of long standing in Latin America. It is a most problematic tradition in a region where public and private performance is intimately interrelated in the task of change. The ideological format adopted does not change the situation. One can no more mount a revolution on the assumption that "government will do the job" than can one pursue development by more conventional means. A mobilization regime, goading its followers into relevant action, is of course one solution. But the task of so mobilizing a society after the assumption of power is, in principle, no easier than the stimulation of participation in the development effort within a more pluralistic order.

Fifth, a pluralistic system of representation provides policy-makers with needed information or "feedback" on the success and failure of policies in progress. When established channels of communication link decision-makers and those affected by government actions, adjustments and changes may be made at the incremental, practical, day-to-day level, prior to sudden crisis or total disaster. Through a more complete process of representation, policy-makers learn of unanticipated consequences to third parties, "by-product" effects of policies in sectors of the society not immediately involved in the program at issue. Furthermore, only through the organization of the clientele of government programs can continuing pressure be exerted on the administrative apparatus of the state. Political leaders, however well-intentioned they may be, are often helpless to overcome the inertia of the bureaucratic establishments they depend on to convert policy intention into social impact.

Sixth, the policy alternatives available to statesmen are far more numerous and flexible when the capacities of private organizations can be coordinated with government powers in the fulfillment of public purposes. It is one thing for the state to mount a program of agrarian reform on its own initiative. It is quite another for the state to add to its efforts those of labor organizations, cooperative federations, the private and public banking community, and existing agricultural associations, in a more comprehensive attack on the problem. However, the potential forms of such coordinated action, and the impetus to such cooperation, is vastly enhanced when the expectation of dialogue and common endeavor between government and private organization is an institutionalized part of the political system.

Seventh, and finally, there is a sense in which democratic process is more pertinent to societies undergoing rapid change than it is to more stable, established ones. The essential point of democratic process is that social goals, public policies, and the relationships of power, should be periodically or continually reassessed in the light of changing circumstances. In an emergent nation, the relationships of productive forces, the aspirations of various groups, the relative political power of various contenders, the character of the society itself—all are in a state of flux. Political coalitions, and development strategies, both become quickly obsolete under conditions of rapid change. The most common criticism of the political institutions of Latin America is that they are no longer adequate to cope with the forces at work in the region, with the needs and demands for change. To many the archaic institutions of government must be replaced by a movement dedicated to the radical restructuring of the political and economic institutions of society. Yet no form of government more quickly tends to obsolescence and nostalgic irrelevance than the mobilization regime that has achieved its objectives. The leadership cadre that shared a total commitment to a vision of change, that struggled to achieve power, that shared the heady experience of building a new society, inevitably finds it hard to adjust to the new order once it has been established. The paradoxes of the "institutionalized revolution" are apparent in virtually every society that has undergone this experience.

If, in fact, pluralistic representation is an important political variable in the effective formulation and implementation of economic development policy, it is worthwhile to give conscious attention to the creation of the appropriate institutions as a critical component of the development effort itself. One can think of such institutions as the "political infrastructure" of development. Much as roads, power plants, and fiscal services are conceded to be prerequisite to the effective performance of the productive forces of the society, so labor unions, mass parties, and cooperative federa-

tions may be essential if the state is to act most effectively in assist-
ing in the development effort.

However, one need not think of a system of adequate representation as a "precondition" of development. In no part of Latin
America are we dealing with a static "predevelopmental" situation.
New forms of political association are constantly being formed, and
development policy is being made using the political resources available. In some cases, new forms of political association will demand
new services from the state. In others, the formation of representative organizations will be an aspect of a total program imposed from
above.

Thus, it need not be assumed that democratic representation requires that the "voice of the people" must provide the sole and
exclusive guide to development goals and programs. What is more
at issue is dialogue and communication. Certainly, development
planning requires the creative intervention of modernizing elites,
and the insights of those who can analyze the technical requirements of a total society in the process of change. However, it is
also necessary that those who possess a total approach to development be confronted as fully as possible with the intricacy of the
environment on which this plan will be imposed. To this end, all
the social science research, all the polls and surveys, all the collection and interpretation of economic data, can only supplement and
clarify the arguments, issues, and data churned up through a competitive political system.

Certainly too, in societies where a large part of the population has
only limited awareness of the greater society about them, the "will
of the people" particularly in the early stages, is not apt to be very
instructive. In a sense, appropriate demands must be created, and
this is indeed the function of the agencies of pluralistic representation. The dual function of these institutions is apparent. They are
instruments of motivation, as the political activist, the political
"broker," communicates his vision of development to those whose
way of life must change if this goal is to be realized. They are also
instruments of communication, as the design for development is
perfected in the light of what is learned in the process of organizing
consent.

The process connotes obligations for he who would serve as the
political broker. A real effort at communication and discussion is
required, as well as certain minimum standards of plausibility in the
promises made and authenticity in the representation provided. It

implies as well that the political activist will in fact go into the villages and farms and slums that lie beyond the extant modern sector, an obligation honored more in the breach than in the observance by most present institutions of mass organization in Latin America.

For some, investment of the resources of political militancy in the creation of responsible demands rather than in revolution or mobilization society may seem to be an effort to reverse an inevitable historic process. Pluralistic society is the outcome of the developmental process, it is not the means to its achievement. However, contemporary Latin American society is in fact most heterogeneous and complex. There is no Latin American nation that could be adequately described in terms of a simplistic model in which a small entrenched oligarchy and a compact modernizing elite compete for control of a population totally submerged in traditional patterns of life. Rather, contemporary Latin American society includes many forms of commitment to the existing modern sector, many degrees of alienation from the prevailing structure of society. Even the premodern sector is far more complex than it superficially appears. Our argument is not that it is desirable to create a more pluralistic society. It is rather that it is desirable that the policy-making process reflect the heterogeneity that does in fact prevail.

It may be argued that Latin America cannot wait for such evolutionary processes to take hold, and must engage in revolution to hasten the pace of imperative change. However, there is a significant sense in which Latin America, because of its urgent needs for change, cannot wait for revolution. To create the revolutionary situation, to undergo the sacrifices that a large-scale reordering of social and economic systems entails, to endure the tumult and disorder that precede the constructive phase of revolution, may involve an extravagance of time, energy, and human and physical resources that Latin America can ill afford.

The economic development of Latin America is "in process." This is not a region that has just begun its efforts to enter the modern world. The urgent needs for change and reform that are present in Latin America are themselves the product of an ongoing pattern of growth and development. The population pressures and rising aspirations that strain existing productivity are themselves symptoms of developmental achievements in earlier periods. The very inequality of wealth and opportunity that is such a glaring defect of the contemporary situation may well reflect a stage in an ongoing process of change. Latin America has a considerable stake in the going concern that has been built up over time. To "destroy the old order" as prelude to further progress may be grossly inefficient. To create the forces that will redirect the product of development, and swiftly increase the proportion of the population sharing in the developmental effort, while the existing processes of change continue, may be less wasteful for a society operating on a rather slim margin for error.

It may be argued that democratic process is inappropriate to Latin American political culture. The prevalence of hierarchical patterns of authority in many social institutions, the attraction to personalistic leadership, the tendency to see politics as an appropriate arena for dramatic and heroic personal action, the weakness of norms of social cooperation—these values seem to run contrary to those required for the effective establishment of democratic institutions and democratic societies. Yet, for each of these "characteristic qualities" of Latin American political life, one can observe others. Equally general in Latin American political culture are the skills of pragmatic statesmanship, including ingenuity in the recombination of institutions and political factors, and a relative tolerance for political dissent and political ambivalence. The classic political systems of Latin America have been in fact pluralistic, though imperfectly so. What indeed is "characteristic" of Latin American political culture? Military "strong men" have dominated the political life of some nations for long periods, but equally characteristic has been intelligent, democratic, civilian leadership. For every Ubico there is also a Sarmiento, for every Perón there is also an Alfonso López. Political processes dominated by conservative elites characterize some countries. But Latin America has also been the scene of creative experimentation in socially conscious public policy —as in Uruguay and Mexico.

The argument for democratic process in development planning may represent a cultural bias in favor of Western institutions. Certainly, the political institutions of the emergent nations cannot succeed as mere imitations of Western models. They must reflect the institutions and values of their own cultures. Although this canon of political development is well-taken, it must be noted that Latin America is not, in any significant political sense, a non-Western area. Despite persistent disappointment and frustration, the goal of Western democracy has remained a remarkably stable culture value in Latin America. When Latin American nations have abandoned democratic process in favor of other forms of government, it has always been with a certain sorrow and wistfulness, and the intention to continue the search for democratic society at a later date has never been completely submerged.

Certainly, this is not to suggest that the institutions and concepts of democratic process in Latin America will look precisely like those of Anglo-America, or any other part of the Western world. It is likely that mass organizations and interest associations will be more closely related to the state, and that many will be created at the initiative of the state. It is unlikely that fully competitive party systems will develop everywhere, and labor organizations will probably be closely related to mass parties, more in the European than in the North American tradition. With the possible exceptions of such nations as Brazil and Colombia, with their historic traditions of regionalism, it is not to be expected that a sense of constituency and decentralization of power will develop as strong and pervasive as that of the United States. Latin America is, after all, a distinctive civilization, and just as it is unnecessarily pessimistic to suppose that democratic process is inappropriate to that culture by analogy to political patterns in other developing regions, so it is a bit perverse to insist that democratic intent can only be satisfied by specific institutions and processes.

However, once all of this has been said, a note of caution should be entered. "Revolution" in Latin America need not imply catastrophe. The term is part of the political culture of the area, and its implications are most ambiguous. For many, in fact, probably for most Latin Americans, "revolution" implies constructive development within a democratic framework. Nonetheless, it is probably to be expected that some nations in the region will undergo more or less prolonged periods of political turmoil and experimentation with what appear to be radical solutions to the developmental problem. In the majority of such cases, it is less likely that the Latin Americans involved will have "gone to extremes" than that fear born of ignorance will cause well-meaning North Americans to "go to extremes" in their interpretation of the situation.

In any event, as the experience of such nations as Mexico and Bolivia indicates, there is nothing inevitable about the process of revolution itself. Revolutionary societies themselves change and mature over time. They are subject, in their own way, to the same conditions of economic development, the same deeply ingrained forces making for political pluralism, as are other types of political regime. Given an atmosphere of relative international tolerance for diversity and experimentation, the paradoxical pragmatism of Latin American statesmanship, the relative stability of Latin American values and aspirations, give promise that revolution need not imply calamity unless fear and impatience make it such.

Latin America is apt to be a "continent in crisis" for a long time to come. The obstacles to be overcome before economic well-being, social justice, and democratic society are widely achieved are most formidable. The process of change is going to be difficult for all concerned.

It is the fate of each of the two distinctive civilizations of the Western Hemisphere to endure the growing pains of the other. As Latin America has had to cope with some of the more unfortunate aspects of the adolescence of North American civilization, so North America must be prepared to sympathetically endure the problems that come with the maturation of Latin America. However difficult the process may be, there is no particularly good reason why Latin America should not come into her full inheritance as part of Western civilization unless we—the people of this "New World"—lose our nerve, and with it, our commitment to the values we share.